SANTA FE, NM

BERLIN DIARIES, 1940–1945

Berlin Diaries, 1940–1945

Marie Vassiltchikov

Alfred A. Knopf   NEW YORK   1987

Library of Congress Cataloging-in-Publication Data

Vassiltchikov, Marie, 1917–1978.
  Berlin diaries, 1940–1945.
  Originally published: London: Chatto & Windus, 1985.
  Includes index.
    1. Vassiltchikov, Marie, 1917–1978.   2. World War, 1939–1945—Personal narratives,
Russian.   3. World War, 1939–1945—Berlin (Germany)   4. Berlin (Germany)—Social life
and customs.   5. World War, 1939–1945—Austria—Vienna.   6. Vienna (Austria)—
History—1918–   7. Russia—Nobility—Biography. I. Vassiltchikov, George. II. Title.
D811.5.V38   1987   940.54'81'47   86–45301
ISBN 0–394–55624–0

The illustrations are from the author's own collection, or have been kindly lent from other
private collections, with the exceptions of 6(c) (courtesy of the Presse Informationsamt
der Bundesregierung, Bonn); 10(a) © André Zucca-Tallendier-Magnum Distribution;
10(b); 10(c) (courtesy of the Berlin Documentation Center, U.S. Mission Berlin); 11(a)
Lichtbildwerkstätte 'Alpenland', Vienna. A. Haushofer quotation from 'Moabiter Sonette',
Deutscher Taschenbuch Verlag GmbH & Co., München, 1982.

'She has something of a noble animal of legend . . .
Something free that enables her to soar far above everything and everyone.
This, of course, is a little tragic, indeed almost uncanny . . .'

Adam von Trott zu Solz, writing about Missie to his wife, Clarita

'There are times when lunacy takes over
And then it is the best heads that are axed . . .'

Albrecht Haushofer, 'Sonnets from Moabit. Companions'.

CONTENTS

LIST OF ILLUSTRATIONS

FOREWORD

The author of this diary, Marie ('Missie') Vassiltchikov* was born in St Petersburg, Russia, on 11 January 1917. She died of leukemia in London on 12 August 1978.

She was the fourth child (and third daughter) in a family of five. Her parents, Prince Illarion and Princess Lydia Vassiltchikov, had left Russia in the spring of 1919 and Missie grew up as a refugee – in Germany; in France, where she went to school; and in Lithuania (between 1918 and 1940 an independent Republic), where her father's family had owned property before the Revolution and where, in the late 1930s, she worked for a while as a secretary at the British Legation.

The start of World War II in September 1939 found her in Germany, where, together with her second sister Tatiana (now Princess Metternich), she was spending the summer with a childhood friend of her mother's, Countess Olga Pückler, in the latter's country home, Schloss Friedland, in Silesia. The rest of the family were scattered; her parents and younger brother George ('Georgie') lived in Lithuania; and her elder sister Irena in Rome. Her eldest brother, the twenty-seven-year-old Alexander, had died of tuberculosis in Switzerland earlier in that year.

Since the world economic depression of the early 1930s it was virtually impossible for a foreigner to get a work permit in any of the Western democracies. Only in Fascist Italy and (even more so) Nazi Germany had unemployment been by and large licked by massive public works programs and, of course, re-armament. Given the required skills only there, therefore, could also stateless persons (such as the Vassiltchikov girls) make a living. In January 1940 the two sisters moved to Berlin in search of work. Missie's diary

* The family name is usually spelled 'Vassiltchikov' in English; Missie herself used the Germanic 'Wassiltchikoff'.

starts with their arrival in the German capital, where, in this first winter of the war, life – apart from the blackout and stringent food rationing – was still surprisingly 'normal'. Only with the German invasion of Denmark and Norway in April do the war and its attendant horrors and, presently, also ethical challenges gradually take over, to eventually dominate all else.

Though not a German citizen, owing to the shortage of qualified linguists, Missie soon found a job first with the Broadcasting Service and then with the Foreign Ministry's Information Department. There she worked closely with a hard core of anti-Nazi resisters who were to be actively involved in what has come down in history as 'the 20th July Plot'. Her day-by-day, sometimes hour-by-hour description of Count von Stauffenberg's abortive attempt to kill Hitler and of the reign of terror that followed (in which several of her closest friends or associates were to perish) is the only known eyewitness diary account in existence. Having finally escaped the ruins of bombed-out Berlin, she was to spend the last months of the war working, again under Allied bombs, as a hospital nurse in Vienna.

Missie was a compulsive diarist. Daily she would type out a summary of the events of the eve. Only the longer accounts, such as that of the bombing of Berlin in November 1943, were written *ex post facto* though immediately following the event. The diary was written in English, which had been familiar to her since her nursery days. The typed pages were kept in a filing cabinet at her office, hidden between sheets of official matter. When the pile of material became too bulky, she would take it home and hide it somewhere there or, occasionally, in country homes she happened to be visiting. At first all this was done so openly that more than once her bosses would say: 'Come on, Missie, set aside your diary and let's get a little work done!' Only with the 20th July plot on Hitler's life did she take more serious precautions: the account of that period was written in a personal shorthand which she transcribed only after the war.

Although she was bombed out of several successive homes and, as the war drew to a close, had to flee for her life from besieged Vienna, much of the diary, including the historically more essential sections, survived. Only parts of 1941 and 1942 and the beginning of 1943 are missing – destroyed deliberately, lost or beyond present reach.

Shortly after the war, Missie typed out the shorthand sections and retyped the rest. This second version remained untouched for over a quarter of a century – until 1976 when, after much soul-searching and considerable prodding from family and friends, she at last decided to make it available to the public. In so doing, however, she made a point of cutting out very little and changing nothing of substance; any modifications were confined to language or the occasional routine editing and the insertion of names in lieu of initials. For she believed very strongly that if her diary had any value at all, this was because, not having been written originally for publication, it was completely spontaneous, outspoken and honest. Her eye-witness accounts and on-the-spur-of-the-moment reactions and emotions spoke, she felt, for themselves. They would lose much of their interest were they to be adulterated by wisdom after the event, let alone censored – to save herself from possible embarrassment now or to spare other persons' feelings.

This third and definitive version was completed by Missie mere weeks before she died.

One of my most heart-warming rewards, when preparing my sister Missie's manuscript for publication, was the instant response and all-out assistance (and occasional hospitality) I received from all those to whom I turned for additional personal or background information, clarifications, or source, or photographic material; and this, whether they had known Missie personally or not. In some cases it meant stirring up memories which, however admirable their political attitude and personal behaviour had been in those times of darkness, they had nevertheless tried hard to put out of their minds; their generosity is all the more appreciated.

My gratitude goes in the first place to Countess Elisabeth ('Sisi') Andrassy (born Countess Wilczek), whose description of the last weeks of the war, which they had lived through together, filled a crucial gap in Missie's own reminiscences; to Dr Clarita von Trott zu Solz, who was one of the few to whom Missie, just weeks before her death, chose to show the completed manuscript, and who has gone on to give me every assistance, including the use of excerpts from her late husband's letters; and to Dr Hasso von Etzdorf, whose encouragement and introductions, let alone fund of personal reminiscences, helped me greatly.

Count Hans Heinrich Coudenhove went through the manuscript with a fine comb; his experience in publishing, knowledge of contemporary history and personal acquaintance with many of the *dramatis personae* were all invaluable; as was the expertise in German and Allied politics during the period in question, and specifically in the history of the German anti-Nazi resistance, of Dr Rainer Blasius, in Bonn, who very kindly did the same with my historical annotations.

A special word of thanks goes to Gordon Brook-Shepherd and the editors of the *Sunday Telegraph*, who were the first to acquaint the English reading public with Missie and her diary.

Missie's daughter, Alexandra Harnden, undertook the painstaking task of preparing the basic name-index.

Mrs Marie Ellis and Mrs Carol Cain showed both skill and patience in typing out what must have been occasionally a baffling manuscript.

The staff of the Goethe Institute in London and of the United Nations library in Geneva (where most of my research was done) were unfailingly helpful, as were those of the Wiener Library in London, of the German Federal Republic Foreign Ministry's Government Press and Information Office in Bonn and Bundesarchiv in Koblenz, and of the U.S. Document Center in Berlin.

Others to whom I am indebted in one way or another include: the Hon. David Astor; Mr Antoni Balinski; Count Andreas von Bismarck-Schön-hausen; Mr Herbert Blankenhorn; the late Mrs Barbara Brooks (born Countess von Bismarck-Schönhausen); Baron and Baroness Axel von dem Bussche-Streithorst; Mr P. Dixon; Count Johannes ('Dicky') and Countess Sybilla von und zu Eltz; Baroness Hermine von Essen; Princess Petronella Farman-Fermayan; Countess Rosemarie von Fugger-Babenhausen; Mrs Inga Haag; Professor Peter Hoffman (of McGill University, Montreal); Mrs Linda Kelly; Dr E. Klausa; Mrs Sigrid Kurrer (born Countess Schlitz von Görtz); Mrs Caroline de Lacerna (born Princess Schönburg-Hartenstein); Dr I. Miller; Mrs M. von Moltke; Mr W. I. Nichols; Mr C. C. von Pfuel; Sir Ronald Preston, Bart.; Mrs B. Richter von Prodt; Mrs E. Rhomberg; the Marquis de Santa Cruz; Baron Anton Saurma von der Jeltsch; Countess Dorothea von Schönborn-Wiesentheid (born Countess von Pappenheim); Princess Carmen zu Solms-Braunfels (born Princess von Wrede); Mrs Christina Sutherland; Baron Philippe de Vendeuvre; Baron and Baroness von Watsdorff and Mrs Lore Wolf.

Last but not least, I wish to thank Pat Kavanagh, of A. D. Peters, Ltd, whose professional experience, wise advice and dedication have been invaluable from the first day she agreed to represent Missie; Elisabeth Grossman (Literistic, Ltd) who handled the U.S. rights; Jeremy Lewis of Chatto & Windus, whose enthusiasm, ability and sensitive understanding for the often complex psychological and ethical challenges Missie and her friends faced, combined to make our lively editing sessions as fruitful as they were enjoyable. A special word of thanks goes to Susan Ralston, of Alfred A. Knopf, for her skill, enthusiasm and dedication in putting together the U.S. edition of Missie's diaries.

London, *November 1986*   George Vassiltchikov

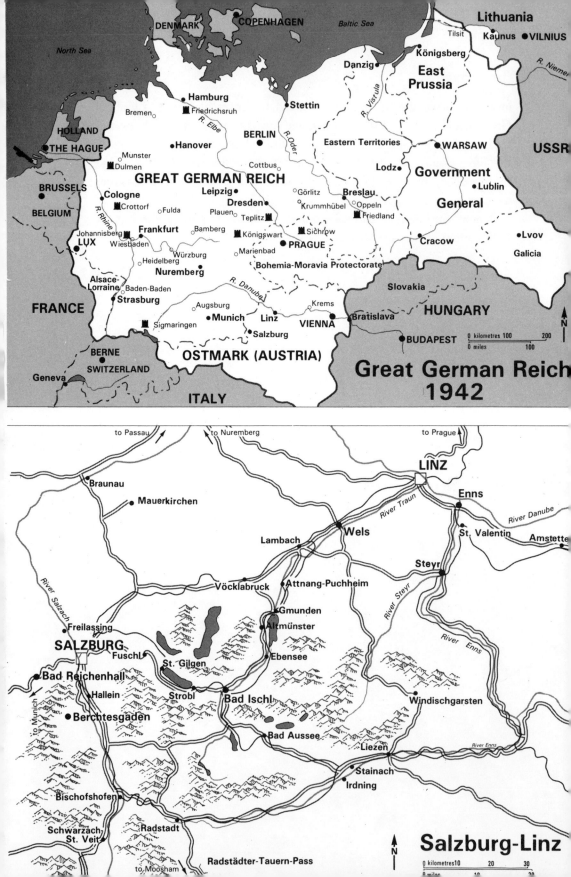

Great German Reich 1942

DENMARK · COPENHAGEN · Baltic Sea · Lithuania · Tilsit · Kaunus · VILNIUS

North Sea · Königsberg · East Prussia · R. Niemen

Hamburg · Friedrichsruh · Stettin · Danzig

Bremen · BERLIN · R. Oder · R. Elbe · R. Visrula · WARSAW · USSR

HOLLAND · THE HAGUE · Hanover · GREAT GERMAN REICH · Eastern Territories · Government

Munster · Dulmen · Cottbus · Lodz · General

BRUSSELS · BELGIUM · Cologne · Crottorf · Fulda · Leipzig · Görlitz · Breslau · Oppeln · Lublin

LUX · Johannisberg · Frankfurt · Dresden · Krummhübel · Friedland · Lvov

Wiesbaden · Plauen · Teplitz · Sichrow · Cracow · Galicia

Heidelberg · Würzburg · Königswart · PRAGUE

Alsace-Lorraine · Nuremberg · Marienbad · Bohemia-Moravia Protectorate

FRANCE · Baden-Baden · Bamberg · Slovakia · HUNGARY

Strasburg · R. Danube · Krems

Augsburg · Munich · Linz · VIENNA · Bratislava

Sigmaringen · Salzburg · BUDAPEST

BERNE · SWITZERLAND · OSTMARK (AUSTRIA)

Geneva · ITALY

0 kilometres 100 200
0 miles 100

N

Salzburg-Linz

to Passau · to Nuremberg · to Prague

LINZ · Braunau · Mauerkirchen · Enns

River Traun · River Danube

Lambach · Wels · St. Valentin · Amstette

Vöcklabruck · Attnang-Puchheim · Steyr

River Steyr

Gmunden · Altmünster · River Enns

Freilassing · SALZBURG · Ebensee

River Salzach · Fuschl · St. Gilgen · Windischgarsten

Bad Reichenhall · Strobl · Bad Ischl

Hallein · Berchtesgaden · Bad Aussee · Liezen

to Munich · River Enns · Stainach · Irdning

Bischofshofen · Schwarzach St. Veit · Radstadt

to Moosham · Radstädter-Tauern-Pass

0 kilometres 10 20 30
0 miles

N

erlin 1940-45

kilometres 1 2
miles 1

N

Key to Numbers

1 Plötzensee Prison
2 Lehterstrasse Prison
3 Police HQ
4 Garrison HQ
5 Wireless Service (DD)
6 Missie's home 1941-42
7 Broadcasting House ('Funkhaus')
8 Reichstag
9 Hotel Central
10 French Embassy

11 Brandenburg Gate
12 Hotel Adlon
13 British Embassy
14 Hotel Bristol
15 Foreign Ministry
16 Reichskanzlei
17 Ministry of Propaganda
18 Hotel Kaiserhof
19 Gestapo HQ
20 Hotel Esplanade
21 Italian Embassy

22 St Mattheus Church
23 Spanish Embassy
24 U.S. Embassy
25 Swedish Legation
26 Czech Legation
27 War Ministry/Army HQ (OKH)
28 Ministry of Navy (OKM)
29 Missie's home 1943-44
30 Missie's office
   (ex-Polish Embassy)
31 Hotel Eden

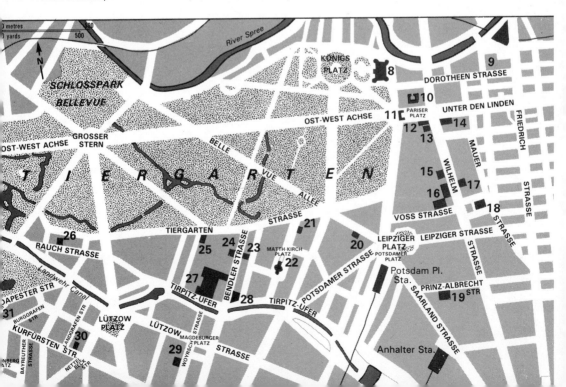

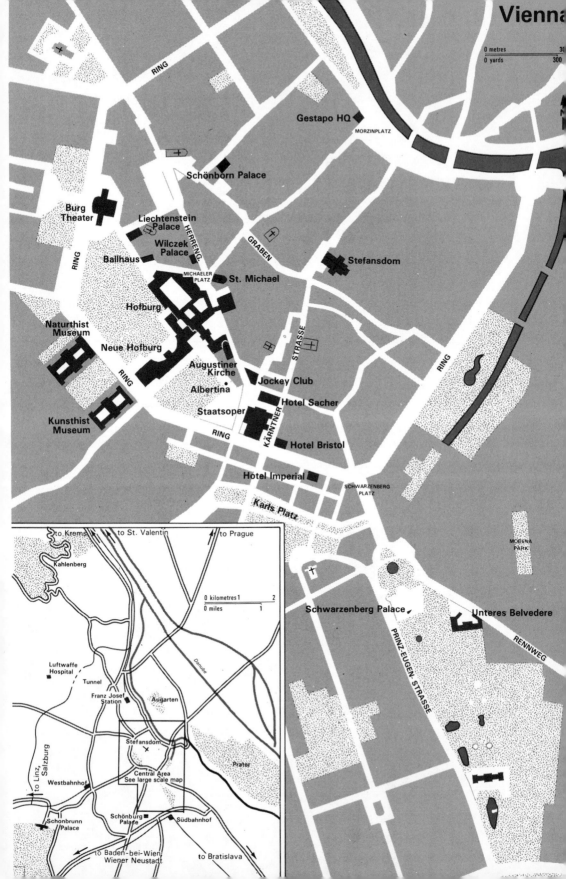

Vienna

0 metres 30[0]
0 yards 300

RING

Gestapo HQ
MORZINPLATZ

Schönborn Palace

Burg Theater

Liechtenstein Palace

Wilczek Palace

HERRENG.

GRABEN

Ballhaus

MICHAELER PLATZ

St. Michael

Stefansdom

RING

Hofburg

STRASSE

Naturhist Museum

Neue Hofburg

Augustiner Kirche

Jockey Club

RING

Albertina

Hotel Sacher

Staatsoper

KÄRNTNER

Kunsthist Museum

RING

Hotel Bristol

Hotel Imperial

SCHWARZENBERG PLATZ

Karls Platz

MODENA PARK

Inset map

to Krems   to St. Valentin   to Prague

Kahlenberg

0 kilometres 1   2
0 miles   1

Luftwaffe Hospital

Danube

Tunnel

Franz Josef Station

Augarten

Schwarzenberg Palace

Unteres Belvedere

RENNWEG

PRINZ-EUGEN STRASSE

to Linz, Salzburg

Stefansdom

Prater

Westbahnhof

Central Area
See large scale map

Schönburg Palace

Südbahnhof

Schonbrunn Palace

to Baden-bei-Wien,
Wiener Neustadt

to Bratislava

BERLIN DIARIES, 1940–1945

SCHLOSS FRIEDLAND *Monday, 1 January* Olga Pückler, Tatiana and I spent the New Year quietly at Schloss Friedland. We lit the Christmas tree and tried to read the future by dropping melted wax and lead into a bowl of water. We expect Mamma and Georgie to appear any minute from Lithuania. They have announced their arrival repeatedly. At midnight all the village bells began to ring. We hung out of the windows listening – the first New Year of this new World War.

When World War II started on 1 September 1939, Lithuania (where Missie's parents and brother George lived), was still an independent republic. However, under a secret protocol to the Soviet–German Boundary and Friendship Treaty of 29 September (which complemented the Molotov-Ribbentrop Non-Aggression Pact of 23 August) it had been included in the U.S.S.R.'s sphere of influence and after 10 October a number of strategically located towns and airfields were garrisoned by the Red Army. Ever since, Missie's family had been preparing to escape to the West.

BERLIN *Wednesday, 3 January* We departed for Berlin with eleven pieces of luggage, including a gramophone. We left at 5 a.m. It was still pitch dark. The estate manager drove us to Oppeln. Olga Pückler has lent us enough money to live for three weeks; by that time we must have found jobs. Tatiana has written to Jake Beam, one of the boys at the American Embassy she met last spring; our work at the British Legation in Kaunas may be of some help to us there.

Washington was to maintain an Embassy in Berlin until 11 December 1941, when, following Japan's attack on Pearl Harbor, Hitler declared war on the U.S.A.

The train was packed and we stood in the corridor. Luckily, two soldiers had helped with the luggage, as otherwise we would never have been able to squeeze in. We arrived in Berlin three hours late. As soon as we reached the flat the Pücklers have kindly allowed us to stay in temporarily, Tatiana started telephoning friends; it made us feel less lost. The flat, in the Lietzen-burgerstrasse, a street running parallel to the Kurfürstendamm, is very large, but Olga has asked us to do without outside help on account of the many valuable contents, so we are only using one bedroom, a bathroom and the kitchen. The rest is shrouded in sheets.

Thursday, 4 January We spent most of the day blacking out the windows, as no one has been here since the war started last September.

Saturday, 6 January After dressing, we ventured out into the darkness and luckily found a taxi on the Kurfürstendamm which took us to a ball at the Chilean Embassy off the Tiergarten. Our host, Morla, was Chilean Ambas-sador in Madrid when the Civil War broke out. Although their own government favoured the Republicans, they gave shelter to more than 3,000 persons, who would otherwise have been shot and who hid out in the Chilean Embassy for three years, sleeping on the floors, the stairs, wherever there was space; and notwithstanding great pressure from the Republican Govern-ment, the Morlas refused to hand over a single person. This is all the more admirable considering that the Duke of Alba's brother, a descendant of the Stuarts, who had sought refuge at the British Embassy, was politely turned away and subsequently arrested and shot.

The ball was lovely, quite like in pre-war days. At first I feared I would not know many people, but soon I realised that I knew quite a few from last winter. [*Missie had visited Tatiana in Berlin in the winter of 1938–1939.*] Among those we met for the first time were the Welczeck girls, both very beautiful and terribly well dressed. Their father was the last German Ambassador in Paris. Their brother Hansi and his lovely bride Sigi von Laffert were also there, and many other friends, including Ronnie Clary, a very handsome boy, just out of Louvain University, who speaks perfect English – which was rather a relief, as my German is not quite up to the mark yet. Most of the young men present are at Krampnitz, an officers' tank training school just outside of Berlin. Later, Rosita Serrano [*a popular Chilean chanteuse*] sang, addressing little Eddie Wrede, aged nineteen, as 'Bel Ami', which flattered him enor-mously. We had not danced for ages and returned home at 5 a.m., all piled in the car of Cartier, a Belgian diplomat, who is a friend of the Welczecks.

Sunday, 7 January We are still searching painfully for jobs. We have decided not to ask any friends to help, but to turn directly to business acquaintances.

Monday, 8 January This afternoon, at the American Embassy, we had an appointment with the Consul. He was quite friendly and at once gave us a test, which rather unnerved us, as we were not mentally prepared for it. Two typewriters were trotted out, also shorthand pads, and he dictated something at such speed and with such an accent that we could not understand all he said; worse, our two versions of the letter he dictated turned out not to be identical. He told us he would ring us up soon as there were vacancies. We cannot wait long, however, and if something else turns up meanwhile, we will have to accept. Unfortunately, as most international business is at a standstill, there are no firms here in need of French- or English-speaking secretaries.

Thursday, 11 January My twenty-third birthday. Sigi Laffert, Hansi Welczeck's fiancée, came for tea. She is strikingly pretty and many describe her as 'the prototype of the German beauty'. In the evening Reinhard Spitzy took us to the cinema and then on to a night club, Ciro's, where we drank champagne and listened to the music; there is no longer any dancing in public.

Saturday, 13 January Mamma and Georgie arrived at crack of dawn. I had not seen Georgie for over a year. He has not changed, is full of charm and is very nice to Mamma, who looks very ill and run-down. In Lithuania, which is gradually becoming Sovietized, they had been through unnerving experiences. It was high time the family left. Papa, however, has stayed on, as he has a big business deal pending.

Sunday, 14 January We have installed Mamma and Georgie in the Pückler flat so that they need not spend money on a hotel. As it is, they only have forty dollars between them. As we still have no jobs, the financial situation is catastrophic. They are thinking of staying on here. This would be a mistake: it is very cold, there is little to eat and the political situation is more than shaky. We are trying to convince them to go on to Rome, where Mamma has many friends and where there is a large White Russian émigré colony. Here she would be lonely, for apart from the foreign embassies, whose numbers are fast dwindling as the war spreads like an oil-patch, there is little family life left. Berlin is nowadays a young bachelors' town, full of our contemporaries, who either are in the armed forces or work all day in offices and then end up in night clubs. In Rome Irena has already settled down nicely; life would be easier, if only for the climate, and as soon as we begin to work, we could send them money regularly.

Monday, 15 January A new government decree: no baths excepting on Saturdays and Sundays. This is quite a blow, as one gets amazingly dirty in a big town and it was one of the few ways to be warm.

Wednesday, 17 January We stay at home a lot – to be more with the family. Mamma's nerves are in bad shape; all she has been through since Alexander's death is beginning to tell.

Thursday, 18 January Georgie has an enormous appetite and our food supplies – we had brought butter and sausage from Friedland – are dwindling fast. This is another argument in favour of their continuing on to Rome. Here, he would get rapidly under-nourished, whereas Italy, thank heaven, is still out of the war and there is no food rationing.

Friday, 19 January Katia Kleinmichel is working with the English department of the D.D. She may be able to find me a job there too. We are getting rather desperate, for we have not heard from the American Embassy and yet cannot harass them. We are very broke and with the arrival of the family, what money we had has dwindled fast. We went to see a man at I. G. Farben, but they need people who can do German shorthand perfectly and that is not our forte.

The D.D. (for Drahtloser Dienst, i.e. Wireless Service) was the news service of the Reichs-Rundfunk Gesellschaft or R.R.G., which was roughly Germany's equivalent of the B.B.C. At one point, one of Missie's superiors was the future West German Chancellor, Dr K. G. Kiesinger.

Monday, 22 January Today, I went to Katia Kleinmichel's office in the Friedrichstrasse and spent the morning taking down English dictation on a typewriter; this was my first test and it could not have been easier. It was a speed test and I was told that I would be summoned later. The place resembles a madhouse, as everything is done in a rush on account of those news broadcasting schedules. Among possible future colleagues, I stumbled upon Roderich Menzel, the former Czech-born international tennis champion.

Saturday, 27 January At the Wrede twins Tatiana met a man who suggested that she should work in his office, which is a part of the German Foreign Ministry. They need people with good French. Most of our friends advise us against working at the American Embassy because, as foreigners, we are probably already under the vigilant eye of the Gestapo. It's bad enough that we should be White Russians – in view of Germany's present alliance with the Soviet Union. Furthermore we have worked in a British Legation. In any case, we are by now so broke that the first job offer must be accepted, whatever it is. The American Embassy remains silent.

The other day, at friends', I was introduced to Frau von Dirksen, who is one of the top official hostesses here. She passed her hand through my hair – something I resented – and asked whether we were White Russians or Red, for if the latter, 'you are our enemies'. A somewhat surprising remark considering how pally Germany and Soviet Russia are these days!

Monday, 29 January Today we both started work: I with the D.D., and Tatiana at the Foreign Ministry, better known as the A.A. [Auswärtiges Amt]. My office does not seem to know who its Top Boss is, as everybody is giving orders at the same time, although the Reich's Propaganda Minister, Dr Joseph Goebbels is said to have the last word. We earn 300 marks each: 110 are deducted for taxes, which leaves us 190 to get on with. We must try to manage.

Tuesday, 30 January My first job was taking down a long story about Ronnie Cross, who is British Minister of Economic Warfare and with whom Tatiana stayed when she was in England before the war. My direct boss, Herr E., has a vast walrus moustache; he seems to have spent most of his life in England. His wife works in the same room with us. They are both middle-aged and will evidently soon become a plague. All day he dictates endless articles, mostly vituperative and so involved that they become often incomprehensible. When they speak another language too well, Germans often get like that. I type from 7 a.m. to 5 p.m. As soon as the paper leaves the typewriter, Frau E. pounces on it to correct possible mistakes. This work goes on in shifts all day and all night.

In a few cases Missie confined herself to first initials – to spare the feelings of survivors or their families, but she did so only if those persons were politically harmless.

Today the American Embassy telephoned offering us jobs, both far better paid than our present ones. But it is too late.

Tuesday, 13 February Mamma and Georgie left this morning to visit Olga Pückler in Silesia. We hope that they will stay there long enough to recuperate a little before going on to Rome.

Wednesday, 14 February I do not see much of Tatiana these days, as I get up at 5.30 a.m. and return around 6 p.m. The trip across town is endless. Tatiana works from 10 a.m. to 8 p.m. and often later.

Thursday, 22 February Today I got a postal order in payment of the two days' test. This is lucky as we were given no salary advance.

Saturday, 2 March A large cocktail party this evening at the Brazilians'. The Ambassador lives just out of town. I did not like seeing a beautiful Russian icon hanging over the gramophone. This craze foreigners have for icons and the way they hang them just about anywhere is rather shocking to us, Orthodox. I left early and got lost on the way home.
Aschwin zur Lippe-Biesterfeld has suddenly appeared from the Siegfried Line [*name given by the Allies to the 1938–1940-built* West Wall, *the German fortifications which ran roughly parallel to France's famed* Ligne Maginot *and which was to be popularized in a British music-hall tune 'We're going to hang our washing on the Siegfried line'*].

Sunday, 3 March This morning at the Russian church the singing was beautiful. Usually I work on Sundays too. Afterwards I stayed at home and, surrounded by Olga's Pückler ghost-like sheet-covered furniture, played the piano.

Monday, 4 March I have a bad cold and am staying home for the next few evenings. Tatiana is out every evening and keeps up a vast correspondence with various boys on the Western Front.

Tuesday, 12 March Mamma (who is on her way from Silesia to Rome) telephoned from Vienna to say that Georgie had disappeared. When the train stopped at some small station on the way, he went to check their luggage.

Without his noticing it, the luggage van was uncoupled from the main body of the train and joined on to another. He is now hurtling towards Warsaw. He has both their tickets, no passport and only five marks to his name. Mamma is waiting for him hopefully in Vienna.

Wednesday, 13 March A party at the Wredes'. The twin sisters Edda ('Dickie') and Carmen ('Sita') were alone when I arrived and chatted with me in the bathroom while I re-did my hair. Letters from Generals Yague and Moscardo were proudly produced, dating back to the time when the sisters had been nurses with the German Condor Legion in Spain during the Civil War. They know all the celebrities of this world, including the Pope. It's a kind of hobby with them.

The Condor Legion was a unit of the Luftwaffe, plus some ground troops, organised in 1936 to aid the Nationalists in the Spanish Civil War. It included medical personnel.

Thursday, 14 March This afternoon after work I went with Ella Pückler to Elena Bennazzo's. She is Russian-born, but does not speak a word of the language, though her parents – both present – seem Russian 100 per cent. Her husband, Agostino, is with the Italian Embassy here. Later, a lot of Italian ladies came around. They are, apparently, knitting tiny garments for Goering's baby. Seems a bit much.

Saturday, 16 March Helen Biron came to tea and also Carl-Friedrich Pückler, our Friedland – and present – host. He is, as usual, optimistic and thinks the war will be over by Whitsun. Although he has been kind to us and is quite intelligent, I never feel quite relaxed with him.

Later we wound up at our neighbour's, Aga von Fürstenberg, where champagne flowed.

Monday, 18 March My free day. Slept till eleven. Fetched Tatiana at her office for lunch. We walked in the Tiergarten, which looks still very wintry. Later in the afternoon there was a big party at the de Witts', the Dutch Ambassador's.

Wednesday, 20 March Tonight we both went to bed early. In France Daladier has resigned.

Three times Prime Minister of France, lastly in 1938–1940 (a function he combined with that of Minister of War), Edouard Daladier (1884–1970) had played a key role in the Munich agreement. He was succeeded by his Finance Minister and political rival, Paul Reynaud (1878–1966).

Friday, 22 March It is Good Friday today, but I had to work my head off just the same. Typed for nine hours without stopping. When he sees me on the verge of collapse my boss, Herr E., produces schnapps, a kind of brandy; it picks me up a bit but tastes horrible. He and his wife squabble all the time. When I see and hear them, I am dead against husband and wife working together. I dislike him cordially and am tempted to give him a shove when he leans far out of the window to get a breath of air after one of their rows. Katia Kleinmichel feels the same. I see a lot of her now, as she works on our shift, and often, when the couple get too much for me, we take turns at the typewriter. We have moved into another building in the Charlottenstrasse. It makes our bosses more independent of Goebbels' constant nagging. Before, when our offices were closer, the Herr Minister would summon them every hour or so. Now he can only get excited over the phone . . .

I come home dead beat.

Monday, 25 March Was free all day. Tatiana and I went out to Potsdam. The weather was lovely. I had never been there before – a delightful little garrison town, full of the charm Berlin totally lacks. We returned to Berlin in time for a concert of the White Russian 'Black Sea' Cossacks. A great success. Germans like that sort of thing.

Tuesday, 26 March Lunched with Katia Kleinmichel. She can be most amusing and it's nice having her in the office. In the streets and restaurants we usually speak English, but nobody here ever objects.

Thursday, 28 March A letter from Rome telling us of Mamma's and Georgie's safe arrival, minus some things that were stolen in Venice. These included many *objets d'art* Mamma had kept from Russian days, Fabergé enamel frames, etc., and Georgie's suitcase with his few clothes, which was substituted for somebody else's that contained none. Their adventures never seem to end.

Friday, 29 March Dinner at the Schaumburg-Lippes' in Cladow. There were only a few people. Later, in front of the fire, Prince August-Wilhelm of

Prussia, the ex-Kaiser's fourth son – a man in his sixties – told many amusing stories about earlier days.

Sunday, 31 March Supper at the 'Roma' with friends. Italian restaurants are most popular just now, on account of the nutritive value of their pastas, for which you do not need ration cards.

Monday, 1 April My free day. Shopped. 'Shopping' these days means essentially shopping for food. Everything is rationed and it takes time, as most shops have long queues. In the evening dinner with Tatiana at Hans von Flotow's. As owner of a factory working for defence, Hans is still a civilian.

Tuesday, 2 April Cinema with Mario Gasperi, the Italian air attaché, and then the Roma. He has a new Fiat car, the size of a wireless set, called a Topolino. It feels strange to be again in a car at all.

Wednesday, 3 April Went to the office only at ten. Working hours are becoming a little less strenuous, as we change shifts now more often. Today I was given my first independent translation to do, probably because my boss is away on holiday. The subject was economics. The morning shift consists of Katia Kleinmichel, myself and a young man from the A.A. He is good-natured but does not speak English very well, so we have him pretty well in hand. He knows it, treats us accordingly, and we live in harmony. It makes me realise all the more clearly what a strain the E.s are to work with. I hear that the latter wants me to be his private secretary, as on his return he is becoming Chef-Redakteur [chief news editor]. I would rather resign!

Thursday, 4 April Every day we get the verbatim monitored record of all B.B.C. news and other foreign broadcasts. Labelled *streng geheim* [top secret], the colour of the paper depends on the degree of 'secrecy', pink being the most secret of all. It makes interesting reading. Nobody in Germany is supposed to know what the rest of the world is up to except what appears in the daily papers and that is not much. Our D.D. is one of the exceptions. This afternoon our Foreign Ministry colleague came in after lunch looking haggard – he had forgotten one of these volumes in a restaurant. This is a most serious offence and visions of the death penalty – by axe (the latest invention of our rulers) – chills his mind. He has raced off to his Ministry to 'confess'.

The normal method of execution in Nazi Germany was beheading by means of a miniature guillotine. But in some cases (such as high treason), Hitler had ordered the re-introduction of the medieval axe.

Tuesday, 9 April Today German troops occupied Denmark and invaded Norway. As a result, we worked like hell, since all these various *coups* must be justified in the eyes of the world at large and endless memoranda are exchanged how best to do this. I came home with a fever. Mario Gasperi telephoned; he was just back from the Siegfried Line, which he had been inspecting with the other military attachés.

The conquest of Denmark and Norway, indeed a war in the West in general, had not been part of Hitler's original plans. But Germany was vitally dependent on the free flow of Swedish iron ore, which came out via the northern Norwegian port of Narvik; moreover, once the Allies had joined the conflict, control of the two countries would open up the Atlantic to the German navy and, conversely, prevent an Allied economic blockade such as had stifled Germany in World War I. For these very reasons, ever since the autumn of 1939 there had been open talk in the Allied camp of a pre-emptive strike there, allegedly to help Finland, which was under attack from the U.S.S.R. Indeed, an Allied force was on its way to Norway when the Germans struck.

Denmark succumbed in one day, becoming a German protectorate until the end of the war. Norwegian resistance continued until June, during which time the Allies made several attempts – all of them unsuccessful – to retain a foothold in Northern Norway. But with Germany's offensive in the West, the Allied forces were withdrawn, the Norwegians capitulated and King Haakon VII escaped to England, there to set up a government-in-exile.

Hitler had gained his second major victory, after Poland: the Swedish ore route was secured (and remained so virtually until the end of the war); the Baltic Sea was to all intents and purposes a German lake; and Germany's armed forces were now poised for further conquests all the way from the North Cape to the Alps.

Wednesday, 10 April This morning I had a temperature of 39.5° C.

Thursday, 11 April Now Tatiana is down with it. She had returned from her office at midday, after a lengthy interview with the Gestapo – they were curious about our correspondence with Rome – and went straight to bed. Our respective offices keep ringing us up – worried, agitated, annoyed.

Friday, 12 April Our 'flu continues. We both feel very weak.

Saturday, 13 April The doctor does not want me to work for five more days. What a relief! Apparently, when one is as under-nourished as we are, this 'flu is bad for the heart.

Sunday, 14 April British troops have landed in Norway.

Tuesday, 16 April Dinner at Lutz Hartdegen's. As is often the case now, there were many more boys than girls. Vetti Schaffgotsch appeared unexpectedly. He was on his way to the United States via Russia, but the Gestapo took objection to his diplomatic assignment and he was summoned all the way back from Moscow. He is now enlisting.

Wednesday, 17 April Went Easter shopping and bought a startling tie for Georgie. No coupons were needed.

Met a man called Hasso von Etzdorf, who is considered very bright and reliable. To me he seemed stiff, but Prussians need time to unwind. He is at present the Foreign Ministry's liaison man with the O.K.H. [Army High Command].

A badly wounded veteran of World War I, Dr Hasso von Etzdorf had entered the diplomatic service in 1928, being posted successively to Tokyo and Rome. When Missie met him, he was an Embassy counsellor and liaison officer between the A.A. and the Chief of the General Staff, Colonel-General Franz Halder (himself hostile to Hitler's aggressive plans). Having close contact with many senior generals who shared Halder's misgivings, Etzdorf had actively sought to stir them into action. But the appeasement policies pursued by the Western powers prior to the outbreak of war, and Hitler's repeated successes once war had started, effectively cut the ground from under the feet of all his opponents.

Palm Saturday, 20 April This morning we went on a semi-official visit to Kira, Prince Louis-Ferdinand of Prussia's wife. He is the Kronprinz's second son and she is the daughter of Grand-Duke Kiril Vladimirovitch, one of the few survivors and present head of the Romanov family. She has two babies.

Monday, 22 April Mamma has come down with a thrombosis of the leg. This is very worrying.

We are fasting rather severely. Our Church allows us to disregard this in wartime, on account of general malnutrition. But we have so little to eat anyhow that we want to save up some coupons for Easter.

Tuesday, 23 April Church.

Wednesday, 24 April Church.

Thursday, 25 April In church in the evening there was the traditional reading of the Twelve Gospels.

Friday, 26 April We have been fasting so conscientiously that by now we are half-famished.

Saturday, 27 April Our respective offices gave us time off for Confession and Communion. The morning Mass lasted until two. The midnight Mass at the Russian Cathedral was so crowded that we were pushed out into the street. Later, we joined a group of friends at Dicky Eltz's and stayed up until 5 a.m. We had not been out for a long time. The Eltz brothers are Austrians with estates in Yugoslavia. Dicky is the only one who is not yet mobilised.

Sunday, 28 April Russian Easter. We went out to Potsdam and ran into Burchard of Prussia's father, Prince Oscar, another son of the ex-Kaiser – an old gentleman in a magnificent red-and-gold uniform.

We managed to make a *paskha* of which we are very proud, ingredients being so scarce. It tasted delicious.

The virtual disappearance of many indispensables since the start of the war has had a comical aftermath at my office: for some time now our bosses had been complaining about the inexplicable consumption of unaccountable quantities of w.c. paper. At first they concluded that the staff must be suffering from some new form of mass diarrhoea, but as weeks passed and the toll did not diminish, it finally dawned on them that everyone was simply tearing off ten times more than he (or she) needed and smuggling it home. A new regulation has now been issued: all staff members must betake themselves to a Central Distribution Point, where they are solemnly issued with the amount judged sufficient for their daily needs!

Thursday, 2 May Chamberlain has announced that the British are abandoning Norway. People here are rather staggered by this precipitous pull-out. Many Germans have still a lurking admiration for the English.

Saturday, 4 May Went to a big diplomatic reception. Foreign Ministry people must now wear an unbecoming uniform, dark blue with a broad white belt. There was a large buffet, but nobody dared approach it too eagerly.

We have a strange man working with us at the D.D. His name is Illion. He walks about in rags, wears thick spectacles, has an American passport, was born in Finland and has spent most of his life in Tibet, living in the entourage of the Dalai Lama and, he boasts, never washing. Although his salary is quite decent, he does not wash now either, which is not pleasant for the rest of us. Occasionally he teaches Katia Kleinmichel and me short sentences in Tibetan.

Tuesday, 7 May Have just got hold of a secret news item – Molotov has asked the German government to give no support to the Russian Church in Berlin, as its leaders are unfriendly to the Soviets!

Had rather a messy supper consisting of buns, yoghurt, warmed-up tea and jam. Yoghurt is still unrationed and, when we are at home, it constitutes our main dish, occasionally supplemented by porridge cooked in water. We are allowed approximately one jar of jam a month per person and, butter being so scarce, that does not go very far. Tatiana suggests our hanging a notice over the kitchen table: 'breakfast', 'lunch' and 'supper', according to the time of day, as the menu remains by and large unchanged. I had struck up a friendship with a Dutch milkman who occasionally kept me a bottle of milk left over from the 'expectant mothers' stock. Unfortunately he is now going back to Holland. I sometimes get desperate at having to queue up after the office, just for a piece of cheese the size of one's finger. But people in the shops remain friendly and seem to take it all still smilingly.

Thursday, 9 May Worked late and then joined a Herr von Pfuel (who is known to all as C.C.) at Aga Fürstenberg's. They were giving a party for the very beautiful Nini de Witt, the Dutch Ambassador's wife.

Friday, 10 May Germany has marched into Belgium and Holland. And yet there was Nini de Witt at the party yesterday, seemingly quite unaware! I rang up Tatiana from the office and we decided to meet for lunch and discuss matters. It comes as a shock as this means the end of the 'Phony War'. Antwerp has been bombed by the Germans and Freiburg-im-Breisgau by the Allies. There are many dead in both places. Paris is being evacuated, Chamberlain has resigned and Churchill is now Prime Minister. This, probably, kills any hope for peace with the Allies now.

In the evening a farewell reception at the Attolicos' (the departing Italian Ambassador). Everybody stands around with forlorn faces.

After the war it came to light that Freiburg-im-Bresgau was bombed in fact, not by the Allies, but by the Luftwaffe, which mistook it for a French town on the other shore of the Rhine.

Hitler had never believed that France and especially England would go to war for Poland. The months of 'Phony War' (the name given by the Allies to the relatively uneventful first winter on the Western Front), the lack of any clear statement of Allied war aims (itself due to Franco–British differences about what to do next) and wishful thinking among wide circles of the German population (which had never wanted war in the first place) contributed to the illusion inside Germany – an illusion Missie echoes – that so long as not too much blood was shed, a negotiated peace was still possible. Indeed, throughout the winter of 1939–1940 repeated feelers had been put out by influential circles on both sides to find a mutually acceptable means of putting an end to the conflict.

The German offensive had started on the night of 9–10 May with a massed airborne drop on neutral Holland and Belgium. On 15 May the bulk of the German armoured divisions had thrust through the Ardennes forest into southern Belgium. Piercing the French lines they drove quickly west to the sea, splitting the Allied forces in two and forcing the northern armies (including the British Expeditionary Force) out of Belgium and back to the English Channel. The Dutch army was to surrender on 15 May; the Belgian army on 27 May. On 3 June the last British ship would leave Dunkirk. Paris would fall on 14 June, and on 25 June France would sign an armistice that abandoned two-thirds of the country to German control, the remainder, under the rule of Marshal Philippe Petain, constituting what was to be known colloquially as 'Vichy France'.

Saturday, 11 May Antoinette and Loulou von Croy drop in to see us. Both are exceedingly pretty. Their mother is Danish-American, their father, the Duke, Franco-Belgo-German. Not easy at times such as these.

Monday, 13 May I have not had a day off for weeks and am saving all my compensatory leave to visit the Clarys at Teplitz, in Bohemia. I have not seen them since Venice and want Tatiana to meet them too.

Burchard of Prussia has written her from Cologne; he is on his way to the front.

Thursday, 16 May As of yesterday there is a big offensive on. It's enough to give one insomnia.

Friday, 17 May I keep reminding my temporary boss of my intended trip to Teplitz. Like the water dropping on to the Chinaman's head, I am hoping that the thought will sink in.

Sunday, 19 May A spaghetti picnic supper in the Wrede twins' kitchen. Tino Soldati, the new Swiss attaché, keeps rushing to the telephone. He says that the Swiss expect to be invaded any time too.

Monday, 20 May My boss, Herr E., returned today, sunburnt but fuming. He chases around in circles shouting 'Schweinerei! Saubande!' – presumably meaning us. For during his absence we had carried out a kind of palace revolution. I was even summoned by a higher boss, a Herr von Witzleben, who asked me whether it was true that I was 'hurling ultimatums' about. Luckily E. is unpopular and 'we' have carried the day.

Tatiana has had a salary raise. I feel peeved for mine seems frozen.

Wednesday, 22 May The new Italian Ambassador, Alfieri, gave a reception. Max Schaumburg-Lippe appeared suddenly – fresh from Namur, with the first personal account of what was going on at the front. Friedrich von Stumm has apparently been killed. His mother was at the Italian reception, but nobody dared tell her.

Saturday, 25 May Tatiana and I left for Teplitz, the Clarys' castle in Bohemia, at 7 a.m. In the taxi a fleeting doubt crossed my mind – whether I had left the electric iron on in the kitchen or not, but I soon forgot about it. We were greeted by Alfy Clary (who is a distant cousin of Mamma) and his sister, Elisalex de Baillet-Latour, who is married to the Belgian President of the International Olympic Committee. She now lives mostly here. We called on Alfy's mother Thérèse, a very beautiful old lady, born a Countess Kinsky, who was once painted by Sargent. The portrait was hanging over her head.

TEPLITZ, *Sunday, 26 May* Corpus Christi. We all went to church, Alphy Clary headed the procession, walking behind the priest. We watched from a window. They have heard nothing as yet from the two oldest boys, Ronnie and Marcus, who are both fighting in France. Only the youngest, Charlie, aged sixteen, is at home. He looks exactly like Harold Lloyd and, having rolled back the carpet, tap-danced very cleverly. [*Later in the war Charlie Clary was called up in his turn; he was to perish in 1944 fighting the Yugoslav partisans.*]

Monday, 27 May Lidi Clary never speaks of the boys, although in church yesterday she cried. Alfy looks worried to death. Today we played bridge and in the evening Tatiana left. I am staying on a little longer. We visited the town. Peter the Great came here once for a cure – Teplitz being a well-known spa – and there are many souvenirs of his visit.

The eldest son of the Kronprinz, Prince Wilhelm of Prussia, died today in a Brussels hospital, after being wounded in the lungs and stomach on the 13th.

Tuesday, 28 May King Leopold of the Belgians has surrendered. Elisalex Baillet-Latour is happy, for she hopes that this may save many Belgian lives.

Letters have at last arrrived from both Clary boys. Ronnie's regiment took their young French cousin prisoner. Alfy is figuring out how to notify his family. His own ideas are those of a nineteenth-century idealistic patriot and he seems very out of touch with present-day realities.

Today we saw a newsreel of the bombing of Rotterdam. Absolutely appalling. It makes one shudder for Paris.

The bombing of Rotterdam, undertaken by the Luftwaffe while negotiations for capitulation were underway, was to be one of Germany's costliest psychological blunders of the war. The bombers did not see the flares sent up by the German ground forces warning them off. Most of the city was razed to the ground, but the casualties (put by Allied propaganda at 25,000 or 30,000) were in fact 814. Nevertheless, the bombing of Rotterdam has come down in history as a typical example of Nazi wanton brutality and, together with the later bombing of English cities, did much to swing British public opinion in favour of the indiscriminate bombings of German cities with their far greater numbers of victims.

BERLIN, *Wednesday, 29 May* Tatiana returned to find me already in bed. She was furious with me, as she had found the iron still plugged in on her return from Teplitz. It had burnt its way through the shelf on which it stood on a metal stand, and had landed, thank goodness, on the stove. But a flame was creeping up the wall as Tatiana entered the kitchen three days later. I am crushed. I do not know what I would have done had the Pückler flat caught fire.

Today was Prince Wilhelm's funeral in Potsdam. Monarchists are said to have staged quite a demonstration.

Thursday, 30 May Had a nice quiet dinner at the Bennazzos'. Agostino is violently anti-fascist and, unlike many of his colleagues, is most outspoken. He predicts a dire fate for the whole of Europe.

Sunday, 2 June Yesterday we went shopping as it was pay day. We never seem to have a cent left at the end of the month, which is not astonishing, considering our salaries. The two of us now earn 450 marks, of which 100 go to the family in Rome, another 100 to repay our debts and about 200 more for food, transportation, etc. This leaves us about 50 marks for our personal expenses, clothes, mail, etc. But this time I had saved and was able to buy a dress I had spotted months ago. I had also had to put aside enough clothing coupons, but the shop forgot to ask me for them!

Tonight a bath. Now that baths are rationed too, this is an event.

Monday, 3 June Paris was bombed for the first time today. The Germans have officially announced their losses in the West to date: 10,000 dead, 8,000 missing and probably also dead. 1,200,000 Allied prisoners have been taken so far.

Thursday, 6 June Aga Fürstenberg's brother Gofi has been granted special leave for bravery. He is being sent to an officers' training school. Apparently, though he had never even done his military service, he behaved like an absolute hero and has been awarded the Iron Cross and the Panzersturm-abzeichen [Tank Combat Clasp]. Yet he hates the war before it broke out lived most of the time in Paris.

Sunday, 9 June P. G. Wodehouse was taken prisoner near Abbeville while playing golf. The German High Command want him to edit a newspaper for British P.O.W.s and have brought him to Berlin.

At the outbreak of war Wodehouse (a British subject, but a longtime American resident) was living with his wife at their home in Le Touquet, where the Germans caught them just as they were about to escape to the west. Interned as an enemy alien, he was eventually released at the request of the U.S.A. (which was not yet at war). In Berlin the representative of the American Broadcasting System talked him into making five broadcasts for the American public, describing his experiences. These broadcasts – witty, slightly ridiculing the Germans – were totally apolitical. But since he had used German broadcasting facilities to do so, he was technically guilty of collaboration with the enemy. In England this caused a furor and he was advised never to set foot in his native land again.

This afternoon after work some Hungarian friends fetched me and we drove out to Helga-Lee Schaumburg's, where we lay in the sun. Gofi Fürstenberg joined us, looking haggard. He seems utterly exhausted and could barely participate in the conversation. Aschwin Lippe has been *fristlos entlassen*, – cashiered without prior notice – because his older brother Bernhard, the Dutch Prince Consort, has joined Queen Wilhelmina in England. This will probably save Aschwin's life eventually, but he is very upset: he loved his men and had fought through the Polish and French campaigns with them, and he now feels an outcast. To make things even worse, their family estate is in his brother's name and it will now no doubt be confiscated.

Monday, 10 June Burchard of Prussia is fuming because, after his cousin Wilhelm's death, all German royal princes have been debarred from frontline duty and at best are still 'tolerated' in staff jobs. Adolf does not want them to distinguish themselves and thereby acquire 'unhealthy popularity' – for all have shown themselves to be good soldiers.

Yesterday Narvik was abandoned by the Allies and Norway surrendered. This afternoon Mussolini announced Italy's entry into the war. Apart from being stupid, this is not very elegant – to march 'triumphantly' into the south of France at this eleventh hour of the French campaign.

Wednesday, 12 June It is rumoured that Paris will be defended. I hope not; it would change nothing.

Thursday, 13 June Went with C. C. Pfuel to the theatre to see *Fiesco* with Gustaf Gründgens. This was a treat as one seldom can get tickets nowadays, these being nearly always sold out or reserved for the military on leave. We had a bite in a little restaurant afterwards and discussed the war. C.C., who is bright, does not think it will end soon and is, on the whole, pessimistic.

Friday, 14 June Paris surrendered today. Strange how lukewarm the reaction is here. There is absolutely no feeling of elation.

Saturday, 15 June Rumours of a French capitulation.

We spent the evening with Sigi Laffert and friends in Grunewald, boating and sitting around in the garden. Suddenly Agostino Bennazzo appeared, drew us aside and whispered: 'The Russians have just annexed Lithuania!' And Papa is still there! We went home at once and spent all night trying to get in touch with those at the A.A. who might prove helpful. They are all more than evasive, for fear of spoiling their *entente* with Soviet Russia.

Sunday, 16 June While Tatiana made another stab at the A.A., Burchard of Prussia came with me to church. He, too, is trying to find a way of rescuing Papa while there is still time.

Monday, 17 June Have hardly slept these last nights. It is rumoured that Lithuanian President Smetona and most of his cabinet ministers escaped across the German border.

President Antanas Smetona, who had ruled Lithuania as a benevolent dictator since 1926, succeeded in making his way to the U.S.A., where he died in 1944. The Soviet authorities immediately proceeded to purge the country: some 5,000 persons were shot and from 20,000 to 40,000 deported; most of them were to die in exile.

Although under the secret protocol of 29 September 1939 Lithuania had become part of the U.S.S.R.'s 'sphere of influence', Hitler had not agreed to its outright incorporation into the Soviet Union. Followed as it was by Moscow's seizure from Rumania of Bessarabia and North Bukovina (which brought the Soviet airforce within striking distance of the Ploesti oil fields, Germany's main source of fossilfuels), this annexation was viewed by Hitler as a breach of faith to which there could be only one possible response – his long-held dream, the conquest of the U.S.S.R.

Albert Eltz has just telephoned that Marshal Pétain has capitulated in the name of France. The French Cabinet seem to have scattered in all directions. It all seems incredible after only two months' fighting.

Tuesday, 18 June France is being occupied with great speed. C. C. Pfuel and Burchard of Prussia have started enquiries about Papa with the help of a Colonel Oster of the Abwehr [Military Intelligence]. No news as yet.

A dashing officer of outstanding ability and a passionate anti-Nazi, the Alsatianborn Colonel (later Major-General) Hans Oster (1888–1945) had, in his capacity of Chief-of-Staff to Admiral Canaris, turned the Abwehr into a safe-house for antiNazi resisters. In the early days of the war he had, possibly with Canaris' knowledge, leaked Hitler's invasion plans to their opposite numbers in the intelligence services of Denmark, Norway, the Netherlands and Belgium. But by 1943 several of his protégés had been arrested and presently he was dismissed, the Military resistance regrouping around General Olbricht and Colonel von Stauffenberg. Arrested in the aftermath of the abortive 20th July Plot, Oster was to perish because of the German mania for keeping records. Once his driver had betrayed their hiding-place, the Gestapo made short shrift of him. He was hanged together with Canaris on 9 April 1945 at Flossenburg concentration camp.

Wednesday, 19 June The Tillmanns family have arrived from Lithuania. Of German-Russian descent, they were important industrialists there. Two hours before the Soviet takeover, both the German Minister, Dr Zechlin, and my ex-boss, the British Minister, Mr Thomas Preston, warned them to get out. Their son has stayed on, hoping that, with his German passport, he can save some of their property.

Thursday, 20 June On returning tonight I found a telegram from Papa. Sent from Tilsit, in East Prussia, it said: 'Glücklich angekommen' ['have arrived safely'], and asked for money to come and join us.

Friday, 21 June A crawfish party at C. C. Pfuel's with Luisa Welczeck and Burchard of Prussia; the latter brought us home in his car, which is strictly illegal. We were just going to bed when the sirens sounded an air-raid warning. We sat downstairs on the steps and chatted with the doorman, who is an air warden as well. Later we learnt that bombs were dropped near Potsdam, but none over Berlin.

Saturday, 22 June Spent the evening at Tino Soldati's. The armistice in the West was announced and the 'Wir treten zum Beten' ['Let us gather together to pray . . .'] was sung over the wireless. Everybody present spoke scathingly about the Italians for having attacked France only once the chestnuts had been pulled out of the fire for them.

Monday, 24 June Dinner at Gatow on the lake with a group of Italian friends. Went home early, as the others were off to a party given by the American-born wife of one of the Italian diplomats here. It strikes me as somewhat indecent to be so jolly, considering what is happening in France.

Tuesday, 25 June On returning home, I found Papa, extraordinarily spry considering what he has just been through. His only earthly possessions now are his shaving things, two dirty handkerchiefs and a shirt. On reaching

German soil, he was apparently treated very well by the frontier police – thanks to Colonel Oster's intervention. He was even offered money to join us. But before that, he had had a scary time, hiding in the woods of his former estate and crossing the border at dead of night with the help of an ex-poacher. This proved difficult, as in the height of summer the underbush was very dry and noisy underfoot.

When the Soviet troops took over Lithuania, Missie's father was visiting Vilnius, the country's ancient capital, which had been returned to Lithuania by the Soviets the preceding autumn following the dismemberment of Poland. Taking the first train back to Kaunas – where he lived – he spent the night with friends, after which, without going home, he took a steamer down the river Nieman to Jurbarkas, where the Vassiltchikov estates had been. The family had remained popular with the local population and in due course guides were found who volunteered to smuggle him across the border into Germany. They happened to be poachers who used to 'work' his forests and when he reached German soil and was about to pay them off, they refused, saying: 'We've had our reward many times over . . . when you still lived here!'

Monday, 1 July After work, paid a visit to Luisa Welczeck and Tatiana at their office in the former Czechoslovak Legation in the Rauchstrasse. Luisa's boss is a very nice diplomat, Josias von Rantzau, who was formerly posted in Denmark and the United States. He has a keen sense of humour, which stands him in good stead, as Luisa writes excellent limericks about the office personnel and rags him a lot. We were treated to a stiff drink and things seemed, generally, very relaxed.

Tuesday, 2 July Dinner with Otto von Bismarck, the Bennazzos, Helen Biron and a young Swede, von Helgow, from their Legation here. We spent the rest of the evening in his flat near the Tiergarten, which is full of Wedgwood bric-a-brac. Dangerous in times like these.

The eldest grandson of the Iron Chancellor, Prince Otto von Bismarck (1897–1975) had started out as a right-wing member of the Reichstag (in which his younger brother Gottfried was to sit for the Nazi party). He had then switched to diplomacy, being posted to Stockholm and London. His career culminated in 1940 to 1943 as Minister-Counsellor with the German Embassy in Rome. After the war, he re-entered politics, serving for a time in the Bonn Bundestag.

Sunday, 7 July Tatiana, Luisa Welczeck and I were invited to the Italian

Ambassador's residence in Wannsee for a 'quiet swim'. This turned out to be in honour of Foreign Minister Ciano, who is here for a memorial service for Marshal Italo Balbo, who has just been killed in an air crash in Libya.

For this occasion the Embassy seemed to have invited all the prettiest girls in Berlin, but none of the men we happened to know. Ciano's own entourage turned out to be rather unattractive, Blasco d'Ayeta, his *chef de cabinet*, being the only exception. To us the whole thing seemed pretty fishy. We were whirled around the Wannsee in numerous motor boats in the pouring rain. On getting back, we three decided to take off for home as soon as we could find a car. But when it came to saying goodbye and thank you to our host, we found him and Ciano in a darkened room, dancing cheek-to-cheek with two of the flightiest ladies Berlin has to offer. And this on a day of alleged official mourning! We departed disgusted, and Luisa has even complained to her father.

Thursday, 11 July My young A.A. colleague is throwing a party and has invited Katia Kleinmichel and me. Katia believes he has asked Baillie-Stewart as well. The latter is a British officer who betrayed some plans to Germany several years ago, was imprisoned for a while in the Tower, and is now here. I asked Katia to tell our colleague that I preferred not to come, as I did not wish to meet the fellow. Our friend took this very badly, saying that Baillie-Stewart was 'the most decent Englishman he had ever met'. I could not help answering that he did not seem to have met many and that if he was right, then God Save the King! He threatened to cancel the party altogether – 'all on account of my stupidity'. So I agreed to attend it after all and spent most of the evening watching the others playing poker. Otherwise we work in harmony.

Our boss, Herr E., has been relegated to a den of his own from which he never emerges.

Friday, 12 July This evening, the Bielenbergs gave a small party in Dahlem. Peter Bielenberg is a lawyer from Hamburg. Nearly seven foot tall, extremely handsome, with the complexion of an Indian rajah, he is married to a charming English girl, Christabel, a niece of Lord Northcliffe, I believe. They have two little boys. The elder one, aged seven, was expelled from his school for having protested when his teacher referred to the English as

Schweine. The parents want to avoid further incidents and she is taking them to the Tyrol to sit the war out there. They are a very attractive couple. An old friend of Peter's since their university days, Adam von Trott zu Solz was also there. I had seen him once before in Josias Rantzau's office. He has remarkable eyes.

The son of a former Prussian minister of education, Adam von Trott zu Solz (1909–1944) had an American grandmother, who was the great-grand-daughter of John Jay, the first Chief Justice of the United States. After studying at the Universities of Munich, Göttingen and Berlin, he had won a Rhodes scholarship at Balliol College, Oxford. Following a spell of law practise in Germany, he had in 1937–1938 spent some time in the U.S.A. and travelled extensively in China. In 1939 he was back in England where, sponsored by the Astors and Lord Lothian, he was received by Prime Minister Neville Chamberlain and Foreign Secretary Lord Halifax. In September 1939 (the war in Europe had already started) he was again in the U.S. at the invitation of the Institute of Pacific Relations. Wherever he now went, to all foreign politicians he met, he advocated a dual, some thought ambiguous, message: stand up to Hitler and encourage the anti-Nazi opposition but respect Germany's national interests. By then, any expression of German patriotism (and Trott, like all anti-Nazi resisters, was above all an ardent patriot) was viewed with suspicion and Trott himself came to be regarded in some Allied circles with distrust. He returned to Germany in 1940, via Siberia. Joining the Nazi party for cover, he took a job with the A.A., where an active anti-Nazi group was forming around two senior officials, the brothers Erich and Theodor Kordt. Eventually his colleague Hans-Bernd von Haeften brought him into Count Helmuth von Moltke's 'Kreisau Circle', the foremost think tank of the Resistance which was planning Germany's post-Nazi future. On its behalf he took advantage of his every trip abroad – and he travelled much – to maintain contact with his friends in the Allied camp.
Christabel Bielenberg was to describe her own experiences in her best-selling 'The Past is Myself' *(Chatto & Windus, London, 1968).*

Saturday, 13 July I accompanied Tatiana to the Gestapo, where we were received by a particularly repulsive character. Our legal situation is becoming more difficult. As far as the Germans are concerned, our Lithuanian passports are no longer valid since the Soviets have annexed the Baltic States and are now demanding that all former citizens of these countries apply for Soviet citizenship. This we will of course not do.

Sunday, 14 July In the evening a friend of Papa's, a Baron Klodt, who is a former Russian naval hero (from the 1904–1905 Russo-Japanese war days) and Misha Boutenev came by. The latter is a very bright Russian youngster who spent a whole winter living with his brothers and sisters in a cellar in Warsaw, after having fled from Russian-occupied eastern Poland. His father has been deported to the U.S.S.R. What irony that this should happen twenty years after his original escape from Russia during the Revolution! Misha has his sister's twins with him, aged seven. They are being treated decently, having been born in the United States.

Tuesday, 16 July Paul Mertz has just been killed flying over Belgium. A young Luftwaffe officer whom we met last summer in Silesia, he left us his dog 'Sherry' when he went off to the war. As we could not bring Sherry to Berlin, we farmed him out.

Today at the office I received, by mistake, a blank sheet with a yellow strip across. These are usually reserved for especially important news. As I had nothing better to do, I typed out on it an alleged rumour about a riot in London, with the King hanged at the gates of Buckingham Palace, and passed it on to an idiotic girl who promptly translated it and included it in a news broadcast to South Africa. The boss, who has to vet any outgoing news item, recognised it as mine because of some German grammatical mistakes. As he was feeling mellow today, he took it well.

Wednesday, 17 July At Tino Soldati's tonight I had a long talk with Hasso Etzdorf about France. He has the reputation of being a very good man, but the *m'en fichisme* in lieu of open criticism, which even some of the best Germans display in public as a kind of self-protection, while dissociating themselves from their country's present rulers and actions, is to me sometimes quite frightening. For if they don't stand up for their beliefs, where will all this end?

It was only after the failure of the 20th July coup that Missie learnt about Hasso von Etzdorf's key role in the anti-Nazi resistance, and that his earlier aloofness when discussing politics was merely elementary caution.

Monday, 22 July Listened at home over the radio to a beautiful concert of the Berlin Philharmonic.

Daroussia Gortchakov has just sent us from Switzerland a list of White

Russian émigré boys who had been fighting in the French army and who have been listed as missing since the end of the French campaign; they include, among others, our first cousin Jim Viazemsky, Misha Cantacuzene and Aliosha Tatishchev. It has not been possible as yet to locate them.

Tuesday, 23 July Misha Cantacuzene has been found, but we are worried about Jim Viazemsky, who was last seen in Flanders. No news either from our cousins, the Shcherbatov girls, in Paris.

Thursday, 25 July Dinner at the Horstmanns' to celebrate Freddie's birthday. For the first time since the Chilean ball we wore long dresses. The conversation centred on gas masks. We do not have any, which caused some surprise, for rumour has it that some gas bombs were found in the wreckage of a recently shot down British plane.

A passionate collector, with the personal wealth to indulge in this passion, 'Freddie' Horstmann was one of the most colourful characters in wartime Berlin. A former distinguished diplomat, he had, when Hitler came to power, been made to resign from the Foreign Service on account of the Jewish background of his wife Lally. At the time Missie writes, the small but exquisite Horstmann flat in the Steinplatz was an island of civilisation in a mounting sea of barbarity. There, amidst Freddie's art collections, a carefully selected group of friends (which invariably included some of the most beautiful ladies in Europe) would periodically gather in an atmosphere that was refined, relaxed and stimulating. Though politics were a taboo subject, the very existence of the Horstmann salon, with its shared interests – and aversions – was a subtle defiance of all Nazism stood for.

Friday, 26 July Albert Eltz dropped in this evening. He brought us cake and Kolynos toothpaste – a valuable item which one can get now only at Siemensstadt. He is an anti-aircraft gunner on the roof of the factory there and was locked up recently for having been caught reading an English novel instead of scanning the skies for English planes.

Monday, 29 July I make a point these days of staying at home on Mondays, on account of the Philharmonic concerts that are broadcast weekly.

Tatiana has been given another raise. I have not. I am lagging sadly behind.

Thursday, 1 August I am getting to know Tatiana's boss, Josias Rantzau, a little better and like him very much. A lazy retriever with a good sense of humour.

Saturday, 3 August Through a neutral country we have finally heard from Mara Shcherbatov. All the cousins are back in Paris, but without jobs. André Ignatiev, an old friend of theirs, lost a leg fighting with the French army.

Sunday, 4 August After church we joined a group of friends at the Hotel Eden, where Luisa Welczeck was lunching with a boy called Paul Metternich, the famous Chancellor's great-grandson, who is half-Spanish. Afterwards, as we were all invited to the Schaumburgs' out in Cladow, we took off in different cars, with Paul Metternich in the rumble-seat with Tatiana, Nagy and me. He has practically no hair on his head, poor thing, just stubble, as he is a simple soldier somewhere. Because of this unannounced intrusion, poor Burchard of Prussia had to take the train. It is obvious that Paul has fallen for Tatiana.

Thursday, 8 August Coffee with Luisa Welczeck and Josias Rantzau in her office. We were later joined by Adam Trott, whose looks fascinate me. It is perhaps his intensity which is somehow so striking. Dined with Tatiana, Burchard of Prussia and Rantzau at Luisa's at her Hotel am Steinplatz. Luisa danced the flamenco, having changed into the appropriate clothes. She is really good at it.

Tuesday, 13 August This evening C. C. Pfuel, two other guests and I managed to consume 120 crawfish. At 11 p.m. Tatiana telephoned that Papa had slipped in the dark and cut his head open on the sidewalk. As he was bleeding profusely and we had no bandages at home, we took off to find an open pharmacy. We had hardly seen to Papa, when there was an air-raid. It needed a great deal of persuasion to make him come down to the cellar (our flat is on the fourth floor) – he feared the neighbours might think he had had a fight. There was quite a lot of shooting and the all-clear sounded only at 3 a.m. There are heavy raids over England these days and this is probably in retaliation.

Following the fall of France, Hitler, hopeful that England would sue for peace, called a pause and on 19 July, in a triumphant speech to his dummy-Reichstag, he extended a formal offer to that effect. Winston Churchill's response was to demand Germany's withdrawal to its 1938 frontiers. Whereupon Hitler set in motion the first stage of

'Operation Sea-Lion', the code-name for the conquest of Britain: on 15 August the Luftwaffe launched an all-out offensive to gain mastery of the British skies. This was to become known as 'The Battle of Britain'.

Friday, 16 August Josias Rantzau has presented us four girls with a variety of good French perfume with exotic and suggestive names – Mitsouko, Ma Griffe, Je Reviens, etc, – of which I had not heard before.

Tuesday, 20 August Tatiana and I had a talk with some members of the Swiss Legation to find out how we could get in touch with our cousin, Jim Viazemsky. We now know that he is unhurt in a P.O.W. camp somewhere in Germany.

Sunday, 25 August Tonight there was another air-raid. Tatiana was out. I first stayed in bed, but the shooting was so violent that at times our whole room was lit up. I ended up in the cellar, forcing Papa to come along with me.

Though cities like Warsaw and Rotterdam had been bombed by the Germans in the opening stages of the war, both they and the British were long reluctant to start massive bombing of one another's civilian targets. Even the Battle of Britain was at first essentially a series of dog-fights for supremacy in the air. But in the night of 24 August German aircraft dropped some bombs on London by mistake. The following night – the one Missie has just described – the R.A.F. retaliated with an 80-bomber raid on Berlin. Incensed, Hitler thereupon ordered the Luftwaffe to cease pounding the R.A.F.'s ground installations and to concentrate on London. This decision was to cost him the Battle of Britain, for just when British air-defenses were at their weakest and German victory in the air in sight, the R.A.F. was able to regain its breath and rebuild its strength. But from then on, also, the green light was on for the indiscriminate bombing of civilian populations everywhere.

Monday, 26 August Yet another raid. We stayed in bed, although the doormen of all houses have now received orders to force everyone into the cellars. Ours came along too, rattling a saucepan to get us up. But this time the racket only lasted half an hour.

Tuesday, 27 August Dropped in on Tatiana at her office after work. One could hear a lot of splashing from the next room, a bathroom. Her boss was evidently taking advantage of the fact that hot water is still freely available in government establishments.

Dinner with friends, including the two Kieckebusch brothers. Both were

badly wounded in France. Mäxchen was paralysed for three months. Claus's
tank caught fire, he was thrown out, his face badly burnt, but he has recovered
well and one does not see much. This is lucky, as he is proud of his looks.
Two members of his crew, however, died.

Wednesday, 28 August Today, as I was passing the Kaiser Wilhelm Gedächtniskirche in a bus, the sirens sounded. The bus stopped and everybody was
hustled into the basement of the K.D.W. department store. The sun was
shining brightly and nothing more happened. But tonight, while we were
dining out in Grunewald, there was quite a to-do. We stood in the garden,
watching the many green and red 'Christmas trees' that were dropped on the
town. We soon had to take refuge in the house, because of all the *flak*
splinters. This time there appear to have been quite a number of victims. We
got home only after 4 a.m.

Monday, 2 September Although we expected a raid, we stayed at home, hoping
to get some sleep. Our cellar is rather well arranged. Small children lie in
cots, sucking their thumbs. Tatiana and I usually play chess. She beats me
regularly.

Tuesday, 3 September Air-raid at midnight, but as Tatiana had a slight fever,
we stayed upstairs. Our beds are in different corners of the room and Tatiana
fears that if the house is hit I might be hurtled into space while she would
remain suspended in mid-air, so I got into her bed and we lay hugging each
other for two full hours. The noise was ghastly. Flashes of light outside kept
lighting up the room. The planes flew so low that one could hear them
distinctly. At times they seemed just above our heads. A most unpleasant
feeling. Even Papa was slightly perturbed and came in for a chat.

Friday, 6 September These nightly raids are getting exhausting, as one only
gets in three or four hours' sleep. Next week we are going on leave to the
Rhineland, to stay with the Hatzfeldts. People tease us for going to the
Rhineland of all places 'to escape the bombs', but the German countryside is
still relatively peaceful and the Ruhr – a major target for Allied bombs – is a
long way away.

Saturday, 7 September Today we moved from the Pücklers' to Ditti
Mandelsloh's *pied-à-terre*. He is at the front and does not wish it to stay vacant
for fear it may be requisitioned by some party fellow. It is in the

Hardenbergstrasse, near the Zoo S-Bahn station – a bad location in an air-raid – but it is tiny and therefore practical. It does not even have an anteroom and consists of a small sitting-room, a bedroom, a nice bathroom (though this seldom has hot water), a tiny kitchen and a corridor running the whole length of the back. We are turning one end of that into a room for Papa. The whole flat looks out on to a dark yard and forms part of a large office building which is not inhabited at night except for a female caretaker who will do some cleaning.

Sunday, 8 September I visited Lally Horstmann, who lives just around the corner, and we chatted about what may have become of our English and French friends. The raids over England have started up again and it is rumoured that terrible fires are raging in London.

Monday, 9 September Another raid. I slept through the whole thing, hearing neither the siren, nor the bombs, nor the all-clear. This shows how exhausted I am.

Tuesday, 10 September Went to bed early. At midnight, another alarm. This time the Hedwig hospital was hit, one of the bombs landing in and setting fire to Antoinette Croy's room (she had just been operated on). Luckily she had been carried down to the cellar just in time. The Reichstag also caught fire and several bombs fell in the American Embassy garden.

Wednesday, 11 September Air-raid. An American friend, Dick Metz, took me to see Antoinette Croy, who is chirpy and rather proudly shows off the wreckage in her room. He is unofficially engaged to her sister Loulou.

Tomorrow we are off for a ten days' stay at the Hatzfeldts'.

Thursday, 12 September We took the sleeper to Cologne. The train went at great speed and I kept waiting for the crash. In many places we passed through the sky was red and one town was on fire. In Cologne we had breakfast with Bally Hatzfeldt, having somehow missed her on the train. We then visited the cathedral. Many of its famous stained-glass windows have been removed to safety. As we wanted to buy something, just anything, we settled for handkerchiefs. At noon we took an incredibly slow train to Wissen, where we were picked up by the Hatzfeldt car.

CROTTORF, *Saturday, 14 September* Schloss Crottorf is a lovely place. Like many castles in Westphalia, it is surrounded by two moats full of water and from the outside looks rather forbidding, but inside it is most liveable, being full of fine pictures, good furniture and masses of books. It is surrounded by hilly woods and at present is inhabited by Lalla, the eldest Hatzfeldt daughter, and her parents. The only son, Bübchen, aged nineteen, is a soldier in the army.

Thursday, 19 September One sinks into nothingness. We rise at 10 a.m., breakfast with the girls, write letters till lunch time, afterwards sit with the Princess and from 3 to 5 p.m. retire to read and sleep in our respective rooms. At 5 p.m. – tea. It rains all the time, but in the late afternoon the weather usually clears a little and we go for long walks in search of mushrooms. Gone is the Bally we knew in Berlin – a real glamour girl. Here she trudges along in thick shoes and motorist's goggles, but she still has the longest and curliest eyelashes I have ever seen. Sometimes we play racing-demon, but only when we feel particularly energetic. At 7 p.m. we bathe and change into long dresses. Afterwards everyone sits around the fire until 10 p.m., when we retire 'exhausted' to bed. The Prince wakes up after dinner and can be witty, although he is very old. The food is always delicious and we look back on our habitual Berlin fare with gloom.

Friday, 20 September Jim Viazemsky has written us in German from his P.o.W. camp. He asks for food, tobacco and clothes. He says that he left all his gear in his car before the town hall of Beauvais. He seems to hope that we may still be able to retrieve it there. Several friends of his are in the same camp and he is allowed to take long walks.

Monday, 23 September Tatiana feels sometimes sick and we fear it may be appendicitis. She is generally rather fragile.

Tuesday, 24 September Tatiana has been to see the doctor at Wissen; his verdict – appendicitis and the beginning of blood poisoning. He wants to operate immediately! We have arranged it for Thursday, as I must leave Friday and would like to see her through it before I go.

Thursday, 26 September The operation went off all right. The doctor is pleased, but Tatiana feels sorry for herself. She must stay in hospital ten days, after which she will go back to Crottorf to recuperate. I stayed all day with her, taking the night sleeper from Cologne to Berlin.

BERLIN, *Friday, 27 September* Arrived to find Papa at breakfast. Apparently air-raids are now a nightly occurrence.

The Three Power Pact between Germany, Italy and Japan was announced today.

Though in November 1936 it had adhered, alongside Germany and Italy, to the Anti-Comintern Pact, Japan had long held back from closer ties with them. Hitler's successes in the West tempted it to throw caution to the winds and link its fate with the European aggressors. Under this agreement, better known as the 'Tripartite Pact', Japan recognised the leadership of Germany and Italy in the establishment of a 'New Order' in Europe, while Germany and Italy reciprocated with regard to Japan in 'Greater East Asia'. The parties also agreed to come to one another's aid if one of them were attacked by a third power (meaning the U.S.A.).

Sunday, 29 September Air-raid. As we live on the ground floor, we no longer go down to the cellar and I stayed in bed. But then people are beginning to distrust cellars. A few nights ago a bomb landed on a house nearby, hitting it from the side. Though the house itself remained standing, in the cellar the pipes burst and all the inmates were drowned.

Monday, 30 September Gusti Biron has not returned from a raid over England. His sister Helen is frantic.

Tonight's raid lasted from 11 p.m. to 4 a.m. I stayed in bed reading most of the time, falling asleep before the all-clear.

Tuesday, 1 October I had supper with friends in Dahlem and was caught by the sirens at the Zoo station. I escaped in time and ran all the way home. I hate the idea of being stuck during a raid in some anonymous cellar. But this is bound to happen sooner or later, as once the sirens start, one is forbidden to stay out in the streets.

Wednesday, 2 October When we stay home, Papa cooks; he is quite gifted but puts too much pepper in everything. He is beginning to give Russian lessons.

There was only a short alarm.

Sunday, 6 October Supper with Konstantin of Bavaria and Bübchen Hatzfeldt. The latter was given a dressing-down by a colonel sitting at the next table because he did not salute him. All very unnecessary and embarrassing for everybody.

Tuesday, 8 October This night's raid was the longest yet; it lasted five hours, with much shooting, a few bombs and subsequent fires. We stayed in bed.

Thursday, 10 October In London, Aunt Katia Galitzine was killed by a bomb which hit the bus she was riding in. There was a memorial service for her here in Berlin this morning.

I am reading Vladimir Soloviov's prophecies, which are hardly encouraging.

Vladimir Soloviov (1853–1900) was a friend and follower of Dostoyevsky and a leading Russian poet, philosopher and mystic. Missie is referring here to his Story of the Antichrist, *an apocalyptic vision of the latter's coming – which Soloviov believed to be imminent – in which the horrors of modern totalitarianism, whether of the Left or the Right, are foretold with chilling accuracy.*

This evening I was at a party when the alarm sounded. The shooting was very loud and poor Mäxchen Kieckebusch, whose nerves have gone to pieces since he was injured in the spine in France, rolled on the floor moaning 'Ich kann das nicht mehr hören' ['I cannot listen to this anymore'] over and over again. After I left, the others went on and a drunken Swiss fired a shot that narrowly missed Mäxchen.

Friday, 18 October Tatiana is back, pale and weak.

Sunday, 20 October Ronnie Clary is here for the day. He is decidedly one of the most attractive and gifted young men of our generation. He has just got engaged.

Evening at Wolly Saldern's in Grunewald. He is on leave and lives with his family. The house is crammed with good books and good music. We had just started for home in Zichy's car when the alarm sounded. As only diplomats are allowed on the streets after the sirens, Zichy drove us back to Wolly's, where we sat listening to records until about 2 a.m. Then I set out for home with Konstantin of Bavaria, a walk of over three miles. After we had crossed the Halensee bridge, the sirens again started to howl. As nobody stopped us, we went on, but the shooting soon became unpleasant and on the Kurfürstendamm a policeman shoved us into a cellar. We sat there on the floor, shivering with cold, for three hours. I had no coat, so we both huddled under

Konstantin's raincoat. Part of the time we dozed or listened to the others talking. Berliners are at their best in times of crisis and can be very funny. At 6 a.m. the all-clear sounded. No trams or taxis, of course, anywhere, so we ran a race down the Kurfürstendamm to warm up and finally found a taxi which brought us home. We had to make a detour near my house – two ambulances had collided just after having dug out some people from the house next door to ours, which is now pulverised, and three people who had survived the bomb were killed in the crash.

On getting home, I found Tatiana very worried about me, for that bomb had just barely missed our own building. I pulled on a sweater, lay down for half an hour and then had to take off for the office. I could not work, I was so tired. At Katia Kleinmichel's suggestion I stretched out on a camp bed (which is there for emergencies) and woke up only three hours later to find my boss studying me with disapproval. All day long people have been calling to enquire whether we are still alive, as our neighbourhood was apparently badly damaged, several bombs falling between us and Luisa Welczeck's hotel around the corner.

Saturday, 26 October After work I drove out in Tino Soldati's car with Tatiana to C. C. Pfuel's place. We sat around the fire, took baths, slept and tried to forget the air-raids.

Monday, 28 October Today the Italians attacked Greece. Hitler is meeting Mussolini. A great to-do on the radio.

Though already involved in Abyssinia and Libya, Mussolini could not allow Hitler a monopoly in redrawing the map of Europe. Fresh from his easy success in France, which had earned Italy Nice and Corsica, he now turned his gaze eastwards – to the Balkans, where in April 1939 Italy had already annexed Albania. Now, on 28 October, the Italian forces crossed the border into Greece.

Not only had Hitler not been forewarned, but he had explicitly advised Mussolini against any such initiative, for he had no illusions about the Italian army. Moreover, he was now intent on his grandest design of all – the conquest of Russia. The last thing he needed was a British intervention on the southernmost flank of the German armies that were beginning to mass in the East, as would inevitably happen were Greece to appeal for British aid. Moreover, the Greek dictator at the time, General Metaxas, was pro-German. Preparations for the Italian offensive were therefore carried out in total secrecy from their German allies; and when Hitler met Mussolini in Florence on

28 October – reportedly one of the stormiest of all their meetings – he could merely record a fait accompli.

Tuesday, 29 October The British have landed in Crete.

Friday, 1 November Tonight we had two raids, one lasting from 9.30 p.m. to 1 a.m. and the other from 2.30 a.m. till 6 a.m. Our ground floor flat is a blessing.

Sunday, 3 November British troops have landed in mainland Greece.

Monday, 4 November As I suffer from lack of exercise, I have started taking gym lessons and feel better already, though somewhat stiff. The teacher seems to think she will make an athlete of me just because I am tall and thin.

Wednesday, 6 November Paul Metternich has been here for the last six days and Tatiana is out with him most of the time.

Friday, 8 November Paul Metternich left today and Tatiana was at home for a change.

Monday, 11 November Sideravicius – the former head of the Lithuanian police, who is our next-door neighbour – related how while he was queuing outside his butcher shop he saw a dead donkey being carried in by the back door; he recognised it by its hooves and the ears, which were sticking out from under the tarpaulin. So that is where our weekly schnitzels may be coming from!

Sunday, 10 November Drove with Luisa Welczeck, Tatiana and Josias Rantzau out to Adam Trott's in Dahlem. He married Clarita Tiefenbach recently. He is a former Rhodes scholar and there is something very special about him. Hitler's private secretary and liaison man to the A.A., Gesandter Walther Hewel, was there. The latter once nonplussed Cartier, the Belgian, by asking him what Luisa and her friends' attitude to the regime was. He is clumsy, but is said to be relatively harmless and is the only member of the 'inner establishment' who occasionally surfaces in other circles. Some people seem to hope they can acquire a positive influence through him.

Thursday, 14 November Paul Metternich is back. Tatiana sees him constantly.

Wednesday, 27 November Dined with Tatiana, Paul Metternich and Dicky Eltz at Savarin's. Ate lobster and other unrationed plutocratic delicacies.

When Tatiana is home after being out with Paul all evening, he usually rings up in the middle of the night and they talk and talk. Luckily the telephone has a long cord so I can chase her out into the sitting-room, otherwise I would hardly sleep a wink.

Like quite a few other features of everyday life in German-occupied Europe, the food distribution system had its unexpected quirks. Thus, while seafood was either unobtainable or strictly rationed, deep-sea fishing fleets having disappeared owing to the mining of coastal waters and the Battle of the Atlantic, shell-fish, including such erstwhile 'plutocratic delicacies' as lobsters and oysters, remained plentiful right up to the Allied landings of 1944. Likewise, though decent beer was soon hard to find even inside Germany, French wine and Champagne, though rationed in France itself, soon inundated the Reich.

Sunday, 1 December Konstantin of Bavaria accompanied me to the Russian church in which he is very interested. We went on to the Zoo and the Aquarium; there were many repulsive water snakes swimming around and other reptiles. It seems surprising they should keep them, with the ever-worsening air-raids.

Monday, 2 December People are dropping indiscreet hints about Paul Metternich and Tatiana. It's a nuisance to have constantly to deny their engagement, but they do not want to announce it now, as they plan to marry only late next summer.

The Greeks are sweeping the Italians out of Albania. The latter still hold Durazzo and Valona. A current Berlin pun: the French have put up a sign on the Riviera: 'Greeks, stop here! This is France'.

Tuesday, 3 December The former Paris Préfet de Police, Chiappe, has been shot down in the Near East when flying to Syria. Lately, two Egyptian cabinet ministers suffered the same fate. German propaganda makes a great play of 'perfidious Albion' popping off foreign statesmen who have become an embarrassment.

Jean Chiappe (1878–1940), a right-wing politician and former Paris police chief, had been appointed by Marshal Pétain High Commissioner in Syria, which was about to be invaded by a joint British-Gaullist force.

Thursday, 5 December We are without news from Rome for some time. Marshal Badoglio has resigned; he was Supreme Commander of the Italian armed forces. Also Admiral Cavagnari, who headed the Italian navy. The Italians seem to have been utterly unprepared for their campaign against Greece; their losses are horrendous.

The Italian invasion of Greece had almost immediately turned into a disaster. Skilfully led by General Alexander Papagos, the Greeks had put up a determined stand and within weeks had not only thrown back the enemy but invaded Albania in their turn. And meanwhile, as Hitler had feared, British troops and material had been pouring into Greece and its outlying islands.

Saturday, 7 December Evening vespers. Was dropped off at our church by Tatiana and Paul Metternich on their way to the theatre. Later I went on to the opera to hear Karajan. He is very fashionable and some people tend to consider him better than Furtwängler, which is nonsense. He certainly has genius and much fire, but is not without conceit.

Sunday, 8 December Lunch at the Hotel Adlon with Tatiana, Paul Metternich and the Oyarzabals (who are with the Spanish Embassy here.) We had hoped to have a good meal there, but it turned out to be *Eintopftag*, 'one-dish day' – a tasteless stew that all restaurants are obliged to serve once a week. We drove out to C. C. Pfuel's much disgusted.

Wednesday, 11 December Now the Italians are being beaten also in Africa. The British have started an offensive there. Already one Italian general has been killed.

In North Africa the Italians had attacked on 12 September and within a week had captured Sollum and Sidi Barrani, but there their offensive had come to a halt. On 9 December the British counter-attacked, expelled the Italians from the Western Desert, captured Tobruk, overran most of Cyrenaica and took some 120,000 Italian prisoners. By early February 1941, General Archibald Wavell would reach the El Agheila line. Six weeks later, General Erwin Rommel would launch his epic counter-offensive which would bring the Axis forces to the gates of Alexandria.

Thursday, 12 December The British announce that they have captured Sidi Barrani. The Italians continue to be systematically driven out of Albania. One cannot help feeling sorry for so many fine people – proud Italian patriots, everything notwithstanding.

Monday, 16 December Last night bombs fell on the Tauentzienstrasse, a main Berlin shopping artery, smashing most of the windows. The whole street is littered with broken glass.

Tuesday, 17 December Yesterday I dined at the San Martinos'. Most of the Italians present whirled around in crazy dances. Their military reverses do not seem to trouble them overmuch.

Wednesday, 18 December Adam Trott has suggested to Tatiana that I work for him as private secretary at the A.A. He is brilliantly intelligent and I would have to live up to his high standards. But the atmosphere at the A.A. is far more congenial than at our D.D. Most of his colleagues have lived part of their lives abroad and have therefore seen more than just *das Dritte Reich*. Besides, my present job is becoming tediously routine-like. However, my contract runs until March. I must therefore find a valid excuse for leaving. In wartime it is difficult to change jobs.

The other day we drew up a list of the food served in our office canteen. It is short and not very imaginative:
Monday: Red cabbage with meat sauce
Tuesday: Meatless day. Codfish in mustard sauce
Wednesday: Stonefish patties (this tastes exactly as it sounds)
Thursday: Assorted vegetable dish (red cabbage, white cabbage, potatoes, red cabbage, white cabbage . . .)
Friday: Mussels in wine sauce (this is a 'special dish' which vanishes within minutes, so that one has to fall back on potato dumplings in sauce)
Saturday: One of the above
Sunday: Another of the above
Dessert all through the week: vanilla pudding with raspberry sauce.

Monday, 23 December After work I had a talk with Adam Trott. The job seems interesting, though difficult to define. He evidently would like to turn me into a kind of confidential factotum. He is doing many things at a time, the whole of it under the official cover of 'Free India'.

Shortly before the start of World War II, the Indian nationalist movement had split – the more extremist wing under Subhas Chandra Bose (1897–1945) advocating the overthrow of British rule in India by force, while Gandhi and Nehru remained true to non-violence. Bose judged Nazi Germany to be a natural ally and in January 1941 he escaped to Berlin, where he was taken in charge by the A.A.'s Sonderreferat Indien *(Indian Special Department). Nominally headed by a Nazi hack, Under-Secretary of State Wilhelm Keppler, this office was in fact run by two staunch anti-Nazis, Adam von Trott zu Solz and Dr Alexander Werth.*

In due course, Bose was allowed to set up a 'Free India Centre' – which enjoyed diplomatic status – and to broadcast anti-British propaganda in various Indian languages. He even declared war on England 'in the name of free India'. But his planned 'Indian Legion' (to be made up of Indian P.O.W.s captured in North Africa) came to nothing for lack of volunteers. Ironically, the main stumbling-block to Bose's plans turned out to be Hitler himself, who had a visceral aversion for all coloured races and had always secretly admired England's imperial role.

In February 1943, off the coast of Madagascar, a German U-boat transferred Bose to a Japanese submarine. With Japanese help, an Indian Legion fought the British in Burma until Japan's defeat in August 1945. Bose was on his way to Manchuria to seek Soviet support when, on 18 August, his plane crashed into the China Sea.

Wednesday, 25 December Midnight Mass with Paul Metternich. When we got to church after trudging through the snow, we learned that the service had been postponed until tomorrow morning in view of possible raids.

Monday, 30 December Paul Metternich left this morning to join his regiment.

Tuesday, 31 December Dined in a *séparé* at 'Horcher's' with Tino Soldati and other friends. Later we went on to Tino's, where numerous people assembled to toast in the New Year. There was a very good band which to everyone's consternation struck up 'Deutschland über Alles' at midnight. Luckily Tino had just slipped out of the house to congratulate his boss at the Swiss Legation.

Thursday, 2 January This morning I handed in my resignation from the D.D. They have agreed to let me go if I can find a replacement. This may prove difficult.

Sunday, 5 January Freddie Horstmann took Tatiana and me to Karajan's concert. It's terribly cold. I am ill for the third time this winter.

Tuesday, 7 January Russian Christmas. We went to evening services. Lovely.

Friday, 17 January Spent most of the morning saying goodbye to colleagues at the office, for I have managed to get away after all. I am very glad to be leaving the D.D.; the neighbourhood is so grey and dismal. Tatiana is in bed with a cold.

Saturday, 18 January Boring evening at the Horstmanns'. Sometimes I wonder why we go out so much in the evenings. It must be a form of restlessness.

Monday, 20 January Supper with Bally and Bübchen Hatzfeldt. They share a huge flat near the Tiergarten. I wandered into Bübchen's room to fix my hair, caught sight of an open cupboard and was staggered by the quantity of suits hanging there with an equal number of shoes. I could not help thinking what Georgie and Alexander would have given to own just a couple. Our penniless émigré life reached its peak just as they got to the age of eighteen, when clothes for boys are often as important as they are for girls.

Wednesday, 22 January First day on my new job with the Information Department of the Foreign Ministry. I feel depressed as everything is unfamiliar. Adam Trott has installed me temporarily in a kind of research institute attached to his India office, as his bosses might get wary were we not only to hold similar political views, but also to work together. My immediate chief is an elderly woman journalist who is a specialist in Indian affairs. Adam seems to hope that once I know more about the work, I will eventually influence her in a way useful to him; but I fear that he over-rates my capacities. When they head big offices, German women can be quite difficult, as their femininity somehow recedes into the background.

Tobruk has fallen to the Australians. Italian losses are heavy.

Friday, 24 January Lunched with Adam Trott, who fascinates me. He is full of constructive ideas and plans, whereas I feel utterly discouraged. But I dare not let him see it.

Saturday, 25 January We have been given a pheasant; and Papa two suits.

Sunday, 26 January Went to church and then for a long walk with Tatiana. We inspected the new Embassies in the Tiergarten; they are in the pretentious monumental style which is to characterise the new Nazi Berlin. All marble and columns, they seem abnormally large, quite beyond human scale. They have even started on a new British Embassy, as the old one near the Brandenburger Tor was allegedly too small. Can they *really* believe that England will give in eventually?

Friday, 31 January My new office appears pleased with me.

Saturday, 1 February Lunch at the Rocamoras' (he is the Spanish military attaché here). They live just opposite my new office. I am getting used to the latter; if only the place were not so cold! There is also hardly any light and we work by electricity, mostly research in small print, which strains the eyes. Adam Trott came by with a friend, Dr Alex Werth. They had a small conference and made me attend. I sat listening to their lofty thoughts.

A close friend of Adam von Trott since their student years at Göttingen University, Dr Alexander Werth had back in 1934 spent some time in a Nazi concentration camp. He had then practised law as a barrister in London, returning to Germany only on the eve of the war. After a brief spell in the army, he had been assigned to the A.A.

Sunday, 2 February This afternoon Marcus Clary bounced in. He is Alfy's second son and in face very like his father. He is perishing for any sort of entertainment, having been until now at the front and being badly wounded in the arm to boot. He is in an officers' training school near Berlin. We took him with us to a party.

Loulou Croy is in the act of running away to Portugal to marry her American friend Dick Metz against her father's wishes.

Tuesday, 11 February Tea at the Horstmanns' to meet 'Loulou' de Vilmorin, at present married to a Hungarian magnate, Count 'Tommy' Esterhazy. Although no longer young, she is very attractive and elegant.

Monday, 17 February Since last week Adam Trott has taken me into his section. I am very glad, as the atmosphere there is much more congenial. Adam has one room; then comes an office for me and two secretaries; then another large room for Alex Werth and a man called Hans Richter, whom everybody calls 'Judgie'; and then there is a tiny hole in the wall with a Herr Wolf (known to all as 'Wölfchen') and Lore Wolf, his secretary. Wölfchen is often slightly tipsy, but he is intelligent and nice. Tatiana works downstairs in the converted garage with Josias Rantzau and Louisette Quadt. Luisa Welczeck has just left for good as her family, worried about the air-raids, has decided to move to Vienna. We miss her much. For the moment Adam drowns me in translations and book reviews. I have one to do right now for which I have been given only two days. Sometimes I must fill in by taking German dictation. I horrify my entourage with my grammatical mistakes.

Thursday, 18 February All these new branch offices of the A.A. are housed in the buildings of the various foreign missions which have left Berlin; they are therefore fully equipped with bathrooms, kitchens, etc. I love the atmosphere here and am much happier. Office hours are, however, most irregular. We are supposed to start after 9 a.m. and work till about 6 p.m. But at lunch time the bosses evaporate; so do we, although this is not officially allowed. The gentlemen hardly ever return before 4 p.m. or even later; we have therefore to catch up afterwards and sometimes go on until ten. The top boss, Gesandter [Minister Plenipotentiary] Altenburg, who was a very nice man respected by all, has just been replaced by quite another bird, a young and aggressive S.S.-Brigadeführer [brigadier] by the name of Stahlecker, who strides around in high boots, swinging a whip, a German shepherd at his side. Everybody is worried by this change.

Together with the infamous Adolf Eichmann, S.S.-Brigadeführer Franz Stahlecker had been involved in the Nazis' early plans for the 'solution' of the Jewish question which envisaged at first only their deportation to the East, not yet their bodily extermination. An opponent of Reinhard Heydrich, the all-powerful head of the R.S.H.A. (the Reich's main security office), he was nevertheless, at the start of the war against Russia, to head Einsatzgruppe 'A', which operated in the Baltic. These special 'task forces', which were made up of S.S., Gestapo and members of the German and local regular police and numbered from 500 to 1,000 men each, had the task of liquidating all Jews, Communists and suspected partisans in the rear of the advancing regular German forces. Stahlecker was to boast that in the first four months of the campaign his unit had accounted for 135,000 people. He was to die in March 1942 in a partisan ambush in Estonia.

Thursday, 20 February Tatiana has high fever. I dined at the Horstmanns' who are celebrating C. C. Pfuel's engagement to Blanche Geyr von Schweppenburg; she is the daughter of a well-known panzer general and a very pretty girl.

The Rocamoras have just returned from Rome with a packet of letters from the family, who are all very excited about Tatiana's engagement to Paul Metternich, which she has just disclosed to them and which came as a surprise.

Saturday, 22 February C. C. Pfuel's wedding. He had asked me to be a bridesmaid. The whole business was very posh with a reception at the Hotel Kaiserhof. Rather strenuous for us as we had to present everybody to the parents of both parties, who had all just arrived from the country and knew no one. C.C. looked harassed. I got so tired that I ended up shaking hands with the taxi driver who brought me home. In return he kissed my hand.

Tuesday, 25 February Dined with Josias Rantzau and discussed Tatiana's engagement, of which he approves. He is a kind of guardian angel and mentor to us all.

Wednesday, 26 February Tatiana and I lunched with Count Adelman, a friend of Papa's. He has just returned from Lithuania, where he was Minister Counsellor at the German Legation. He has helped many non-Germans escape the Soviets by simply issuing them with German passports.

Under a second secret protocol to the Soviet-German Boundary and Friendship

Treaty of 29 September 1939 (which had consecrated the partitioning of Poland and brought Lithuania into the U.S.S.R.'s sphere of influence), ethnic Germans residing on Soviet territory were to be repatriated to Germany. Though, in theory, only genuine Volksdeutsche *(i.e. persons of German blood) qualified and the whole operation was run by the S.S., who were later to forcibly enroll many repatriates in their ranks, the German diplomatic authorities on the spot often applied generous criteria. Some 750,000 persons, including thousands of non-Germans, were to escape death or captivity in the U.S.S.R. thanks to this arrangement.*

There are rumours that King Alfonso of Spain has died. He is Paul Metternich's godfather; if true, this will be a big blow for Paul and his mother. After his abdication in 1931 he had spent much time at Königswart, the Metternichs' country place in Czechoslovakia.

Following a Republican landslide in the 1931 elections, King Alfonso XIII had left Spain and thereafter lived in exile.

Thursday, 27 February Paul Metternich, Josias Rantzau, Tatiana and I lunched at 'Horcher's' and simply gorged. As the best restaurant in town, they scorn the very idea of food coupons.

Wednesday, 5 March Pan Medeksha, a Polish landowner in Lithuania and an old friend of the family, came to supper. He has recently escaped, leaving everything behind. His large old wooden mansion was a typical 'nest of gentlefolk' – lavish hospitality, masses of food, huge unkempt garden, an overgrown pond, a portrait gallery . . . Poor fellow, it must be hard to start life again after sixty.

The German army has marched into Bulgaria.

Italy's invasion of Greece, and the British intervention which followed, brought the R.A.F. within reach of the Rumanian oil fields at Ploesti – Germany's main source of fossil fuel. Hitler now ordered the conquest of Greece, for which he had to secure transit rights for his troops through Hungary, Rumania and Bulgaria. To this end he brought them into the Three Power Pact. Hungary and Rumania had joined on 23 November 1940. Bulgaria's Tsar Boris III showed himself more reluctant. But ever since Rumania had been forced, in June 1940, to yield Bessarabia and Northern Bukovina to the U.S.S.R., Bulgaria, too, had wanted a share of Rumanian spoils. Germany offered its 'mediation', and in August 1940 Rumania had ceded to

Bulgaria the Southern Dobrudja. Since then, German pressure – and influence – in Bulgaria had been stepped up and on 1 March 1941 it, too, had joined the pact. The very next day Field Marshal Siegmund List's Twelfth Army, to which had been assigned the task of subduing Greece, marched into the country.

Thursday, 6 March For once we have a little money and are planning to go to Italy on leave. It would be lovely to see the family again. Paul Metternich has gone to Kitzbühl to ski. Many people are away skiing now and life in Berlin is calmer.

It looks as if a Serbian crisis is looming.

Sunday, 9 March In the evening Albert Eltz, Aga Fürstenberg and Claus Ahlefeldt dropped in with Burchard of Prussia. Papa was shocked at Claus sitting with his arm around Aga. 'In my days . . .'

On 11 March 1941 the United States had passed the Lend-Lease Act, by means of which, even before it was provoked into active belligerency, America became the 'Arsenal of Democracy'. By the time the war ended, some $50 billion worth of armaments and supplies had been funnelled to the various Allies.

Saturday, 15 March We have been much at home lately, leading a very quiet life. Tatiana, especially, is tired out and we think longingly about our coming trip to Rome.

Monday, 24 March Our entire staff has been roped in for some special very urgent work connected with a Japanese exhibition. Adam Trott is the only one left out; he is delighted and scoffs at us, as we toil away over our typewriters until late at night. Wölfchen is our saving grace as he maintains more or less civil relations with our nasty new boss Stahlecker and thus shields us from possible trouble. The rest avoid Stahlecker as much as possible. There is something sinister about him.

Father Shakhovskoy dined with us at home.

One of the most distinguished clerics of the émigré church, Father (Prince) John Shakhovskoy was to become, after the war, Russian Orthodox Archbishop of San Francisco.

Thursday, 27 March There is much excitement because the Yugoslav ministers, who had signed a pact with Germany in Vienna recently, were arrested on their return to Belgrade by a group of pro-Allied military. A new provisional government has been set up and Prince Paul, the Regent, has fled to Greece. This may mean war with Yugoslavia too. What a mess!

Yugoslavia had long also been under German pressure, but Greece's successful repulsion of the Italian invasion and the arrival of the British on the Balkan scene, together with the latter's successes in North Africa, had encouraged it to resist. Only on 25 March 1941 did it join the Three Power Pact. Two days later a military coup deposed the Regent Prince Paul, proclaimed the seventeen-year-old Crown Prince Peter as king, and set up a pro-Allied government.

German plans for the invasion of the U.S.S.R. were by now far advanced; faced with the emergence on his southern flank of a British-supported Greek-Yugoslav bloc, Hitler ordered Yugoslavia to be crushed 'with merciless brutality'.

Saturday, 29 March Went with Paul Metternich, who has made himself a new suit and is still a little self-conscious about it, to Espinosa – he is a Spanish diplomat – and listened to the latter's very good Russian records. Paul's wardrobe definitely needs freshening up. He wears a black stringy knitted tie day in day out, a tired green tweed jacket and flannels. Apart from his uniform, I have never seen him in anything else – and the uniform is beginning to look tired too. Since the age of eighteen he has seen only war, starting with the Spanish Civil War, where he volunteered with the Nationalists.

Dicky Eltz took me out to Potsdam to meet Gottfried Bismarck, Otto's brother, who is Regierungspräsident [District Civil Governor] there. I liked him very much. He is married to Melanie Hoyos, who is half-Austrian, half-French; an Austrian cousin of his, Loremarie Schönburg, was also there. We all returned to Berlin together very late.

A younger grandson of the 'Iron Chancellor', Count Gottfried von Bismarck-Schönhausen (1901–1949) had at first sympathised with the Nazi movement, which, he believed, would ensure Germany's 'national rebirth'. He even held the honorary rank of S.S.-Standartenführer (colonel) and was for many years an N.S. member of Hitler's dummy Reichstag, a function he combined with that of Regierungspräsident of Potsdam. But by 1941 he had become a convinced anti-Nazi and was from the first one of the most active civilian members of what became the 20th July Plot.

Thursday, 3 April Had supper with Josias Rantzau at the Trotts' in Dahlem. Professor Pretorius, an art historian, stage designer and a great authority on China, was there. Adam Trott is passionately interested in China, where he spent some time and where he became a close friend of Peter Fleming's. The conversation centred mainly on the Far East.

It is rumoured that Count Teleki, the Hungarian Prime Minister, has committed suicide.

As Prime Minister since 1939, Count Paul Teleki had tried unsuccessfully to prevent German domination of Hungary. He had already refused a German request to surrender Polish soldiers and civilians who had sought refuge there. The pro-Allied coup in Yugoslavia led to increased German pressure. Rather than yield, Teleki shot himself.

Friday, 4 April Supper with the Hako Czernins. There were only Austrians present, including Dicky Eltz and Josef Schwarzenberg. They lingered nostalgically over the 'good old days' in Vienna and Salzburg, telling amazing tales about the life of the *jeunesse dorée* in the Twenties.

Sunday, 6 April This morning the German army invaded Yugoslavia and Greece.

Friday, 11 April After work yesterday I raced to the Stettiner Bahnhof, where Dicky Eltz was meeting me to go out to Reinfeld, Gottfried Bismarck's place in Pomerania, for the long Easter weekend. We travelled seven hours instead of the usual three. At the station we were met by the Bismarcks' horses, who drove us over to Reinfeld by moonlight. We arrived at 3 a.m. to find Gottfried Bismarck waiting up for us with a light supper and a lot of fresh milk. Bliss!

This morning, breakfast – a real breakfast, followed by a hot bath. Reinfeld is a charming mixture of small farm-cum-country house – whitewashed, comfortable furniture, and many books. We walked in the woods and Dicky Eltz shot a jay. In the afternoon we went riding. It was my first time on horseback, but my muscles, mercifully, did not hurt afterwards, probably thanks to those gymnastics.

REINFELD, *Saturday, 12 April* I went riding again with Gottfried Bismarck and later we went deer stalking.

Belgrade was taken today and Croatia has declared itself independent.

Easter Sunday (Western style), 13 April After tea we did some target rifle-shooting through the sitting-room window. The target was pinned to a tree. I had never shot before and started by closing the wrong eye. Nevertheless my shots were the best – beginner's luck. But when we tried pistols I was a total failure. The gun was too heavy and kicked back hard. We hid Easter eggs for the children, but they were too young to understand. They are all very well fed, indeed they are a bit too plump; the little boy, Andreas, though hardly a year old, is full of personality with red hair and a blue stare, like his great-grandfather, the Iron Chancellor.

Monday, 14 April The weather has spoilt; it is warm but without sun. Dicky Eltz left for Berlin. He works for the Ritter Bank, where his job has so far saved him from being called up. I am staying on one more day. This afternoon we again went riding. It rained in heavy gusts. On our way home, Gottfried Bismarck saw some children stealing straw off the roof of a barn. He galloped after them, my horse followed suit, and there I was, clinging to its mane, absolutely desperate.

BERLIN *Thursday, 17 April* The reading of the Twelve Gospels this evening in the Russian church. This is *our* Easter week, and my feet are beginning to ache from standing through the long services. Tatiana plans to leave for Rome on 6 May. Alas, I cannot accompany her as I am too new at my job.

Yugoslavia has capitulated.

Saturday, 19 April Office for two hours and then church and Communion. Paul Metternich is here on his way to Spain and then Rome. The whole trip – an official mission of sorts – is being arranged by Wölfchen, who has a soft spot for both him and Tatiana. Our Midnight Mass was at 7 p.m. on account of the air-raids. It was held in a Lutheran church, ours being too small for the crowds who invariably attend. We took along Paul Metternich and Loremarie Schönburg.

Sunday, 20 April Russian Easter. Papa insisted that we accompany him on his traditional visits to the entire Russian colony here.

We have just heard that, at the time of the Belgrade *coup*, poor little King Peter of Yugoslavia was pulled out of his bed at night to witness the execution of his tutor, a general. [*This turned out to be a false rumour.*]

Tuesday, 22 April I am still sweating away at translations. Adam Trott wants me to take all his routine work in hand, so that he can retire to more Olympian heights and not be bothered by red tape. I started by trying to clean up his writing table while he was away at lunch. I sat on the floor scooping out drawer after drawer and nearly cried at the mess. His little secretary, who is devoted to him, came in and comforted me: 'Herr von Trott ist ein Genie und von einem Genie kann man so etwas wie Ordnung gar nicht verlangen' ('Mr von Trott is a genius and you cannot possibly demand that a genius be tidy as well!'). I repeated this to him on his return and he was visibly touched. He spent several years in England as a Rhodes scholar, as well as in China and the U.S.A., and we usually speak English together. I feel more at home with him that way. When he speaks German he becomes so intellectual that I cannot always follow, or rather I cannot do so when he dictates. He throws the beginning of a sentence into the air, pauses for a second, and then the rest comes tumbling after it. Later, when I am faced with my hieroglyphs, I usually seem to have missed half. My German is simply not yet good enough. Judgie Richter and Alex Werth also often speak English to me – Judgie having spent much of his life in Australia. We are sometimes referred to as the 'House of Lords'.

Wednesday, 23 April Inès Welczeck is working as Landjahr–Mädchen [young women's compulsory rural service] at Hanna von Bredow's in Potsdam. Hanna is the Bismarcks' sister and has eight children. The three youngest are now looked after by Inès. She washes and dresses them and takes them to school. On the whole, she has an easy enough time, as otherwise she might be working in the fields or milking cows. We celebrated her birthday in the 'Atelier' today. Paul Metternich sat in another corner with the Spanish Ambassador and kept winking at us.

Friday, 25 April Dined with Tatiana at the Hoyos'. Our host, Jean-Georges, is Melanie Bismarck's brother. Gottfried Bismarck, Helen Biron and the Czernins were there. We are slowly giving up the big parties and only see the same dozen or so people in their own often rather cramped quarters.

   Tonight there was again a raid. Our flat is near the Zoo bunker, which has just been built of heavy concrete. It is very high and sprouting with *flak* guns, and is considered the safest air-raid shelter in this part of the town. When the guns start firing the earth trembles, and even in our flat the noise is ear-splitting.

Saturday, 26 April Yesterday only two bombs were dropped but both weighed 500 kilograms each. We have discovered a door leading into a back garden. It may serve as an emergency exit in case we get cut off by fire. But of course the garden is walled in on all sides. My gym lessons may prove helpful in enabling me to clamber over those walls.

Went to the Italian opera which is visiting here from Rome: *Romeo and Julia* by Sandomai. I had never heard of it before. The singing was good.

Sunday, 27 April After church lunched with Steenson, the Danish chargé d'affaires, an elderly man with five little children and a charming wife.

The war in Greece is virtually over.

Hitler's conquest of the Balkans was to be his last major victory. It was marked by yet another deliberate atrocity: the Luftwaffe's destruction of Belgrade, with a loss of 17,000 lives. Following the Yugoslav army's capitulation on 17 April, the country ceased to exist: Croatia became independent; Dalmatia was annexed by Italy and what remained of Serbia was administered by a German puppet. Only in the central mountains did resistance continue until the end of the war – first by General Draža Mihajlovic's monarchist 'Chetniks', later by Josip Tito's Communist partisans. Greece held out until 29 April, when the remnants of its forces and most of the British expeditionary corps were evacuated to Crete. However short-lived, Yugoslavia's and Greece's heroic stand had for Hitler fateful consequences: for the first time in eighteen months of war he had suffered a rebuff; in a Europe that had already tacitly accepted his 'New Order', two small countries had dared to challenge him; more important still, the Balkan campaign caused him to unleash his panzers against the U.S.S.R. six weeks later than planned.

Thursday, 1 May A national holiday ever since Hitler came to power – to steal the Communists' thunder. Sat in the Tiergarten reading letters from the family.

Sunday, 4 May Went to the new little Russian church in the Fasanenstrasse. The choir sings beautifully, boosted by a former Soviet opera bass.

Monday, 5 May After hectic preparations, Tatiana left today for Rome. Helen Biron had telephoned me that she would leave with the porter of her flat a letter for Tatiana to take to Rome by hand. When I went to fetch it, I was told that a gentleman had just called for it in my name and that the porter had handed it to him. I was aghast, for I knew it contained important information on the whereabouts of Polish prisoners-of-war which Helen had acquired illegally through the Red Cross office where she works. We forget all too often that even our office telephones can be tapped. I am now mentally preparing myself for a summons to the Gestapo.

It is pouring with rain.

Thursday, 8 May Air-raid. Am getting more nervous about them. Now my heart begins to beat whenever the siren starts. Josias Rantzau teases me about this.

Friday, 9 May Albert Eltz, Dicky's youngest brother, dropped in at the office to see me. He has failed his officers' exams and is rather depressed.

Monday, 12 May This afternoon I went to try on hats. Now that clothes are rationed and hats are not, they have come into their own. They provide a sartorial diversion and we are slowly accumulating them. At least they change one's appearance a bit.

During a small supper party this evening the B.B.C. announced that Rudolf Hess had landed in England! Much speculation as to why he did this, with everybody coming up with a different interpretation.

An early Nazi, Rudolf Hess was one of Hitler's most trusted confidants, his Deputy as Führer of the party and successor-designate (after Goering) as Chancellor of the Reich. The preparations for the invasion of the U.S.S.R. were nearing completion when, on 10 May 1941, Hess took off alone in a Messerschmitt 110 and crash-landed on the Duke of Hamilton's estate in Scotland. They had met at the 1936 Olympics. With the Duke's help, Hess hoped to contact influential British politicians known to be opposed to Churchill and anti-Communist, and to convince them that it was in Britain's best interest to put an end to the war and allow Germany a free hand in Eastern Europe. Alternatively, he said, Britain would lose its empire and a large part of Europe would be dominated by the Soviets for at least a century. To his surprise, he was treated like a common P.O.W., interned until the end of the war, and then brought to trial at Nuremberg. Sentenced to life imprisonment, he was incarcerated at Spandau prison in Berlin, where he remains to this day. The way this bizarre episode was handled in Germany but also in Britain – where some of the relevant papers are still under wraps – immediately sparked the suspicion, shared at the time by Roosevelt and Stalin, that moves towards a compromise peace were underway by both sides.

Tuesday, 13 May At the Lanzas', of the Italian Embassy, I sat in a corner with Hasso Etzdorf discussing Hess and future developments. Everybody finds it rather comical.

Wednesday, 14 May Lunched with Paul Metternich at the 'Atelier'. He is just back from Rome. He gave a graphic description of his meeting with 'the family'. He was rather funny about it, but it must have been quite an ordeal for him all the same.

After lunch we tried to buy a picture postcard of Hess, but they seem to have been withdrawn overnight and cannot be had for love or money. Indeed in one shop a woman said aggressively, 'Wozu brauchen Sie ihn denn? Er ist ja wahnsinnig geworden!' ['What do you need him for? He has clearly gone crazy!'] – the official version. To calm her down, we pretended we were interested in the whole zoo and bought one each of Goebbels and Goering.

In Tatiana's absence Paul haunts the place. He hates Berlin and has no close friends here. As at the D.D., every day we receive stacks of pink papers marked *streng geheim* which contain the latest international news and press excerpts from abroad. Nobody is supposed to read them but a chosen few, yet a messenger distributes them unsealed. Paul, avid for information, devours all this, since the German papers nowadays contain strictly nothing. Should anybody walk in there would be hell to pay, but as Tatiana's office (where I temporarily work) is in a garage, we usually communicate with the rest of the department by telephone. The only exceptions are Rantzau and Louisette Quadt, who work below, and they couldn't care less.

After lunch I met Edgar von Üxküll, an elderly Baltic baron who before 1914 was in the Russian diplomatic service. He spoke charmingly of Papa, saying that he had been one of the most promising young men in Russia and that in time he would certainly have become Prime Minister. Poor Papa!

There is a rumour that Stalin has agreed to cede the Ukraine to the Germans for ninety-nine years. I am quite indignant! [*This was yet another false rumour, sparked probably by wishful thinking among the German population that the much-dreaded looming conflict with the U.S.S.R. could be avoided by a last-minute 'deal'.*]

Sunday, 18 May The Berliners, who are noted for their wit, have already concocted a few jokes about Hess's escape. Examples:
'Augsburg [the town he took off from], Stadt des deutschen Aufstiegs'

['Augsburg, town of the German ascent'].

B.B.C.: 'Weitere Einflüge von deutschen Staatsminstern fanden in der Nacht zu Sonntag nicht mehr statt' ['On Sunday night no further German cabinet ministers flew in'].

'O.K.W. Bericht: Goering und Goebbels sind noch fest in deutscher Hand' ['German High Command Communiqué: Goering and Goebbels are still firmly in German hands'].

'Das 1,000-jährige Reich ist nun ein hundertjähriges geworden; eine Null ist weg' ['The 1,000-year Reich has now become a hundred-year Reich. One zero is gone'].

'Det unsere Regierung verrückt ist, det wissen wir schon lange, aber det sie es zugibt, det is neu' – in broad Berlin accent: ['That our government is mad, is something that we have known for a long time; but that they admit it, *that* is something new'].

'Churchill fragt Hess: "Sie sind also der Verrückte?" – "Nein, nur der Stellvertreter"' [Churchill asks Hess: 'So you are the madman?' – 'No, only his deputy'].

To all of which Aga Fürstenberg, known for her snobbism and wit, adds: 'Wenn es so weiter geht, sind wir bald wieder unter uns' ['Well, if this keeps up, we will soon be back among our cosy selves'].

Saturday, 24 May Paul Metternich has been called back to Berlin, where he will work at the O.K.W. [High Command of the Armed Forces]; this is a great relief. People are speaking more and more of troop concentrations on the Russian border. Nearly all the men we know are being transferred from the West to the East. This can mean only one thing.

In fact, the conquest and colonisation of Eastern Europe and the U.S.S.R. had been one of Hitler's theme songs since Mein Kampf; all his other political moves had been mere stepping-stones to this end. The campaign in the West was barely over when on 21 July 1940 – the day after Stalin annexed the Baltic states – Hitler had informed his generals of his intention to destroy the U.S.S.R., 'the sooner the better'. None of them raised any objections. That summer the first German divisions were transferred back to the East. On 18 December 1940 Hitler had approved the final campaign plan. Code-named 'Barbarossa', the operation was supposed to be launched in May 1941 and to take only four to five weeks. It was to drag on for four years and end with the total destruction of Nazi Germany.

There has been a huge battle at sea between the *Hood* and the *Bismarck*. The *Hood* was sunk by a single salvo which landed in the munitions hold and almost all the crew perished. Ghastly! The *Bismarck* is now on the run, but she is in difficult straits as she is being chased by the entire British fleet.

Monday, 26 May Dined at the Hoyos' to meet an American couple, the George Kennans, who have been for many years with the U.S. Embassy in Russia. They are now posted temporarily at the American Embassy here. He has highly intelligent eyes but does not speak freely, but then the situation is of course ambiguous, as the Germans are still allies of Soviet Russia. Instead of serious talk, therefore, Claus Ahlefeldt and Vinzi Windisch-Graetz gave a demonstration of the respective charms of the Hungarian and Danish languages. We unanimously settled for Hungarian, but found neither exactly music to the ears.

Tuesday, 27 May The *Bismarck* was sunk today. The German Admiral Lutjens went down with her.

Completed in 1941, the 42,000-ton Bismarck was one of the largest, fastest, most powerful and best-built ships in the war. On 18 May it set out with the heavy cruiser Prinz Eugen *to raid British shipping in the Atlantic. British reconnaissance planes quickly discovered the enemy raiders and the Admiralty dispatched a strong force to intercept them. The first encounter took place off the coast of Iceland and within minutes the battle cruiser* Hood, *flagship of Vice-Admiral Lancelot Holland and pride and glory of the British navy, blew up and sank with all but three of its 400-man crew. But the* Bismarck, *too, had been hit. The German ships now separated. While the* Prinz Eugen *slipped back into Brest, the limping* Bismarck *was lost for the next thirty-one hours. From the Admiralty in London came orders for every available warship from Newfoundland to Gibraltar to 'hunt the* Bismarck'. *After an epic chase by virtually the entire British Home Fleet, it was finally located in the Bay of Biscay and further crippled by torpedo planes from the aircraft-carrier* Ark Royal. *The next day, after a heroically fought battle against overwhelming odds, the* Bismarck *went down with all hands but one.*

Friday, 30 May Stayed at home to wash, iron, mend, etc. This keeps us pretty busy as nothing can be done elsewhere. Real soap is non-existent and one has to make do with smelly synthetic substitutes which are also rationed.

Tuesday, 3 June Adam has given me a lot of books to read for him. If they are worth his while, I pass them on to him; otherwise they wander into some file and are never seen again. He gets most of the books that are published just now in England and the United States. Sometimes they make light reading, such as Peter Fleming's *Flying Visit*, which is being passed from hand to hand and makes us all roll with laughter. The competition is great as to who gets a book first, but I usually manage rather well.

Thursday, 5 June The ex-Kaiser, Wilhelm II, died at Doorn, his Dutch place of exile since 1918. The news is being handled with surprising restraint.

Sunday, 8 June Russian Whitsun. Paul Metternich and I went to the station in a car lent to us by the Spaniards to meet Tatiana. She appeared wth lots of new things and looking radiant, very rested after such a change of scene. She was a pleasure to see. We had supper together.

Monday, 9 June Paul Metternich and Tatiana have finally decided to announce their engagement formally. It will come as a surprise to no one. Papa wishes Paul to pay him an official visit to ask for Tatiana's hand. We tease Paul and remind him to wear white kid gloves for the occasion. Tatiana is far more nervous at the thought of this visit than Paul.

Tuesday, 10 June Dinner with Josias Rantzau, Louisette Quadt and Herr Ulrich von Hassell, who was German Ambassador in Rome for ten years. He is a most charming and erudite man.

Later we dropped in at Aga Fürstenberg's, who was giving a farewell party for Albert Eltz, prior to his departure for Greece.

Most of the German army seems to be massing on the Russian border.

A veteran diplomat, Ulrich von Hassell (1881–1944) had been gravely injured on the Western Front during World War I. Rejoining the Foreign Ministry in 1919, his career had culminated as Ambassador to Italy from 1932 to 1938. A liberal conservative of the old school, he was a passionate anti-Nazi and one of the most active civilian members of the plot to overthrow Hitler. At the time Missie met him, he held an academic post which enabled him, despite wartime conditions, to travel abroad, each trip being an excuse to cultivate his many contacts with influential Allied and neutral circles.

Wednesday, 11 June Albert and Dicky Eltz dropped in. On their way home later, they stumbled over a man lying dead in the street. He must have been hit by a bus but, owing to the blackout, nobody had noticed. This would happen to Albert of all people.

Saturday, 14 June Loremarie Schönburg came to borrow clothes for a party. She is studying acting. She was to make her debut in some Shakespeare play, but the leading man fell off a ladder during a rehearsal and everything has been called off. Who knows? Perhaps a career nipped in the bud!

Friday, 20 June Adam Trott rang up. He is one of the few men I know who likes to chat on the telephone. He has some job in view for me 'to take my mind off other things', meaning the war with Russia which seems imminent now.

Sunday, 22 June The German army is on the offensive along the entire eastern border. Hako Czernin woke me at dawn to break the news. A new phase of the war begins. We knew it was coming. And yet we are thunderstruck!

Missie's note [September 1945]: From this day on, nearly two years of my diary are missing, even though I kept on writing it almost daily. Some pages I destroyed myself. Others I concealed in the country home of a friend in what is now Eastern Europe, where they may still be to this day; or where, as likely as not, they were discovered and removed to some local archive or, even more likely, burnt as rubbish.

But then in the confusion of the hectic years that followed, it seems a miracle that so much of my diary survived at all.

INTERLUDE JULY 1941 TO JULY 1943

Missie's note [written in the spring of 1978, the year of her death]: Since I continued to write my diary almost daily, trying to recall the minutiae of everything I experienced between 22 June 1941 and 20 July 1943 is practically impossible. But I will try to give a short account of those events that had a lasting impact on our lives and of what happened to me, the family and some of my friends during that period, so that the reader may find it less difficult to go on with the daily account when this resumes.

By then Missie's strength was failing so fast that she was able to write only two accounts, that of her sister Tatiana's marriage, and that describing her mother's relief activities for Soviet prisoners-of-war.

Fortunately, the Vassiltchikov family have always been compulsive letter-writers. Many of these letters – by Missie or to her – survived the war. From them and from random scraps of diary found among her papers after her death, it was possible to reconstitute to some extent her life during the period June 1941 to July 1943 for which the original diary entries are not available.

For the rest, this annotator has limited himself to a brief summary of the main events in Missie's and her family's lives during this period and of the historical background against which they took place.

Missie in Berlin to her brother George in Rome, 1 July 1941 Burchard of Prussia was just here, after being sent back from the Russian front because he is a 'royal'. He says it is absolutely beastly. Hardly any prisoners are being taken by either side. The Russians fight and torture like criminals, not soldiers, putting up their hands and then, when the Germans come up to them, shooting them *à bout portant*; they even shoot from behind the German medical orderlies who try to help their wounded. However they are very courageous and the fighting everywhere is very heavy. All three Clary boys are now out there, which must be ghastly for their poor parents.

Met the Wrede girls, who have just heard that their brother Eddie has been killed. He was only twenty and always so bursting with beans. In general, the losses this time are incomparably greater than during the earlier campaigns. Nevertheless the German advance is progressing well, as was to be expected . . .

Hitler's invasion of the U.S.S.R. was probably the largest military assault in history, 153 German divisions – about three quarters of the Wehrmacht's strength being supported in due course by 18 Finnish, 16 Rumanian, 3 Italian, 3 Slovakian and one Spanish divisions, 3 Hungarian brigades, some Croatians and, later, numerous Waffen-S.S. levies from all over occupied Europe – some 3 million men in all. Opposing them at the start of the campaign were 178 Soviet divisions with some 4.7 million men. But whereas Germany's reserves were soon stretched to the limit, the U.S.S.R. could mobilise a further 12 million. All depended, therefore, on yet another German Blitz victory. But Hitler was totally confident: 'We need only break open the door and the whole rotten building will collapse'. And many qualified Western experts predicted as much. Indeed at first even Stalin panicked.

'Barbarossa' provided for a simultaneous three-pronged attack against Moscow, Leningrad and Kiev; the Soviet armies were to be destroyed early in the campaign, through the usual German method of deeply penetrating armoured pincers; the final objective – to be achieved before winter set in – was a line stretching from Arkhangelsk to Astrakhan. After a victory parade in Red Square, Moscow would be levelled to the ground, lost forever to the eyes of 'civilised people'. The campaign, heralded as an 'Anti-Bolshevik crusade', had, in fact, no other objective but the plain brutal conquest of Russian lands, the plunder of their natural resources and the massive extermination of their inhabitants, the survivors being expelled beyond the Urals or reduced to slavery for the German settlers who would take their place.

But then, as Hitler put it frankly to his generals on the eve of the campaign, this would be no ordinary war; the Russians being by definition sub-humans, there could be no question of soldierly chivalry towards them; indeed not even the most criminal acts committed by Germans in Russia were to be prosecuted, let alone punished. And for a start, all captured political commissars and Communist party members, generally, were to be summarily shot! In other words, not only anything was permitted but the worst was prescribed. Though in some cases privately aghast, none of the generals batted an eyelid. It is to the honour of quite a few German military in the field that when the time came, they ignored these criminal orders. From their ranks would come many of the plotters of 20 July 1944.

To begin with, all went according to plan. Despite massive German preparations spread over many months and numerous indications received by Stalin from many sources, the Soviets were taken almost completely by surprise, with their forces strung out in the open along the country's western frontier, much of their equipment obsolete or in the process of replacement, and their senior officers' corps decimated by Stalin's recent purges. Within weeks the German land forces had penetrated deep into Soviet territory and in a series of gigantic encirclement battles had put out of action or captured most of the Soviet front-line armies. But time and again (and this, despite the initially large number of Soviet deserters) their progress was slowed down or stopped altogether by the extremely tough resistance of the Russian soldier. If often out-manoeuvred, he could never be out-fought, surrendering (when at all) only after mostly merciless fighting. Over-confident as the result of their relatively bloodless successes in Poland, the West and the Balkans, the Germans' reaction was one of surprise, followed by indignation; soon it would turn to reluctant admiration and fear.

From Missie's 1978 recollections Tatiana married Paul Metternich on 6 September 1941. It was a joyous event that was attended by all our friends except, of course, those who were at the front or who had already been killed or were too badly injured. Even Mamma, Irena and Georgie had been able to travel up from Rome for the occasion. The reception took place at the Rocamoras', the food having been saved for months in Königswart by Paul and his mother.

That night Berlin had one of its worst air-raids to date. Luckily the bombs fell mostly in the suburbs.

Tatiana and Paul had already left for Vienna, from where they later went on to Spain, where they remained until the following spring. Irena went back to Rome at once, but Mamma and Georgie decided to stay on for a couple of months. This turned out to be a fateful decision, for as the situation on the Eastern Front deteriorated, the authorities put a ban on travel by foreigners in and out of the country – the family still carried Lithuanian passports – and so they found themselves stuck in Germany, Mamma until the end of the war and Georgie until the following autumn, when he managed to slip over to Paris.

I missed Tatiana enormously, for we had been very close since infancy and had been together during most of the difficult times in our lives. Fortunately, Georgie moved into the Hardenbergstrasse flat and stayed there with me until the following spring . . . [*Missie got no further.*]

In November 1941 Missie was able to take a few weeks' holiday in Italy. Three letters written to her mother during this trip have survived.

Missie from Rome to her mother in Berlin, 10 November 1941 I find the food here quite decent, with infinitely more variety than in Berlin. The green leaves on the trees, after the greyness of our Berlin streets, are also most refreshing.

The Via Veneto, packed with young men about town, rather shocked me when I think what it is like in Germany these days.

Am going shopping tomorrow but am not very hopeful, as that which does not require coupons (and very few of these are issued) can only be bought by presenting one's identity card. Even Irena, after three years in Italy, has not yet got one, so you can imagine what chances I have. And so I walk around with hungry eyes, unable to spend a cent . . .

Missie from Rome to her mother in Berlin, 13 November 1941 The Russian colony here is in a great state of agitation. Last month an article appeared in one of the local papers, signed with a pen-name, in which the author voiced his surprise and indignation because so many White Russians were showing a marked lack of enthusiasm about the campaign in Russia; this being the case, they should perhaps be invited to transfer their domicile elsewhere. Immediately the rumour went round that the article had been inspired 'from above' and this, of course, caused even greater emotion among our compatriots, with some of them gathering to draft a scathing reply, while others went around trying to find out who the author of the article was.

Two days ago Lony Arrivabene invited Irena and me to dinner at the Circolo della Caccia, together with one of his cousins, who turned out to be a journalist, and in due course the conversation shifted to the famous article. Whereupon the cousin admitted that *he* was the author, that nobody 'at the top' had inspired it, but that it was just a *cri du coeur* in the light of some discussion he had had with one of our fellow-Russians here. Needless to say, I gave him a piece of my mind. But poor Lony was in agony throughout . . .

Missie from Capri to her mother in Berlin, 20 November 1941 . . . On Monday in Rome I had supper with Hugo Windisch-Graetz and a friend of his, a Prince

Serignano, who, on hearing of my intention to come here, suggested that I stay in his house, as he wouldn't be going back for several weeks and meanwhile it stood empty. This is where I am now.

The house is a tiny bungalow affair, all whitewashed, with a terrace overlooking the whole of the island and the sea beyond. It stands quite isolated on a hill opposite the larger villas. It has two rooms; a very smart green-tiled bathroom, the water of which, however, must be pumped up for hours; and a kitchen. It is surrounded by vineyards and cypresses. I live alone, except for a little Italian maid called Bettina, who comes up from the village every morning to clean up and to prepare my breakfast and run my bath. I intend to read a lot, sleep a lot, walk and swim if there is sun, and see no one. Otto Bismarck (who is Minister at the German Embassy here) has lent me plenty of books. Today I am going shopping to lay up provisions and will then go into retirement.

Vesuvius is more active than it ever has been in recent years and they say that were it not for the war, people would begin to worry. At night you see the red lava erupting from the top and trickling down the sides. Most exciting! You can also watch the air-raids on Naples, but from here they seem pretty harmless. However on Capri all the lights go out; the first time I was in rather a fix as I hadn't had time to buy candles and they came early . . .

By now the German offensive on the Eastern Front, after spectacular first successes, was beginning to encounter difficulties. For the deeper the invading armies advanced into Russia, the more they had to fan out, the longer became their front-line and the longer also (and the more vulnerable, once partisan warfare started) the supply-lines they had to keep open. Moreover, with every Russian division they destroyed or captured, fresh ones, better trained, better equipped, seemed to spring from nowhere. Gradually, the Germans found themselves sucked into the vastness of Russia, with their main goal – the destruction of all Soviet armed might – an increasingly elusive will-o'-the-wisp and their own losses far greater than in any earlier campaign. In Missie's own circle, apart from Eddie Wrede (whose death she mentions in one of her last entries for 1941), three other close friends – Ronnie Clary, Bübchen Hatzfeldt and Gofi Fürstenberg – had been killed within weeks of the start of the campaign.

Yet Hitler remained confident and on 25 October, after another series of spectacular encirclement battles, he proclaimed that 'Russia is already beaten!'. True, by now, the U.S.S.R. had lost one-third of its industrial output and half its agricultural lands. But much plant had been evacuated east of the Urals (where it was soon back in production) and the ruthless scorched earth policy carried out as the Russians retreated was beginning to affect the Germans too. And now, as so often in the past, 'General Winter' came to Russia's help. On 4 December, within sight of Moscow's Kremlin, the German tanks ground to a halt amid flurries of snow in a sea of mud. The following day, fresh Russian divisions from Siberia launched a first major counter-offensive, in the course of which they regained considerable terrain. By the spring of 1942, German losses would reach one million. And even though Russian losses would be far greater (some 5 million casualties, some 4.5 million prisoners), to many senior German generals the war in the East was already lost.

On 7 December the Japanese attacked Pearl Harbor and the United States came into the war; and though that winter the Allies suffered spectacular reverses in the Pacific and most of South-East Asia fell to the Japanese, from now on America's 'arsenal of democracy' would assure the Allies ever-growing material superiority.

By the spring of 1942 the Metternichs were back in Germany – Paul in an officers' training school from which he would eventually be posted as liaison officer to the Spanish Blue Division on the Leningrad front, while Tatiana lived mostly in Königswart, their estate in northern Bohemia, where the family would occasionally visit her.

Two letters from Missie to her mother from that period have survived, as well as an extensive excerpt from her diary.

Missie from Berlin to her mother in Schloss Königswart, 17 July 1942 Yesterday Georgie and I were invited for dinner to the Chilean Embassy. Among the guests – the actress Jenny Jugo and Victor de Kowa (who is also a well-known actor and producer) and his Japanese wife. The party lasted very late, with lots of dancing.

By now all public dancing was prohibited and offenders severely punished, the only exception being the diplomatic world.

I had a long chat with Victor de Kowa (for whom I used to sigh as a young girl in Lithuania!). He now wears a huge pair of spectacles as he is short-sighted. He turned out to be a very shy but witty man. When I complained that it was virtually impossible nowadays to get tickets to the theatre, he said I had only to telephone him and I would have a whole box at my disposal, but that even if I was bored, I would still have to sit it out until the end, as he would be keeping an eye on me. Although he absolutely refused to dance, claiming he didn't know how to, I dragged him onto the dance floor, whereupon he went ploughing around the room with a martyr-like expression. Later he and Jenny Jugo plunged into a violent altercation with the Wrede twins, who had again attacked me because of my alleged 'lack of enthusiasm' about you can guess what [*meaning the campaign in Russia*].

Georgie is going around these days with hair so long that people keep urging me to talk him into having it cut. He has acquired the reputation of being the best dancer in Berlin – much to Hans Flotow's sorrow . . .

Though Missie did not know this at the time, Victor de Kowa (1904–1973) was not only one of the most popular stage and screen actors in Germany, but, since 1940, an active resister. After the war he was to become prominent also internationally as a director and teacher, combining his professional work with the promotion of various ethical causes such as Moral Re-armament.

Missie from Berlin to her mother in Schloss Königswart, 30 July 1942 I have been going out here every night for the past three weeks and have reached a state of complete exhaustion. But this is the only way to have at least one decent meal a day, as the food in our office canteen has become awful.

Antoinette Croy has been sacked from her job in Paris with just a couple of days' notice and sent back to Germany, solely on account of her title and foreign connections. As a special favour Ambassador Abetz (who represents Germany in the Occupied Zone) had allowed her to stay on for a few weeks to see her mother.

On Sunday she and I went out to Alfieri's (the Italian Ambassador), where we had a delicious tea and then lolled around on the terrace, which overlooks the lake. Yesterday he invited me again, but I refused. Whereupon he invited me for dinner tonight. This time I accepted, as the Emos are going too.

Random excerpts from Missie's diary discovered after her death:

Tuesday, 11 August 1942 That beastly personnel officer has refused to let me off for the four weeks I had requested and is only allowing me sixteen days. I will apply to the A.A. doctor to let me take four weeks this winter and will then go to the mountains. Took the train out to Potsdam with Georgie to dine with Gottfried Bismarck.

KÖNIGSWART, *Wednesday, 12 August* Took the night train to Eger, where I arrived at 1 a.m. Paul Metternich's secretary Thanhofer met me and drove me over to Königswart. The house was asleep. Only Tatiana sat up half-dozing, with a cold supper awaiting me at her side. Had a quick bath and a long chat and fell asleep only at three.

Thursday, 13 August This morning Mamma heard in the village rumours that heavy air-raids were underway in the Rhineland. Mainz had been practically wiped out, with 80 per cent of the town in ruins. Later a telegram arrived from Paul Metternich, saying he was going to fetch his mother. What does this mean? After all, Schloss Johannisberg, where she is living, is quite some distance away from Mainz.

Sunday, 16 August After church Tatiana was called up from Berlin. The conversation lasted an hour. Meanwhile I sat in the garden mending stockings. When she reappeared, she was white in the face. 'Johannisberg no longer exists!' she said with a catch in her throat.

It appears that on Thursday night Paul Metternich's mother Isabel was awakened by a resounding crash: a bomb had fallen on the castle. She and her cousin Marisia Borkowska donned dressing gowns and slippers and together with the maid ran downstairs and across the courtyard into a cellar. By now bombs were raining down one after the other – on the house, the church and the out-buildings. All in all, some 300 of them were dropped, of every type – so-called 'air torpedoes', explosive bombs, incendiary bombs, etc. One torpedo hit the church, which immediately burst into flames – at which a young man rushed in, seized the Host and carried it out, badly burning his hands so doing. Fifty planes took part in the raid, which lasted for two hours. One airman, who had been shot down over Mainz, was found to have a map with three clearly marked targets: Mainz itself, Schloss Johannisberg and Schloss Assmanshausen. All three were duly wiped out. By the time the firemen arrived, there was virtually nothing they could do. The estate staff, including the manager, Herr Labonte, behaved wonderfully, rushing in and out of the house trying to salvage some of the pictures, china, silver, linen, etc. The Mumms (who live next door) had seen the flames and hurried over. Olili Mumm, with a steel helmet poised rakishly at an angle of 45 degrees, jumped onto chairs and cut some of the pictures out of their frames with scissors. They managed to save quite a lot of things from the ground floor, but everything upstairs perished, including all Isabel's clothes, furs and personal belongings. To make things easier for Tatiana, she had tactfully insisted on moving her things from Königswart to Johannisberg, which was going to be now her home. The last two packing cases had left just two weeks ago and we hope that they are still underway. Fortunately she had given a pair of shoes to be mended in the village and these she is now wearing. Paul, coming up the hill next day on foot from Rüdesheim, found snippets of fur strewn about their vineyards, blown all over the countryside by the air pressure caused by the explosions. With the exception of one of the pavilions that flank the entrance to the castle, nothing but the outer walls of the various buildings remain, all the roofs and top floors having collapsed. Most of the cows and horses had been chased out into the fields, but twelve of the animals perished in the holocaust. Apparently, fire-proof doors were installed between all rooms five years ago, but of course they were of no avail against an air attack.

Tuesday, 18 August Drove this morning with Thanhofer to Marienbad to look for a cosmetic which I couldn't find anywhere else.

Mamma is sometimes full of beans, sometimes deeply depressed.

BERLIN *Wednesday, 19 August* Left this morning with Tatiana for Berlin. Thanhofer and the chauffeur brought us to Eger and gave us a pompous send-off. How very pleasant it is to be a plutocrat for a brief moment and have people packing your bags for you and even carrying them!

In Berlin we waited at the station for hours for a taxi, as Georgie had turned up to meet us without one. Dined with him at Schlichter's, where he told me all about his current girl-friend, who, he complains, is pestering him with amorous declarations. The other day, on returning home, I found a telegram which I opened by mistake: 'Still angry? Kisses . . .'

Tomorrow I am off to Schloss Dülmen in Westphalia to stay a few days with Antoinette Croy. From there I may go on to Konstantin of Bavaria's wedding to a Hohenzollern girl at Sigmaringen.

DÜLMEN *Thursday, 20 August* Met Antoinette Croy at the Zoo station. The train was as usual packed, so until Osnabrück we stood in the corridor, after peeling off our stockings because it was so unbearably hot. We passed through Osnabrück at a snail's pace, as the tracks had been badly damaged in the recent bombing. The town looked ghastly, with many buildings pulverised and others gutted shells. At Dülmen we were met by a carriage drawn by recently broken-in wild horses (these are one of the Duke of Croy's hobbies), in which we drove at a scary pace to the castle. We found the Duke waiting for us with a cold supper and then literally collapsed into bed.

Friday, 21 August Slept until 11 a.m.; had breakfast in Antoinette's room in dressing-gowns and went down just in time for lunch. The Duke is aloof to the point of curtness and his children are clearly terrified of him. And yet he is visibly devoted to them, even though he rules them with a rod of iron. He is very much a French *grand seigneur* of the old school.

After a delicious lunch, we sat around chatting in the library and then went for a bicycle ride, returning in time for a sumptuous tea on the terrace. Then the Duke took us for a drive around the game park, where besides his famous wild horses, he raises various types of deer and a rare strain of pitch-black wild sheep. Then a bath. Then a delicious dinner. Then another chat in the library and then early to bed.

Saturday, 22 August The restful life continues. Today we visited the orchard, where we stuffed on lovely grapes, apricots, peaches, plums and berries of every sort.

Sunday, 23 August At 11 a.m. we departed for church, where the Duke, the Duchess, Antoinette and I sat solemnly in the family pew. After tea we were taken to see the nutria farm, which is laid out in a special mud field.

Monday, 24 August Visited the garage, where we found about twenty-five vehicles of every type, more than half of which belong to the family.

NORDKIRCHEN *Wednesday, 26 August* After lunch the Duke drove us over to 'Nordkirchen', the Arenbergs' place – they are cousins of the Croys – where we will be staying for a few days.

'Nordkirchen' is more a palace than a country castle. It is surrounded by beautiful *pièces d'eau* and French gardens. At the moment the family occupies only one wing; this is charmingly arranged with a *volière*, an indoor swimming pool, a special enclosed garden for sun-bathing and every other form of luxury. The food is even better than at Dülmen. At tea I drank gallons of milk and then we sat around chatting with our hostess Valerie, while the Duke and the Prince went shooting. I have a charming room and share a bathroom with Antoinette Croy.

Thursday, 27 August Got up at 9 a.m. and after a scrumptious breakfast, Enkar and Valerie Arenberg took us for a long walk around the estate. After lunch we changed into shorts and lay sunning ourselves in the garden, occasionally dipping into the pool to cool off.

That night, after dinner, I lay reading in bed, when there was suddenly the sound of many planes overhead, the *flak* of the neighbouring town opened fire and all hell broke loose. A full moon lit up the moats while searchlights swept the sky, and as I leaned out of the window I was for a brief instant caught up by the rather scary beauty of it all. Then, remembering what had just happened to Johannisberg, I ran out into the corridor, where I barged into the whole family, who were on their way to fetch me. We trooped down into the main courtyard, where we sat on the cellar steps eating peaches and drinking milk, while Enkar went around the house opening all the windows (to save them from being shattered by the air pressure caused by exploding bombs). After about an hour the noise quietened down and we went back to our rooms. Antoinette Croy and I were standing by the window chatting, when all of a sudden there was a terrific bang and we were hurtled back into the room, as though a door had been slammed in our faces. Later we learnt that this was caused by a bomb that had dropped twenty kilometres away, and yet the gust of air caused by the explosion was so strong that we were practically thrown off our feet. Extraordinary feeling! A neighbouring castle was destroyed in the raid.

Friday, 28 August I had still not decided whether to go on to the wedding or not, when Konstantin of Bavaria called up from Sigmaringen to say I simply *had* to come, that there would be a fearful confusion if I did not, that it was going to be a very solemn affair, that all the table seatings, the order in which the family and guests would proceed to and from church, etc., had been pre-arranged, that my escorts for the various events had been assigned, and so on. And so I spent the rest of the evening with Enkar Arenberg and the housekeeper studying time-tables. Owing to recent air-raids many railway lines are cut or damaged; the trains often slow down to a crawl, when they run at all, and yet I must be there by Sunday at the latest.

SIGMARINGEN *Saturday, 29 August* I had left the bulk of my luggage in Dülmen, so we had first to call the Duke to ask him to send someone down to the station with it. The Arenbergs had plied me with books, provisions, wine,

Enkar's lighter-cum-alarm watch (I had mislaid my own clock) and a solitary rose (which I found afterwards in my overnight case). Thus equipped, I reached Dülmen station, jumped out, recovered my luggage and with it my mail and settled down for the long journey southwards.

One letter was from Loremarie Schönburg, who announced casually that Hugo Windisch-Graetz was dead, killed in an air crash (he was an officer in the Italian air force). We had known each other since childhood and I had seen a lot of him just before the war in Venice. I sat miserable all through the journey, thinking of Lotti, his mother, and of his twin brother, Mucki, from whom he was inseparable. Loremarie announced other deaths – those of Vetti Schaffgotsch and Fritz Dörnberg. A short while ago the Duke of Kent crashed to his death in Scotland; his wife Marina had just had a baby. The son of the Hungarian Regent, Admiral Horthy, has perished in the same way. One wonders whether this succession of plane accidents may not be due to faulty wartime construction. Or is it a sort of curse, punishing mankind for inventing those beastly things?

The voyage was plain sailing at first, with the carriage, surprisingly enough, almost empty. We passed through the Ruhrgebiet, which is the industrial heartland of Germany and where many towns are now mile after mile of ruins. In Cologne only the cathedral was still standing. We continued up the Rhine valley past those well-known mediaeval castles, the ruins of which are somehow almost beautiful compared to the ghastly havoc man is causing everywhere nowadays. Someone pointed out Schloss Johannisberg to me (I have never yet been there); from afar it looked almost intact, except that the roof was missing. Actually, of course, nothing remains of it. Then came Mainz, 80 per cent of which is said to be destroyed. At Frankfurt I again changed trains. This time I travelled less comfortably, crammed with three other girls into the first class w.c., while two Italian students plied us with plums, peanuts and English cigarettes. After two more train changes I finally reached Sigmaringen this morning at 8.30 a.m.

Sunday, 30 August I had rung up Konstantin of Bavaria and they had sent a man to the station to help carry my bags. We walked up to the castle, which stands perched on top of a rock in the very middle of the little town, all roofs, gables and turrets like one of those gingerbread castles in German fairy tales. We entered a lift at the bottom of the rock and were taken up about ten floors.

A housekeeper showed me to my room and brought me some boiled eggs and a peach. I took a hasty bath and then jumped into bed, hoping to get a little sleep while the family was at Mass in the castle chapel. But the organ played so loudly that I couldn't close my eyes, so instead I sat up reading the guest list, which seems to include millions of Hohenzollerns and Wittelsbachs, most of them well advanced in age.

At noon I got up and dressed and upon opening my door caught sight of Konstantin tying his tie; his room is just opposite mine. We had a cosy chat, after which he took me along endless corridors, upstairs, downstairs, upstairs again and eventually into the so-called 'children's wing' to meet his bride (whom I do not yet know). Young men looking like little archdukes in picture books – very slim, fair and well-mannered – kept popping up from all sides to be introduced: brothers and cousins of the bride. Thus escorted, we reached her sitting-room. From there we trooped down to one of the drawing-rooms, where the two families were assembled. On the way we met the bride's mother, my hostess, who seemed both surprised and relieved that I had made it in good time after all. The house guests include Louis-Ferdinand of Prussia and his Russian wife Kira, the ex-reigning house of Saxony *au complet*, Didi Tolstoy (who is a distant cousin of ours) and his half-brother and sister, Georgie and Lella Mecklenburg, the Hassells, the Schnitzlers, the Rumanian Minister Bossy and the Max Fürstenbergs.

We settled down to lunch at little tables in the so-called Ancestors' Hall. I sat next to Bobby Hohenzollern, who is the eldest son of our host's twin brother. A young soldier of twenty-one, very fair-haired, blue-eyed, effusive and touching, he has not left my side since. Our table included Konstantin's brother Sasha, very shy and 'proper', who looks the spitting image of Emperor Franz-Josef of Austria in his youth (which is hardly surprising, since he is his great-great-grandson).

A Prince Albrecht of Hohenzollern, who is serving as liaison officer with the Rumanian army, spoke to me at length about the Crimea, where he had just been. He had visited Aloupka, Gaspra and various other former family homes there and had found them in perfect condition. He was full of admiration for the Russians and especially for their women, who, he says, show amazing courage, dignity and fortitude. It is nice to hear this!

After lunch we strolled about the roof terraces and then Bobby took me for a running tour of the castle, which seems to have as many cellars and attics as it has rooms. With people popping out of every door, the place looks like a gigantic hotel, run most efficiently by a multitude of menservants in very smart liveries covered with decorations, and teeming with guests, whom I am gradually getting to know. A pretty extraordinary atmosphere considering the times we live in! . . . Our host, Prince Hohenzollern-Sigmaringen and his twin brother Franz-Josef have each three sons, of whom four are more or less grown-up; the other two, looking very sweet in Eton collars, will be the bride's train-bearers. They spend their time guiding me to and from my room. 'You need only ring up the children's floor and ask for us and we will be down in a jiffy to fetch you!' Something I do often, as I keep losing myself.

We then went to have a look at the wedding presents. After tea we, the younger generation, seized our bathing things and rushed down through the town and across several fields to the Danube, which in these parts is still quite narrow, with the water barely reaching one's shoulders. The Duke Luitpold *in* Bavaria (as distinct from the royal house *of* Bavaria) – an elderly sportsman, who is the 'last of his name' – was already there; we lay in the grass chatting with him until it was time to rush back to change for dinner.

There followed a mad struggle for the bathroom (of which there is only one on our floor). As we dressed, the men kept popping in to have us help them with their ties or powder their freshly-shaven chins – all very family-like and *gemütlich*. At last we got Konstantin on his way and were able to finish our own preparations. We found the older generation already assembled in one of the drawing-rooms, the ladies covered with jewels, most of the men in uniforms, some of them of unfamiliar pre-World War I vintage, and all sparkling with decorations. The host's brother wore that of an Admiral; Louis-Ferdinand of Prussia that of a Luftwaffe officer with the yellow ribbon of the Order of the Black Eagle. They all looked very impressive!

At a given signal we paired up with our appointed escorts and marched solemnly into the dining-halls: the bridal couple, their immediate families and the 'notables' being seated at a long table in the Ancestors' Hall; the rest of us at small tables in the neighbouring King's Hall. I sat between Bobby's brother Meinrad and Ambassador von Hassell. In the middle of dinner Louis-Ferdinand got up and made a speech on behalf of his father, the Kronprinz. He spoke of the close ties that had always bound the two houses of Hohenzollern – that of the North and that of the South – and, turning to the youngsters in our room, he said that 'all these glowing young people' were a living guarantee that the Southern branch would continue to prosper as the Northern one had done.

After supper we assembled in yet another room to hear the local church choir serenade the bridal couple. While this went on, most of the guests slipped away. I stayed, as they sang very well and I found it all very moving. Konstantin made a short speech of thanks and then we, the younger generation, made for another, more distant hall to dance (although, because of the war, our hosts had forbidden this). But we retired early, as tomorrow, the Big Day, will be long and tiring.

Monday, 31 August Konstantin of Bavaria awakened me at seven and then went off to confess and take communion. After a hasty breakfast we rushed back upstairs to put on our hats. We were wearing short dresses, I my green one with a very pretty hat. The men wore a white tie or uniforms, with all their decorations and ribbons. At 10 a.m. on the dot we started off, again in pairs, I myself arm-in-arm with Didi Tolstoy. Slowly and solemnly the procession, the guests first, the bridal party and their immediate families last, wound its way out of the castle, across the many courtyards, down the wide ramp, through the town and into the church. The whole neighbourhood seemed to line the streets to watch, as had a score of photographers and newsreel cameramen. The ceremony lasted almost two hours, owing to an endless address by the officiating bishop, devoted essentially to extolling the Christian virtues of past generations of the two families. Then a telegram from Pope Pius XII was read out and this was followed by a very beautiful High Mass with good singing and Bach's Toccata. When it was over, we started back to the castle, this time in reversed order – the bridal party and families first, the guests last – and now the photographing and filming began in earnest. I, too, broke ranks and took quite a few snapshots.

When we arrived back at the castle we found the main reception rooms crowded with people gathered to congratulate the newlyweds, each room being allotted to a given group according to their position, i.e. the local officials in one, the staff in another, the outside guests in a third and we, the house guests, in a fourth. Luncheon, a veritable banquet, was served in the so-called Portuguese Room (named after its magnificent wall tapestries). The food was delicious, starting with crab cocktail and vol-au-vents filled with caviar, and the wines out of this world. I sat between Franzi Seefried (a cousin of Konstantin) and Bossy, the latter in full gold-braided diplomatic regalia, his plumed hat under his chair. The bride's father made a speech; this was answered by Konstantin's father, Prince Adalbert of Bavaria (who has a charming voice and a very simple manner) and then the eldest son of the house, aged eighteen, got up and said: 'We, the young ones, will always stand by you [meaning his sister] even though you are no longer one of us!' and he went on to read the dozens of telegrams. Then the signing of the individual menus started and of course mine got stuck half-way round (I retrieved and completed it later). It is scribbled all over with names such as 'Bobby', 'Fritzi', 'Sasha', 'Willy', 'Uncle Albert', etc. And then comes, in rather childish writing, a huge solitary 'Hohenzollern'. This turned out to be the youngest brother of the bride, aged nine!

After lunch we tore off for a swim. Supper was again at the small tables, but this time in short dresses and without the newlyweds, who had already taken off for a brief honeymoon on the Wörthersee. I retired early, dead tired.

Hardly was I in bed when there was a knock on the door and the so-called 'Hereditary Prince of Saxony' and the second son of the host sneaked in, pulled up chairs and asked whether they could stay awhile to chat: '*So gemütlich!*' The former, a sixteen-year-old called Maria-Emmanuel, begged me to help him find a bride, as he feels that his dynastic obligations (the family was dethroned in 1918!) made it incumbent upon him to start a family early. I suggested that most of his potential brides were probably still making mud patties; he sadly agreed and presently they departed.

BERLIN *Tuesday, 1 September* As by now most of the house-guests had left, we lunched at the long table. I sat next to Louis-Ferdinand of Prussia, who is very well-disposed towards all things Russian and spoke nicely about our country. He is quick and intelligent. I had had a long chat with his wife Kira the day before; she is a Romanov; her father, the Grand-Duke Kiril, grew up with Papa's family.

After tea there was a last bout of photography, after which the family walked us down to the station, where Didi Tolstoy, Georgie Mecklenburg, Franzi Seefried and I took the night train back to Berlin.

Since this may well be the last event of its sort until the war is over (and God knows what Europe will be like after that!) I have kept the programme. It reads:

Celebration of the marriage of
H.H. Princess Maria-Adelgunde of Hohenzollern with
H.R.H. Prince Konstantin of Bavaria

Castle Sigmaringen, 31 August 1942

Sunday, 30 August 1942:
Birthday of H.R.H. the Prince and H.H. Prince Franz-Joseph of
Hohenzollern

8.15:   Holy Communion in the Castle Chapel

8.30:   Congratulations in the King's Room Followed by Breakfast in the
        Ancestors' Hall

9.30:   High Mass in the town church followed by congratulations by the
        Court and Town officials in H.R.H.'s drawing-room; by the Staff in
        the Watercolours Room.

13.00: Luncheon in the Ancestors' Hall and King's Room.

16.00: Civilian wedding in the Red Drawing-Room.

16.30: Tea in the Old-German Hall.

20.00: Supper in the Ancestors' Hall and King's Room. Guests to
        assemble in the Green and Black Drawing-Rooms.

        Dress: Gentlemen – white tie or full-dress uniforms with decora-
               tions and ribbons; ladies with decorations, without rib-
               bons, without tiaras.

21.00: Wedding eve Party.

21.30: Serenade by the Church choir in the French Hall.

Monday, 31 August – WEDDING DAY

8.15:   Holy Communion in the Castle Chapel.

8.30:   Breakfast in the Ancestors' Hall and King's Room.

10.00: Guests to assemble in the Green and Black Drawing-Rooms.

10.15: Procession to the town church.

10.30: Wedding ceremony and High Mass in the town church.

        Following the ceremony: – congratulations:

        1. Staff – King's Room

        2. Officials – Ancestors' Hall

        3. Invited outside guests – French Drawing-Room

4. Relatives and house-guests – Green and Black Drawing-Rooms

13.30: Wedding luncheon in the Portuguese Gallery. Guests to assemble in the Green and Black Drawing-Rooms.

Dress: Gentlemen – white tie or full-dress uniform with decorations and ribbons; ladies – short dress with hat, with decorations, without ribbons.

16.30: Tea in the Old-German Hall.

17.30: The newlyweds depart by car.

Sigmaringen was to acquire brief notoriety in the final stages of the war as 'Provisional Seat of the French State'. Here, following the liberation of France, Marshal Pétain and a raggle-taggle of discredited collaborationists sat out the last months of the conflict.

Wednesday, 2 September After a hasty breakfast with Tatiana, I went on to the office; I was a little uneasy, as I had overstayed my leave by three days. But nowadays, what with the constant bombing of the railways, one can get away with such things fairly easily.

Friday, 4 September After lunch – in the office canteen – went with Tatiana to see the film *G.P.U.* This was very well done. But they were also showing a long newsreel about the attempted British landing at Dieppe and seeing that, we were nearly sick; hour after hour of close-ups of torn and mangled bodies. When I next meet one of those responsible for their news films, I will give him a piece of my mind. When in so many countries nearly everyone has already lost a brother, or a son, or a father, or a lover, to go on to show that kind of horror, presumably in order to prop up German morale, is not only shocking but plain idiotic, as it is bound to be counter-productive. And if it is shown abroad, the effect will probably be even more disgraceful. And with good reason!

In order to test the German defences along the Atlantic Wall, as well as their own landing tactics, the Allies staged on 19 August 1942 an amphibious assault on the

town of Dieppe. Carried out by some 6,000 men, most of them Canadians, the operation was a total disaster.

Almost none of the German objectives were reached, and three-quarters of the assaulting forces were killed, wounded or captured. Though an easy propaganda triumph for the Germans, the terrible lessons of Dieppe were duly taken into account by the Allies when planning the Normandy landings of June 1944.

Afterwards we were very hungry and wandered over to the Hotel Eden, where we found Burchard of Prussia, Georg-Wilhelm of Hannover and the Welczecks, so we dined with them and then went on to the Wrede twins for coffee.

The German advance in southern Russia is progressing fast. It looks as if they are trying to cut off the Caucasus.

It had taken the German armies six months to recover from their reverses of the preceding winter. But in June 1942 they had resumed the offensive with fresh vigour. Their objective – the North Caucasian oil fields and the Volga. By mid-September they had reached the Caucasus (though not the desperately defended oil fields) and General Paulus' Sixth Army had encircled Stalingrad. This was to mark the zenith of Nazi power.

For with every month, the Russians' resistance had stiffened. Not only did they now fight as well as ever, they had also learnt to retreat. There would be no more spectacular German breakthroughs, no more colossal encirclement battles with millions of prisoners, only local tactical successes of an increasingly defensive nature against an ever stronger, better led and more confident enemy. While partisans harassed the Germans' rear, the number of prisoners itself dwindled. For the mass deaths from starvation and ill-treatment in the German P.O.W. camps (reaching by March 1942 into more than 2.5 million!); the brutal policies of the invaders in the occupied territories and wanton killings of civilians there, as opposed to Stalin's widely-proclaimed policy of national reconciliation in defense of the Russian Motherland, coupled with the ruthless punishment of Red Army waverers and deserters in the field – all that was now combining to rally the Russian people around their leaders irrespective of how they felt about Communist rule. And a change of heart was occurring also among many White Russian émigrés, including Missie's own mother.

Saturday, 5 September Mamma read out a letter she had just received from Irena in Rome, who gives a perfectly dreadful description of Hugo Windisch-

Graetz's death. Apparently he was trying out a new plane which promptly disintegrated, hurtling him out into space. They found him completely mutilated, with one leg missing. His mother, Lotti, arrived just in time for the funeral. Luckily Carlo Robilant was there to help his twin brother Mucki, who is utterly broken; they were the closest of friends all their young lives and I am so afraid that now that Hugo is gone, Mucki may go and do something to himself. At the funeral, Irena writes, he knelt throughout the service next to the coffin, stroking it and talking to Hugo. It is perfectly heart-rending. I wept all the rest of the day and came home totally drained.

In the evening we went out to dine at the Schaumburgs' – a cosy, intimate evening with all our best friends. But my heart was simply not with it anymore. One feels so little gaiety left in oneself nowadays. Almost daily one hears that this friend has been killed; or that one. The list is getting longer and longer . . .

Late in September Missie's brother Georgie departed for Paris. In October 1942 Missie herself arranged to visit Paris, ostensibly for the purpose of research in the German photo-archives there; in fact to see how Georgie was doing and to re-establish contact with her cousins there. In two letters to her mother she summed up her impressions of the trip and what she found when she got back to Berlin.

Missie from Berlin to her mother in Schloss Königswart, 30 October 1942 Paris was lovely, much warmer out of doors than here. But there is no heating anywhere and as a result I was laid up with a nasty cough which still bothers me and Georgie had 40 degrees fever the day after I arranged for him to move into my hotel (which was the only way we could get to see each other).

The town is as beautiful as ever, with the leaves turning red and the autumn just starting. I did all I had to do on foot so as to be able to take in as much of the scene as possible. Life is still most agreeable so long as one can afford it. This does not mean that things are particularly expensive; but to have a decent meal (say, with oysters, wine, cheese and fruit, plus a tip) you must fork out about 100 francs per person; which is, after all, only 5 marks . . . There are many excellent plays on, and Georgie and I went to the theatre a lot and generally the whole place has much more 'go' and is far more jolly, smart and optimistic than Berlin.

Georgie himself has a nice room in a pension off the rue de l'Université, which will be heated in winter – a rare advantage. He seems well settled . . .

The other day he and I went out to St Germain-en-Laye to see what had happened to the trunks you had stored with the Boyds before the war and which contained, among other things, part of the eighteenth-century family library from Lithuania. The house is now an annexe of a neighbouring German military hospital and we were received by a Dr Sonntag, a charming Bavarian, who heads all the medical services in occupied France. He turned out to be himself an amateur collector. He was most friendly and helpful, lent us gloves and pinafores so that we should not dirty ourselves while we repacked things and assigned an orderly to help us. And when we had finished, he fed us a delicious tea by the fireplace and then took us around the house (which is in impeccable condition) so that Georgie can reassure old Mr Boyd, who is said to be in a nursing-home nearby.

Dr Sonntag promised to have the attic, where the trunks are, placed 'under the protection of the German Wehrmacht' after Georgie had roped them up and stamped them with the family seal; and once he has found a place in Paris to store them, Georgie will have them brought there in a German army lorry.

Incidentally, Georgie asks us urgently to obtain from the Berlin authorities a certificate that he was not given any new food coupons before he left; until they do so, he is not being delivered any in Paris. Meanwhile he must buy everything on the black market, which is of course ten times more expensive.

Missie and Georgie were not to meet again until the war was over.

Missie from Berlin to her mother in Schloss Königswart, 3 November 1942 I have had a very unpleasant surprise: my salary has been cut, so that I now get, after various deductions, only 310 marks. As the same has happened to everybody else, I can't really protest. But since the new flat costs 100, with another 100 going to pay off the furniture, plus what I must pay for heating, telephone, electricity, laundry, food, etc., I will have to find someone to share it with me . . .

Two weeks after Missie's last entry for 1942, on 19 November, the Russians defending Stalingrad counter-attacked, and five days later they succeeded in cutting off the twenty divisions of General Paulus' Sixth Army. On 2 February 1943, after

*one of the bitterest battles in modern military history, what remained of Paulus' army
– some 91,000 men – surrendered. Only 6,000 of them were to see their homeland
again. The victory of Stalingrad was to be the turning-point of the war in Europe.
From them on, led by a constellation of mostly new, young, talented generals, the
Russian armies were to hold the initiative, virtually without stop, until Germany
capitulated in May 1945.*

*But in the Far East and the West also the tide was turning. On 4 June 1942, off
the island of Midway, the Japanese navy had suffered its first major defeat, thus
losing control of the Pacific. In North Africa, the battle of El Alamein (October–
November 1942) had routed Field Marshall Rommel's famed 'Afrika Korps'; its
remnants would surrender in Tunisia the following May. On 8 November the Allies
landed in French North Africa, the Germans reacting by occupying Vichy France. In
July 1943 the Allies would debark in Sicily, thus initiating the liberation of Western
Europe that would culminate in the invasion of June 1944.*

*For the first two years of the war, the R.A.F. had lacked the numbers and technical
capacity for the large-scale penetration of enemy skies. Moreover, the daytime
bombing of military targets without fighter escort – long-range fighters would appear
only much later in the war – turned out to be so costly that in November 1941 they
had been called off, to be replaced by occasional night-forays, fateful mainly to the
civilian population. But in February 1942 Air-Marshall Arthur Harris had been
put at the head of the R.A.F.'s Bomber Command with a War Cabinet directive to
commence a systematic offensive against Germany's cities 'with the morale of the
civilian population and particularly of its industrial workers to be the chief focal
point'. Harris believed (as it turned out, erroneously) that by concentrating night after
night, for weeks on end, hundreds of aircraft dropping the new 4,000- to 8,000-
pound High Capacity bombs on a single city, the enemy could be literally smashed to
his knees. In the two years that followed, every major city in Germany and Austria
and quite a few in the rest of occupied Europe would be reduced to ashes. The cost in
civilian lives: some 600,000 (as compared to Britain's 62,000!). The attendant
horrors would soon begin to loom ever larger in Missie's diaries, to become eventually
one of its main themes.*

*This turning of the tide had sparked a series of measures inside Germany itself, as
a result of which the last vestiges of decency would eventually succumb to brute force.
Already on 1 September 1941 a decree had ordered all Jews to wear a yellow star. On
20 January 1942 a top secret meeting of senior officials at Wannsee had worked out
the modalities of the so-called 'Final solution of the Jewish problem' following which,
from haphazard, the killing of Jews, and later gypsies and other declared 'sub-
humans', would become methodical, relentless, scientific, with much of Germany's
resources and organisational talent being diverted from winning the war to*

murdering innocent people. On 26 August 1942 the dummy-Reichstag had voted a law conferring on Hitler discretionary powers in the administration of justice. The preamble to the law read: 'at present in Germany there are no more rights, only duties. . . .' A few days later, in his weekly 'Das Reich', Goebbels made clear what lay ahead: 'The bourgeois era with its false and misleading notion of humaneness is over. . . .' The doors to barbarity had been flung wide open.

By now everyday life in Berlin had also changed radically. The U.S.A.'s entry into the war had been followed by a mass exodus of Latin American diplomatic missions – until now the last bastions of social life in the capital. And the heavy losses on the Eastern Front, which were beginning to affect every family in Germany, in themselves discouraged frivolity. From now on, the daily efforts of the author and her friends – or rather of those who were not on the fighting fronts – would be focussed essentially on physical but also ethical survival – against hunger, Allied bombs and, presently, ever-worsening political tyranny and persecution.

Almost incongruously (considering what was happening in the background), one of Missie's letters from Kitzbühel to her mother in Schloss Königswart described a short holiday she took with Tatiana early in 1943:

8 February Tatiana and I have now been here a week and are feeling very rested. We lead a healthy life – we go to bed at 9 p.m. and rise at 8.30 a.m. We have a very nice room, with hot and cold water, but no bath. We must supply our own provisions for breakfast and usually take our meals in town in a very nice little restaurant called Chizzo. The food is very wholesome (schnitzels, delicious cheese, various fruit tarts, etc.) and comes in large portions. The town is really a big village, with coloured houses and gabled roofs and a single main street, with nice sidewalk cafés and shops.

The altitude here is only 800 metres, but when the weather is fine we take a cable-car and go up another 900 metres. There we lie in the sun on a large terrace, from which the others descend to the valley on skis (we don't). People are constantly having accidents, usually poking their ski sticks into one another's faces. I have started taking skiing lessons and am getting along quite well. I crash all the time but without doing myself much harm.

We hardly know anything about the political situation, as only very few newspapers get through and they are immediately bought up. If it were not for the Wrede twins, who keep sending us clippings, we wouldn't know what is going on . . .

A couple of months later, the Germans announced the discovery in the forest of Katyn (in the western part of the U.S.S.R.) of a mass grave containing the decomposed bodies of some 4,400 Polish officers, captured by the Soviets during the brief Polish campaign of October 1939. All had been shot in the back of the head. Missie's diary will later shed new light on this episode.

But there also had been other developments within Germany itself which would dramatically affect her own life and those of some of her closest friends: the anti-Nazi resistance movement was regaining momentum.

Ever since Hitler had made clear his intention of starting a war, influential circles within the armed forces, but also outside their ranks, had been seeking to put an end to what they regarded as both a crime and a folly, if necessary through his overthrow and even assassination. But as Germany went from victory to victory, the conspirators' ranks thinned – through defections, demotions, arrests and even executions. Hitler himself seemed to enjoy a charmed life as every attempt to kill him came to naught. Nor were the resisters' efforts made any easier by the demand of the Western Allies at the Casablanca Conference of January 1943 for Germany's unconditional surrender.

It would require the debacle on the Eastern Front and the subsequent successful Allied landings in the West, coupled with the ever-growing power of the S.S. and the ever-worsening brutality of Nazi policies and methods of warfare (which went against the grain of the best elements in the German armed forces), to give body and urgency to the plans of a new group of plotters, with some of whom Missie would be in almost daily touch.

And now her daily diary resumes:

BERLIN *Tuesday, 20 July* Have just seen the Wrede twins, who have decided to move to Bayreuth. They are not alone in wishing to leave the capital. Besides, since their only brother Eddie was killed early in the Russian campaign, they are restless. Both are Red Cross nurses and can easily get themselves transferred.

A 'Free Germany Committee' has begun to broadcast from Moscow. Reaction of some of my friends here: 'That's what we should have done in Russia from the start!'

On 12 July 1943 a 'National Committee for Free Germany' had been founded in the P.O.W. camp of Krasnogorsk. Its first manifesto, issued a week later, called on the German people and the Wehrmacht to rise up against Hitler. Aside from several veteran Communists (e.g. Wilhelm Pieck and Walther Ulbricht), the Committee included a few senior generals who had been captured at Stalingrad, such as Field Marshal Paulus and General von Seydlitz-Kurzbach. But owing to the German soldiers' fear of Soviet captivity, its success was limited, and though its Communist members were among the founders of the future German Democratic Republic, it played no role in the post-war organisation of the Soviet zone of occupation in Germany.

Thursday, 22 July Lunched with Burchard of Prussia, who is at a loose end now that, as all royal princes, he has been kicked out of the army. He is hoping to get a job in industry, but this will not be easy. He is a typical representative of the decent 'old school' element of the German officer corps and has really been trained only for a military career.

After Prince Wilhelm of Prussia, the Kronprinz's eldest son, was mortally wounded in 1940 during the campaign in the West, all members of former German ruling houses were withdrawn from front duty. Later they were discharged from the Wehrmacht altogether. These measures, which had been taken by the Nazis to avoid a possible monarchist backlash from such 'glamour deaths', were in fact counter-productive: They saved the lives of one of the elements the Nazis hated most.

Sunday, 25 July On my way to Potsdam today I met Henri ('Doudou') de Vendeuvre, one of the many French boys working nowadays in Germany. His brother Philippe was sent here by force under Vichy's S.T.O. and Doudou has followed to keep in touch with him. Here they divide their time between sweeping the corridors of the Deutscher Verlag (an important German publishing house) and 'investigating' conditions in Germany generally. They are both brilliantly intelligent and consider the whole thing a crazy lark.

On 4 September 1942 the Vichy Government had instituted the so-called 'service du travail obligatoire' or S.T.O. (compulsory labour service). Thereafter, all Frenchmen of military age, many of whom had until then, under the system of the 'relève', volunteered for work in Germany, thus enabling a given number of older P.O.W.s to return home, were obliged to do so. This measure, against which thousands naturally rebelled, contributed more than anything else to the proliferation of maquis – resistance centres in remoter areas of the country.

I spent the night at the Hotel Eden with Tatiana, who is here for a few days. Mamma rang up to tell us of Mussolini's dismissal and arrest. Badoglio has now taken over.

On 10 July the Allies had landed in Sicily. Two weeks later, on 24–25 July, the Fascist Grand Council had invited King Victor Emmanuel III to reassume full ruling powers. Mussolini thereupon resigned and was promptly arrested on the King's orders and interned in the Abruzzi mountains. Marshal Badoglio, a former Chief of the General Staff and Viceroy of Ethiopia, was appointed to form a government.

Tuesday, 27 July Tatiana is off to Dresden to undergo treatment, together with Maria Pilar Oyarzabal. On our way to lunch we were followed by a man who moved from tram to bus and kept behind us until we got quite worried. We tried to get rid of him by diving into a house, but he waited outside until we came out, finally buttonholed me and gave me to understand that he objected to our speaking French. This sort of thing used not to happen, but the bombings are making people more bitter.

Wednesday, 28 July Hamburg is being bombed daily. There are very many victims and it is already so badly hit that practically the whole town is being evacuated. There are stories of little children wandering around the streets calling for their parents. The mothers are presumed dead, the fathers are at the front, so nobody can identify them. The N.S.V. seems to be taking things in hand, but the difficulties are enormous.

During the raids of 24, 25, 26, 27 and 29 July and 2 August, nearly 9,000 tons of bombs were dropped on Hamburg, leaving over a million persons homeless and killing an estimated 25,000 to 50,000 people (the German blitz on Coventry killed 554). The Hamburg raids were notable for several 'firsts': they marked the first application of round-the-clock 'area bombing', with the Americans attacking by day and the British by night; for the first time phosphorus bombs were used on such a scale as to create 'fire storms' – hurricane-like winds which started hours after the raid was over and destroyed and killed even more than the bombs themselves; and for the first time the Allies used 'windows', metallic strips dropped in bundles to confuse enemy radar and flak.

Thursday, 29 July I am trying to persuade Mamma to join Tatiana in Königswart, but she refuses, saying I may need her here. I would be far happier these days knowing the parents were safe and not having to worry about them – especially Mamma, who is in real danger here.

From Missie's 1978 recollections: In the autumn of 1942 Mamma had spent some time with Olga Pückler in Silesia, where her husband Carl-Freidrich happened to be passing through on leave. The Allies had just landed in North Africa, and Mamma was her usual outspoken self about what would happen to Germany if the present policies in Russia continued.

Two weeks later Josias Rantzau walked into my office, closed the door and silently handed me a letter signed by Count Pückler and addressed to the Gestapo. Its approximate wording was as follows: 'Princess Vassiltchikov – a childhood friend of my wife's – is strongly opposed to our policy in Russia and criticizes our treatment of prisoners-of-war. She has many influential connections on the Allied side and the information she might give them would be dangerous for Germany. She must not be allowed to leave the country.' The Gestapo had forwarded the letter to the A.A. with orders not to issue an exit visa to Mamma were she to ask for one.

In wartime Germany such a denunciation usually landed its victim in a concentration camp. Josias told me that Mamma should on no account try to leave Germany; indeed the wisest course would be for her to vanish from sight for a while, for instance by going to stay with Tatiana in Königswart, especially as she was beginning to attract a lot of attention through her efforts to organise relief for the Soviet prisoners-of-war.

Mamma had always been fiercely anti-Communist – which is not surprising considering that two of her brothers had perished in the early days of the Revolution. She maintained this unbending attitude for twenty years, going so far as to view even Hitler in a favourable light, according to the principle of 'My enemy's enemies are my friends.' When she arrived in Berlin for Tatiana's wedding in September 1941, she still believed that the German invasion of Russia would result in a mass popular uprising against the Communist system; after which the Germans would be dealt with in their turn by a resurrected National Russia. Not having lived in Germany for any length of time during the Nazi period, it was not easy to convince her that Hitler was no less a fiend than Stalin. Tatiana and I, who had lived in Germany for some time now, had witnessed the unholy alliance between Hitler and Stalin for the purpose of destroying Poland and had first-hand accounts of German atrocities there, had no such illusions.

But as the brutal stupidity of German policy in the occupied territories became known, and the tide of victims mounted both there and inside the Russian P.O.W. camps, Mamma's love for her country, combined with a latent Germanophobia that went back to the years spent as a nurse at the front during World War I, supplanted her earlier anti-Soviet feelings, and she decided to do her share in alleviating the suffering of her people and, in the first place, of the Russian P.O.W.s.

Through some of our friends she got in touch with the responsible offices of the German High Command; she also contacted the International Red Cross in Geneva through their representative in Berlin, Dr Marti. Unlike pre-revolutionary Russia, the Soviet Government had refused the assistance of the International Red Cross. This meant that Russian prisoners, being in the eyes of their own government traitors to their country, were abandoned to their fate – in most cases a hungry death – unless assistance could be provided otherwise.

Mamma then contacted her aunt, and my godmother, Countess Sophie Panin, who worked for the Tolstoy Foundation in New York. She also roped in two world-famous American aircraft constructors of Russian origin, Sikorsky and Seversky, as well as the Orthodox Churches in North and South America. In due course a special relief organisation was set up, which was able to assemble several shiploads of food, blankets, clothing, medical supplies, etc. By now the U.S.A. had entered the war, so that all this had to be purchased in neutral Argentina. The ships were about to set out on the long trek across the U-boat-infested Atlantic when the whole operation almost collapsed: the donors had laid down one condition, namely that the relief be distributed in the camps under the supervision of the International Red Cross. The German military had agreed to this. Only one last thing was needed – Hitler's personal consent. When Mamma next visited her contact, a colonel at the army High Command, he led her out into the neighbouring Tiergarten and there, far from possible prying ears, he said: 'I am ashamed to admit it, but the Führer has said "No! Never!"' Mamma retorted: 'Very well then, I will write to Marshal Mannerheim. He will not say "No!"' Which is what she promptly did. Baron Mannerheim, who had liberated Finland from the Reds in 1918 and now commanded the Finnish army, was a former officer in the Russian Guards Cavalry and knew our family well. Thanks to his influence, the Finnish forces (unlike their German counterparts) had always fought a decent war against the Soviets; the prisoners they captured were treated strictly according to the Geneva Convention and as a result, most of them survived. Within no time Mamma received an enthusiastic response from Mannerheim and in due course the relief shipments reached Sweden, from where the contents were promptly distributed, under international Red Cross supervision, in the Finnish P.O.W. camps.

Sunday, 1 August The fate of Hamburg arouses great anxiety here for last night Allied planes dropped leaflets that called upon all women and children in Berlin to leave at once, as they did before the raids on Hamburg began. This sounds ominous. Berlin may well be next.

Yesterday I had the night shift. After riding in Potsdam all afternoon, I turned up at the office at 11 p.m. My departing colleagues came over to wish me a solemn goodbye, for they had heard that a raid was expected. Slept on a sofa till 9 a.m. without being once disturbed and went home for a bath and breakfast. But I am moving out to the Bismarcks' in Potsdam tomorrow, to be away from town at night.

Monday, 2 August Notices have been put up in every house, ordering the immediate evacuation of all children and of those women who are not doing defence work. There is a tremendous rush on the stations and great confusion, as many evacuated Hamburgers are coming through Berlin on their way elsewhere. There are also rumours that government offices will be moved out of town *in corpore* and we have been given orders to pack, but I am not taking this very seriously. Mamma now spends the nights out in the country at Wanda Blücher's and has at last agreed to join Tatiana soon.

Lunched with Ambassador von Hassell. He told me interesting stories about Mussolini, whom he knew well. He is retired now and writes articles on economics, which he keeps sending me. I confess I don't understand much.

Later I dragged a suitcase over to Potsdam and went to bed early, as I was very tired. Unfortunately sleep was postponed by the arrival of Gottfried Bismarck, Loremarie Schönburg and Count Helldorf, who is Polizeipräsident [Chief of Police] of Berlin. He comes to Potsdam often and they all confer late into the night. It is all very hush-hush, but Loremarie, who has also moved out to Potsdam, keeps me informed about what I call 'the Conspiracy'. She is feverishly active, trying to bring various opposition elements together and acts often in a headstrong and imprudent way. Gottfried, however, never breathes a word.

This is Missie's first allusion to what was to become known as the 20th July Plot.

Helldorf does not think that heavy raids on Berlin will start soon.

Unlike many of his future fellow-conspirators, Count Wolf-Heinrich von Helldorf (1896–1944) had started out as an early, convinced and active Nazi. After World War I (in which, as a subaltern, he had fought with distinction), he had joined the notorious Rossbach Freikorps – a freebooting unit set up by former veterans to fight leftist uprisings in the early days of the Weimar Republic. Following the 1923 Kapp putsch, he was exiled. Returning to Germany, he joined the Nazi party, in which he soon rose to high rank in the S.A., became a member of the Reichstag and served from 1935 on as Berlin Chief of Police. For all this background, Helldorf seems to have had serious reservations about such Nazi policies as anti-Semitism and notably the

Kristallnacht *(anti-Jewish pogrom) of 1938, which set him apart from his erstwhile party comrades and gradually drew him into the centre of the anti-Hitler conspiracy.*

Tuesday, 3 August Today Welfy and Georg-Wilhelm of Hannover came out to Potsdam for supper. Their mother is the late Kaiser's only daughter. Gottfried Bismarck insists that we invite our friends over – I suspect partly to 'size them up', but also because he does not want us to stay late in town. As it was very hot, we sat with our feet in the fountain.

KÖNIGSWART *Monday, 9 August* I had a rough day. I intend to spend a few days at Tatiana's in Königswart, where, thank God, Mamma is now installed. But since one is not allowed to leave the capital without a special permit, I had first to take a commuter train out of Berlin, get off at the small station of Neustadt and buy my ticket to Marienbad there. Loremarie Schönburg helped me drag an enormous suitcase containing the things I wanted to evacuate – mainly photo albums. The train was full of Hamburgers in burnt rags going home, as they prefer to rough it out in their own ruins to being knocked about by the inhabitants of other towns, who are not at all kind to them. They seemed a wild lot, very bold and outspoken. On trains people say pretty much what they think of the regime nowadays. At Neustadt I had just time to buy my ticket and leap back onto a train returning to Berlin, where I had again to change stations and trains. Once more most of the passengers were from Hamburg. One little girl had a badly burnt arm and was laughing all the time hysterically. I arrived in Königswart at two in the morning.

Tuesday, 10 August We spend most of the time driving around the beautiful woods and discussing what we should do 'if and when'.

Saturday, 14 August The weather is rotten, it rains and rains. Tatiana has left to resume her treatment in Dresden. While Mamma goes for long walks, I rest. When one lives in the country, it is surprising how little one knows about what is going on.

DRESDEN *Sunday, 15 August* After lunch I, too, left for Dresden to see Tatiana and visit my cousin Jim Viazemsky, who is in a P.O.W. camp in the neighbourhood. I took along some wine to keep my spirits up during the tedious journey, which took over ten hours. Tatiana had promised to send a car to the station, but when I arrived after midnight I found none and had to walk through the whole town to the clinic. There had been an air-raid warning and there was a full moon, which made things very eerie. I had never been in Dresden before and dreaded getting stuck in some anonymous cellar, but I reached the clinic safely. I found Tatiana looking very seedy with a night nurse in attendance. I was put to bed on a rickety sofa, prolonged by two chairs which kept parting, but I was so tired that I soon fell asleep.

Monday, 16 August Departed at dawn for Jim Viazemsky's camp. I had trouble getting on to a bus, as special travel papers were required, but things were smoothed out eventually. Whenever necessary I present a *laissez-passer* issued by our friend General von Hase, the Military Commandant of Berlin. Actually, he has no authority whatsoever over P.O.W. camps, but thus far it has worked wonders for the entire family, as we visit Jim in turns.

Alighting at some village, I had to walk for half an hour through the fields. Found Jim's camp surrounded by barbed wire. At the principal entrance I again presented my paper. No hitch there. Unfortunately, the Camp Commandant kept me chatting for nearly an hour before summoning Jim and, wishing to keep him mellow, I could do nothing about it. But he seemed good-natured and later Jim confirmed that he is always very decent to them. He is in fact a military doctor and the camp a kind of field hospital, where prisoners of all nationalities spend some time in transit, before being transferred to permanent camps.

While his orderly was preparing a picnic lunch, Jim and I sat chatting in the Commandant's office, which the latter had very kindly placed at our disposal for the duration of my visit. Presently we left the camp and set off on foot for our picnic. Cars with German military kept passing us, but nobody seemed to notice or mind a woman strolling through the woods with a French officer in uniform. This struck us as most bizarre.

Jim is steeped in work, interpreting in English, Russian, German, French, Polish and Serbian. The feeling that he is so badly needed here stops him from thinking too much about escaping. All his life his ears have stuck out and now, availing himself of the enforced leisure, he has decided to have them operated on and pinned back. He seems in good shape and high spirits. They have a secret radio and are therefore well-informed. Apparently, Allied war communiqués are read aloud every night in the dormitories!

Our lunch consisted of corned beef, sardines, peas, butter and coffee, all things we civilians have not seen for a long time. I had brought a roast chicken and champagne from Tatiana and received from Jim a gift of tea and a record of Tchaikovsky's Manfred Symphony. At the bus station he kissed me goodbye, which prompted a passenger to ask whether I was the French officer's *Braut* [fiancée].

I spent another night at Tatiana's clinic. She is progressing satisfactorily, but every time I say something to cheer her up, she bursts into tears from pain. In the night, apparently, I shouted so much that the nurse had to give me a tranquilliser. She says it's the Berlin air-raids.

BERLIN *Tuesday, 17 August* On the way back to Berlin and Potsdam the train was so packed that I stood all the way.

Wednesday, 18 August At the Bismarcks' this evening I talked long with Heinrich Sayn-Wittgenstein, who has been recalled from Russia to defend Berlin. He has already shot down sixty-three enemy bombers and is Germany's second most successful night fighter. But because he is a prince and does not share their ideology (he is descended from a famous Russian field marshal in the Napoleonic wars), he is being cold-shouldered by the regime and his exploits are being played down. I have seldom known a nicer and more sensitive boy. I met him two years ago and he has become one of my closest friends. Having grown up in Switzerland, he hardly knew Germany and so I would take him around everywhere and all my friends adored him.

Friday, 20 August It is dreadfully hot and so after work we drove out to the Golf Club, where Loremarie Schönburg, Heinrich Wittgenstein and I sat on a green, making plans for the future. We discussed what we would do when everything collapsed and the authorities started bumping off non-sympathisers – such as hopping into Heinrich's plane and taking off for Colombia or somewhere. The question of whether we would have enough fuel to get across the Atlantic remained unsolved. Loremarie has a cousin in Bogotá, whom she vaguely proposes to marry one day. She would thus kill two birds with one stone.

Monday, 23 August Instead of going to work, Loremarie Schönburg pretended she had had a sunstroke, and since I felt seedy anyhow, we seized the opportunity and bicycled over to Werder, to try and buy fruit. We took along a rucksack. It is a long way, and when we got there we were joined by a man with a basket, who said that he too wished to buy some fruit. We finally latched on to a farmer who was willing to sell us fifteen pounds of apples. While I muttered that fifty pfennigs a pound seemed a bit expensive, our companion helped me fix the rucksack on the bike. To our amazement, when we had left the orchard and were passing through a tomato field, he produced a paper showing that he worked for the Price Control Board and announced that we had been swindled, that he was going to make a report and that we would have to testify against the farmer in court. He then asked for our names, which we refused to give, saying the poor fellow should be left alone. He insisted. I again refused, whereupon Loremarie, with a blank expression, gave that of Hans Flotow, together with his address. At this I could not suppress a smile and the man grew suspicious, but since we had no identity papers on us, he could not verify anything. He then went to the length of suggesting that, in future, we act as decoys for the police; they would drop us off by car at various farms . . . We told him what we thought of that.

Loremarie is constantly in trouble with the police. In Potsdam, she insulted some cop and has now been summoned to account for it.

Tuesday, 24 August Yesterday there was a heavy raid. Gottfried Bismarck was away. His brother-in-law, Jean-Georges Hoyos, slept through the whole affair. I alone smelt a rat and despite their violent protests, got him and Lore-marie Schönburg up. There was a red haze over Berlin, and this morning Jean-Georges telephoned me to say that he had taken three hours (instead of the usual twenty minutes) to get to town as entire streets had collapsed.

At 6 p.m. we went into town ourselves – to fetch Gottfried and to see whether anything had happened to our respective flats. Martha, the Gersdorffs' cook, fell into my arms sobbing. She had been scared silly, but the house was all right. Not so Loremarie, who has a gaping hole in the ceiling over her bed. She is greatly impressed and announces that she is evidently predestined for bigger and better things. We looked up Aga Fürstenberg, who is very shaken as all the top floors of the houses on and around the Kurfürstendamm near where she lives, including the Pückler flat in the Lietzenburgerstrasse where we had lived when we first moved to Berlin three years ago, had burnt down. After the raid Goebbels toured some of the worst-hit districts, but when he asked for thirty volunteers to fight the fires he got, we are told, a cool reception.

After being bombed out of a succession of flats, Missie and her father were at this point living as paying guests in the villa of friends, Baron and Baroness von Gersdorff. A person of great charm, warmth, refined intelligence and integrity, Baroness Maria von Gersdorff had turned her home in the Woyrschstrasse into what, under the circumstances of a bombed-out city, came closest to a political and intellectual salon, where like-minded people could meet in an atmosphere of complete tolerance and mutual understanding. Thanks to her husband's connection with the powerful Siemens dynasty, to whom he was related, and his wartime duties at Berlin's military H.Q., this salon spanned every sector of German society – from the landed aristocracy (Maria's own background) to industry and business, the academic world, diplomacy and the military.

Wednesday, 25 August Tonight there was again a raid, but little damage was done and the railway to Potsdam is running normally.

Thursday, 26 August Tatiana telephoned from Königswart that the Berlin-Leipzig line had been hit and rail communications with them are severed.

Dined with Loremarie Schönburg and her Hamburg friend, Hanni Jenisch, who is for the moment out of the war, as both his older brothers have been killed. He drives around in a handsome Mercedes without a licence, but the police, unable to believe their eyes, leave him alone.

Friday, 27 August Alex Werth and another man from the office, Professor X, were bombed out yesterday and are now homeless. The latter was blinded into the bargain, after rescuing a woman from a burning house. But his injuries, thank God, are only temporary. He comes from Baden, loathes the regime and keeps repeating that it is the German women who are responsible for it all, as it is they who voted Hitler into power. He says that from now on all toys with military overtones, such as trumpets, tin soldiers and swords, should be banned.

Saturday, 28 August Met Victor de Kowa's Japanese wife, Michiko. He is not only one of Germany's most talented and attractive actors, but he also directs. We went to a rehearsal of his current play.

Sunday, 29 August Drove out with Gottfried Bismarck and Loremarie Schönburg to the country to spend the day with his mother, a charming old lady, half-English, who remembers her father-in-law, the great Bismarck, very well. On the way home Loremarie insisted on driving through pouring rain. As she is totally inexperienced, we got very nervous.

Wednesday, 1 September Four years ago the war started. It hardly seems possible. Last night the Allies staged a 'celebration' and quite a lot of damage was done to Berlin's shopping district.

This evening I went to the opening of *Phline*, Victor de Kowa's new play. Afterwards we went back to his house and I had a long talk with Theo Mackeben, the composer, who is a great admirer of Russia.

Friday, 3 September The Allies have landed on the Italian mainland.

By 17 August the liberation of Sicily had been completed and the Allies were poised to invade the mainland. Meanwhile, with Mussolini's dismissal and arrest on 23 July, Italy was moving fast towards joining the Allied camp and on 19 August Marshal Badoglio had started secret negotiations to this effect. The Allied landings in southern Italy, which began on 2 September, were to greatly accelerate Italy's defection from the Axis' cause.

Saturday, 4 September Tonight I dined with Nagy of the Hungarian Embassy and the Victor de Kowas. The latter is terribly jumpy. With tears in his eyes he announces that he cannot take it anymore; his entire neighbourhood (he lives not far from Tempelhof airport) was wiped out last night. Yesterday's raid was very bad. Even out in Potsdam we assembled downstairs. Since Hamburg Melanie Bismarck has developed an obsession about phosphorus, for there entire pavements were turned into rivers of fire. Now, when a raid starts, she appears with her head draped in a wet towel.

Monday, 6 September It is rumoured that something has happened to the Horstmanns. They had moved out to the country recently for greater safety. Tino Soldati, who lives with them, was expected last night at some official dinner and never turned up, nor did he give a sign of life, which, for a correct young diplomat, struck his hosts as strange.

Tuesday, 7 September This morning Loremarie Schönburg and I took our bicycles into town for the first time. Actually they belong to the Bismarck household. We had trouble, at first, keeping out of the way of trams and buses. Once Loremarie took a flying leap over her handlebars. It was quite a sight!

We had an appointment with Berlin's Chief of Police, Count Helldorf –
Loremarie for her own mysterious ends, I to talk shop. I have been asked to
build up a photo-archive for the A.A. and as all pictures showing bomb
damage are nowadays censored, I wanted Helldorf to release a few for
publication. He promised to do so.

As we had feared, Kerzendorf, the Horstmanns' country place, was badly
damaged two nights ago. I sat at the Gersdorffs' and listened with Gottfried
von Cramm to Fia Henschel's account of the catastrophe; she was staying
there at the time. Fortunately, nobody was killed, but Freddie, who had just
finished installing the priceless antiques they had evacuated from their house
in Berlin, has lost practically everything. It seems odd to think of Tino Soldati
– a Swiss diplomat – streaking across the lawn in his pyjamas at 2 a.m. under a
shower of bombs.

*One of the greatest players in tennis history, Baron Gottfried von Cramm, was to be
dogged by bad luck: though repeatedly in the Wimbledon finals, the cup was always to
elude him. He had run foul of the Nazis early, had even spent some time in a
concentration camp, and until the war had lived mostly abroad.*

Spent most of the afternoon in Adam Trott's office. Our Chief of
Personnel, Hans-Bernd von Haeften, dropped in for a chat. He is a close
friend of Adam's. With his deathly pale, inscrutable face, he reminds me of
some mediaeval tombstone.

*An early anti-Nazi militant, who as far back as 1933 had denounced Hitler's
'robber chieftain mentality', Dr Hans-Bernd von Haeften (1905–1944) had, like
Adam von Trott, studied in England. In 1933 he had joined the diplomatic service
and, when Missie met him, he was a Legation Counsellor. But unlike some of his
fellow-conspirators, he had never become a Nazi – for reasons of Christian ethics. An
early member of Count von Moltke's 'Kreisau Circle', he had gone on to recruit for it
several other prominent resisters, including Adam von Trott himself.*

We discussed the general situation, also the latest mobilisation measures.
The authorities seem to be deliberately calling up the last opposition
elements in the Foreign Service that are still around, replacing them,
wherever they can, with their own men, most of them S.S., like our

Stahlecker. And nobody is allowed to resign of his own free will, unless it is to volunteer for the front. This, of course, complicates greatly the clandestine activities now apparently afoot. It is said that Foreign Minister von Ribbentrop never leaves his lair in Fuschl, near Salzburg. Some internal quarrel has erupted between him and Under-Secretary of State Luther – another hound, if there ever was one. All this, of course, is never discussed openly in my presence, but I can guess much of what is happening. Anyway, as a result, the A.A. is at present without an effective head. If people only knew how inefficiently this whole machine operates under the semblance of a well-oiled bureaucracy, they would be amazed. But then in a way the very existence of our little conspiratorial group is proof of it.

In the evening I dined at Hans Flotow's. Four of us then rode out to the Potsdam station on two bicycles without lights – quite a *tour de force*.

Hans-Georg von Studnitz's diary entry for this day reads: 'Hans Flotow gave a small dinner-party, attended by Missie Wassiltschikoff, Loremarie Schönburg, Aga Fürstenberg and Bernd Mumm among others. We talked about nothing but air-raids. The whole thing reminded me of a meeting of persecuted Christians in the Roman catacombs!' (from While Berlin Burns. Diaries 1943–5, *London, Weidenfeld & Nicolson, 1963).*

Wednesday, 8 September We again took our bicycles into Berlin, where I picked up a Rose Valois hat – a large, bright green sombrero with black ribbons – somebody had sent Tatiana from Paris. After work, Gottfried Bismarck dropped Loremarie Schönburg and me at Scapini's. During dinner a secretary burst in with the news that Italy had capitulated. We excused ourselves and rushed off to warn Otto Bismarck, Gottfried's older brother, who had just arrived from Rome (he was long Minister-Counsellor at the German Embassy there) and who was dining at 'Horcher's' with Helldorf and Gottfried, all three supremely unaware of the event. They were in a *séparé* when Loremarie and I burst in with the news and were thunderstruck. Scapini had also been floored. He is here as Acting French Ambassador to negotiate the return of French prisoners-of-war in exchange for 'voluntary' labour. He is a pathetic figure; blinded in the last war, he is always attended by an Arab servant, who acts as his eyes and describes everything going on around him.

Thursday, 9 September On my way into town I bought a paper and was amused by the expression of a man sitting opposite me, who saw for the first time the news about Italy's capitulation. For all their sacrifices, the Italians manage to cut a very poor figure indeed!

Friday, 10 September Albert Eltz and Aga Fürstenberg dropped by at the office shortly before closing time and we hurried over to the Italian Embassy, where I had hoped to find somebody who would be leaving soon and who would take a letter to Irena, before we get cut off for good until the end of the war. The poor girl will worry so.

Found the entire Italian colony seated on suitcases around the building, with many cars and ambulances waiting. Albert remarked that they would probably be given a hiding before being transported to the station. I finally caught sight of Orlando Collalto, who promised to give Irena verbal messages but would take nothing in writing.

I then proceeded to Potsdam, taking along a valuable carpet plus Albert, who though himself in the Luftwaffe, is full of wholesome respect for Allied aircraft and prefers to spend his nights out of town. In the evening Adolf delivered a long diatribe about the Italian 'stab in the back'.

Saturday, 11 September The Germans have occupied Rome. Let us hope this does not mean that the town will now be bombed by the Allies.

This evening Loremarie Schönburg had invited Helldorf to dinner to discuss politics. Albert Eltz too was interested to hear his views. As he has not the best of reputations (he is a veteran party member and an S.A.–Obergruppenführer), Helldorf's present conspiratorial activities leave some of the more intransigent anti-Nazi plotters dubious. Loremarie and Albert were in their respective baths when Aga Fürstenberg arrived unannounced. She is a notorious chatterbox, so we all hid, pretending to be out. When she departed, I went in search of the others and found them cowering in the cellar draped in nothing but their bath towels. Unfortunately all these preparations proved to be in vain, for when Helldorf arrived, he was monosyllabic. Albert tried hard to needle him, but he was clearly on his guard. I fell asleep.

Sunday, 12 September Tonight the radio suddenly burst out into a rendering of the Italian fascist anthem, 'Giovinezza', and went on to announce that Mussolini had been rescued by German parachutists from his mountain prison, the Gran Sasso d'Italia, in the Abruzzi, and was on his way here. We were struck dumb.

In a daring commando-type raid, S.S. parachutists led by Lieutenant-Colonel Otto Skorzeny had landed by glider on top of the Grand Sasso d'Italia, freed Mussolini and flown him to Germany. He was later to set up a rump neo-fascist administration – the Italian Social Republic – in northern Italy, with its capital in Salò.

Wednesday, 15 September Dined alone with Otto and Gottfried Bismarck. The former told us a lot about life in Rome. Anfuso has apparently declared himself for Mussolini (he was Ciano's former *chef de cabinet*), but most of the other fascist big-wigs have, now that he is losing, turned against him.

Thursday, 16 September Georgie has just written from Paris, enclosing a white tassel – all that was left of one of his window panes after a bomb fell nearby.

The Allied raid on Paris on 3 September had caused some 110 deaths.

Later I bicycled over to Wannsee to see Dr Marti, the Swiss Red Cross representative with whom Mamma has been working to organise relief for the Soviet prisoners of war. I came just in time, for he was leaving next day for Switzerland.

Mussolini spoke at length on the radio. I understood nearly everything.

Sunday, 19 September A 'Union of German Officers' has broadcast an appeal from Moscow. It is signed by several German generals who were captured at Stalingrad.

KÖNIGSWART *Tuesday, 28 September* I have taken a short holiday to visit the parents and Tatiana. The latter looks a little better. I went for long walks with Mamma, who insists that I quit my job and join them in the country. She cannot understand that this is impossible and that I would automatically land in a munitions factory. Slept both nights with Tatiana, to give us a chance to chat.

BERLIN *Monday, 4 October* Lunched with Josias Rantzau, Ambassador von Hassell and the latter's son. On returning to the office Josias was given to understand from 'higher up' that our meetings outside office hours are frowned upon.

Tuesday, 5 October Went to a Hungarian concert with Philippe de Vendeuvre and another French boy, Hubert Noël, who, although deported to work in Germany, has managed to obtain a medical certificate that he is half-deaf; he is now returning to France.

Thursday, 7 October Lunched at the Golf Club with friends but had to hurry back, as I had made an appointment with Philippe de Vendeuvre to accompany him to the headquarters of the S.D., of which the Gestapo is merely a part. He had just heard that one of his best friends, the son of a French banker by the name of Jean Gaillard, had been arrested near Perpignan while trying to cross into Spain. He had been transferred to a camp in Compiègne still dressed in the tennis shirt and shorts in which they had caught him. He had managed to notify his fiancée of his plight. But there had been no further news of him, except that he had been bundled into a sealed box-car heading for Oranienburg, a dreaded concentration camp outside Berlin. Our planned strategy was to act dumb, make naive enquiries and treat the S.D. officers as we would officials of a normal institution. I would give the A.A. – oh, irony! – as a reference. We even planned to ask for permission to send Gaillard some food and clothing. In case I did not return, I had told Loremarie Schönburg where I was going.

Once inside the building – a vast compound surrounded with barbed wire a little out of town – and after they had removed a camera I had by some aberration of the mind taken along with me, we were handed over to a succession of officials, who passed us down the line from one to the next like tennis balls. Each time we had to give a full account of ourselves. When asked why I was interested in the case, I said that Philippe and I were cousins. We stayed there a full three hours but got nowhere. They even condescended to go through the files of the recent arrivals at Oranienburg; Gaillard was not among them. Finally they suggested that Philippe go to Oranienburg and enquire on the spot. I begged him later not to, as he would have ended locked up there himself. They were taking down all kinds of particulars about us, when I was suddenly called to the phone – Loremarie was at the other end: 'Lebst du noch?' ['Are you still alive?']. I assented hurriedly and hung up. We left, utterly discouraged, barely daring to raise our eyes; everywhere black uniforms, guns and grim faces. It was a relief to be in the bombed-out streets once more.

Eventually Philippe de Vendeuvre learnt that his friend was interned not in

Oranienburg but Buchenwald and, disregarding Missie's warnings, he proceeded there – but without success. In 1945 young Gaillard was liberated by the advancing U.S. troops, but as these had no spare transport, the survivors were dispatched to the rear of the advancing armies on foot. Many of them, including Gaillard, perished on the way. His body was never found.

Sunday, 10 October Spent most of the day waiting for a call from Uncle Valerian Bibikoff, an elderly relative from Paris, who early in the Russian campaign had volunteered for service with the German navy as an interpreter. Little did he guess what he was getting into! Now he was on his way back to Paris on leave. I was planning to give him letters, one for Georgie and another from Philippe de Vendeuvre. Philippe had urged me to read his, which I at first refused to do. But after he left, I did so. Consternation! For it was a detailed report addressed to the Archbishop of Moulins by a priest of the resistance working in a German concentration camp. I went through terrible qualms of conscience, not wanting to let Philippe down, but knowing full well what I might be doing to poor Valerian. I finally put everything in a sealed envelope addressed to Georgie, asking *him* to forward it to Moulins from Paris, and handed Valerian this little parting gift. Before he left we drowned our sorrows in vodka. Am praying all goes well.

The letter reached Georgie safely and was in due course delivered by him to its addressee. Its author, the Abbé Girardet, perished.

Monday, 11 October Spent the evening with Sigrid Görtz. The Gestapo have arrested her mother, who is Jewish, and have calmly announced that she is being sent to the ghetto in Theresienstadt, in Czechoslovakia. Sigrid's father (who was not Jewish) was killed in World War I and she herself is a beautiful tall blond girl. Thus far she has managed to obtain a reprieve, during which time she is sending out SOS in all directions, but the chances are thin. At S.D. headquarters she was told: 'Schade, dass Ihr Vater nicht mehr lebt. Dann wäre es nicht nötig. Sie haben halt Pech' ['It's a pity your father is no longer alive, for in that case this would not be necessary. Your tough luck!'].

Tuesday, 12 October Loremarie Schönburg and I are throwing a cocktail party in her flat in town and are lugging things back to make it liveable. We have two bottles of wine and half a bottle of vermouth, but we optimistically hope the guests will contribute something.

Wednesday, 13 October The party was a success, although Gretl Rohan, Loremarie Schönburg's aunt, emptied one bottle of wine while I was buying stuff to put on sandwiches. This came as a shock, but people brought ice and champagne and we poured everything together, a weird mixture; but it was consumed without complaints. Am trying to take the Vendeuvre boys down to Tatiana for a weekend, but so far Frenchmen are not allowed to travel from where they have been assigned to work. We discussed how we could get around this while frying potatoes after most of the guests had left.

The new Badoglio government in Italy has declared war on Germany.

In his proclamation announcing the armistice, Badoglio had ordered the Italian armed forces to end all acts of hostility against 'the enemy forces' but to resist any other attack wherever it came from (meaning the Germans). Though the alliance with Germany had never been popular in Italy and the war even less so, this about-turn, involving the betrayal of recent companions-in-arms, caused much agonising soul-searching in the Italian armed forces and some refusals to comply.

Thursday, 14 October Dropped by to see Count von der Schulenburg. The last German Ambassador in Moscow, he is a charming old man, well-disposed towards all things Russian and very outspoken. I am trying to get Katia Kleinmichel a new job, for she is just now at a loose end.

A diplomat of the old school and a staunch supporter of Bismarck's traditional policy of friendship between Germany and Russia, Count Werner von der Schulenburg (1875–1944) had, as Ambassador to Moscow since 1934, worked tirelessly to maintain a modus vivendi *between the two dictators. Hitler's attack on Russia in June 1941 had been for him a harbinger of national disaster (he did not doubt Germany's ultimate defeat), that alienated him even more from a system he had always abhorred.*

Monday, 18 October Today I was on night duty. I arrived at 7 p.m. The two girls who were to hold the fort with me were at a concert. I wrote a few letters and was about to go out again to call on Dickie Wrede next door, when the doorman warned me there had been rumours of an air-raid. I said I would be back in a jiffy.

I had hardly reached Dickie's front door when there were three loud crashes. I rang and rang but nobody seemed to be at home, so I sprinted back to the office, where I learnt that three bombs had fallen in our immediate vicinity. Though one could hear the planes droning overhead, the alarm sounded only a few minutes later. After the all-clear I returned to Dickie's, who had by then come home, and we had some coffee. The night in the office was uncomfortable; I lay wrapped in a rug on a bed hard as a board.

Sunday, 24 October Maria Gersdorff's birthday. It was difficult to find a present. I brought her scent. She had many guests, including Adam Trott, who later came with Papa to Loremarie Schönburg's flat. We fed our guests bread, wine, fried potatoes and coffee.

I have a new urgent assignment: the translation of the captions for a large number of photographs of the remains of some 4,000 Polish officers found murdered by the Soviets in Katyn forest near Smolensk. The mind boggles.

This is all very hush-hush. I have seen the confidential report sent by von Papen, the German Ambassador in Ankara. He had authorised a member of his staff to become chummy with a Polish diplomatic representative in Turkey who, in his turn, is a friend of Steve Early's, President Roosevelt's special representative there. Roosevelt has expressed the wish to receive the full, unadulterated story – a thing he is, apparently, unable to do in the States because his entourage (Morgenthau?) intercept and suppress any report unfavourable to the Soviet Union.

After a brief spell in 1932 as German Chancellor, Franz von Papen (1879–1969) had, to lull conservative opinion, been named in 1933 Hitler's Vice-Chancellor. In 1934–1938, as German Ambassador to Austria, he had done his share in facilitating the Anschluss, and in 1939–1944, as Ambassador in Ankara, he was not unsuccessful in helping keep Turkey from joining the Allies. Brought to trial in 1946 in Nuremberg for war crimes, he was acquitted on all counts, but in 1947 a German court sentenced him to eight years in a labour camp and loss of property. Released two years later, he was to live out his last years in relative obscurity.

The translations must be ready in two days. I feel very strange when I think that my prose will land on President Roosevelt's desk in less than a week.

What a responsibility! It is also hard work. But above all the detailed evidence that has come to light is harrowing.

On 13 April 1943 the German radio had announced that the bodies of thousands of Poles, mostly officers, had been discovered in a mass grave in the forest of Katyn, near Smolensk, in German-occupied Russia. All had been shot in the back of the neck – the traditional Soviet method of execution. The Germans immediately accused the Soviets of the deed and appointed a commission of enquiry made up of doctors from twelve neutral or German-occupied countries. A second commission, from German-held Poland, included agents of the Polish underground. On 17 April, without consulting the British Government, the Polish government-in-exile in London (which had long suspected the truth) announced that it had asked the International Red Cross to investigate. The latter said it could not act without the consent of the Soviet Government, which, of course, was not forthcoming. Instead, Moscow broke off relations with the London Poles, accusing them of collusion with the enemy; they were never to be resumed.

Both commissions came to the unanimous conclusion that the 4,400-odd victims – all of them officers – were part of the 230,000 Polish military personnel captured by the Soviet armies following their invasion of Poland in the fall of 1939. Of these, some 148,000 – including 12,000 to 15,000 officers – had vanished without trace, all enquiries by the Polish government-in-exile until the discovery of the charnel being met even by Stalin himself with the same response: the Polish prisoners 'had all been released' or 'had escaped'. Only Beria, Stalin's police chief, was once heard to murmur: 'There, we made a great mistake . . .' All the material evidence indicated that the victims had been shot in the spring of 1940, i.e. almost one year before the Germans took over the spot. Lastly, they all came from the same Soviet camp for Polish captured officers, the former Orthodox monastery of Optina Poustyn', near Kozel'sk, from which all correspondence with their relatives had suddenly ceased in April 1940. The inmates of the two other officers' camps, Ostashkov and Starobiel'sk, have not been accounted for to this day; their bodies lie, presumably, in other charnels 'known only to God'.

Upon re-occupying the area, Moscow appointed its own commission of enquiry which shifted the blame to the Germans and this charge was included in the initial Allied indictment against the major Nazi war criminals at the Nuremberg trials. But the final verdict passed it over in silence, thus leaving no doubt as to who the actual murderers were.

The discovery of the Katyn charnel was, of course, highly embarrassing to the Allies. The U.S.S.R. was still bearing the brunt of the fighting in Europe and its continuing good will and participation were essential. Besides, there was a vast and influential body of sympathy for the 'gallant Soviet allies' that rebelled against the thought that Moscow was capable of such an iniquity. And so a conspiracy of silence, to which all Allied leaders were parties, stifled any further mention of the matter until the war had ended.

According to post-war Eastern European sources, following his denunciation of Stalin's crimes at the Twentieth Congress of the C.P.S.U. in 1956, Nikita Khrushchev urged his Polish counterpart, Wladyslaw Gomulka, to publish the truth. Gomulka refused, fearing that this would lastingly jeopardise the two countries' relations. Since then, additional evidence has come to light which not only confirms Moscow's responsibility for the crime, but even reveals the identity of many of the executioners.

Since the victims of Katyn included 21 university professors, over 300 doctors, over 200 lawyers, over 300 engineers, several hundred schoolteachers, and many journalists, writers and industrialists, the massacre is regarded in Poland as an attempt to wipe out all those non-Communists who could have led the country after its liberation.

Loremarie is suddenly very afraid of air-raids. Last night she slept at my house and punched me in the eye in her sleep.

Most of the South American diplomats are departing.

Thursday, 28 October There are air-raids now every night but they seem pretty harmless. They usually catch me in the bath tub.

KÖNIGSWART *Saturday, 30 October* Aga Fürstenberg and I are in Königswart for the weekend. The Vendeuvres were refused permission to travel. Our journey was strenuous; we stood half the way, the carriages being packed with *Mutter und Kind* evacuees; there were also many wounded; the rest of the trip we sat on our suitcases in the corridor. Here I go for long walks with Mamma and try to recover from town life.

Sunday, 31 October Yesterday we were still in bed when there was a loud thump. A plane had crashed in our woods. The pilot, who was flying to Nuremberg, had wanted to wave to his family, who live in a village nearby; something went wrong and his aircraft dropped like a stone. The pilot was killed instantly but his crewman lived for several hours. All the men of the neighbourhood have been mobilised to put out the fire, which spread fast, as the countryside is very dry.

BERLIN *Monday, 1 November* Our return journey was even worse. I got separated from Aga Fürstenberg, who slipped and fell. I could hear her squeaks and moans at the end of the carriage, as people trampled on her where she lay. Even though Tatiana had given us a lot of sandwiches and wine to tide us over the journey, we arrived thoroughly exhausted.

Saturday, 6 November The Russians have retaken Kiev.

Wednesday, 10 November The Bismarck house in Potsdam is filling up and Loremarie Schönburg and I are moving back into town; we have been enjoying Gottfried and Melanie's hospitality too long as it is. And now that autumn has come, it does not look as if the raids will be too heavy. Still, I am only taking back the indispensables, as it seems more reasonable nowadays to travel light.

Thursday, 11 November Supper with the Gersdorffs, followed by another harmless raid. I slept thirteen hours.

Saturday, 13 November Coffee at the Wrede twins' with Sigi Welczeck, the automobile racer Manfred von Brauchitsch and the actress Jenny Jugo.

Everybody is aghast because a well-known young actor has been executed for his 'subversive' remarks: he had forecast Germany's probable defeat. Manfred von Brauchitsch (who is a nephew of the former Commander-in-Chief of the Army) is also in trouble, having been denounced for much the same thing.

Went to a concert conducted by Furtwängler and then came home and played the piano. Martha, the cook, in a musical vein, insisted on singing all her favourite Naughty Nineties ditties. Maria Gersdorff and Papa were out. There was another raid. I packed a small bag but things quietened down, so we stayed where we were.

Tuesday, 16 November Night duty. One always feels bad the next morning – a sort of muscular hangover. Went home for half an hour after taking a bath at the office – the only place that seems occasionally to have hot water. Sadly, I and my photo-archive have been moved to the former Czech Legation in the Rauchstrasse.

Everybody is agog over the news that the boss there has been fired. The Gestapo had got hold of a letter from him to his ex-wife in the Ruhr, warning her of impending raids. The wife's second husband had denounced him. What a gang!

Dined tonight at Gottfried Bismarck's in Potsdam with Adam Trott, the Hassells and Furtwängler. The latter, who is terrified of the possible arrival of the Russians, disappointed me. From a musical genius I had somehow expected more 'class'.

Commenting on this dinner in a letter to his wife, Adam Trott added: 'Drove back with Missie and was again astonished and impressed by her . . . She has something of a noble animal of legend about her, that one can never quite understand . . . something free that enables her to soar far above everything and everyone. This, of course, is a little tragic, indeed almost uncanny . . .'

Wednesday, 17 November We were summoned *in corpore* to meet the new temporary boss of the Rauchstrasse office, a young man by the name of Büttner. He is straight 'from the wars', limps and has a gash in his forehead. He delivered a sermon about the heroic life of the soldiers at the front and about what was expected of us people in the rear.

In the evening I took Adam Trott to the Horstmanns'. They have moved back into a tiny flat in town; it has literally three rooms, but these are as usual beautifully arranged and they continue to be as hospitable as before.

Spent the night at Loremarie Schönburg's, as there was a raid on and my own home in the Woyrschstrasse was too far away. She is in bad trouble, having left a 'top secret' American book, *Hitler's Girls, Guns and Gangsters*, in the lavatory of the Hotel Eden, where she was lunching with a friend. She was supposed to read and review it in the office. To make things worse, it bears the official stamp of the A.A. She dares not admit it and is trying desperately to find it and to mobilise influential friends were she to suddenly disappear. She even went to the length of calling up some man she had met only twice, who works at Foreign Minister von Ribbentrop's hideout in Fuschl. When the call came through, she was not there and I had to behave as though I knew nothing.

Thursday, 18 November I am gradually learning to go without lunch. Our canteen is perfectly horrible, though they have many of our coupons for the concoction they call *Mittagessen* [lunch].

Gottfried Bismarck took me around town on some errand. He feels a bit embarrassed: our respective families – mine and Loremarie Schönburg's – keep writing to thank him for sheltering us in Potsdam; apart from Papa, who lives with me at the Gersdorffs', they do not know that we have moved back to Berlin.

Spent most of the afternoon looking at newspapers and magazines published abroad. They are on file in my former office in the Charlottenstrasse and I go there regularly under various specious pretexts.

In the middle of supper at home with Maria and Heinz Gersdorff there was suddenly a lot of violent shooting. As there is no cellar, we took refuge in the kitchen, which is half underground, its windows overlooking a small garden, and sat there for two hours. There were several fires in our neighbourhood and it became quite noisy. We later heard that several hundred planes reached the outskirts of Berlin, but only about fifty got through the *flak* barrage.

Air-Marshall Harris' attempt to 'smash Germany to its knees' consisted of a number of major air battles named after their main target. The first, in the spring of 1943, had been the 'Battle of the Ruhr', which had wiped out Germany's industrial heartland, together with such cities as Cologne, Mainz and Frankfurt. The 'Battle of Hamburg' had followed – in July and August. By the fall of 1943 Harris' bombers were poised to tackle their prize target – the capital of the Reich. Unsuspecting, Missie has just described the opening shot of what was to become known as the 'Battle of Berlin'.

Friday, 19 November Dined with Rudger von Essen from the Swedish Legation and his wife Hermine. They have just finished decorating a ravishing flat near our house, full of glass and china from Denmark, which seems a bit imprudent. I came late as the trams were running only sporadically. We had oysters – a treat!

Sunday, 21 November Went to Mass with Papa at the large Russian cathedral near Tempelhof. The singing was lovely. Loremarie Schönburg and a badly-wounded young officer friend of hers, Tony Saurma, came too and were much impressed, although Tony was distracted by the sight of the many Soviet women, some of them suckling their babies in church. They come from the German-occupied areas of Russia and their numbers are steadily growing. Some work in agriculture, others in munitions factories. The church on Sundays is their favourite meeting place – more, I suspect, because it gives them a feeling of home than from religious zeal. Loremarie caught sight of a Russian pianist she knew in Vienna, Ogouze, and invited him out to Potsdam. We drove out in two cars. For Tony, being a wounded officer, is also motorised. After several glasses of brandy Ogouze played – mostly Russian music. He is a good pianist but not a very nice man.

Towards midnight I managed to convince Tony and Loremarie that it was time to start for home. The weather was very bad. Tony lost his way and missed the Wannsee entrance to the Avus. After driving in the wrong direction for a while, he realised this, turned around and promptly punctured a tire. By now he had also run out of gas. While he started working on the wheel, Loremarie and I got out to look for help. After quite some time a large car approached from the opposite direction. We waved it to a stop. Out jumped a gentleman in civilian clothes and an S.S. chauffeur; they agreed to give us some petrol and while it was being poured into ours, we got into their car and played the wireless. The civilian asked us whether we were actresses and what country we came from. We enquired slyly to whom we should return the borrowed petrol. He replied that this would not be necessary; he said they were coming from the Führerhauptquartier [Hitler's Supreme H.Q.], but would not reveal his identity.

By now, to make up for their huge losses on the Eastern Front and release more ethnic Germans for front-duty, millions of men and women from all over occupied Europe were being lured or deported to Germany to work in agriculture, mining, industry, rebuilding bombed factories or railway lines, constructing coastline fortifications, etc. By 1944 they would number some 7.6 million, i.e. one fourth of the total workforce. At least one third of them came from the Soviet Union – P.O.W.s (whom otherwise a hungry death awaited in the camps) or civilians from the occupied territories, the so-called 'Osts'.

Monday, 22 November I am so tired after last night's adventure that tonight I plan to go to bed at seven. Went without lunch and am staying on in the office late, as we have a boring conference. It is raining cats and dogs.

Today is Georgie's birthday.

Tuesday, 23 November Last night the greater part of central Berlin was destroyed.

In the afternoon there was heavy rain. I had been sent out to fetch a document that was needed for the conference. Our new boss Büttner has a mania for such conferences; they take place almost daily. He probably just likes to 'review his troops'. I find them a complete waste of time. I got drenched on the way and arrived late at the meeting, which went on until shortly after 7 p.m. I was rushing down the stairs to go home when the hall porter intercepted me with the ominous words 'Luftgefahr 15' ['air-raid danger 15']. This meant that large enemy air formations were on their way. I took the stairs back two at a time to warn those of my colleagues who lived far away to stay put, since they might otherwise be caught out in the open. The sirens sounded just as I was leaving the building. It was still raining hard and since the buses would be stopping shortly, I decided to walk home. On the way I popped a long letter I had just written to Tatiana into the mail box on the corner.

The streets were full of people. Many just stood around, for the visibility was so poor on account of the rain that nobody expected the raid to last long or cause much damage. At home I was met by Maria Gersdorff, who told me that her husband Heinz had just telephoned from his office at the Stadt-Kommandantur [H.Q. of Berlin's garrison] to warn her that the enemy air formations were larger than usual, that the raid might therefore be serious and that he was staying on at the office for the night. Having had no time for lunch, I was ravenous. Maria asked old Martha the cook to warm up some soup while I went upstairs to change into slacks and a sweater. As one does now in such cases, I also packed a few things into a small suitcase. Papa was in his room, giving a language lesson to two young men. He told me that he did not wish to be disturbed.

I had just finished packing when the *flak* opened up. It was immediately very violent. Papa emerged with his pupils and we all hurried down to the half-basement behind the kitchen, where we usually sit out air-raids. We had hardly got there when we heard the first approaching planes. They flew very low and the barking of the *flak* was suddenly drowned by a very different sound – that of exploding bombs, first far away and then closer and closer, until it seemed as if they were falling literally on top of us. At every crash the house shook. The air pressure was dreadful and the noise deafening. For the first time I understood what the expression *Bombenteppich* ['bomb carpet'] means – the Allies call it 'saturation' bombing. At one point there was a shower of broken glass and all three doors of the basement flew into the room, torn off their hinges. We pressed them back into place and leant against them

Missie
during the early years
of the war (1939-1941)

George Vassiltchikov

Missie, 1942

Curt-Christoph von Pfuel ('C. C.') and Irena Vassiltchikov

Tatiana and Missie
with their mother

Schloss Crottorf

Prince Paul Metternich

Prince Konstantin of Bavaria and his bride, Maria-Adelgunde of Hohenzollern
The Gersdorff villa in the Woyrchstrasse, Berlin
BELOW: Schloss Sigmaringen

Schloss Königswart
Baron Johannes von Flotow ('Hans')
Baroness Maria von Gersdorff

ABOVE: Prince Heinrich zu
Sayn-Wittgenstein; RIGHT: Count
Hieronymus Clary ('Ronnie')

Missie with Countess Sigrid von Welczeck ('Sigi') and Princess Antoinette von Croy

Prince Hugo zu Windisch-Graetz
Princess Antoinette von Croy

Prince Ivan Viazemsky ('Jim')
as a prisoner of war

LEFT: Baron Rudger and
Baroness Hermine von Essen
ABOVE: Princess Eleanore von
Schönburg ('Loremarie')
BELOW: Prince Burghard of
Prussia with Missie and
Baroness Agathe von Fürsten-
berg ('Aga')

'Loremarie' von Schönburg
and Dr. Hans Peter Frey ('Percy')

Herbert Blankenhorn

Officials of the Information Department of the German Foreign Office (from left to right): Büttner (first name unknown), unidentified man, Dr. Alexander Werth ('Alex'), Dr. Johannes Richter ('Judgie'), Adam von Trott zu Solz, Josias von Rantzau

Adam von Trott zu Solz in the dock of the People's Court

Ilse Blum ('Madonna') and Hans-Georg von Studnitz

ABOVE LEFT: Hans-Bernd von Haeften in the dock of the People's Court;
ABOVE RIGHT: Werner von Haeften; BELOW: Count Gottfried von Bismarck during
interrogation before the People's Court

LEFT: S.A.-General Count Wolf-Heinrich von Helldorf; RIGHT: Dr. Hasso von Etzdorf

Dr. Rudolf Schleier (far left) and Pierre Laval, Prime Minister of Vichy France (second from right)

ABOVE LEFT: S.S. Colonel Dr.
Franz Six; RIGHT: Dr. Roland
Freisler

Missie and Count Friedrich-Werner von
der Schulenburg

ABOVE: Luftwaffe Hospital in Vienna, photographed in 1986; BELOW LEFT: Tunnel in the Türkenschanzpark, Vienna, photographed in 1986; BELOW RIGHT: Mews of the 'Königinvilla,' Gmunden

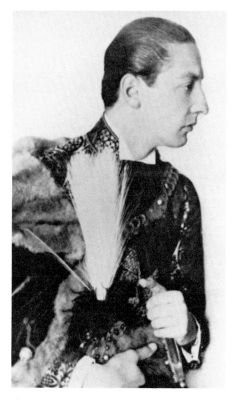

ABOVE LEFT: Count Geza Pejacsevich; ABOVE RIGHT: Palais Wilczek, Vienna, photographed in 1986; BELOW: Missie and Princess Carmen von Wrede ('Sita') in nursing uniforms

LEFT: Countess Elisabeth von Wilczek ('Sisi'); RIGHT: Missie at the end of the war, 1945; BELOW: Missie's wedding day, January 28, 1946, in Kitzbühel (left to right): Paul Metternich, Missie, her husband Peter Harnden, Tatiana Metternich, unidentified family members.

to try to keep them shut. I had left my coat outside but didn't dare go out to get it. An incendiary flare fell hissing into our entrance and the men crept out to extinguish it. Suddenly we realised that we had no water on hand to put out a possible fire and hastily opened all the taps in the kitchen. This dampened the noise for a few minutes, but not for long . . . The planes did not come in waves, as they do usually, but kept on droning ceaselessly overhead for more than an hour.

In the middle of it all the cook produced my soup. I thought that if I ate it I would throw up. I found it even impossible to sit quietly and kept jumping to my feet at every crash. Papa, imperturbable as always, remained seated in a wicker armchair throughout. Once, when I leapt up after a particularly deafening explosion, he calmly remarked: 'Sit down! That way, if the ceiling collapses, you will be farther away from it . . .' But the crashes followed one another so closely and were so ear-splitting that at the worst moments I stood behind him, holding on to his shoulders by way of self-protection. What a family *bouillabaisse* we would have made! His pupils cowered in a corner, while Maria stood propped against a wall, praying for her husband and looking desperate. She kept advising me to keep away from the furniture, as it might splinter. The bombs continued to rain down and when a house next to ours collapsed, Papa muttered in Russian: 'Volia Bozhia!' ['Let God's will be done!']. It seemed indeed as if nothing could save us. After an hour or so it became quieter, Papa produced a bottle of schnaps and we all took large gulps. But then it started all over again . . . Only around 9.30 p.m. did the droning of planes overhead cease. There must have been several hundreds of them.

Just then, marvel of marvels, the kitchen telephone rang. It was Gottfried Bismarck, from Potsdam, enquiring whether we were all right. They had heard hundreds of planes flying very low over their heads, but because of the poor visibility they could not tell how much damage had been done. When I said: 'It was awful!' he volunteered to come over and fetch me, but I told him that it was not worth it, as the worst seemed over. He promised to find out where Loremarie Schönburg was and ring back.

The all-clear came only half an hour after the last planes had departed, but long before that we were called out of the house by an unknown naval officer. The wind, he told us, thus far non-existent, had suddenly risen and the fires, therefore, were spreading. We all went out into our little square and, sure enough, the sky on three sides was blood-red. This, the officer explained, was only the beginning; the greatest danger would come in a few hours' time, when the fire storm really got going. Maria had given each of us a wet towel with which to smother our faces before leaving the house – a wise precaution, for our square was already filled with smoke and one could hardly breathe.

We went back into the house and Papa's pupils climbed up on the roof to keep an eye on the surrounding fires. Then the Danish chargé d'affaires Steenson (who lives next door) appeared, hugging a bottle of brandy. While we stood in the drawing-room, talking and taking an occasional gulp, the telephone rang once more. It was again Gottfried and he sounded desperately worried. He had called up Berndt Mumm's flat, where Loremarie had been dining with Aga Fürstenberg, only to be told that Loremarie had disappeared immediately after the all-clear and no one knew where she had gone. Gottfried thought that she might be trying to rejoin me, but as we were inside a ring of fire, I doubted whether she would get through.

Strangely, as soon as he hung up our telephone broke down; that is, people could still call *us*, but *we* could not get through to anyone. Also the electricity, gas and water no longer worked and we had to grope our way around with electric torches and candles. Luckily we had had time to fill every available bath tub, wash basin, kitchen sink and pail. By now the wind had increased alarmingly, roaring like a gale at sea. When we looked out of the window we could see a steady shower of sparks raining down on our and the neighbouring houses and all the time the air was getting thicker and hotter, while the smoke billowed in through the gaping window frames. We went through the house and found to our relief that apart from the broken windows and the unhinged doors, it had not suffered any real damage.

Just as we were swallowing some sandwiches, the sirens came on once more. We stood at the windows for about half an hour, in total silence. We were convinced it would start all over again. Then the all-clear sounded again. Apparently enemy reconnaissance planes had been surveying the damage. Maria, who had until then been a brick, now burst into tears, for her husband had given her as yet no sign of life. Though by now I was terribly sleepy, we decided that I would keep vigil near the phone. Putting it on the floor near me, I rolled myself up in a blanket on a sofa. About 1 a.m. Gottfried and Loremarie called from Potsdam. We were cut off almost immediately, but at least we were spared further anxiety on her account.

Towards 2 a.m. I decided to sleep for a while. Papa came and held his torch over me as I took off my shoes and tried to wash. Towards three, Maria also lay down. Presently I heard the telephone ring and then her ecstatic 'Liebling!', which meant that Heinz was all right. Soon she, too, fell asleep. Every now and then a crashing building or a delayed time bomb would tear one awake and I would sit up with a pounding heart. By now the fire storm had reached its peak and the roar outside was like a train going through a tunnel.

Wednesday, 24 November Early this morning I overheard Maria Gersdorff talking anxiously to Papa. A house nearby had caught fire. But I was so tired that I dozed off again and staggered up only around 8 a.m.

By then, Papa's pupils had gone home after spending the night on our roof and Maria had gone out to buy some bread. She soon returned with an old lady on her arm, wrapped in a white shawl. She had stumbled into her at the street corner and, peering into her grimy face, had recognised her own eighty-year-old mother, who had been trying to reach her, walking through the burning town all night. Her own flat had been completely burnt out, the firemen having arrived late and concentrated their efforts on saving a hospital nearby (which, thank God, they had done); but all the other houses in the street had been destroyed. Soon Heinz Gersdorff himself appeared. He said that as he had come straight home, he had had only a bird's-eye view of the effects of the raid but, as far as he could judge, the Unter den Linden area (where his office is located) had suffered just as badly as our neighbourhood: the French and British Embassies, the Hotel Bristol, the Zeughaus [Arsenal] and the Wilhelmstrasse and Friedrichstrasse were all very badly damaged.

Towards 11 a.m. I decided to go out and try and reach my office, in the hope – wildly optimistic, as it turned out – of jumping into a hot bath as soon as I got there. Clad in slacks, my head muffled in a scarf and wearing a pair of Heinz's fur-lined military goggles, I started off. The instant I left the house I was enveloped in smoke and ashes rained down on my head. I could breathe only by holding a handkerchief to my mouth and blessed Heinz for lending me those goggles.

At first our Woyrschstrasse did not look too bad; but one block away, at the corner of Lützowstrasse, all the houses were burnt out. As I continued down Lützowstrasse the devastation grew worse; many buildings were still burning and I had to keep to the middle of the street, which was difficult on account of the numerous wrecked trams. There were many people in the streets, most of them muffled in scarves and coughing, as they threaded their way gingerly through the piles of fallen masonry. At the end of Lützowstrasse, about four blocks away from the office, the houses on both sides of the street had collapsed and I had to climb over mounds of smoking rubble, leaking water pipes and other wreckage to get across to the other side. Until then I had seen very few firemen around, but here some were busily trying to extricate people trapped in the cellars. On Lützowplatz all the houses were burnt out. The bridge over the river Spree was undamaged, but on the other side all the buildings had been destroyed, only their outside walls still stood. Many cars were weaving their way cautiously through the ruins, blowing their horns wildly. A woman seized my arm and yelled that one of the walls was tottering and we both started to run. I caught sight of the mail box into which I had dropped that long letter to Tatiana the night before; it still stood but was completely crumpled. Then I saw my food shop Krause, or rather what remained of it. Maria had begged me to buy some provisions on the way home, as the one in which her coupons were registered had been destroyed. But poor Krause would be of no help either now. [*The German food-rationing system required one to register one's coupons in a given shop from where alone rations could be drawn.*]

Somehow I could still not imagine that our office too was gone, but on reaching the corner I saw that the porter's lodge and the fine marble entrance were burning merrily. In front of it stood Strempel (a high official of the A.A.) and the Rumanian Counsellor Valeanu, surrounded by a small batch of the latter's swarthy compatriots. Valeanu threw himself on my neck, exclaiming: 'Tout a péri, aussi l'appartement des jumelles! J'emmène mon petit troupeau à la campagne, à Buckow!' For all foreign missions now have emergency quarters outside of town. And true enough, the Rumanian mission further down the street, together with that of the Finns, was a smouldering ruin. I asked Strempel what we should do. He growled: 'Didn't you have any contingency orders?' 'Certainly,' I answered sweetly. 'We were quote not to panic and to assemble at the Siegessäule, [the Victory Column halfway down the Ost-West Axe], where we would be picked up by lorries and taken out of town unquote!' He shrugged his shoulders angrily and turned his back to me. I decided to go home.

By now the sight of those endless rows of burnt-out or still burning buildings had got the better of me and I was beginning to feel panicky. The whole district, many of its houses so familiar to me, had been wiped out in just one night! I started to run and kept on running until I was back in Lützowstrasse, where a building collapsed as I passed. A fireman shouted something unintelligible to me and some people close by: we all flung ourselves to the ground, I hid my head under my arms, and when the rumble and clatter of yet another collapsing wall ceased and we were covered with mortar and dust, I looked up across a puddle into the smudged Japanese face of Count C.-K. Although Tatiana and I had been studiously cutting him for the last four years (he has a soft spot for pretty girls and does not always behave), I said to myself that in times like these all men are brothers and, trying a friendly smile, I exclaimed in English: 'Hullo!' He eyed me coldly and enquired: 'Kennen wir uns?' ['Have we met?']. I decided that this was not the time for formal introductions and, scrambling back to my feet, hurried on.

When I got home I found some hot soup waiting. Papa took my goggles and went out to have a look in his turn. Then Gottfried Bismarck rang up and said that he would pick me up at 3 p.m. I told him which streets to take so as not to get stuck. Maria's sister, Countess Schulenburg (who is married to a cousin of the Ambassador), turned up on her bicycle. She lives at the other end of the town, which, apparently, has suffered only slight damage. That very morning three workmen had arrived at her house to replace the window panes that had been smashed during a raid in August and although all central Berlin lost its windows last night, they repaired hers.

The only material loss I have as yet sustained is my monthly ration of Harz cheese; I had bought it yesterday, and as it smelt vile and looked equally so, I had stored it outside on the window sill; in the morning it had vanished, probably blasted by the air pressure onto a neighbouring roof.

When Papa returned I took the goggles and walked over to our other office in the Kurfürstenstrasse. The ex-Polish Consulate on the corner, where Tatiana, Luisa Welczeck and I had all worked together for a long time, was burning brightly, but the Embassy building next door seemed undamaged. I took a flying leap past the former and dived into the latter's entrance, where a sorry little bunch of people had collected. Seated on the stairs were Adam Trott and Leipoldt, both with sooty faces. They had been there all night, as the raid had caught them still at work. As nothing seemed to be happening, we agreed to meet there again the following morning at eleven.

At 3 p.m. on the dot Gottfried appeared with his car. We piled my luggage into the back, together with some blankets and a pillow. As his house in Potsdam was crammed with other bombed-out friends, he explained, we would have to camp. In addition to Loremarie Schönburg, there are the Essens, who also turned up in the middle of the night, wet, bedraggled and exhausted.

Rudger Essen had been in his office just down the street from our office when the raid started; Hermine was at home (she is expecting a baby soon). He telephoned her to hurry over to the Legation, beneath which some Swedish workmen had just built a solid-concrete bunker with walls 2.5m. thick. Until last night none of the diplomatic missions and homes had suffered any damage and they probably imagined that their immunity extended to bombing too! Hermine reached the bunker safely and, after the all-clear, they emerged only to find the Legation burning like a torch. They spent several hours salvaging the most precious archives and then, jumping into their car, headed for home. That, too, was now past saving, whereupon they got back into the car and drove through the burning city straight out to the Bismarcks' in Potsdam.

After picking up Rudger, we drove to the still smouldering Swedish Legation to collect some of his surviving belongings there. While Rudger was inside, Gottfried and I got out of the car to re-arrange the luggage. Just then, tottering towards us wrapped in an expensive fur coat, I saw Ursula Hohenlohe, a famous Berlin belle. Her hair was straggly, her make-up was running. She stopped before us, sobbing: 'I have lost everything. *Everything!*' She was trying to reach some Spanish friends who had promised to drive her out to the country. We told her that the Spanish Embassy, too, had been destroyed. She turned away without a word and staggered off towards the smoking Tiergarten. A big piece of fur was torn out of the back of her coat.

Soon Rudger re-appeared and we threaded our way up Budapesterstrasse between straggling lines of people tugging along babies' prams, mattresses, odd bits of furniture, etc. Brandl's, Tatiana's favourite antique shop, was still burning; the flames licked at the curtains in the windows and curled around the crystal candelabra inside. As most of the materials in the shop were silks and brocades, the pink glow looked very festive, indeed sumptuous. The whole Budapesterstrasse was gutted, with the exception of the Hotel Eden, so we picked that as our meeting place in town next day. We then turned down the Ost-West Achse. We could hardly believe our eyes: not a single house on either side had survived.

When we reached Potsdam the contact with the fresh, cold air at first made me dizzy. At the 'Regierung', the Bismarcks' official residence, Gottfried's wife Melanie was bustling around, busily making up beds. Hermine Essen was sitting up in hers, her hair freshly washed and stiff as a little girl's. I took a bath too, Loremarie scrubbing me; the water turned black! Melanie is quite disgusted with the soot and dirt which every new arrival brings into their hitherto spotless home.

We had just finished supper when the call we had put through to Tatiana in Königswart came through and we were able to reassure her and Mamma; they had been trying all day to contact us – without success. Immediately after, Gottfried was informed that large enemy air formations were once more heading for Berlin. I rang up the Gersdorffs and Papa to warn them. I felt bad about breaking such bad news to them when I myself was safe, but at least it gave them time to dress. And sure enough a little later the sirens sounded. The others stayed in the sitting-room but Loremarie and I, still shaken by the events of the past night, went up to Jean-George's room to keep watch. The planes came flying over Potsdam in wave after wave but this time they headed farther west, towards Spandau, and so we worried less. The raid lasted about an hour, after which we collapsed into bed.

Thursday, 25 November This morning Loremarie Schönburg and I were up early. The Essens were giving us a lift into town in their battered car, as Hermine was catching a plane to Stockholm. As the doors were jammed, we had to climb in through a window. The window panes, too, were smashed and many smithereens were still stuck to the edges; as we drove they kept flying into our faces, which we muffled up as best we could. We were due at the office at 11 a.m., but since Rudger wished to exchange his car for one in better condition in some garage near Halensee, we made a detour that way.

Soon we realised that last night's raid had caused further destruction in town after all. Although the Halensee bridge still stood, all the houses around it were gone. Rudger's garage was badly battered and deserted. We drove on along Pariserstrasse. This part of town looked a little better, though shabby.

But when we reached the Hotel Eden, we found to our astonishment that it, too, had changed much in the past twenty-four hours. The walls were still there, but all the windows were gone, and their openings were crammed with mattresses, broken pieces of furniture and other debris. We heard later that three mines had crashed through the roof, destroying everything but the outside shell. Fortunately the bar, which functioned also as an air-raid shelter, had held out, for it was filled with people at the time. The Zoo, opposite, had suffered badly. A mine had landed on the aquarium, destroying all the fish and snakes. The wild animals were shot early this morning, as their cages had been damaged and it was feared they might escape. As it is, the crocodiles tried to jump into the river Spree; they were hauled out and shot, too, just in time. What a sight *that* would have been! On leaving the Eden, we decided to meet again in the afternoon at five in front of the Swedish Legation, so as to return to Potsdam together.

We were dropped off at the Lützowplatz and, muffling up our faces in large wet towels (many buildings were still burning and the air was unbreathable), we made our way to the office. There we found the same chaos as before; nobody knew what was to happen to us next; some said that we would be leaving town immediately for our *Ausweichquartier* [emergency quarters] in the country. Foreign Minister von Ribbentrop was said to be in town; he had even visited some of the diplomatic missions as they burned. It was rumoured that he was taking a personal part in the deliberations about 'whither from here' in what remained of the Foreign Ministry complex in the Wilhelmstrasse. After chatting a bit with various colleagues, who kept turning up in the weirdest clothes, since most of them had lost all they possessed, I waylaid the head of our Technical Division, who had attended our last conference on the day of the first raid. He told me that he had saved my bicycle, which he had found standing in the yard, but that he would be holding on to it for the time being, as he had no other means of getting into town. This seemed only fair, since I had given it up for lost, but I wonder what Gottfried will say, as it happens to be his! In the end we were told to return again tomorrow at 11 a.m., when things might be a little more settled.

Just as we were about to leave, Papa appeared. He looked terrible, his hair on end, his face grey. He seemed upset that I had not come to the Gersdorff house first. I had not thought that our neighbourhood would be hit again and was planning to pay them just a casual visit. Apparently last night a mine came down behind it; all the doors and windows are gone and the roof and some of the walls have caved in. They had been fighting the fires ever since, this time with less success, and a house opposite ours in the little square had burnt to the ground.

Papa, Loremarie and I thereupon returned to the Woyrschstrasse. The sight was truly horrifying. As most Berlin bakeries had been destroyed or had closed down, I had bought several loaves of white bread in Potsdam and we hastily had some soup. Then Loremarie went off to look up some friends who had disappeared and I spent the better part of the afternoon nailing cardboard and carpets over all the window openings to keep out the cold and smoke. Maria's eighty-year-old mother, dauntless as ever, insisted on helping, handing me the nails as I perched atop a ladder. I was also helped by an English lady to whom the now destroyed house opposite had belonged. She had not been able to save anything and was leaving for the country shortly.

Since yesterday, people keep dropping in from other parts of the town, having usually made the trip on foot, just to enquire how we all are. Nearly all agree that though bombs have fallen all over Berlin, our neighbourhood, the diplomatic sector off the Tiergarten and the Unter den Linden, have suffered most. At one point a Lieutenant-Colonel von Gersdorff (a relative of Heinz) arrived in a military car with his orderly and they helped put up a temporary roof, nailing wooden planks over the holes.

Lieutenant-Colonel Baron von Gersdorff was an early military member of the conspiracy to overthrow Nazism (though at the time, of course, Missie did not know this). In March 1943, at a ceremony in the Berlin Arsenal, he himself had come close to assassinating Hitler. He was among the few major conspirators to survive.

Later I went out in search of Dickie Wrede. When we had passed Rauchstrasse yesterday her house had burnt down and when I got there today, there wasn't a soul to be seen. I crawled in nevertheless. Her flat had been on the ground floor and I thought I might still save something. But as I stood in the hall looking up at the wrecked staircase, there was a crash and a charred rafter came hurtling down. I made a flying leap and landed in the street again. I then crossed over to the Alberts, whose house was still standing.

Mrs Albert is an American married to a German industrialist with chemical factories in the Rhineland. When the war broke out, their son came back from the U.S.A. to join the German army, leaving his American wife and his children in California. There is also a daughter, Irene, a gifted guitar player and singer, who has been a friend of ours for a long time.

I found mother and daughter standing in the entrance. Falling on my neck, they announced that they were hoping to leave for Marienbad, the famous spa in the Sudetenland (which, incidentally, is quite close to the Metternichs' Königswart) and that Papa should accompany them. They had a car, some gasoline, but no driver. However, since their house had now been taken over by the Swedes, who are roofless, they hoped that, in exchange, they would provide them with a chauffeur. They urged me to come too, but it is unlikely that my office will let me go. By a curious irony, they had arrived from the Rhineland only yesterday and had sat out the raid in their cellar.

I walked back to the Woyrschstrasse to tell Papa about this new plan, but he refuses to leave without me and since he has no other reason to stay on in Berlin, I have decided to ask the office for a few days off. I then took Papa with me to the Swedish Legation, from where we all drove with Rudger Essen back to Potsdam. Papa had not slept for two nights and was totally exhausted. The Bismarcks welcomed him very kindly; we fixed up a bed for him and he collapsed into a steaming bath.

We had hardly finished dinner when the sirens sounded. But it turned out that these were, once more, reconnaissance planes surveying the damage.

Friday, 26 November At 8 a.m. today Papa, Loremarie Schönburg and I returned to Berlin. As we thought we might be leaving with the Alberts for Marienbad, we had packed a few things. I tried to take a minimum, storing the rest in two large suitcases in the Bismarcks' basement. Rudger Essen's car was filled with Swedes and so we boarded the S-Bahn, changed at Wannsee and got out at Potsdamer Platz. The train was full, people fighting their way into it at every station, as this seemed to be the only line still running. The Potsdamer Platz station is underground and was still spotlessly clean, white tiles, etc. The contrast was all the greater when we emerged into the street, for the whole neighbourhood was one smouldering mass of ruins; all the large buildings surrounding the square had burnt down with the exception of the Hotel Esplanade, which looked shabby but still comparatively intact, though without a single window pane, of course.

We started out for the Alberts', dragging our luggage through the mud and ashes of the Tiergarten. The houses on all sides were black and still smoking. The park looked like a battlefield in France in the 1914–1918 war, the trees stark and gaunt and broken-off branches everywhere, over which he had to clamber. I wondered what had happened to the famous rhododendrons and what it would be like in the spring. As transport was non-existent, we had to walk all the way.

Actually, in the last two days private cars have re-appeared like mushrooms, after being hidden away, doubtless in anticipation of just this sort of emergency. Most are without licence plates but nobody gets stopped. On the contrary, orders have been issued that all vehicles should give a lift to anyone they can, so that gradually, despite the destruction, Berlin's traffic is assuming an almost pre-war appearance. Unfortunately we were out of luck: all the cars that passed us were already crammed. At one point we were stopped by an extraordinary-looking soldier who had probably just been called up – a cross between a decadent aesthete and a comic cabaret artist. Gesturing elegantly, he advised us not to go any further, as five time bombs had fallen in front of the Swedish Legation. We turned down Bendlerstrasse, where the offices of the O.K.H. [Army Command H.Q.] are located. Or, rather, *were* located – for they, too, had been destroyed and dozens of officers and soldiers in the grey-green uniforms of the army were crawling about the debris, trying to salvage their archives. When we reached the Ministry of the Navy further down the road we found an identical sight, except that here naval officers and ratings in blue were performing the same acrobatics among the ruins. Funnily enough, the only foreign missions which have not been too badly damaged by the Allied bombs are those of their enemies, the Japanese and Italians! And yet, being both recently built and gigantic in size, they seem perfect targets.

As part of his scheme to turn Berlin into a worthy capital of his 'Thousand-Year Reich', Hitler chose the Tiergarten district, once the hunting ground of Prussian kings, as the new diplomatic quarter. Work started in 1938 on an ensemble of new embassies, all of them in the impersonal monumental style fancied by Hitler himself and his chief architect, Albert Speer. The Italian and Japanese Embassies were the largest of all, as befitted Germany's main allies. Completed in 1942, both were badly damaged – by Allied bombs and house-to-house fighting in the end weeks of the war.

After nearly an hour's walk we reached the Alberts', where we learnt that there was a last-minute hitch: the Swedes had discovered a chauffeur all right, but he had not eaten for four days; they had thereupon tried to buck him up by giving him some brandy as well as food and now he was dead drunk and useless. We said that we would return in the afternoon, once I had obtained official permission to leave.

Loremarie and I then wandered down Landgrafenstrasse, as we had heard that Kicke Stumm's house had been hit. Though his only brother was killed in France, he is in Russia. Not a single house in that street had survived and, as we approached his, we feared the worst, for only the outer walls remained. We asked some firemen whether the inmates were all right. They said they thought so, but those next door were still trapped in the cellar. 'As to that one over there,' and they pointed to a large six-storeyed building on the other side of the street, 'they are all dead, 300 of them!', the cellar having received a direct hit. We crossed over to Kurfürstenstrasse, where friends lived in almost every house; most of them had been hit too. The Oyarzabals' huge granite apartment building was a heap of stones. The corner of Nettelbeck-strasse (including our favourite little restaurant, the 'Taverna') had been literally pulverised, only small piles of rubble remaining. Wherever we looked, firemen and prisoners-of-war, most of them so-called 'Badoglio Italians', were busy pumping air into the ruins, which meant that some people were still alive in the collapsed cellars.

After Italy's capitulation in September 1943, all Italian military personnel in German-occupied territories were made to choose between serving Mussolini's rump republic in Salò or being interned and put to hard work. The latter were known as 'Badoglio Italians'.

In front of another wrecked building a crowd was watching a young girl aged about sixteen. She was standing atop a pile of rubble, picking up bricks one by one, dusting them carefully and throwing them away again. Apparently her entire family was dead, buried underneath, and she had gone mad. This part of the town looked truly ghastly. In some places one could not even tell where the streets had been and we no longer knew where we were. But eventually we reached Rauchstrasse and our own office.

Miraculously, it had survived. Downstairs I ran into one of our personnel officers. I told him that I had an aged father, whom I had an opportunity to take to the country. At first he was reluctant, but on hearing that we were *Bombengeschädigte* [bomb victims] – a life-saving word in times like these! – he agreed. I assured him that I would return as soon as I was needed again and, giving him Tatiana's address and telephone number, I took off before he could change his mind.

After some hot soup at the Gersdorffs' just around the corner, Loremarie and I continued on our round, combing the town street by street in search of lost friends.

These last days innumerable inscriptions in chalk have appeared on the blackened walls of wrecked houses: 'Liebste Frau B., wo sind Sie? Ich suche Sie überall. Kommen Sie zu mir. Ich habe Platz fur Sie' ['Dearest Frau B., where are you? I have been looking for you everywhere. Come and stay with me. I have room for you'] or 'Alle aus diesem Keller gerettet!' ['Everyone from this cellar has been saved!'] or 'Mein Engelein, wo bleibst Du? Ich bin in grosser Sorge. Dein Fritz' ['My little angel. Where are you? I worry greatly. Your Fritz'.], etc. Gradually, as people return to their homes and read these messages, answers start to appear, chalked underneath. We discovered the whereabouts of several of our friends this way and on reaching the ruins of our own office we, too, picked up some chalk in the rubble and wrote in large square letters on the pillar next to the entrance: 'Missie und Loremarie gesund, befinden sich in Potsdam bei B.' ['Missie and Loremarie are well, staying in Potsdam at the B(ismarcks')]'. Our top boss doubtless would have disapproved, but we were thinking above all of our various beaux, who are in the habit of telephoning at all hours of the day and who might come by to look for us.

Suddenly Moyano of the Spanish Embassy appeared in his car. He told me that his ambassador and many other Spaniards had been dining at the Eden that first night and that, luckily, Maria Pilar Oyarzabal and her husband had not had time to get home, for when their house collapsed, everyone in their cellar, including their servants, had perished. Federico Diez (another Spanish diplomat) was at home and when his house, as well as all the neighbouring ones, started to burn and the streets filled with people, he fished out his family cognac and started handing around drinks.

Around 4 p.m. I went back to the Alberts' to await developments. The Albert house was an ice-box, as the glass roof and window panes had been blown to smithereens and all the doors had been torn off their hinges. We sat in our coats in the kitchen, freezing, while a Georgian friend of the Alberts, Prince Andronikov, who was leaving for Marienbad with us, sat in the drawing-room muffled in scarves, a hat pulled over his eyes, playing the piano beautifully all afternoon. During the first raid the poor fellow had managed to escape his burning hotel with all his things and had found a room at the Eden. But the following night that, too, had been wrecked and he was now left with only the clothes on his back. He especially bemoaned the loss of four brand-new pairs of shoes.

While we waited Aga Fürstenberg burst into the room and fell on my neck squealing: 'Missie, ich dachte Du bist tot!' ['Missie, I thought you were dead!']. She had returned home after the first raid to find the house in which she and Dickie Wrede lived a pile of ruins. Until the next day she thought that she had lost everything; then she ran into Jean-Georges Hoyos, who told her that some of her things had been saved, and now she was in high spirits.

Hardly had Aga left, when the film actress Jenny Jugo appeared in a car. She embraced me and announced that Dickie Wrede had now moved to her house in Cladow and that she had come to fetch some of *her* things. Thus, gradually, one begins to know the whereabouts of some of our friends, but progress is very slow; and the news sometimes ghastly.

After the first raid Papa had gone to look for some Russian friends, the Derfeldens. Their house had collapsed. The husband had been rescued from the cellar alive, but she was dug up only many hours later, headless. The poor woman had always been terrified of air-raids and had insisted each time on dragging a large Bible into the cellar with her. Though I am more and more frightened, somehow I feel I will not end that way.

After what seemed like hours of waiting, the Swedes let us know that our departure was postponed for another twenty-four hours.

While Papa returned to Potsdam for the night, I went over to the Gersdorffs' for tea. I found the tennis champion Gottfried von Cramm there. He had just arrived from Sweden and had nearly burst into tears, he said, at the sight of the town. Then old Baron Üxküll drove up in a military car wearing his porter's overcoat. He had fought the fires on his roof until dawn, but then it became hopeless. His flat was on the top floor of the house; he had had a lovely collection of books but had not been able to save anything. Indeed one woman in the building had been burnt to death. I missed Rudger Essen and had to return to Potsdam by train. Luckily Üxküll dropped me off at

Charlottenburg station. On the way, completely imperturbable, he offered me tickets for Karajan's concert next Sunday. The Bismarcks were not particularly surprised to see me.

In the night there was again an alert, but nothing serious.

Saturday, 27 November In the morning Loremarie Schönburg, Papa, Gottfried Cramm (who had joined us in Potsdam) and I again piled into Rudger Essen's car. The latter was going back to Sweden.

Everywhere in town large fires are still burning in the backyards and it is, apparently, impossible to put them out. These are Berlin's recently-delivered coal supplies for the winter! We often stop before them to warm our hands, for these days it is colder indoors than out.

Towards midday, armed with my now habitual load of white bread from Potsdam, I dropped by at the Gersdorffs' and found Gottfried Bismarck there. We had our usual soup. The Gersdorff house is really the only one where, notwithstanding the cold and draughts, one can relax a bit.

In the middle of 'lunch' Loremarie and Tony Saurma walked in. The poor fellow was badly shaken. The day before, he had driven his office staff out to the small village to which they were being evacuated. During the night's raid (which I had described as 'nothing serious') his driver had been killed and he himself buried in the cellar of his house, which had caved in; he had only managed to crawl out in the morning. He announced – and this is typical for our times! – that he had just bought one hundred oysters, whereupon Loremarie and I jumped into his car and we drove over to his flat to fetch them.

We passed Wittenbergplatz, which I had not seen since these heavy raids began. The whole vast square was strewn with the carcasses of burnt-out trams and buses – it's an important traffic junction. Bombs had fallen everywhere, even on the underground station, and the K.D.W. – a big department store – was now merely a skeleton. On the way, we overtook Sigrid Görtz riding a bicycle. I congratulated her because her house was one of the few still standing, but she announced that a phosphorus flare had landed in her top-floor bedroom and that all her clothes were gone. She had now moved to friends in Grunewald. I remembered some lovely fur coats! A little later we were stopped by a fireman and asked to drive a woman with a lot of bundles to Charlottenburg station. We did so and it took us thus quite a long time to reach Tony's. We ate some of the oysters on the spot, washing them down with brandy. I had never realised how difficult they are to open and cut myself. The rest we took back, together with some wine, to Maria's, where a feast followed, people dropping in all the time to participate. It lasted until quite late, with many gashed thumbs, as nobody else seemed very expert at opening oysters either.

The morning after the first raid I had had an appointment to try on a hat at a small neighbourhood shop. All around the houses were burning, but I wanted that hat badly and so I now went over and rang the bell and, wonder of wonders, was met by a smiling saleswoman: 'Durchlaucht können anprobieren!' ['Your Highness may try it on!']. I did so, but as I was wearing muddy slacks it was difficult to judge the effect. Tony and Loremarie then dropped me off at the Alberts', where at long last, at 4 p.m., a lorry appeared before the door. It was taking a lot of furniture and trunks belonging to the Swedish colony out of town and the Minister had allowed us to leave with it. We would be dropped at the nearest railway station beyond the city limits, from where we would have to find our way around Berlin to the main line going south. While Mrs Albert climbed up in front next to the two helmetted Swedish drivers, the rest of us – Papa, Prince Andronikov, Irene Albert and I – crawled into the back. We sat on the luggage, surrounded by plaid suitcases and baskets, my new hat in a large paper bag; the only thing missing was the proverbial canary! A third Swede got in with us, the oil-cloth flap was buttoned down, plunging us into total darkness, and we were off.

As we could see nothing, we could not tell where we were going, but after an hour of bumping along rather bad roads, we reached a village called Teupitz, sixty-three kilometres from Berlin, where we were invited to alight.

As we all wore tags inscribed *Bombengeschädigte* and, owing to our drivers, were taken for Swedes, the local clean little *Gasthaus* agreed to take us in for the night. Surrounded by our luggage, we assembled in the tap room. While our rooms were being prepared, we were given some real tea and ate the tuna sandwiches which we had wisely prepared before leaving, washed down with a jeroboam of champagne. In the middle of this 'supper' an air-raid warning sounded – a kind of trumpet blown in the backyard by the innkeeper's son. We had hoped to hop into bed nevertheless, but the locals, who clearly took air-raids seriously, eyed us with such disapproval that we stayed where we were. Actually, they were probably right, for we were, after all, still very close to Berlin, and Tony Saurma's experience proves that even remote villages are not safe. Very soon the shooting started and then we heard the by now all too familiar droning of planes overhead. They dropped a few bombs nearby, whereupon we all trooped down into the cellar, a weird place full of hot-water pipes and boilers. Mrs Albert chose a moment when the shooting was particularly violent to drawl in broad American: 'We can be proud of one thing ... We have just witnessed one of the greatest disasters in modern history!' Nobody seemed to resent this statement.

I confess that these last nights have made me rather jumpy and even at this distance it was obvious that the raid was again a heavy one. Later we learnt that a mine hit the house that arches over the entrance to our little square. Maria and Heinz Gersdorff had been sitting it out in the cellar of that very building, as it seemed safer than their own basement. It collapsed, nevertheless, burying them under the debris. Fortunately they were dug out in the morning, unhurt.

After our own all-clear, we were shown to our rooms – one for us, the three women; the other for Papa and Andronikoff. The beds were damp but comfortable, with heavy eiderdowns, and Mrs Albert snored loudly most of the night. Actually, this was heaven, as we had resigned ourselves to sleeping on floors until we reached Königswart.

Sunday, 28 November We got up early to take a bus to the nearest railway station. It was so full we had difficulty squeezing in. We made some train, however, and two hours later were in Cottbus (an important junction south of Berlin). The train to Leipzig took off before our very noses, as we could not drag our luggage across the tracks fast enough. Fortunately some Hitler Youth boys were very helpful. Carrying everything, they led us to a special waiting-room reserved for *Bombengeschädigte*, where we spent several hours waiting for the next train and where we were offered marvellous sandwiches with plenty of butter and sausage and some thick soup, all free of charge. This is the work of the N.S.V., which has proved itself most efficient in emergencies. In Berlin the same N.S.V. had on the very first day of the raids organised field kitchens in every wrecked street, where all passers-by could, at any hour of the day, get delicious soup, real strong coffee and cigarettes, none of which can be found in the shops.

Finally at 1 p.m. we piled into a slow train for Leipzig. Standing most of the way, we arrived at six. By then we had been travelling twenty-four hours (instead of the usual two!). Throughout the journey we had considerable trouble with the Alberts, who just would not abandon their habit of speaking all the time in loud English, calling out 'Honey!' – 'Yes, lovey! Are you all right?' from one end of the car to the other. Papa was in a cold sweat, but the other passengers did not seem to mind and there were no incidents.

At Leipzig we went straight to the station restaurant, where we were able to clean up a little and had a very decent supper of *Wienerschnitzel* washed down with wine. There was even an orchestra playing Schubert! When the Berlin express pulled in half an hour later, it was, needless to say, jammed and we had literally to pummel our way aboard. A woman was pushed onto the track just in front of me and pulled back by the hair in the nick of time. It was a little annoying to learn that several passengers had calmly boarded it in Berlin only a couple of hours earlier. True, Goebbels had recently issued a proclamation ordering all young people to remain in Berlin, and Irene and I had feared that we might be turned back at the station.

We had hoped to be met at Eger by the Metternichs' car, but there was no one and we had to wait another two hours for a local train, which brought us to Königswart only at five in the morning. We found a cold supper waiting. Afterwards I slept in Tatiana's bed and we chatted almost until dawn.

KÖNIGSWART *Monday, 29 November* Spent the whole day describing our adventures; it is very difficult to convey what Berlin looks like now to those who have not lived through it. After supper we all immediately went to bed.

The total silence here is difficult to get accustomed to.

Missie's note (written at the time): I took advantage of this respite to put down in writing the events of these last days. Foolishly, before being called to supper I left the only copy on a pile of wood in a basket near my writing table. On my return it had vanished, fed into the tile stove by an over-zealous maid. I immediately re-typed the whole saga, knowing full well that I would never want to do so again.

Between the first massive attack on Berlin on 18 November 1943 and the end of the main onslaught in March 1944 (though the city continued to be bombed intermittently until its capture by the Russians in April 1945), Berlin was bombed 24 times. By now, each attack involved some 1,000 planes and the dropping of some 1,000 to

2,000 tons of bombs. But while most of the buildings were reduced to rubble and tens of thousands of its inhabitants were killed or maimed and some 1.5 million made homeless (and this figure does not include the thousands of P.O.W.s and foreign workers, of whom no count was ever held), German air defenses – an elaborate combination of massive flak and radar-guided free-prowling night-fighters – proved so effective that most of Berlin's industries continued to churn out war material in scarcely diminishing quantities. In the words of the British historian Max Hastings: 'In the operational sense, the Battle of Berlin was more than a failure. It was a defeat . . . Berlin won, it was just too tough a nut to crack.' ('Bomber Command', London, Michael Joseph, 1979).

But then generally, Air-Marshal Harris' 'area bombing' (the official Allied term) or 'terror bombing' (as Nazi propaganda promptly dubbed it not without justification) never achieved its purpose. For all the material destruction, including that of countless treasures of world civilisation (hence also another cruel propaganda term – 'Baedecker Bombing'!) and for all the losses in civilian lives (often aged persons and children and therefore not engaged in production), many primary targets such as the armaments plants (now mostly dispersed or underground) and the railway lines (repaired within hours) functioned virtually to the end. As for the population's morale, though dulled by grief, physical exhaustion and malnutrition, it was never broken. It would require traditional conventional warfare, with the physical occupation of enemy territory by the converging Allied and Russian armies, to bring Germany to its knees.

Tuesday, 30 November A telegram from my office: 'Erwarten sofortige Rückkehr' ('We expect immediate return'). Consternation! Meanwhile, Papa and I have a bad cough. The doctor thinks it is a sort of bronchitis, the result of the draughts in Berlin, combined with all the involuntarily absorbed smoke. In Marienbad both Alberts are also in bed.

Wednesday, 1 December I am in bed, as a precautionary measure after last summer's pleurisy. The doctor has written out a certificate.

2, 3, 4, 5, 6, 7 December All these days I have been in bed, leading a very relaxed and pampered existence.

Wednesday, 8 December Prince Andronikov has left for Munich. He is a typical Georgian, with a strong oriental slant. We were talking about somebody who had married the widow of a brother who had been killed in the war, at which he remarked: 'Only in Europe can such things happen – *pravda dikari*' ['they are truly savages'].

Last week there was another massive raid on Berlin, which makes four in a row. On Friday (3 December), I woke up in the middle of the night – outside a queer bugle was sounding mournfully at intervals. Tatiana said this was their air-raid warning. One could hear heavy shooting far away. Later we learnt that this was the raid on Leipzig, which practically obliterated the town.

This afternoon Paul Metternich telephoned from Potsdam, where he is staying at the Bismarcks', to announce his arrival tomorrow with his colonel. Tatiana is in seventh heaven to know that he is away from the front for a while.

Friday, 10 December Paul Metternich is shattered by his impressions of Berlin.

Letters have come through from Irena in Rome; she is very depressed at being cut off from us. Family discussions continue as to what she should do. Papa and Mamma do not agree on the subject; Mamma wants her to stay on in Italy; Papa suggests she should join us, to face the ultimate collapse *en famille*.

Monday, 13 December We go for long walks in the snow. Paul Metternich's colonel seems a good-natured fellow and his very complimentary remarks about Russia and the Russians please the parents.

Tuesday, 14 December Paul Metternich and the colonel have departed. Although this trip does not count as leave, Paul does not think he can return for Christmas. But he may stop by for a couple of days on his way back to the front.

Tuesday, 16 December A telegram from Loremarie Schönburg (who is now in Vienna), suggesting that I take over the job of Count Helldorf's secretary (all this in veiled terms). This must be her doing, for he hardly knows me. But I know something of his conspiratorial activities and he probably needs a person he can trust. I must consult Adam Trott and will not answer until I do.

Spent the afternoon with Tatiana in Marienbad, where we visited the Alberts, who wish to return to Berlin!

Monday, 20 December We went to Marienbad again, where Tatiana had a permanent wave and I something simpler, more suited to air-raids.

Tuesday, 21 December Last Friday there was again a heavy raid on Berlin; we tried to telephone Maria Gersdorff, but could not get through, so we telegraphed instead. Today the answer came: 'Alle unversehrt. Schreckliche Nacht. Brief folgt' ['Everyone safe. Dreadful night. Letter follows'].

I have applied for permission to stay here until after the Christmas holidays.

Wednesday, 22 December We play Ping-Pong all the time. I am reading many trashy books – to the disgust of the parents. I cannot concentrate on anything else, although Mamma keeps plying me with contemporaries' memoirs about the Congress of Vienna and the Napoleonic Wars. But *this* war seems to me quite enough, obliterating for the moment anything else.

Innsbruck has been bombed repeatedly, so that the Austrians' hope that Vienna will be spared seems pretty naive. The Allied advance in Italy is not proceeding very fast. It looks as if these ghastly raids are intended to help their progress by breaking the Germans' morale, but I do not think that much can be achieved that way. Indeed they are having the contrary effect. For amidst such suffering and hardship, political considerations become second-ary and everyone seems intent only on patching roofs, propping up walls, cooking fried potatoes on an upturned electric iron (I myself fried an egg that way!), or melting snow for water to wash with. Furthermore, at such times the heroic side of human nature takes over and people are being extraordinarily friendly and helpful to one another – '*compagnons de malheur*'.

For a long time, the Allies had indeed spared Austria – that first victim of Hitler's attempt to dominate Europe. Indeed, so secure had its fame as 'the air-raid shelter of the Reich' become that much war-essential industry had been moved there. And that sealed its doom. Already on 13 August 1943 a first raid against the aircraft factories of Wiener–Neustadt had signalled the end of Austria's immunity. In due course, also most of its larger towns would be reduced to rubble.

Friday, 24 December Christmas Eve. It is again snowing and it is very cold. Tatiana and I have been working all day making paper chains for the tree, as we have nothing else. Gretl Rohan, Loremarie Schönburg's aunt, had sent us two parcels of decorations from Bohemia, but they arrived in smithereens. We have made a lot of stars and have some angel hair, so the tree looks nice all the same. Lisette, the housekeeper, even managed to find twelve candles in the village. In the evenings we now play bridge. Went to Midnight Mass in the chapel, very cold but pretty. Afterwards we drank champagne and had some biscuits.

Sunday, 26 December I have received several letters from the office, one of them unsigned, informing me that we are being evacuated to the mountains (small wonder, since all our buildings are wrecked). They add that this will also do my health good and that they therefore bank on my early return. I have decided not to mention this to the family, as I want to postpone my decision until I am back in Berlin. For I may want to remain where the action is and that, of course, *is* Berlin.

A letter from Maria Gersdorff. On Christmas Eve there was apparently another raid, our neighbourhood was hit again and again and has suffered dreadfully. I find this disgraceful; even in the first world war (which was bad enough) both sides suspended hostilities that night. The Gersdorffs now live in the basement, having fixed up a bedroom beside the kitchen, with the famous double bed in which all of us have slept in turns.

Friday, 31 December Paul Metternich telephoned to say he was arriving today at 2 a.m. I am glad I will see him before I depart for Berlin tomorrow.

KÖNIGSWART *Saturday, 1 January 1944* Paul Metternich arrived only at dawn. The tree had been lit in Tatiana's room. We celebrated the incoming New Year and her birthday with champagne and jam-puffs, burned wishes written on little bits of paper and fed tit-bits to the Scotty Sherry – with disastrous results.

Now I am packing, as I am catching the midnight train to Berlin.

BERLIN *Sunday, 2 January* Mamma accompanied me by car to the station in Marienbad. It was snowing hard. The train was, as usual, late. We sat for an hour in the freezing station. Just as it was pulling in, the sirens sounded. I had hoped that by taking a late train I would avoid the now almost nightly raid and arrive in Berlin early in the morning. The lights went out and I climbed into the wrong carriage; it was full of sleeping soldiers returning from the Balkans in various states of disarray, most of them with beards several weeks old. They immediately started combing their hair and putting on bits of clothing. Later on, the female train controller told me to change carriages, but as planes were still flying overhead I chose to remain under the protection of those Mamma calls in her letters ironically 'the brave boys in blue' (she has probably picked this up in a corny novel). I worried about her having to drive back to Königswart during a raid. I was also worried about ourselves, as, with the snow on the ground, our train was far more visible. But the Allied planes were apparently heading for a more important target and we got to Leipzig safely, just in time to make our connection.

We had reached the outskirts of Berlin when we were held up for another four-and-a-half hours. Many tracks were torn up and trains had to await their turn. Some of the passengers got hysterical, climbed out through the windows and took off on foot. I stayed on and reached Anhalter Bahnhof at 3 p.m. I found a bus still running and headed for the Woyrschstrasse.

As far as I can see, Berlin has not changed much since my departure five weeks ago, but things have been cleaned up a bit and the streets swept clear of debris. Our neighbourhood looks worse than the others I passed through: two mines fell on either side of Lützowstrasse and a third at the entrance to our little square and all the villas around ours are gone. I went through the house with old Martha, the cook. It is a dreary sight: the windows are gaping holes, the rain comes in onto the piano . . . I deposited the turkey and wine I had brought from Königswart, restored myself slightly with some soup and took the train out to Potsdam.

There everything was quite peaceful. The cook gave me coffee (Rudger Essen had left some as a present to the staff at Christmas). Although the housekeeper had once complained to Loremarie Schönburg that when we were both in the house 'es ging ja zu wie im wilden Westen' ['things were as rowdy as in the Wild West'], she seemed pleased to see me.

After supper I unpacked only a little, as I do not expect to stay very long, and went to bed. At 2 a.m. the sirens went off. There was a lot of firing in and around Potsdam and as I was alone with the maids, we retired prudently to the cellar. My nerves are not improving and I was jolly frightened when some bombs came whizzing down in our vicinity. Also having to sit up every night, sometimes for hours, is becoming exhausting.

Monday, 3 January Punctually at nine I was at the office. The former Polish Embassy building is now all that remains of our once extensive Information Department and work is pretty much at a standstill, with everyone leaving at 4 p.m. so as to be home by nightfall when the raids start. Some people travel several hours to get into town; one of the secretaries takes seven hours to make the return trip, so she spends only about an hour at work. In her place I wouldn't come in at all.

We work eight in one room, which is the former dressing-room of the Polish Ambassador, Lipski. With its luxurious closets and mirrors and a beautiful carpet, it has otherwise little to commend it for use as an office. Everyone's nerves seem on edge; the other day two secretaries downstairs got into a fist fight. Indeed I find the harassed faces of the people more depressing even than the desolate aspect of the town. It must be this constant insomnia that never gives one time to recuperate, be it only a little.

Judgie Richter is frantic, as during the last two raids some bombs fell also on the village of Werder, where his family – wife and two kids aged one and two – live in a house without a cellar. As he is about to join Ambassador Rahn in Italy for six weeks, I suggested that he take them down to stay with Tatiana. She is taking in refugees from many bombed towns these days and would surely be happy to put them up.

My immediate boss, Büttner, is very fussy and edgy, perhaps on account of his head wound; but he has enrolled Loremarie Schönburg and Usch von der Groeben to join our section, which makes things nicer for me. I am happy to see that aside from him, practically all the nicest people in the Department are still in Berlin, although rumour has it that we are about to move to Krummhübel, a village in the Riesengebirge on the Silesian-Czechoslovak border, where the whole A.A. is being relocated and where I will be expected to build up a new photo-archive (the old one was destroyed in the November raid). This is an entirely new occupation and not an easy one, considering the scarcity of material.

Spent the morning chatting with colleagues. Then Loremarie, Adam Trott and I went over to Maria Gersdorff's for a bite. As usual, we found a lot of people there.

Tuesday, 4 January The other day Loremarie Schönburg was asked by Büttner to draw up a list of all those who were *not* back at work on Monday. She presented him with a list consisting of the entire staff of our Department, without exception. His reaction was a rather understandable explosion.

Luckily, there is a new young man, who acts as A.D.C. to Hans-Bernd von Haeften, our chief of personnel (himself one of the best elements in the A.A.), and who is both kind and understanding and smoothes out many a difficulty. This we need.

Another time Haeften himself asked Loremarie to quickly fetch some twenty-pfennig stamps for him. She found none and came back trailing a snake of one-pfennig stamps in her wake. This was met with a smile.

Wednesday, 5 January Ran into Dr Six, the newly appointed head of our Information Department; he wishes to see me tomorrow at 1 p.m. Apart from the fact that we avoid him as much as we can, as he is a high S.S. officer and a stinker, it's rather inconvenient, as I want to go to church, it being our Russian Orthodox Christmas Day.

A 'Nazi intellectual' Professor Dr Franz Six (b. 1906) had headed the faculty of Foreign Economics at Berlin University, a function he combined with that of department head successively for 'Scientific Research' and 'Ideological Research and Analysis' in the R.S.H.A., the main state security office. In 1940 he had been appointed head of the S.D. team which, in German-occupied Britain, would have presumably 'purged' the country. When that invasion plan was abandoned and Hitler turned against the U.S.S.R. instead, Six was assigned to head the team which, in captured Moscow, would have taken over the Soviet state archives. But Moscow too proved elusive, and meanwhile Six and his men were posted to Smolensk to hunt down Jews, commissars and partisans. Ever a prudent man, he soon got himself transferred back to Berlin, to the A.A., which the S.S. were busily infiltrating – first to its Cultural Affairs Department and then to that of Information, in which Missie worked.

Katia Kleinmichel came around to borrow some shoes, as she has lost all her clothes in a raid. Luckily mine fit her.

Thursday, 6 January Rushed to church with Loremarie Schönburg. The Mass was beautiful, but there were very few people. We just managed to get back to the office in time for my confrontation with Dr Six. He was very solicitous about my health and said I should 'take the pill which saved Churchill' (who was stricken by pneumonia last winter at Casablanca). Then, turning to more serious matters, he went on to insist on the total war effort that is now required of everybody and to threaten 'all shirkers' with transfer to ammunition factories, as street-car conductors, etc. He ended by ordering me to leave as soon as possible for Krummhübel. Oh, what a horrible man he is!

I cannot make up my mind whether I am glad about this or not. Somehow I feel that these days my every decision can have fateful consequences and that it is better not to swim against the tide. On the other hand, I am tempted to stay where my friends are.

Friday, 7 January That part of Berlin where most of us used to live has become too depressing for words. At night there is not a light to be seen, just street after street of burnt-out houses. Tatiana says that in Madrid, after the Civil War, hooligans would hide out in the ruins and attack one at night; this does not seem likely here, but the silent emptiness is eerie.

This afternoon Claus Kieckebusch and Clemens Kageneck appeared at the office, the latter with his Ritterkreuz – Knight's Cross of the Iron Cross – dangling over his fur collar. He is on his way back to Russia. Seeing them so handsome and laughing, I felt a bit worried lest our boss, Dr Six, descend on us, but they refused to budge, so I settled them on a wooden bench near the stairs and Clemens produced a bottle of brandy, from which we drank in turns. Judgie Richter happened along and, as he knows Claus, joined the party.

Later I went over to Hans Flotow, who was having friends in for drinks. His flat has miraculously survived. Claus then drove me to the station in a borrowed Mercedes and presented me with a bottle of vermouth, as it is soon my birthday. He is leaving in two days for Paris and then going on to ski for a month, ostensibly to teach it to fresh recruits. How he does it is a mystery to all, but he gets away with it. Ever since his tank blew up in France, burning him badly, and his youngest brother Mäxchen was killed in Russia, he considers all this his due.

I had supper with the Alberts, who are now back in Berlin and are nearly always at home. Irene's brother was there, on leave from Guernsey; he told me that Charlie Blücher was killed while serving with the British army in Tunisia. Tatiana will be very sad: she had stayed with them before the war.

Descended on their father's side from the famous Prussian Field Marshal of the Napoleonic wars and on their mother's – a distant cousin of Missie's mother – from the Polish Radziwills, the Blücher boys had been educated in England, had become British subjects and, when the war broke out, enrolled in the British forces.

Saturday, 8 January This evening, in Potsdam, I was alone with Gottfried Bismarck, when Heinrich Wittgenstein dropped in for supper. He looks pale and tired. Suddenly the papers are full of his exploits. The other night he shot down six bombers in half an hour. Though only twenty-seven, he is now a major and has been given command of a night-fighter group. He looks so fragile! I urged him to take some leave, but he only wants to do so at the end of the month. He stayed overnight. Luckily there were no alarms.

Tuesday, 11 January My birthday. Spent the morning with another girl from the office in the underground of the Friedrichstrasse station. We were caught by a raid on our way to the photo-archive which belongs to the Scherl publishing house in Tegel. The tunnel was crowded because it was lunch time. Somebody remarked that all would be well, so long as no babies were unexpectedly born. We chose what we thought was the safest part of the tunnel, under some heavy iron girders which, we hoped, would stand the strain. After the all-clear, which was followed by heavy shooting – this happens often nowadays – we proceeded on our way, only to realise soon that it was useless as it would take us another four hours to get to our destination. We returned to the office empty-handed to face a boss who was not pleased. Dr Six wants results and cares little how one obtains them.

I reached Potsdam at 7 p.m. to find that Melanie Bismarck had touchingly prepared a very nice birthday dinner, with Chesterfields from Rudger Essen, much champagne, and a real cake with candles.

Wednesday, 12 January Today I went again to the Polizeipräsidium to pick up some pictures of bombing damage. As the sight of mangled bodies is considered the most demoralising of all, these are not available to the general public.

I had some sharp words with Count Helldorf's A.D.C., a handsome but cheeky young man who refused to let me take a look, claiming that he needed his chief's authorisation. I told him airily that I was seeing the latter tomorrow morning and would then discuss the matter with him personally. His eyes popped and I strode out.

Thursday, 13 January Count Helldorf had kept changing the hour of our appointment. Finally he appeared in the doorway and ushered me into his sanctum. We talked at length of cabbages and kings; also of his proposal, some time ago, that I become his secretary. I suspect he is wary of his own entourage and wants to bring in someone he can trust. God knows, he needs it! I asked for more time to think this over. I must consult Adam Trott, as the prospect scares me. Many people distrust him because of his high-level Nazi past, and yet Gottfried Bismarck likes and respects him; indeed they seem very close. I had many questions on what he calls my *Speisezettel* [menu]. He gave me good advice, especially as regards Count Pückler's denunciation of Mamma to the Gestapo. He did not seem surprised. They are hardened fellows, all of them, and are seldom shocked! I feel he will always help me in an emergency, but I think I should not change horses, as it were, in mid-stream, or rather mid-torrent. As he escorted me to the door, we ran into his cheeky A.D.C., who was dumbfounded.

Friday, 14 January Spent the whole morning at the Scherl publishing house in Tegel – this time my colleague and I made it – searching for photographs. I found a couple of ancient shots of the Russian Revolution, which I am adding to my personal collection; also some good portraits of the last Russian Emperor and his family which I had not seen before and which I permitted myself to 'requisition' too; the few surviving members of the Romanov family might like to have copies. The building was unheated and by the time we had finished, we were stiff with cold. We hitch-hiked back to town aboard private cars and even, for part of the journey, in a bright red post-office van.

Paul Metternich arrived in Berlin today. We lunched together at the Gersdorffs'. He then went out to Potsdam. He looks well and rested. It's so dreadful to think that he must now go back again to Russia for several months.

I was walking home from the station in Potsdam when suddenly several bombs crashed nearby. I ran as fast as I could at least a mile and just as I reached the Regierung, the sirens sounded, somewhat belatedly. Loremarie Schönburg and I were nervous as usual, but the men refused to go down to the cellar and so we sat down to dinner instead. The raid, this time, was short and I must say that we felt less helpless with Gottfried and Paul present.

Saturday, 15 January Rose at 6 a.m. to make Paul Metternich some sandwiches. To my surprise, on arriving at the Gersdorffs' for lunch, there he was; his plane had developed engine trouble and had turned back. Adam Trott was also there.

I am putting up a fight at the office to stay on here a few more days. Frankly, this plunge into a totally new atmosphere frightens me. For the moment my boss Büttner is adamant and is even battling with our other superiors about it.

On my way home, I was able to have my hair done at one of the only hairdressers still operating. I also picked up whatever cosmetics were available there, as I am unlikely to find any in Krummhübel.

Later, Loremarie Schönburg, Paul, Tony Saurma and I piled into the latter's car and toured the surviving restaurants in search of oysters – among the few remaining edibles that are not rationed. This wandering around in the evenings is what night life in Berlin in 1944 has become. We tried 'Horcher's', hoping to get some wine; it was closed. Finally, Loremarie and I were deposited in the wrecked bar of the Hotel Eden, while the men continued their search. We groped our way through the lobby into the front hall – it was a shambles: chandeliers on the floor, bits of splintered furniture, debris everywhere. We had been there so often during the last few years, it was as though we had become our own ghosts. And yet they want to re-build it!

Sunday, 16 January Got up at 5 a.m. to see Paul Metternich off for the second time, then returned to bed and rose again at nine. Was hoping to go riding with Rudger Essen (who is back in Berlin) – we get no other exercise nowadays – but on arriving at the stables, we found it deserted. We returned crestfallen to the Regierung – for breakfast. And there, again, was Paul! This time the plane had taken off under his very nose, so he is staying on yet another day. Rudger volunteered to get him a seat on a Swedish plane flying to Riga but, as Loremarie Schönburg wisely said, the fighting on the Leningrad front is worse than ever and the longer he takes to get there the better.

I have lost my battle with Büttner and am leaving for Krummhübel tomorrow.

Spent most of the morning packing and chatting with Paul and Loremarie. Later Anfuso came over to fetch us for lunch at his out-of-town residence. He is now Mussolini's Ambassador to Germany. While Loremarie took a nap – she felt seedy – Anfuso and I went for a long walk along the lake. I had known him before the war in Venice. He is very shaken by the recent execution of Ciano and eleven other top fascists. Ciano was a close friend of his. Anfuso himself is one of the few high-ranking Italian diplomats to have remained faithful to Mussolini. Many rats have left the latter's sinking ship. What Anfuso is doing may not be wise, but I respect him for this. He is a clever man, but his job is very difficult, particularly since he has no real sympathy for the Germans. He lent me some books for Krummhübel.

A professional diplomat, Filippo Anfuso (b. 1901) had from 1937 to 1941 been Foreign Minister Ciano's chef de cabinet. He had then served as Italy's Minister to Hungary and, following Italy's defection in September 1943, had been appointed Ambassador of Mussolini's 'Salò Republic' in Germany. The end of the war found him a prisoner of the French, who accused him of complicity in the 1934 assassination of King Alexander of Yugoslavia and the French Foreign Minister,

Louis Barthou. Cleared of all charges, he returned to Italy, where he went back into
politics to become a neo-fascist deputy in the Italian Parliament.

Married to Mussolini's daughter Edda, Count Galeazzo Ciano (1903–1944)
had always been against Italy's entry into the war. Though he had resigned as
Foreign Minister early in 1943, he remained a member of the Fascist Grand Council
and as such had voted against Mussolini on 25 July 1943. Charged by the Badoglio
government with corruption, he had fled to the north, where the Germans handed
him over to the neo-fascist government in Salò. On 11 January 1944 he and eleven
other senior fascist leaders who had in July 1943 turned against Mussolini were tried
and shot – with the latter's reluctant consent.

I then met Paul at Adam Trott's. As it was already six by the time I got
there, we combined tea with cocktails and then soup. Peter Bielenberg joined
us. Later in the evening, Adam phoned Count von der Schulenburg in
Krummhübel to discuss where I would live when I got there. The Count, who
was Germany's last Ambassador in Moscow, is a sort of *doyen* of the A.A.
officials down there, and also a good friend. He occupies a large house and
has offered to put me up, but it might be wrong to separate me from my
colleagues, at least at first, and so I will remain with them for a while. Adam
also phoned another of his friends, Herbert Blankenhorn, whom I do not yet
know. The latter is in charge of protocol and of re-locating the foreign
missions and has, therefore, many houses at his disposal.

KRUMMHÜBEL, *Monday, 17 January* Today our office was evacuated to
Krummhübel. Rudger Essen and I drove to Berlin alone, as Paul Metternich
had decided to travel back to the front by train. It was still quite dark. Rudger
helped me drag my two very heavy suitcases to the waiting lorry. I had refused
to send anything on ahead, fearing that my only possessions might get lost. I
was most relieved to find a Herr Betz in charge of our little group. He will be
chief of personnel in Krummhübel, and is very nice and helpful. We were
dropped with all our bags at the Görlitzer station, where we found another
group of thirty, headed by our boss Büttner himself, very pale and barely civil.
His secretary whispered to me that he thought I would not show up. Evidently
a strong mutual dislike prevails. I was relieved to find that a very pretty girl
called Ilse Blum – nicknamed 'Madonna' because of her sweet expression –
had brought along even more luggage than I had. We were both frowned
upon but, assisted by the bus driver, helped each other tow our respective

belongings. Lists were produced and consulted, our names were called out, the whole thing began to take on the aspect of a school outing. Betz, clutching an umbrella and an ivory-topped cane under one arm, helped us on to the train. Angered by the sour mien with which Büttner had greeted me, Madonna and I picked a separate compartment, third class alas, and very hard (none of us are very fat these days).

At 3 p.m. we arrived in Hirschberg, where the line to Krummhübel branches off and where we were met by our local quartermaster. He was in skiing clothes – rather an anticlimax. We changed to a little electric local train and half an hour later were in Krummhübel.

We were greeted by half the resident staff of the A.A. and, in the waiting crowd, I caught sight of Count Schulenburg, a smart Astrakhan fur hat set jauntily on his head – probably a memento of Moscow. He had come to meet me. I felt a little conspicuous. This was not quite the anonymous debut I had planned. We had some difficulty finding Haus Christa, where I am billetted. Depositing my luggage there, we returned to the Count's chalet for tea. We had some delicious coffee and sardines on toast, then Schulenburg's assistant, a Herr Sch., brought me back to my own chalet.

The village of Krummhübel is rather charming; it is on a steep hill, with the chalets set quite far apart and surrounded by gardens with many fir trees. My fear of air-raids is beginning to fade. The offices are all at the bottom of the hill, so most people ride down to work on little sledges, taking them back up the hill home again. From what I can see, the more important the people, the higher up the hill they live. Our Information Department seems to have missed out – we are latecomers – so our chalets seem less attractive than most.

As a visitor to Krummhübel noted at the time, 'The Ministry has evacuated five hundred people to Krummhübel . . . The pensions and hotels are primitive . . . (Count) Schulenburg . . . lives under such primitive conditions that he has to go to Missie Wassiltschikoff's once a week to have a bath. As all the servants in the place are Czechs and all the workmen in the sawmills are Serbs and Badoglio-Italians, Krummhübel has become a spy's paradise. As an emergency headquarters it is quite unsuitable, for not only is it readily visible from the air and therefore extremely vulnerable, but the rapid Russian advance has also rendered it geographically unsafe.' (H. G. von Studnitz, op. cit.)

I had not specified with whom I wished to share a room and so I have been paired off with a Fräulein Dr K., a good-natured soul whom I hardly know. I found her looking disconsolately round a huge unheated room with a veranda. The lighting is foul, with nothing one could read in bed by and, to add insult to injury, we have been told that on account of the room's size, we may get a third lodger. If so, I will go to war and accept the Count's offer of a room in his chalet. Otherwise Haus Christa is quite nice. There are eleven of us, seven women and four men, headed by a Herr W., with whom we all got on very badly in Berlin. But here he seems to have turned over a new leaf, acts as our benevolent papa and greets us with a friendly speech about *Hausgemeinschaft* [community spirit]. We are even fed a reasonably good supper and then retire. I have decided to be a difficult room-mate so that if I leave, I will not be missed. As a first move I have insisted on keeping all the windows wide open. For her part Fraülein Dr K. snores. We wake up blue with cold.

Tuesday, 18 January After breakfast we ventured down the hill to our temporary office, the Tannenhof – an inn not far from the station. The ground is very slippery, as our sledges flatten the fresh snow immediately.

I have suddenly another housing option – that of moving in with one of Papa's former Russian pupils, a Frau Jeannette S., who not only works here too but owns a chalet and has offered to put me up. Herr Betz judges this preferable to my accepting Count Schulenburg's hospitality. Though he does not say this in so many words, 'public opinion' might frown at 'aristocrats joining forces', as it were. One way or the other I have decided to move tomorrow.

Wednesday, 19 January The A.A. has taken over every *Gasthaus* in the neighbourhood and the Tannenhof is to become one of its offices. When we had assembled, Büttner tried to make a speech, which fell flat as the place was crammed with soldiers lounging around drinking beer. They made no sign of leaving and listened with interest.

The local population does not seem over-enthusiastic about our arrival, as they fear that it will make Krummhübel a target for bombs. Also it has killed tourism.

This afternoon I tied my suitcase on to a sledge and hauled it over to Jeannette S.'s small chalet, which is in a wood. Then I joined Count

Schulenburg at the Tippelskirchs' – who were members of his Moscow staff – from where we all took the train to the nearest little town to see a play. It was quite good, the actors coming from an important theatre in the Rhineland that has been bombed out.

Friday, 21 January Madonna Blum and I have decided to take up skiing seriously in our free time and also to learn to play the accordion properly. We both have one.

Most of our Berlin colleagues look rather comic here. One was used to seeing them with their noses glued to their desks – real chancery rats. Here they trot around in baggy trousers, bright mufflers, knitted caps, pulling their little sledges behind them and looking very self-conscious.

In Russia, the fighting on the northern front is getting very violent. I worry about Paul Metternich. Tatiana writes frantic letters.

Tuesday, 25 January Work is extremely erratic. We sit eight in one tiny room. To help me build up the new photo-archive I have been given a secretary. The photographs are sent down from Berlin in large batches. Every picture needs a caption; she takes care of most of that, while I select the pictures and organise the files. I have won her heart by allowing her to do the typing at home. Actually, this gives us more space.

Tonight I dined with Count Schulenburg (or 'the Ambassador', as he is known, although there are several of them here). Midway through dinner he announced casually that Heinrich Wittgenstein had been killed. I froze. He looked at me with surprise, as he did not know we were such close friends. Only a few days ago, in Berlin, Heinrich had rung me up at the office. He had just been to Hitler's H.Q. to receive from the hands of 'the Almighty' the Oak Leaves to his Knight's Cross. He said on the phone 'Ich war bei unserem Liebling' ['I have been to see our darling'] and added that, to his surprise, his handgun had not been removed before he entered 'the Presence' (as is customary nowadays), so that it might have been possible 'to bump him off' right then and there. He went on to elaborate on the subject until I remarked that it might be preferable to continue the conversation elsewhere. When we met a little later, he started to speculate about the possibility, next time, of blowing himself up with Hitler when they shook hands. Poor boy, little did he suspect that he had only a few more days to live! And yet he seemed so fragile that I always worried about him. He had become Germany's most successful night fighter, was constantly in action and was clearly worn out. He often spoke of the agony he felt about having to kill people and how, whenever possible, he tried to hit the enemy plane in such a way that the crew could bail out.

At the time of his death at the hands of a British long-range Mosquito fighter, Major Prince Heinrich von Sayn-Wittgenstein had destroyed eighty-three Allied planes, six of them in one memorable sortie. The night of his death he had shot down another five.

Thursday, 27 January A girl colleague on a rush visit here from Berlin brought me some pictures of Heinrich Wittgenstein. She had often seen him when he dropped in to visit me at the office. She had also made enquiries about the circumstances of his death, but no details are as yet available. His parents live in Switzerland and must be notified first.

Friday, 28 January Yesterday there was again a heavy raid on Berlin. But there are as yet no details, as all communications are cut.

I met Blankenhorn at last under the lantern of a local inn. It was pouring with rain. We climbed a steep hill to his house and settled down for a long chat in the parlour with a bottle of wine and some chocolates. He strikes me as an extremely quick-minded Rhinelander. To say that he foresees the collapse of Germany is putting things mildly. He seems actually to look forward to it and has very definite ideas about Germany's post-defeat future – partition of the country, the creation of individual autonomous *Länder*, etc.!

This was to be, in fact, the consitutional structure of the post-war Federal Republic, in which Dr Blankenhorn became one of Chancellor Adenauer's closest advisors.

The Russians have broken through to Leningrad; the siege had lasted almost three years.

The siege had lasted 872 days – since 8 September 1941. Cut off from its southern supply lines by the Germans and the Spanish 'Blue Division', and from the north by the Finns, the city's only link with the rest of the country had been across Lake Ladoga. Although more than 500,000 people were evacuated in this way, about a million of its inhabitants perished, mostly from starvation or exposure. With

Stalingrad, Leningrad has become a legend in the annals of the U.S.S.R.'s 'Great Patriotic War'.

Sunday, 30 January I have acquired a pair of white skis which were originally destined for the troops in Russia, but which apparently never caught up with them.

In the afternoon Count Schulenburg took me to visit a Baron von Richthofen, a former Minister in Sofia, who is married to a charming Hungarian. They live in the country, quite far away. Very nice relaxing atmosphere and the conversation very open.

I am deeply depressed: Tatiana has still no news of Paul Metternich and Heinrich Wittgenstein is dead . . .

Monday, 31 January Yesterday there was yet another heavy raid on Berlin, the worst, they say, since the November ones. Every time this happens, we are completely cut off here. One wonders how the A.A. can ever work.

The snow has melted and the weather is spring-like. I walked to another village to see a half-American girl I knew in Berlin. She is running another archive. I found her in bed. People seem to take things pretty easy down here. She lent me a lot of English and American magazines.

Wednesday, 2 February Büttner, who had been in Berlin for two days, is back. He has been bombed out of house and home and is nastier than ever.

Thursday, 3 February Count Schulenburg arrived today in pouring rain with a rucksack full of things to drink. He and Jeannette S., a twittering 'starlet' type, get on beautifully. She likes elderly gentlemen. She also has a crush on Papa and writes to him constantly. We baked some cakes and had quite a spread.

Friday, 4 February While typing some urgent stuff in another office, I was called to the phone from Berlin. It was Adam Trott's secretary. Our Woyrschstrasse has been bombed to smithereens and I had better come up immediately to see to things. Indeed a girl has already been sent down to replace me. I suspect that is not the only reason for this sudden summons. Büttner is again away, but the assistant chief of personnel has agreed to let me go.

BERLIN *Saturday, 5 February* Got up at 5 a.m. and trudged down to the station to find that Blankenhorn was going up to Berlin on the same train. He, too, was travelling in a semi-truant fashion. There is an idiotic regulation that nobody can leave our village without special papers, but we keep breaking loose, simply because no one can stand being cooped up here, cut off from where so many friends are in constant danger. The train to Berlin was packed and we stood all the way, but Blankenhorn had a car waiting and he dropped me off at the office, where I found Adam Trott and Alex Werth still working.

Alex is a bright and exceptionally decent man; luckily for us, having been bombed out of his own house, he has been billeted with our top boss, Dr Six, and though we all loathe and despise the latter, so long as Alex has a foot in that door he can occasionally use his influence to good purpose. As a result, things are not quite as unpleasant as they used to be. Alex is very displeased with Büttner's performance, which takes a weight off my mind.

The short glimpse I have had of Berlin is terribly depressing. Since the January 30 raid nothing seems to function any more.

Adam and I then went over to the Woyrschstrasse to see Maria Gersdorff. Although it had been badly hit already before, the whole street seems now to have collapsed and we stood in a crowd watching them pull down a remaining wall. Our little square is totally burnt out, with one exception – the Gersdorffs' house.

After lunching with Adam, I spent the rest of the afternoon with him. He is not at all well. I wish he were down in Krummhübel with us, but I know he would never agree to leave Berlin at such a moment. He gave me some books and drove me to the station, where I caught a train for Potsdam. Gottfried and Melanie Bismarck were alone. It was like coming home.

Sunday, 6 February Went back to Berlin, to church, walking through half the town on foot. Much of the Kurfürstendamm is now destroyed. Tried to look up Sigrid Görtz, who lived just behind it. Her house was the only one still standing. I went up the stairs but they stopped in mid-air and her flat at the top was gone; nobody knew where she was. Lunched with Hans Flotow, who has also at last been badly hit. He has emptied his flat of all the surviving furniture, has somehow propped up the sagging walls and camps there in a tent like a Bedouin. Afterwards I returned to Maria Gersdorff's and she told me a horrifying story:

On 26 December, our old postman, whom she had allowed to use my wrecked room under the eaves, fell ill with pneumonia. His family had been evacuated, so Maria and Heinz brought the old man downstairs and fixed up an improvised bed in the kitchen. No doctor could be reached and he died on the 28th. For three days nobody came for the body and he lay in state on the kitchen table, surrounded by candles. Finally Professor Gehrbrandt dropped in to see Maria and, appalled by the sight, alerted the authorities. Still nobody came for the body. On the 30th bombs again rained down on our square and the surrounding houses caught fire. Ours did too but was saved thanks to the efforts of Kicker Stumm and several of his friends. As they fetched water to douse the roof, the rescue party kept bumping the body, while Maria sat at its feet making sandwiches for the hungry men. Some neighbours volunteered to throw the body into the ruins of a burning house; Maria favoured the idea of digging a hole in the so-called garden, which is now a mere strip of debris. The poor postman remained another two days in the house and only then was at last removed.

Gottfried and Melanie Bismarck have returned from his mother's country place, Schönhausen. It is there that Heinrich Wittgenstein's plane was shot down. Melanie brought back some earth and odd bits of his plane, such as the windshield and parts of the motor. She thought his parents in Switzerland might want some relics. I hardly think so. It only makes things worse. If only they had not sent the three boys back to Germany when the war started! What with their Russian and French ancestors, they were barely German in the first place. It is thought that Heinrich was unconscious when he hit the ground, as his parachute never opened and he was found, shoeless, quite some distance from the plane. He usually wore light pumps, with just a coat thrown over his civilian clothes. I remember him going up once in a raincoat thrown over a dinner jacket. He had become such an ace that he did whatever he pleased. The rest of his crew survived, as he made them jump when the plane was hit. Either he injured his head jumping out last or else he was wounded and could not pull open his parachute. Melanie gave me some scraps of metal as a keepsake. Maybe this will make me realise at last that we have truly lost him.

Monday, 7 February Tatiana has had a telegram saying that Paul Metternich is dangerously ill at the front outside Leningrad. It is impossible to get any information here. Since Juan Luis Rocamora, the Spanish military attaché, left, no one seems to know anything about what is happening to the Spanish 'Blue Division' to which Paul is attached as liaison officer.

Ferdl Kyburg has turned up from Vienna, where life seems still pretty carefree. He is very much struck by the contrast with Berlin. Since he was kicked out of the navy – as a Hapsburg – his life seems without purpose. He was serving on the cruiser *Prinz Eugen* in the legendary battle in which both the *Hood* and the *Bismarck* were sunk. He now studies at Vienna University.

Later, a lovely dinner at the Bismarcks' in Potsdam.

Rudger Essen is back from Sweden, bringing lobsters, American *Vogue*, etc. Another world!

At night a call from Loremarie Schönburg in Vienna: she has overstayed her leave and is again in trouble. Then another call – from Count Schulenburg in Krummhübel. I should not be scared, but in my absence he had opened an official letter to me: Büttner was firing me for having gone to Berlin without his leave. Luckily, I had asked that my mail be opened in case of news from Paul. I may thus be able to discuss my plight with Adam Trott and Alex Werth. The dear old Count sounded deeply worried and was most relieved to hear me take it so lightly.

Tuesday, 8 February Loremarie Schönburg is back from Vienna.

On hearing of my dismissal, Alex Werth got very angry: abuse of authority, etc. I told him jokingly that I would not mind a little holiday while the matter was being cleared up, but it appears that the top brass, Dr Six, refuses to hear of it.

I took advantage of the situation and went to the hairdresser. Maybe I should grasp this opportunity and quit; but nowadays unless one has a job in a government office, one is immediately assigned to a munitions factory – or worse. *Qui vivra – verra.*

Wednesday, 9 February This morning Loremarie Schönburg and I turned up at the office looking rather sheepish. My dismissal had not yet been revoked; she had been absent without leave for three whole weeks. The comic part is that I had always warned Loremarie about her light-hearted attitude towards 'total war', yet here she is unscathed, and I am the one who is fired.

Alex Werth sent me off at once to beard Dr Six in his den. The upshot of this interview: I am to ignore the whole thing, go back to Krummhübel and then return to Berlin on the 21st to collect additional material. Büttner will be dealt with here.

On my way home to Potsdam I bought some tulips. I was stopped by several people who asked where I had found them. It's pathetic how one tries to keep up a semblance of civilised life.

Spent the evening alone with Gottfried Bismarck. We telephoned Admiral Canaris' office as I had been told by Hasso Etzdorf that a colonel in the Abwehr had just returned from Paul Metternich's sector of the front and might know more about his condition. When, thanks to Hasso, I finally got through to this colonel, he first took me for Tatiana and sounded guarded. This worried me, particularly as when he heard I was leaving Berlin soon, he insisted on seeing me. We agreed to meet tomorrow at the Hotel Adlon. Gottfried tried to cheer me up by saying that he probably just wants to meet a pretty girl. But I am frankly scared.

Thursday, 10 February Rudger Essen drove us into town. The Abwehr colonel was very friendly and told me all he knew: Paul Metternich has double pneumonia, is now at a base hospital in Riga and will be brought back to Germany as soon as he can be moved. But nothing can be done at present as his condition is very serious. The colonel tried to sound optimistic. Actually, all this may well be a blessing, as his regiment had suffered very heavy losses during the recent Russian offensive and Paul had told us that this was only the beginning.

Later, I had a long talk with Hans-Bernd von Haeften, our Berlin chief of personnel. He had already received all the papers concerning my dismissal. He was very decent about it. Everything seems to have been smoothed out but he wants me to apologise to Büttner: '. . . after all, he is in trouble anyhow . . . you left without his consent . . . he has been badly wounded . . . his nerves are shot . . .' As I was leaving, I ran into Büttner himself on the stairs and as I wanted to get it over with, I started to apologise. Just then the siren sounded, he muttered 'nicht jetzt, nicht jetzt' ['not now, not now'] and that was that.

Adam Trott drove me to the station; on the way we got lost as one cannot always find one's bearings amidst the ruins. He stayed with me in the train until it left. It was, as always, crammed. I stood in the corridor and even that was a squeeze. At Hirschberg I missed the connection and got back to Krummhübel only at midnight, totally spent.

KRUMMHÜBEL *Friday, 11 February* The snow is almost one metre high. After putting in a short appearance at our Tannenhof headquarters, I went up to see Count Schulenburg and, with his help, tried to telephone Tatiana, who is again in hospital in Dresden. Am joining her there for the weekend. What a dear that old man is, and how marvellous it is to have him here! We lunched together and I returned to the office, where I found a telegram from Hasso Etzdorf addressed to Tatiana. He confirmed Paul Metternich's serious illness, but added 'ausser Gefahr' ['out of danger'], which is encouraging.

Tatiana has sent me some fresh eggs. Jeannette S. is in seventh heaven.

Saturday, 12 February Worked all morning and left for the station at 2 p.m. Luckily I had taken along some sandwiches, as the journey to Dresden was appalling. I missed every connection. Then I boarded the wrong tram and got to the hospital only at midnight. Poor Tatiana was asleep and when I woke her up, she burst into tears. She is undergoing a harmless check-up, but feels weak. Paul Metternich's news does not help.

Sunday, 13 February Spent the whole day with Tatiana. I had brought her some *Tatlers* from the office; she recognised several old friends from pre-war days. She is getting a little impatient about the constant and rather overwhelming presence of both parents and I don't blame her. I suggested that she visit me in Krummhübel. It will do her good to get away for a while.

Monday, 14 February The trip back from Dresden this morning was once again endless. Our offices have been moved from the Tannenhof to some pre-fabricated barracks and I headed straight for them. Though they are not quite ready, we had moved all our files there nevertheless and had even installed some quite decent furniture. As I approached, their alignment appeared strange and then I realised that one whole row of pre-fabs was missing – burnt to the ground. Our building, too, had disappeared. Apparently, they had caught fire on Saturday night and burnt down in one hour. The Arbeitsdienst [labour service] boys, who have their camp nearby, saved a lot of the furniture but most of my precious photo-archive has perished for the second time. So have all Büttner's files (no loss!) and a valuable picture belonging to Dr Six, as well as office equipment and copying machines worth 100,000 marks apiece. This – the work, probably, of some unfriendly P.O.W. – means that we will have to start all over again. I was told that when Dr Six heard about it in Berlin, he roared with laughter: to think that we had been sent here to escape 'the vicissitudes of war'!

As there is nothing I can do for the moment, I took off for home and went early to bed. One gets easily sleepy here; it must be the mountain air.

Tuesday, 15 February We have moved back to the Tannenhof. With a colleague I towed what remained of our stuff to an upstairs room, where I have installed my office. I have a wonderful view and the windows lead straight on to the roof, which is good for sun-bathing. Two Russian P.O.W.s helped carry up the furniture; I gave them bread coupons and cigarettes.

My photo-archive is in a sorry state, as most of the pictures are drenched with water and unfit for use. The rest are stuck together. I spent much time trying to unstick them, drying them on a bed, and afterwards placing a stack under the seats of my colleagues to press them flat.

A telegram from Mamma: 'SOS. Tatiana wants to join Paul in Riga. Stop her, etc. . . .' As Tatiana is arriving here on Thursday, I prefer to wait and discuss things quietly then. Count Schulenburg is putting off a trip home in order to see her.

Wednesday, 16 February After lunch Madonna Blum and I had our first accordion lesson with a Czech musician called Holinko, who himself plays beautifully.

Thursday, 17 February Tatiana arrived today.

The famous monastery of Monte Cassino has, apparently, been destroyed by Allied bombs.

Friday, 18 February Madonna Blum's boss, a nice old gentleman who was Consul-General in Istanbul, is very upset as he can find no refuge for his family who have been bombed out of their home. I suggested to Tatiana that she install them too in Königswart. Nowadays no private house can remain incompletely occupied and they would be preferable to total strangers.

Saturday, 19 February Lunched with Tatiana and then took off with Madonna Blum to ski on a steep hill behind a large pompous-looking house which, it is rumoured, will eventually be occupied by Foreign Minister von Ribbentrop himself. On our return, we found Tatiana and Jeannette S. feverishly making sandwiches as Count Schulenburg was coming for supper with his assistant, Sch., it being the latter's birthday. Jeannette had even baked a cake and a supply of wine had just arrived from Königswart, so things became quite animated. Madonna played the accordion but later passed out, probably as a result of the good fare combined with a bad fall on her head while skiing this afternoon.

Sunday, 20 February After lunch, the weather being exceptionally good, five of us took off on a long tour, Madonna Blum and I on skis and the others on sledges. All this involved much climbing, as there are of course no ski lifts.

Up on the mountain we heard an air-raid siren far down below in the valley. It sounded quite unreal. It is sometimes hard to realise here that there is a war on.

Tatiana has received a very 'low' letter from Paul Metternich, who complains of sleeplessness, a bad pain in the chest, etc. Count Schulenburg has promised that if Paul does not get evacuated back to Germany soon, he will try and help her join him in Riga. I am against this, as train travel is chaotic these days, especially in the East.

The news from the Russian front is extremely contradictory – both sides, as usual, claiming successes.

By now the Russians were re-occupying the Baltic States and had reached the borders of pre-war Poland. Further south, ten German divisions surrounded near Cherkassy had just been destroyed. Though, even after Stalingrad, the Germans had been able to mount several successful local offensives, after the battle of Kursk (July–August 1943) – the greatest armoured battle in history, in which the Germans lost close to 3,000 tanks! – their successes were strictly tactical, with the Russians retaining the initiative throughout. By October the latter had reached the Dnieper and liberated Kiev and at the end of March 1944 they would cross into Rumania.

Monday, 21 February I was supposed to go back to Berlin today to show Dr Six my plan for setting up the new photo-archive. But my trip has been postponed, as he is away.

This evening we saw *Ochsenkrieg* [*War of Oxen*], a film about war in the Middle Ages. It was particularly restful to see people whacking away at one another with wooden clubs. After five or six hours' fighting the battlefield was strewn with seven bodies!

Wednesday, 23 February At lunch at the Goldener Frieden today we were given microscopic pieces of inedible meat, although we had handed in our coupons. Tatiana complained and we got a little sausage instead.

In the evening Blankenhorn came and stayed for supper. He has promised to ring up Paul Metternich's doctor in Riga. This is a great relief, as Count Schulenburg has gone home for a week and we are not on the same close terms with his assistant. Alas, the man who had promised Tatiana an S.S. *laissez-passer* to Riga has just been killed in a motor accident.

On the 15th there was again a heavy raid on Berlin. A large bomb hit the Hotel Bristol, one of the few surviving hotels in town, during a big official dinner. Sixty people were buried alive, including several well-known generals. It took fifty hours to dig them out and by then most of them were dead.

Thursday, 24 February Blankenhorn cannot get through to Riga.

Friday, 25 February Blankenhorn got through to Riga at last this morning. Paul Metternich, it seems, is out of danger but is considered still too weak to travel.

In the afternoon I ran a fever and, to Büttner's glee, retired to bed. It appears that he hopped around the Tannenhof rubbing his hands and chuckling 'Jetzt habe ich sie, jetzt habe ich sie' ['Now I've got her, now I've got her!']. Weird!

Saturday, 26 February Now Tatiana is in bed.

Sunday, 27 February At last a cheery letter from Paul Metternich.

Monday, 28 February Missed work again this morning, as I don't feel at all well. Blankenhorn was shocked to hear of our condition and promised to find a doctor. He arrived in the afternoon – young and *sportiv*. Jeannette S. took an immediate fancy to him, which he clearly reciprocated and he is returning, presently, to see *her*. Having heard from Blankenhorn that Paul Metternich had an abscess in the lung, he said that this is a very dangerous thing that hardly ever happens.

Tuesday, 29 February Went back to work.

Louisette and Josias Rantzau have just sent me a magnificent ham from Bucharest. Josias was posted to the embassy there some time ago. It came as a blessing, for we are short of food coupons and do not know how to feed Tatiana, who is unable to go out yet.

Yesterday Count Schulenburg returned. What a relief!

Saturday, 4 March Loremarie Schönburg appears to be again in trouble. I have just had a letter from Hans-Bernd von Haeften (our chief of personnel in Berlin). He would like me to use my influence to talk her into resigning; the political situation is getting increasingly dangerous and her lack of caution worries them all greatly. She had just written me from Vienna that she was about to return to Berlin, so this will come to her as a shock.

Sunday, 5 March Tatiana left this morning.

Blankenhorn is depressed by Churchill's latest speech and the Allies' attitude generally. He had been hoping that it would be possible for Germany to reach an understanding with them 'under certain circumstances', but now this seems unlikely. 'Unconditional surrender' is all they will stand for. Lunacy!

This was Winston Churchill's speech to the House of Commons on 22 February in which he laid down as a principle that once the war was won, Poland should be compensated in the West (i.e. at Germany's expense) for any territory it might have to yield to the U.S.S.R.

Monday, 6 March Another heavy raid on Berlin, this time in broad daylight. For the Americans are now bombing too and their planes can fly higher than the British. Day raids are even worse than night raids, as everybody is in town or on the move. It is said that the U.F.A. film studios in Babelsberg were destroyed. I fear that Potsdam, which is nearby, may also have been hit.

In fact, round-the-clock raids against Germany, with the U.S.A.F. bombing in the daytime and the R.A.F. at night, had started as early as 1943. The first U.S. attack on Berlin – by 29 B-17 'Flying Fortresses' – had taken place two days earlier. The one Missie records here turned out to be the costliest U.S. bombing mission of the whole war in Europe, with a loss of 69 aircraft out of the attacking 658.

Photographs of the battle of Monte Cassino are piling up. The destruction of that beautiful monastery is horrifying. What will happen to Florence, Venice, Rome? Will any of them survive? How strange: we never imagined that this war would be as bloody and destructive as it is now becoming . . .

Tuesday, 7 March Rang up Vienna, hoping to stop Loremarie Schönburg from returning to Berlin, but she had already left.

Wednesday, 8 March Another heavy day raid on Berlin. We cannot get through on the telephone.

Both Jeannette S. and I are expecting parcels: I, wine and she, butter; but nothing has arrived.

Tatiana has sent me a large parcel of letters, many of them from Paul Metternich, in which he describes his life in Riga – they are feeding him well, egg-nogs, scrambled eggs, real coffee, etc. It makes one's mouth water. He is far better now but still weak. It appears that a medical commission investigated his case and was very impressed, for he had had an abscess in the left lung which spread around the heart. He could not be operated on and was only saved because it burst by itself.

Antoinette Croy has written to Tatiana from Paris to say that some time ago Georgie was summoned to the Gestapo on account of some letters of 'advice' he had received from Papa. One sometimes wishes the parents would interfere less in our lives and act more cautiously, especially since we do not always tell them what we are up to.

At the Gestapo Missie's brother had been confronted with letters that the censors had of course opened, in which his father expressed anxiety about his rumoured 'activities'. This logically implied politics, in other words, the Resistance. With some difficulty he was able to laugh off his father's faux pas *by suggesting that he probably meant the black market, in which many people in France were involved at the time.*

Saturday, 11 March Went skiing with Madonna Blum in search of vegetables to go with a hare she is cooking in her house for us all.

Sunday, 12 March The organisational side of life in Krummhübel is chaotic. There is hardly any coal (and yet we are in Silesia, the heartland of coal); and when there *is* coal, the offices become furnaces. Thus we alternately freeze or roast.

Madonna Blum's hare was delicious and the guests stayed late. I must be up at five again, as I am off to Breslau, to pick up replacement photographs for my archive.

Monday, 13 March Dressed in the dark and felt quite strange wearing a skirt.

Luckily, rail communications with Breslau are still working and I was there by ten. I found it a dreary town, although thus far it has been spared. Fortunately, I finished my business early, cast a rapid glance at the market-place and the cathedral, and then tried to have a bite at a local restaurant, but the fare was so poor that I gulped down some nondescript soup and sped back to the station.

Several ladies shared my compartment. One old woman, waggling her head from side to side ceaselessly, was suffering from shock after a raid. Another had lost half an arm but seemed quite cheerful. She was on her way to a hospital in the country. I felt grubby and, as if guessing my thoughts, someone produced some eau-de-Cologne and sprinkled it around the compartment. At Hirschberg an A.A. girl joined us. She was coming from Berlin. She had seen Loremarie Schönburg, who now wishes to join me in Krummhübel.

Tuesday, 14 March A letter from Mamma. She has long had no news from Irena. Conditions in Italy seem chaotic. I felt suddenly terribly low and went and sat in the church for a while to think all this through. Irena seems to be getting desperate all alone in Rome and wants to join us before the war ends. What a mistake *that* would be!

Wednesday, 15 March A letter from Loremarie Schönburg confirming her wish to come here. We will write her an official letter, inviting her to join our group permanently. In Berlin she is too restless, thereby endangering the lives of vitally important people.

Supper at the Preussischer Hof. They had just killed a pig and everybody gorged on its insides. I stuck staunchly to cheese.

The telegraph service has now broken down completely throughout Germany; this is clearly the medium to use if one wants messages to get lost, as one sometimes does nowadays.

Thursday, 16 March Still no food parcels, so today we had a supper of toast soaked in turkey fat.

Yesterday evening General Dittmar (the official military radio commentator) admitted that things in the East looked bad, as the *Schlammperiode* [muddy season] favoured the Russians. We should be prepared for heavy reverses, he said.

For their part, the Allies have bombed Rome, also Stuttgart. Berlin has been left in peace lately.

Friday, 17 March Nothing particular happens to ruffle our bovine existence, except that Count Schulenburg has sent us a turkey.

Saturday, 18 March Came home from a day out skiing with Madonna Blum in heavy snow to find Jeannette S. struggling with a case of Metternich wine, which the Ambassador's assistant Sch. and the chauffeur had just delivered on a sledge. We immediately opened up a bottle and settled down to a quiet evening. I presented Jeannette with half the case to thank her for her hospitality.

Sunday, 19 March More skiing.

At home we found Count Schulenburg. He had just received a parcel of nuts, raisins and dried figs from Turkey. He had also brought some coffee and brandy, so we had quite a spread.

Jeannette S. wants to go back to Berlin for a week. As there have been no raids there lately, she even wants to take along her little girl, who lives here with her. I think this very imprudent.

Tuesday, 21 March This afternoon we had our first conference with Büttner since he fired me. He tried to be pleasant. I gather he has decided to bury the hatchet.

Count Schulenburg's assistant has told Jeannette S. that the German army has overrun Hungary, while the Russians are occupying Rumania. This news is still unofficial. Pleasant prospects in store!

Wednesday, 22 March Up bright and early. After breakfast with real coffee, Jeannette S. and child departed in a snow flurry, accompanied by Count Schulenburg's assistant Sch., who is decidedly assiduous. I am glad to be alone for a while. I will now see to my clothes and put things in order generally.

In some ways Krummhübel has definite rustic charm: this morning I was food-shopping when I was hailed from a neighbouring lane by the postman; he had seen me at the baker's and had then searched all the inns for me – in vain – as he had a registered letter. Touching!

Worked late, as piles of photographs and office supplies have arrived from Breslau and we are now trying to find a cart to tow the stuff up the hill. The A.A. has a special supply of cigarettes to bribe the locals into carrying loads for us, as there is hardly any transportation.

I am inviting people in while the wine lasts. We are still short of coal. The house is getting steadily colder; when I have guests, I switch on two wheezing electric fans.

Thursday, 23 March It is now official: Hungary has been occupied by 'our' troops. The new Premier is the former Minister in Berlin, Sztojay, whom I met several times at Valerie Arenberg's dinners, for she too is Hungarian. Not at all Machiavellian, as far as I can remember.

Even though Hungary had done well by its friendly relations with Nazi Germany, retrieving much of the territory it had lost after World War I, this association was at best half-hearted and its contribution to Hitler's war in the East slight. Following the virtual annihilation of its forces at the time of Stalingrad, its wily Regent Admiral Horthy had made contact with the Allies. This became known to Hitler, who on 17 March summoned Horthy to Berchtesgaden. In his absence, German forces took over the country and installed Field-Marshal Doem Sztojay as Premier.

Friday, 24 March My food supplies are growing thinner and thinner.

In the evening I dropped in to see Count Schulenburg, who showed me a telegram from Madrid: On the night of the 17th the Paris-Hendaye express was derailed by the French Resistance and the two Oyarzabals were killed. There were no further particulars, only that the funeral was held in Madrid. They were going home on leave, Maria Pilar having just returned from Switzerland, where she had visited their little boy at school at Le Rosey. He had carried Tatiana's train at her wedding. This is a tragic blow for us all, as they were among our dearest friends. Spent the evening at home in a state of total dejection.

Saturday, 25 March Finished work at noon; then, after changing, I joined Count Schulenburg and his assistant and we drove in a sleigh drawn by A.A. horses to the Pfaffenberg, a wooded hill in the middle of our valley. The A.A. now has quite a stud here. The Asiatic-looking coachman turned out to be an ex-Soviet P.O.W. from Azerbaijan. There are a number of them here, as the Germans do not want to use them on the Eastern Front. Clad in ill-fitting German uniforms which make them look very strange, they are on the whole good-natured.

Much to the Germans' surprise, virtually from the start of the campaign in the East, large numbers of Russian prisoners kept volunteering for service with the invaders. They came from all parts of the Soviet Union, but especially from the non-Russian minorities (such as Missie's Azerbaijanis) whose lands had been absorbed into the Russian empire but relatively recently and who bore both a nationalistic and (in the case of the Moslems) a religious grudge against their atheist rulers in Moscow. Some did so from opportunism – to escape a hungry death in the P.O.W. camps; but many were ideologically motivated, having come to regard Stalin (whose purges had only recently decimated their country) as a worse enemy even than Hitler. By war's end, they numbered anywhere between 1.5 and 2.5 million!

Already early in the campaign, quite a few German field commanders had realised that their only hope of winning the war in the East was to secure the support of the Russian people against their Communist rulers and so soon ex-Red Army units in German uniform made their appearance, first in auxiliary jobs in the rear and then as regular combat units that served also as poles of attraction for further defectors. In 1942, a much-decorated Soviet general, Andrei Vlassov, who had distinguished himself in the defence of Moscow, was captured. Together with several other Soviet generals, he dedicated himself to creating a free-Russian movement. Though it enjoyed the support of many senior German commanders and even of some high-ranking S.S. (and in the end, of Himmler himself), it never really took off because of Hitler's adamant opposition. For in his plans there was never any place even for anti-Communist Russians – except as slaves. Only in November 1944 (when the Soviet armies were already closing in for the kill) was Vlassov allowed to establish a 'Committee for the Liberation of the Peoples of Russia' and a 'Russian Liberation Army' consisting of two poorly-equipped divisions, whose only achievement was to liberate Prague before the Soviets marched in. They then made their way to the West and surrendered to the Allies who, invoking the Yalta agreement, handed them over to Stalin's tender mercy. Many of these 'Victims of Yalta' were to commit suicide rather than go home. The others were either shot on the spot or shipped off to the Gulag, from where few returned. Vlassov himself, together with his senior generals, was hanged in Moscow in August 1946.

At the top of the hill there is a small *Schloss* belonging to a Baron X., who takes in paying guests, where, after giving advance notice, one can dine. We were received charmingly by host and hostess, but when dinner was announced they withdrew. We were ushered into a delightful little dining-room, all faded blue and white chintz, soft lights, everything we, living our dreary life down in the village, had long not heard of. We were given a de-licious dinner, topped with whipped cream and peaches. We were as gleeful as children at a party. Later, our hosts joined us again and showed us around. They have even a little greenhouse and proudly produced their first rose. After a brandy the sleigh reappeared and we drove down to Krummhübel again.

Monday, 27 March Another ham from Josias Rantzau, bless him!

Tuesday, 28 March Last Friday there was again a heavy raid on Berlin. I worry, as there has been no sign of life from Jeannette S. since they left.

Supper at Madonna Blum's. Later, the cartoonist Bruns dropped in and we played on three accordions. He is here for a fortnight; he usually works at night and spends the day skiing or playing the accordion to us while *we* work. He is exceedingly gifted, has an endless repertoire and has taught us quite a lot. A tiny man, he is a highly talented painter and, I suspect, a secret Communist. He has very 'original' views on present-day Germany.

Wednesday, 29 March It snows and snows.

Hans-Bernd von Haeften rang me up from Berlin to enquire whether Tatiana could put up the Richter family in Königswart, for they, too, have been bombed out. Judgie was sitting in the office bunker during a day raid when a mine hit his house, scattering his family in all directions. Nobody was hurt, thank God, but they have nowhere to go. I am now trying to reach Tatiana, but as usual the long-distance lines don't work.

Thursday, 30 March A letter from Berlin asking me to come up after Easter. I am delighted as it is very difficult to stay away for so long from the 'scene of action'. Our sedentary existence here is purely a physical recuperation exercise.

This evening Madonna Blum and I were cooking potatoes for supper, when Jeannette S. lurched in with her little girl, dragging a huge suitcase. The night of her arrival in Berlin, one of the heaviest types of bomb hit her house there. The cellar collapsed, burying eleven people alive. By some miracle they themselves were saved, but her mother has nowhere to go now and I must move out to make room for her. Berlin must be perfectly ghastly: no water (each family gets two pails a day, delivered by soldiers), no light and no gas . . . Jeannette was sneered at several times in the street on account of her 'provocative' make-up, which nowadays is considered 'unpatriotic'. Hats are no longer worn; at best, scarves around the face, to muffle the smoke fumes.

Friday, 31 March The whole Department is feverishly active. Dr Six arrives tomorrow with Judgie Richter and a few other senior officials and will be visiting each chalet and *Gasthaus* in turn. For this important occasion coal has reappeared from nowhere and the barracks are being heated for practically the first time this winter. Furthermore, the Tannenhof has a fresh coat of

paint and carpets have been laid out. In a dither, Büttner has issued an Order
of the Day asking us to be at our desks on Sunday from nine to twelve. One
might think the Pope was on his way.

The weather is beginning to clear up at last and we are therefore
exceedingly peeved.

Saturday, 1 April Went to the office deliberately late, because of tomorrow, to
find Büttner already prowling the premises. Pointedly he announced that he
had been there since eight. The current object of his wrath – now that he has
given *me* up – is a Professor Michel, who, when attacked, is apt to remark 'das
kostet mich nur ein müdes Lächeln' ['a tired little smile is all that can get out
of me'].

Sunday, 2 April Arrived at the office shortly after nine. The weather was
sunny and bright. For once Bruns's accordion had been hidden away and
every desk or table was graced with an identification panel, such as *Bildarchiv*
(photo-archive), *Schrift und Wort* (the written word), etc., to indicate the
various branches of our activities, and everyone was standing nervously
around awaiting the appearance of the Great Moghul. I was sitting outside on
the veranda in the sun with Bruns and a lady colleague from Berlin when I
was hauled in, as Büttner wanted to discuss some texts and captions.

We were in the middle of this when in marched a procession headed by Dr
Six, followed by Judgie Richter looking as if he had a tummy ache, Böhm,
Blahnt, and Six's secretary Frau Seuster, plus the powers-that-be in Krummhübel, i.e. Betz and so on. The gentlemen from Berlin were in a state of
disarray; being unaccustomed to slippery ice and snow, they had visibly taken
a few tumbles on the way up. Everybody then assembled on the veranda,
where to our general embarrassment Büttner launched into an interminable
speech about our 'immensely important' activities. What a farce! As Six
stared at him silently, he got confused and started to stammer. I stood at the
back, leaning against the door. When Büttner's speech was over, Six said a
few words about the need to provide more space for the photo-archive (*ergo*
myself!), etc., and off they staggered down the hill again, while we took off to
ski.

During the next three days Six will be busy elsewhere, so we will not be
bothered, but he has announced another inspection visit on Wednesday.

Yesterday his secretary Frau Seuster paid me a surprise visit to entreat me to be present this morning. Apparently they had feared I would go skiing instead! They must be crazy: with the Tiger in our midst? He is far too dangerous a man for me to take things flippantly in his presence. Besides, it would be a grave mistake on my part to alienate him at this, of all times, knowing what lies ahead.

Frau Seuster had promised Judgie and the other two gentlemen from Berlin, who had helped her during their journey with her heaviest parcels, a cup of coffee for their pains. I suggested that she receive them in our house, as she has nowhere else to go. Madonna Blum and I got home just in time to tear off our boots and warn Jeannette S. before Judgie, Böhm and Blahnt appeared. Frau Seuster provided the coffee and I the wine. We had quite a good chat, as these three are among the last remaining decent elements in the Department. They are at a loss what to do with Six and asked us whether they could return with him after dinner! Actually, it might be good politics.

So return with him they did and the evening dragged on until very late, the only levity being provided by Jeannette.

Monday, 3 April The Rantzaus are sending all their more valuable belongings from Bucharest to his sister-in-law here. They appear to be very much on the alert there, as the front is moving closer and closer.

Tuesday, 4 April The weather is rapidly spoiling and, taking advantage of Judgie Richter's presence here, I am planning a weekend in Königswart with him. He is resettling his family with Tatiana at last and I may manage to wangle the permission to accompany him. The train trip will be tough; it now takes eighteen hours instead of five.

Wednesday, 5 April Not only has Judgie Richter obtained Dr Six's permission for me to accompany him to Königswart, but by claiming that he has more things to discuss with me, he has arranged that we leave on Friday.

Today the sun is so hot that Frau Seuster and I climbed on to the roof of our veranda. We talked shop there and were soon joined by Judgie and Professor Michel, while Bruns, shirtless, lay sunning himself in a corner. It suddenly dawned on Judgie that Bruns had never sat in on any conference. Since everything here is immediately labelled *streng geheim* [top secret], it was decided that as soon as we got off the roof, Bruns would take the oath of special secrecy.

Thursday, 6 April This morning I was asked to report to Dr Six after coffee, as he wanted to speak to me alone. I did not quite understand what 'after coffee' meant. Luckily, on my way to lunch I barged into Six himself. He looked ostentatiously at his watch. Was I leaving too early or something? One can never tell. With such a man it is difficult to strike the right note and to conceal one's utter dislike and fear behind a mask of bravado and *je m'en foutisme*. Later, Judgie Richter dropped in to say that we were both expected at five. What a relief not to be alone with him! At the Tannenhof we were met by Six himself. We were offered buns, coffee and brandy and general matters were discussed – if one can call it a discussion: he usually ends every argument by stating flatly that he is the highest paid man in our establishment, *ergo* his decisions must prevail.

Good Friday, 7 April Got up this morning at five. At the station, I found Dr Six and Judgie Richter about to board the train, while the authorities-that-be in Krummhübel, i.e. Betz *et alia*, stood on the platform to see 'us' off. Luckily our ways parted at Görlitz. The train we had proposed to take arrived so full that Judgie and I could not climb in even via the windows, so we waited three hours for the next, arriving in Marienbad at eleven at night after a journey of nearly twenty hours; but Judgie was in high spirits and time passed quickly.

On reaching the house, I undressed rapidly and had some supper. Then Mamma appeared. I was happy to see her, as I had not been back since Christmas. We immediately got into a political argument. This life of enforced inactivity is very hard on someone so dynamic. Paul Metternich arrived from Riga yesterday. He looks very tired but less thin than I had expected and is in good spirits.

KÖNIGSWART *Saturday, 8 April* The weather is lovely. There is much less snow here than in Krummhübel. I went with Mamma into the village and met the Richter family taking a constitutional. After a copious lunch – *what* it is, these days, to own a country place! – we went for a long drive. Paul Metternich gets easily breathless, but is otherwise cheerful. What a pity that Krummhübel is so far away that I cannot come here more often! The Metternichs are hoping to go down to Spain this summer – Paul on sick leave. He even wants to drive down in his mother's car, which has been hidden away in a barn here since the outbreak of the war. He gets a great kick from doing so at a time when no other private vehicles are allowed on the roads.

Easter Sunday, 9 April The Richters came to lunch. Judgie makes a lot of sense. It is so reassuring to know that there are at the A.A. still a few persons one can trust.

KRUMMHÜBEL *Tuesday, 11 April* Up at 4.30 a.m. The train was very full and all the way we were pursued by the sound of air-raid sirens. Arrived at Krummhübel at 7 p.m. and headed straight for home, where I found many letters and several parcels.

Wednesday, 12 April The parcels were from Hanni Jenisch and contained butter, bacon and sausage. I am really touched. We immediately organised a spread, followed by coffee.

In the afternoon there was a general roll-call at the barracks to hear what Dr Six had found wrong during his visit: among other things, he had noticed that we did not show enough respect for work hours. On the other hand, in the event of an air-raid here, we were free to disperse and go where we liked. Sound advice, seeing there is no other alternative! . . .

Had supper with Count Schulenburg and then went to the cinema.

Though Missie at the time did not know this, while in Krummhübel on 3–4 April, Dr Six addressed a seminar of 'Jewish experts' attached to German diplomatic missions in Europe. His subject was 'The political structures of world Jewry', in the course of which he stated that 'the physical extermination of European Jews deprives Jewry of its biological reserves'.

Thursday, 13 April This morning Hans-Georg von Studnitz rang up. He is here with Gesandter [Minister Plenipotentiary] Schmidt, the Head of the Foreign Press Department of the A.A. They are meeting with the latter's Slovakian counterpart, Tido Gaspar, who is also Propaganda Minister. Later Hans-Georg dropped in at the office and we sat on a bench in the sun. He is full of the latest Berlin gossip. I believe he invents much but he is a good *raconteur.*

During lunchtime he accompanied me up the hill to look at a room which Count Schulenburg has found for me in another chalet, since Jeannette S. needs mine for her mother. It is rather primitive as things go, but has running water, which is a great advantage. Loremarie Schönburg is arriving one of these days, we will share it and we can probably manage to make things fairly comfortable. On the bridge overlooking the waterfall we collided with Gesandter Schmidt himself; he is, to my surprise, a quite young man. He was arranging a *Kameradschaftsabend* or office party for his Press Department at the Teichmannbaude and invited me to join them.

With Madonna Blum and a few others we drove out there in a horse-drawn carriage.

Apart from us, the girls were all from the Press Department. We sat at long tables, I next to Studnitz, who continued his Berlin sagas. In the course of the evening Gesandter Schmidt emptied a glass of wine into Madonna's lap. His Slovakian guest, Tido Gaspar, invited us to his country and promised me his latest book – *Mille et une femmes* – he is a poet and a playwright. The drinks were copious – brandy, all sorts of wines, champagne; and there were very good sandwiches. The Bürgermeister of Krummhübel was also present and whispered to me confidentially that he was highly intrigued by me – qu'est-ce-que je fichais dans cette galère? The party was to go on until late, but at 2 a.m. I suggested that our group leave.

Friday, 14 April It is spring: crocuses are springing up everywhere.

Madonna Blum and I have decided to hitch a ride to Berlin with Hans-Georg Studnitz's bus, which is going back tomorrow. Madonna is going on leave. I will be playing truant.

Saturday, 15 April Got up at 5 a.m. and met Madonna Blum at the agreed rendezvous. A huge white charcoal-driven monster appeared, driven by a jolly Austrian. The three other passengers were also Austrian. The bus normally carries thirty. Part of the journey was by *Autobahn* and we kept having to stop while the driver stoked his boiler. At Königswusterhausen, where we dropped off one of our passengers, an air-raid was in progress; many fighter planes were circling overhead and there were several craters on the side of the road. But soon the all-clear sounded and we drove on to Berlin, where we were dropped off at the Innsbrücker Platz.

At the Gersdorffs' I found Maria and Baron Korff. She boiled some eggs for me and suddenly Papa walked in. He is in Berlin for Russian Easter. I rang up Gottfried Bismarck, who informed me that Loremarie Schönburg was staying at the Hotel Central, near the Friedrichstrasse railway station. Since it is very difficult to get a hotel room nowadays, this must be Count Helldorf's doing. I called up and asked her to book me one too. Spent most of the afternoon with Maria and then walked over to the hotel through the Tiergarten, which is a sorry sight. Generally, the shabbiness of Berlin is striking and depressing.

On Unter den Linden I passed the Hotel Bristol. At first glance it did not look too bad, as the front façade is still there, balconies and all. But the back is a complete shambles: telephone receivers, bath tiles, chandeliers, bits of carpet, broken mirrors, chipped statues and plaster everywhere.

At the Hotel Central I was received with marked politeness and was immediately given a room. I ordered supper and hopped into bed for a nap. Two hours later, Loremarie, Tony Saurma, Alexandra von Bredow (Gottfried's niece), Kicker Stumm and another friend appeared and we sat drinking brandy and chatting till midnight.

Despite all efforts to hide her and the endeavours of her very capable lawyer, Dr Langbehn (who was at the time himself under a cloud and is now in jail), Sigrid Görtz's Jewish mother has again been arrested – this time for good. Nothing more can be done about it and I am desperately sorry for her. All this reminds me of a memorable session a couple of years ago with her and Loremarie in the Lehndorff kitchen, where we had discussed these monstrous anti-Jewish persecutions. Somebody had given me a bottle of Benedictine and we sat drinking it out of beer glasses with our 'supper', which consisted of dry sausage. It is the only time I ever got tipsy. I woke up still at the Lehndorffs'; Loremarie had made herself up a bed in the sitting room.

Dr Carl Langbehn had long been close to the anti-Nazi group centred around former Ambassador von Hassell and former Prussian Finance Minister Dr J. Popitz. Thanks to his occasional visits to Switzerland, he had also acted as contact with Allied circles there. But he had also had contacts to Himmler, whom Popitz hoped to detach from Hitler. Arrested in September 1943, he was cruelly tortured and finally executed.

BERLIN *Sunday, 16 April* On an empty stomach I sped off to church to take Communion; alas in vain. There was such a crowd, mostly refugees and deportees from Soviet Russia, that I could not even get near the entrance. After a fist fight with some brute who burst into the telephone booth and tried to push me out, I rang up Loremarie Schönburg and returned to the hotel. Presently Tony Saurma appeared and we drove over in his car to the Hotel Eden for lunch. One goes in now by the service entrance, as the front is still non-existent. But it already has fifty habitable rooms! We got a table easily and had an extraordinary meal, consisting of radishes with butter and delicious venison schnitzels (unrationed). We first had cocktails, then several wines, then champagne, topping it off with a bottle of Tony's brandy. We had not eaten so well in months.

We packed up part of the meal in paper napkins and took it over to Maria Gersdorff's, where we found Gottfried Cramm and Papa. Gottfried is at present very low as he has been asked by Sweden not to return. He was a frequent visitor there, owing to his friendship with the old King, with whom he shared a passion for tennis. Could this be a British intrigue?

We stayed at Maria's nearly all afternoon; then Tony left and I headed for the hotel alone, as I had to be back at Krummhübel on Monday morning and could not afford to miss my train.

KRUMMHÜBEL *Tuesday, 18 April* Have left Jeannette S.'s chalet and moved to my new room, which is half an hour's walk from the office; this has many advantages. The room has a large balcony with a lovely view.

At Krummhübel I ran straight into the Betze's, to whom I confessed where I had spent the weekend; otherwise nobody seems to be aware of my escapade.

Then Loremarie arrived with a huge suitcase. We towed it up the hill together. She is pleasantly impressed by the pretty surroundings but is determined to stay only a short while.

Saturday, 22 April I am beginning to realise how difficult it is to work with Loremarie Schönburg, precisely because we are such close friends.

Monday, 24 April A long talk with Loremarie Schönburg, who is sulking as she blames *me* for her having been transferred to Krummhübel. It is difficult for me to tell her that the real reason why she is here is that because of her imprudent scheming, her very presence in Berlin endangers people who (though she does not know this) are far more involved in what is to come than she is. Over supper we had another long talk and this cleared the atmosphere somewhat.

Tomorrow I go back to Berlin for a couple of weeks.

BERLIN *Tuesday, 25 April* Loremarie Schönburg brought me to the station and helped carry my suitcase. Until Görlitz – two hours away – things were fairly comfortable; I even had a seat. But at Görlitz our carriage was for some unknown reason uncoupled and we all had to get out and find seats elsewhere. I stood all the way to Berlin.

Was delighted to see Alex Werth and Adam Trott again. It was like old times. We had a long talk before I joined Judgie Richter in his office. Everybody is furious, as they have been assigned new premises in a neighbouring house where working conditions are more than primitive; there is not even a telephone. So they have decided to move to the Karlsbader Hotel, which still has vacancies. Adam took me back to his house for tea, after which he drove me to the S-Bahn.

I reached Potsdam rather late to find Gottfried Bismarck, Rudger Essen and Jean-Georges Hoyos waiting for me for dinner. Melanie is in the country. Hitler's interpreter, Ambassador Paul Schmidt, has had a bad motor accident – two skull fractures. I hope he recovers, for he is a nice and decent man. There has also been a bad plane crash in which Generaloberst Hube was killed. He had just received the diamonds to his Oak Leaves.

Wednesday, 26 April Am struggling with the layout of a new magazine Dr Six is trying to put out.

Spent the evening with Maria Gersdorff. I see so little of them both and they are invariably such dears and so kind to me! They have fixed up the ground floor somewhat, so one can sit there, but it is still very cold. The little square in front of the house looks better too; peach trees and hyacinths bloom among the ruins – a small oasis.

Thursday, 27 April Saw Count Helldorf this morning. Some rude official tried to stop me, but I got in nevertheless. He was charming to me, as usual, which makes it very difficult for me to form an opinion of what he is really like; so many of my friends distrust him. However, I do value Gottfried Bismarck's judgement highly and am therefore determined to like him. He dropped me off at the Hotel Adlon. I sat next to him in front; behind sat two important police officials. I felt pretty 'safe', there being nobody higher in rank in the Berlin police force than these three.

Lunched with Tütü Stumm. The Adlon is a Tower of Babel, where the last of the Mohicans converge. Cocktail parties being now 'out', anybody and everybody I have ever met at such functions and who have thus far survived drift in here at least once a day. Today, for instance, I found Franz-Egon

Fürstenberg, Helga Nehring, Lally Horstmann, Fritzi Schulenburg (a former Vice-President of the Berlin police under Helldorf), the Lorenz girls, Karl Salm . . . There is something weird about this last-ditch atmosphere.

After lunch I dropped in on Percy Frey at the Swiss Legation. It's good, occasionally, to feel neutral ground under one's feet. Then went off to see the artist Leo Malinowski, who lives in Nikolassee, a delightful Berlin suburb at this time of the year, with the crocuses blooming everywhere, and almond trees in blossom.

Sat over coffee with Leo in his little flat. He has a charming old mother who lives with him; nice, typically Russian intellectual atmosphere. Leo is deeply depressed. One of his closest friends, who worked for *Das Reich* (Goebbels' sheet) and was often in our office, has just committed suicide in prison. Leo suspects he was made to do so. The artists are having a particularly hard time these days. The young ones are all mobilised, if not dead; and the older ones seem to have gone into hiding, as, needless to say, their views are mostly highly non-conformist; so either way they are having trouble surviving.

I drank so much coffee that everything seemed vague and wobbly for the rest of the day. Coffee is the only thing I drink in great quantities whenever I can: it seems to act as a substitute for everything else that is missing. I have practically given up smoking.

I then went straight back to Potsdam. Gottfried Bismarck was alone. One can talk about anything with him, he is always so understanding; but when he is surrounded by people who irritate him, he gets skittish and acts like a nervous horse.

Friday, 28 April Rudger Essen drives me into Berlin every morning. Unfortunately he is about to go back to Stockholm for good very soon. We will miss him much; he is as calm as a rock in a stormy sea and his pipe never leaves his mouth. His colleagues are now throwing goodbye parties for him from which he returns early in the morning in a rather inebriated state.

At the office I found everyone very jumpy: 'Luftgefahr 15 – höchste Alarmstufe'. This means an imminent very heavy raid. Surprisingly, nothing happened. At 2 p.m. Dr Six and Alex Werth suggested that I accompany them to the Foreign Press Club to talk shop over lunch. The Club is now in the suburbs, as the very handsome building in the centre of town which used to house it has been reduced to rubble. We drove through parts of Berlin where nothing is left standing and found Adam Trott going in to lunch with two of his own friends. We got a table in the middle of the room surrounded by German newspapermen and A.A. people. Hans-Georg Studnitz's boss, Gesandter Schmidt was there too. He does not get on well with Six (who does?) and in order to irritate him, he now came up to me to shake hands and in an audible whisper muttered: 'Don't tell him what we talked about in Krummhübel.'

Thanks to Alex Werth lunch went off satisfactorily. We talked about Krummhübel personnel problems; some of the girls there are getting restless. Six seems to be getting used to my turning up here, sometimes unexpectedly. Apart from enquiring what I am doing and when I plan to leave, he no longer asks any questions.

Supper at Studnitz's with Berndt Mumm and Vollrat Watzdorf. Hans Flotow had lent him his flat for the occasion. I was the only girl. Studnitz always keeps a party going. He is witty and cruel, loves a good story and is ready to sacrifice anybody for it. We laughed so much this time that I got a kind of cramp. This does not happen often and does one good.

Saturday, 29 April The morning started lovely. Rudger Essen dropped me off at the U.F.A. film studio offices in the Leipzigerstrasse, in the centre of town, where I was to collect some photographs of German actresses. I had hardly begun wading through their material when the sirens started to howl. We were fast hustled into a deep and roomy cellar. There were more than 500 people, all of them employees of U.F.A. Two girls with whom I sat near the entrance were learning poetry by heart and I had plunged into Mme Tabouis's autobiography, *Ils l'ont appellée Cassandre*, when there was a crash and the lights went out. Immediately auxiliary generators came on. Notwithstanding the seemingly efficient organisation here, the thought that I might be buried alive, with nobody knowing where I was, was very depressing. The *flak* was very violent and bombs kept exploding nearby. Several nurses flitted around with their first-aid kits and every ten minutes two men had to volunteer to go and pump fresh air into the cellar.

An hour later it was over. Hurriedly I finished choosing pictures of pretty faces and went on to the Deutscher Verlag, the floors of which the Vendeuvre boys used to sweep, but which has become chaotic after several bombs hit it a few months ago.

The air was already heavy with smoke and my eyes smarted badly. I had hoped to catch a tram back to the office, but gave up at the sight of a vast crater at the Leipzigerstrasse-Mauerstrasse junction. A mine had just exploded there, wrecking the lines. The hole was about four metres deep and equally wide and the buildings on all sides were burning brightly. But because it was broad daylight it somehow did not look quite as frightening.

It took me more than an hour to walk back to the office. This time, it is the administrative centre of the town that has been hit. As I passed the Karlsbader Hotel, to which our office had planned to move, I saw much commotion. The building itself was no more: three bombs had gone through it. I ran into Frau von Carnap looking rather shaken. She and Hannele Ungelter were sheltering in the cellar to the right of the corridor when the left-hand cellar got a direct hit. Two girls lost their lives there and many people were wounded. I heard later that it took forty-eight hours to get them all out. Hannele said it had happened so quickly that they did not even have time to be scared. The neighbouring house, in which there was army personnel, collapsed on top of those who were standing in the street with a hose. One man went on screaming from inside the building for hours afterwards 'Wenn ich nur bewustlos wäre!' ['If only I were unconscious!']. Nobody could reach him.

I put in a hasty appearance at the office and then went on to lunch at Maria Gersdorff's, where I found Gottfried Cramm, the Bagges and others. Hans-Georg Studnitz joined us; he said that a car was waiting for us at the Wilhelmstrasse to drive us out to the Pfuels', where we are spending the weekend.

We started off for the Wilhelmstrasse by Underground, but had to get out on the way and continue on foot as the line ahead was wrecked. The back of the Anhalter station looked pretty grim. During this morning's raid an express train had come hurtling into it, burning like a torch. Three other trains were waiting to leave; two got off before the bomb came down, but the third was blocked.

On reaching the Wilhelmstrasse, at last, we were told that there was no car. We waited hopefully for a bit and then decided to take the train.

At the station we ran into Blankenhorn, a rucksack on his back. He was in the happiest of moods, being just back from Italy. He was now headed for Switzerland by some devious route. In the rush I forgot Mme Tabouis's book on the ticket counter. Instant panic, for the book is banned in Germany! I finally retrieved it from the ticket vendor – some passenger had handed it in. But meanwhile we had missed two trains. Hans-Georg started telephoning all his friends for help and finally we were picked up by some good Samaritan and deposited at C. C.'s, where we had a whacking supper and coffee, cooked on a spirit lamp fed with eau-de-Cologne, as there is no other fuel available.

C.C.'s house is surrounded by estates that have been rented by foreign diplomats who have been bombed out of their homes in town. We live in the attic, as most of the house is occupied by Spaniards and Rumanians.

Sunday, 30 April I had a long talk with two Russian maids whom C. C. Pfuel employs. One of them, aged twenty-four, has lost her husband and her only child in a raid; she is quite alone in the world: a friendly nice girl who is delighted to speak Russian, she has a very realistic attitude towards her plight and sees the future very dispassionately. The other girl is only eighteen. Dressed in black, with a white apron, she curtseys whenever she is spoken to, is very pretty and could be a little French *soubrette* out of a play. She is fresh from Kiev and we talk a mixture of Russian-Polish-Ukrainian but under-stand each other very well. The servants in Jahnsfelde are a motley group: these Russian girls, a German cook and nurse, many Spaniards for the diplomats and a French butler, who rules the roost and is addressed by the others as *Moussiou*.

After lunch we listened to the official communiqué: yesterday's air-raid was described as a *Terrorangriff* [terror raid]. I fear that the parents will again be very worried, as I cannot telephone and reassure them. Later Tony Saurma drove us over to Buchow for tea with the Horstmanns. The Spanish Ambassador, Vidal, and Federico Dies were there. The latter told me the sad details of Maria Pilar and Ignacio Oyarzabal's death. He was sent to identify the bodies. They had won their *couchettes* from another Spanish couple in a card game; the losers survived. The only consolation is that they died instantly. Vidal asked many questions about Krummhübel, as all the foreign missions will be evacuated there eventually. I wonder whether they will ever make it. Lally Horstmann said that Elisabeth Chavchavadze now heads an Allied ambulance unit in Morocco. We had all been such close friends before the war . . .

In the evening at Jahnsfelde we sat around the fire discussing Rasputin.

Monday, 1 May Am back in Berlin. The weather continues bad. It is rumoured that the R.A.F. dropped a wreath over Heinrich Wittgenstein's grave; it makes all this killing even more futile.

After work I sat for a long time at Maria Gersdorff's with Gottfried Cramm, with whom I am getting to be good friends. Reserved at first, he now begins to impress me as exceptionally warm-hearted. He showed me a red leather frame with three photos of the same girl. I recognised Barbara Hutton.

In the evening Mozart's *Entführung aus dem Serail* with Percy Frey. Then a late snack at the Adlon. Percy is a cosy person; he is detached and yet he understands some things *à demi-mot*, in which he is more like an Anglo-Saxon than a Swiss. He escorted me home on foot through the Tiergarten and was staggered by the ruins around our house. We had to climb over hillocks of rubble and he was quite fascinated. I am not. It has been too uncomfortable too long living like rabbits in a warren.

Dr Hans ('Percy') Frey was at the time in charge of the section of the Swiss Legation in Berlin that safeguarded the interests of some of the countries with which Germany was at war.

Tuesday, 2 May This morning I managed to exchange Percy Frey's meat coupons, which had expired, against a big sausage. Then, at the office, I staged a small auction and a girl bought it off me for a little less than it was worth, but paying for it in valid coupons, which I will now return to Percy. I am very proud!

Stayed at the office until late; then drove with Adam Trott back to his home and had supper with him there. Our friendship is somewhat overwhelming, and I have consciously avoided this so far. He is a man completely out of the ordinary. All his thoughts and efforts focus on things and values of a higher order, to which neither the mood of this country, nor that of the Allies seem attuned. He belongs to a more civilised world – something, alas, neither side does. He drove me home late.

Wednesday, 3 May Had supper at Hanna Bredow's, Gottfried Bismarck's sister, in Potsdam. Hanna's daughter Philippa was at the Air Ministry during Saturday's raid. She tore out from there, with the porter trying to stop her, because she had a suitcase stashed away at the Hotel Esplanade that she wanted to save. The Ministry was hit by eighteen bombs, some of them going right through its seven storeys. In the cellar (where she should have taken refuge) fifty people were killed and many more wounded. I myself was quite close when this happened and could easily have sought shelter there too. So it does seem only a question of luck after all.

The fifteen-year-old Bredow son, Herbert, is about to be mobilised in the *flak*. He has beautiful eyes. If he survives the war, he will be a lady-killer. It is astonishing how precocious he is and how violent his feelings about the present regime. Last year his mother read my hand and predicted that I would leave Germany, never to return. I now asked her to read my hand again. She did and confirmed her prediction.

Thursday, 4 May In the afternoon before going back to Potsdam, Adam Trott and I went for a long walk in the Grunewald. It rains in showers but still it is spring and although cold, there are flowers and shrubs in bloom everywhere. Adam told me of his first love and his life in England and China. There is always another angle to him.

Sunday, 7 May Got up early to go to a small Russian Orthodox church, not far from the Zoo. It has no cellar. Was waiting for my turn to confess, when the sirens sounded. There were not many people and most of them were *Ostarbeiter* [Russian workers], some of them praying aloud with set faces. Nobody moved and the choir continued to sing. How much nicer it was to be there, rather than to cower in some anonymous shelter! All the candles round the icons were alight and the singing sounded truly inspired. I confessed to an unknown priest who spoke of 'love your neighbour', 'when you go home', etc. – all that while the sirens howled. Outside, at first, there was total silence and I was beginning to think that the planes had been turned back when, all at once, they were right over our heads. Masses of them, wave after wave. The weather being very cloudy, the *flak* could not shoot and they flew very low. The droning of their engines was as loud as the crashing of the bombs, the one indistinguishable from the other. It was as if one was standing under a railway bridge with an express train thundering overhead. Suddenly the choir stopped dead. The congregation tried bravely to take over, but it sang falteringly. At one point my legs simply gave way and tottering over to the altar, I sat down on the steps. Near me stood a nun with a lovely face and it comforted me somewhat to be near her. She bent down and whispered: 'One must not be frightened, for God and all the saints are with us!' and when I looked dubious, she added: 'Nothing can ever happen during Holy Mass.' She seemed so convinced that I was instantly reassured. Father Michael went on chanting as if he did not even hear the noise outside and towards Communion time it abated. By the time the service was over, I felt fifty years older and completely drained.

Later I heard that there had been fifteen hundred planes over Berlin that morning. In the early days of the war thirty seemed to us dangerous enough. It is strange that although I feel, theoretically, perfectly resigned to the idea of dying under the bombs, when the droning of the planes and the crash of the explosions start, I get physically paralysed with fright and with every raid this fear seems to increase.

Lunched at the Gersdorffs', where I found Maria and Gottfried Cramm alone. Trapped in a cellar in Wilmersdorf, Gottfried had tried to read Schopenhauer, but could not keep a straight face, as he found himself surrounded by old ladies with towels tucked round their chins and wet sponges stuck protruding from them like beards; this supposedly affords protection against phosphorus burns.

Later we walked about the centre of the town. Unter den Linden, Wilhemstrasse, Friedrichstrasse had all been badly hit. There was much smoke and many new craters, but American bombs – the Americans come during the day, the British at night – seem to cause less damage than English ones. These explode horizontally, whereas the former go deeper, so that the neighbouring buildings collapse less easily.

Monday, 8 May Arrived at the office early. It was rather deserted. They had again announced 'Luftgefahr 15', the highest degree of danger. I tried to get hold of some 'important' papers but the secretary would not let me have them, as all documents must apparently stay in the safe downstairs until the danger is over. Found instead a story in *Life* that commented flatteringly on the work of our office, as compared to similar information jobs done in the United States.

Alex Werth had just returned from some trip with a large tin of Nescafé. We settled down to a second breakfast and a smoke.

Presently, we were told that the planes had flown on elsewhere. We had hardly sat down again to work when the sirens began to wail and we filed downstairs into a bunker in the square, a funny little box of concrete with a flight of steps leading into the bowels of the earth – the Underground station Nollendorfplatz. This has endless corridors with a rather thin layer of earth overhead. All along the corridors there are little tile walls jutting out in different directions; they have been put up hastily at half height – ostensibly to catch the air pressure 'if . . .'

We tried to avoid standing under what we thought were houses, preferring the open streets, where nothing could crash down on top of us except the bombs themselves. People kept streaming in. Judgie Richter and I stayed together. As the explosions came nearer, Judgie got fidgety; he is altogether in a bad way, worrying about his family, etc. I tried to distract him with small talk but he interrupted me – 'if it bursts in through the ceiling, you must throw yourself on your tummy and hide your head in the crook of your arm . . .' Another colleague chose this moment to tell us the gory details of how his house got a direct hit again last night and was totally destroyed. This raid seemed to be a heavy one, but soon the all-clear sounded.

On returning to the office we found that the water pipes had burst. I went down to the street to fetch a canful from the corner pump, as we wanted to cheer ourselves up with some more of Alex's coffee.

Percy Frey, with whom I had a luncheon date, turned up and we wandered down the street to the Hotel Eden. Here three bombs had crashed into the courtyard, blowing the whole inside to smithereens again, although the walls still stood. Managers and waiters, their napkins tucked under their arms, were running about in the street, trying very inefficiently to clear away bricks and mortar. In the middle of the street there was a huge crater where a bomb landed near the exit of the cellar. As all the water pipes had burst, people trapped in the cellar were now swimming their way across the crater. So many bombs have fallen in Berlin again that the streets are half-submerged. The town also smells heavily of gas.

We went on to the Hotel am Steinplatz, lunched there and walked back to the office through the rain. Percy may come to Königswart at Whitsuntide.

In the evening Claus B. fetched me at Maria Gersdorff's and after supper drove me back to Potsdam. At times such as these 'all men are brothers' and I am beginning to speak to him, after avoiding him for years. He had started by following me in the streets and then one day strolled into the office, just like that. I was amazed at his cheek. I have never understood who he is or what he does. His looks are striking, but it seems peculiar that a man of his age should be travelling around Europe freely, as he does, without being clapped into uniform. He has tried again and again to become friends and has even offered to act as 'family postman' between us and Georgie and our cousins in Paris, where he seems to go often. All this I have politely but firmly declined. On the other hand, he has contrived to meet the cousins in Paris anyway and has brought me a letter from them. He also knows Antoinette Croy. But his occupation remains a complete question mark.

Tuesday, 9 May Am going back to Krummhübel tomorrow. Adam Trott drove me over to his house for supper. I am dragging many books back to Krummhübel and he helped carry them. Later, a young friend of his, Werner von Haeften (a brother of our personnel chief, who is on the staff of the Replacement Army here), dropped in and they had a long talk in another room. Shortly after Adam had brought me back to Potsdam, the sirens wailed. This was another *Störflug* [nuisance raid], when many planes circle around, dropping bombs haphazardly. I packed and did not go to sleep until they had flown away.

KRUMMHÜBEL *Wednesday, 10 May* Was up at six and after a big breakfast left, lugging a very heavy suitcase. As I had no special travel permit, I feared I might have to stand all the way, but a good-natured conductor agreed to let me use a private compartment reserved for the *Reichsbahndirektion* [railway management]; he locked me in and I travelled this way all alone, lying flat on my back on a well padded seat, the sun shining pleasantly.

I reached Krummhübel at three to find that Loremarie Schönburg was still there, in bed, feeling sorry for herself.

She wants to get back to Berlin come what may; for her nothing else matters; she is even unwilling to keep up appearances. I do understand that if one stays here all the time everything gets just too unreal and remote. Luckily for me, from now on I must be in Berlin for at least ten days every month.

The Russians have retaken Sebastopol. The Germans do not seem to have put up much of a defence.

Friday, 12 May Count Schulenburg is back from Paris and has brought us many small presents. Loremarie Schönburg's aunt, Gretl Rohan, has invited us for the weekend to Sichrow, their place in Bohemia. The Count has agreed to come too, but we are anxious to be rid of his assistant. Could the latter be there just to keep an eye on him?

SICHROW *Saturday, 13 May* After lunching off an excellent goose, we left for Sichrow. Since the Germans took the country over in March 1939 the Protektorat (as Czechoslovakia is now known) can only be visited with a special *laissez-passer*. Count Schulenburg has obtained one for me; it is valid for several months. Our drive through the mountains was beautiful – vast deserted forests with much snow atop the hills. The guards at the Czech border examined our driver very carefully. He is a soldier and there appear to be many deserters hiding out in the Protektorat these days. The authorities often descend on the villages, hoping to sniff them out.

On reaching Sichrow, we found only one daughter – out of six – at home; the entire family had taken off to the neighbouring small town – Turnau – where the youngest Rohan girl had just had an appendix removed. They did not seem to expect us, which is a bit embarrassing. Luckily, Prince Rohan and Count Schulenburg get on well. I have just enjoyed the rare luxury of a real hot bath.

Sunday, 14 May Church, with beautiful singing in Czech, and then a tour of the grounds. The weather is mild but the famous azaleas and rhododendrons are not yet out, although spring is further advanced here than in Krumm-hübel. Everywhere tulips and daffodils are shooting up out of the grass. Gretl Rohan joined us for lunch. Before that, I went to have a look at the cows being milked. One of the daughters, Marie-Jeanne, then distributed some among the tenants and I had a good drink myself on the sly.

After an excellent meal that consisted mainly of game with cranberry jelly, we all lay in the sun on the lawn and even got quite tanned. We must leave very early tomorrow morning.

KRUMMHÜBEL *Monday, 15 May* The Rohan children came to say goodbye before their lessons. They study hard from eight to one and then again all afternoon. There are quite a number of tutors staying in the house, which also shelters refugees from various bombed-out towns.

We loitered over breakfast and got back to Krummhübel only at eleven. Our offices had been notified of our absence, but someone saw us getting out of Count Schulenburg's car and that immediately caused envious irritation. Our friendship with him is decidedly frowned upon.

Tuesday, 16 May The Allied invasion of Europe is expected any day now, with the papers full of 'our preparedness'. It is difficult to work; one lives from one day to the next. Colleagues keep vanishing for 'family reasons', which usually means bombed-out homes.

Wednesday, 17 May My accordion is progressing.

Thursday, 18 May Discovered that while I was in Berlin someone broke into my cupboard and stole my baptismal cross and chain, also my supply of coffee. The loss of the cross makes me desperate. Had a talk with our housekeeper and she called in the police. In the evening we were awaiting Blankenhorn when in strode a moustachioed Wachtmeister [sergeant] who seemed far more interested in my accordion playing than in the theft. He drew up a report and searched our two rooms unsuccessfully. At that juncture Blankenhorn arrived and thought I was being arrested.

Friday, 19 May Blankenhorn has suggested that Loremarie Schönburg and I move to what they call the *Gästehaus* – a very pretty and large chalet in the middle of a small wood reserved for important visitors who have never yet shown up.

KÖNIGSWART *Friday, 26 May* Took off with Loremarie Schönbürg for a short stay in Königswart. Count Schulenburg gave us a lift, as he was driving down to his own country place, which is not very far from the Metternichs' – a wonderful way of avoiding a dreadful train journey. Although I had informed the office of our absence, we met like conspirators behind the station, Loremarie and I going by different ways so as not to attract attention. We even carried our clothes in bundles, to avoid being seen with suitcases.

The weather was not too good but the countryside was perfectly lovely, with lilacs and apple trees in blossom. We lunched by the roadside. Our progress was slowed a little by Loremarie, who every now and then caught sight of the castle of one of her numerous relatives and suggested, to the indignation of our driver, that we turn off *zum Jausen* [for tea]. We finally did stop off in Teplitz and had tea with Alfy Clary and his sister, Elisalex Baillet-Latour. It was wonderful to see them again. I had not been here since 1940, during the French campaign. Even then they were so worried about their boys. Now Ronnie, the eldest and most promising, has been killed in Russia and Marcus and Charlie are both at the front. I found poor Alfy very changed. The Count dropped us off in Marienbad. He is coming to Königswart on Sunday.

We arrived famished, and while we had a bite, the parents and Hans-Georg Studnitz kept us company (he has come down from Berlin for the weekend). Then Paul Metternich and Tatiana themselves arrived from Vienna. Tatiana has brought back a lot of new clothes. We sat up till 5 a.m. Paul is still very thin and nervous but he is in a happier mood.

Saturday, 27 May Got up very late and did nothing until lunch time. The party is growing larger: Meli Khevenhüller and Marietti Studnitz, Hans-Georg's wife, are arriving tonight. The weather is now marvellous.

Have had long and difficult talks with both parents. They seem more interested in past history than in the way present events may affect our individual lives in the near future; also they keep worrying about Georgie in Paris, who is, admittedly, in a precarious position studying at the Sciences Po with no money and, we hear, involved in something risky.

Soon after Missie's brother moved to France in the autumn of 1942, he became involved in Resistance activities, which continued until the liberation of Paris in August 1944.

After supper Percy Frey arrived. Paul Metternich and Tatiana took care of him. Both Mamma and Papa invariably raise their eyebrows at any new male friend of mine.

Sunday, 28 May After an early Mass we all lay on rugs in the garden, soaking up the sun. Hans Berchem and Count Schulenburg joined us for lunch. This kept the parents busy and amused, while we packed tea in a hamper and took off in the carriage for a picnic.

More and more weekend guests with less and less space in the house. I am spending the night in Tatiana's sitting-room. Judgie Richter is also here, walking his kids around the garden.

Monday, 29 May Spent the day again out of doors. Both Papa and Mamma are annoyed that I do not devote more time to them. They simply cannot see that after the frequent horrors of our daily life, every brief moment of relaxation and gaiety is a gift of the gods, which one tries to enjoy to the utmost.

Marietti Studnitz told depressing stories about the nastiness of the people whom she has taken into her house after they were bombed out of their own home. This war is beginning to turn many people into embittered animals.

KRUMMHÜBEL *Saturday, 3 June* Loremarie Schönburg left for Berlin this morning, this time for good. She was delighted, as she really hated the place, but I feel pretty low; for all our problems with her, I know I am going to miss her.

Gesandter Schleier, who was until now the right-hand man of Abetz, the German Ambassador in Paris, has been appointed to head our Personnel Department. He replaces Hans-Bernd von Haeften, who has been often sick recently. I am afraid that, compared to the regime under the latter and his predecessor, Josias Rantzau, we are going to have a rough time. Schleier is said to be a nasty fellow and his activities in Paris have given him an unsavoury reputation. He certainly looks the part: a fat walrus with a Hitler-type moustache and tortoise-shell spectacles. He is now in Krummhübel to look us over. Today, we were ordered to the Tannenhof to meet him. He made a thunderously patriotic speech.

A former businessman, Dr R. Schleier had, after the fall of France, headed the Nazi party organisation there and then been appointed deputy to and watchdog over ambassador Abetz (who was occasionally at odds with Berlin policies). Later in the war Ribbentrop was to assign him to prepare anti-Jewish drives abroad. One of the consequences would be the extermination of the Hungarian Jews in the summer of 1944.

This evening there was a *Kameradschaftsabend* at the Goldener Frieden, which we were all obliged to attend. Luckily, some of the people here have a sense of humour and we could exchange a wink occasionally, especially when the glee singing began. Madonna was made to play the accordion and they were all very disappointed when I refused to perform.

Sunday, 4 June Today the Allies occupied Rome. Am wondering how Irena managed, whether she stayed on or went to Venice. At least for her, the war is now over.

Tuesday, 6 June The long-awaited 'D-Day'! The Allies have landed in Normandy. We had been told so much about the famous *Atlantikwall* and its supposedly impregnable defences; now we shall see! But it is dreadful to think of the many probable victims of this last round.

It would indeed take another 8 months and millions of more lives lost to bring the war in Europe to an end.

We spend the days very quietly, visiting each other for tea. I seem to be the only one who is not too unhappy here. The thought that one can sleep through the night is such a relief. Of course, my situation is easier because whenever it gets too claustrophobic, Adam Trott in Berlin sends a telegram or I invent some meeting there and board a train without asking anybody's permission. This is in theory forbidden, but they have got so used to seeing me periodically disappear for a couple of days that even Büttner no longer protests.

BERLIN *Wednesday, 14 June* On arriving at the office this morning, I found that I had been summoned to Berlin for a meeting with Dr Six tomorrow. I took the afternoon train and arrived in Berlin at nightfall to find that Loremarie Schönburg has been catapulted back to Krummhübel, so I have just missed her.

Thursday, 15 June Am living at the Gersdorffs'. Now that I come to Berlin for only a few days at a time, I prefer to stay in town rather than commute back and forth from the Bismarcks' in Potsdam.

Had both meals with Maria. Tonight we were alone as Heinz is on duty at the Kommandatur. An air-raid is in full swing. The usual mines which I fear far more than the bombs, although they only drop about eighty each time.

Friday, 16 June Dr Six is in Stockholm and I must now await his return. This happens often: he flies into a rage and summons me up from Krummhübel; by the time I get here he has usually forgotten what it was all about and I can then relax for a few days.

Judgie Richter gets into a stew about Six badgering us all the time in this manner, but Adam Trott considers our problems peanuts compared to his own present preoccupations and he is quite right. I feel often ashamed and frustrated at not being more deeply involved in something really worthwhile, but what can I, a foreigner, do?

By now even Himmler had lost faith in Germany's victory and was seeking to establish secret contact with the Allies. Dr Six's trip to Stockholm in June 1944 (on which Alexander Werth accompanied him) was one such attempt. It was unsuccessful, the British having refused to have anything to do with him.

Saturday, 17 June Dr Six returned today and immediately hauled Judgie Richter and me into his office to discuss the new illustrated publication he is thinking of putting out. He does not seem to realise that no technical facilities exist anymore for *any* kind of publication, whether illustrated or not, as everyone we would need has been called up, so that one just talks in circles.

Sunday, 18 June A friend arrived from Paris with letters from Georgie and Antoinette Croy. She has just married a dashing, much decorated officer by the name of Jürgen von Görne.

Monday, 19 June In the morning, the office. I no longer put in a regular appearance. For the building has been bombed so repeatedly, everybody is so cramped, that no one objects if I do not claim a desk of my own. I usually camp in Judgie Richter's secretariat, but the four girls there make so much noise, sometimes even playing the gramophone or telling one another's fortune, that I can never get anything done. So I just keep up with current developments, see my friends, grab as many foreign magazines as I can get hold of and head back to Krummhübel.

Lunched at Sigrid Görtz's. Nothing has been heard of her mother since her arrest; presumably, she has been sent to a ghetto in the East.

This was the 'model ghetto' of Theresienstadt – a 'Potemkin village' concentration camp to which, occasionally, foreign visitors would be brought and which, barring the armed guards, looked almost like an ordinary settlement. Countess von Görtz was one of the relatively few survivors.

Supper with friends. I was the only female; this happens a lot nowadays, as most women have left or been evacuated from Berlin because of the raids.

KRUMMHÜBEL *Tuesday, 20 June* Took the early train back to Krummhübel, where I found Loremarie Schönburg and a Hungarian cousin installed at the house.

Loremarie does not get on too well with our housekeeper, who keeps ringing up Blankenhorn to complain. He says he feels like a nursemaid.

Loremarie really is the limit sometimes, washing sweaters, dumping them wet on the bed and forgetting to remove them. Next morning even the mattresses are soaked. We have been so lucky, Blankenhorn has been so kind, allowing us to stay here in the first place, that I wish she were more considerate.

Wednesday, 21 June Blankenhorn announced himself to come and read to us tonight. Last time he read Ronsard; he has good taste and reads well, in German better than in French. He is interesting to talk to and completely independent-minded, but one has the feeling that he is awaiting the collapse before venturing to put his hand to the tiller. In this he is very different from Adam Trott, which perhaps explains their friendship.

Thursday, 22 June Loremarie Schönburg is trying to get a certificate that will enable her to go back to Berlin, otherwise Dr Six will not allow her to leave Krummhübel. We make up a thermos full of the strongest coffee possible and some hard-boiled eggs which she will down just before being examined; she hopes this will set her pulse racing and do something to her general metabolism. Doctors are nowadays usually very severe. Actually, I myself cannot complain, as I have been sent twice to the mountains and once even to Italy. Monday I must again be in Berlin for a couple of days for what is supposed to be a 'very important' meeting.

KÖNIGSWART *Friday, 23 June* Arrived this morning very punctually at the office, had long talks with various people, made my presence well felt generally and then departed with a clear conscience to spend the weekend in Königswart. I had told Personnel I was merely stopping off there on my way to Berlin.

The journey was pretty awful. At Görlitz I had to wait hours for the Dresden train and when it arrived I could hardly squeeze in. Somebody tossed a bouncing baby into my arms and jumped into another carriage and I had to hold it all the way to Dresden. It screamed and fidgetted and I was in agony. I had had the unfortunate idea of taking my accordion along and that made my luggage still more unwieldy. But this time I had planned to leave a lot of my things with Tatiana, as I intend to move back to Berlin permanently soon, so as to be with my friends at this particular moment. And there I must be burdened with a minimum of belongings.

At Dresden the mother retrieved the infant and I waited another three hours for a train to Eger. On reaching Königswart I found the family for once alone.

Sunday, 25 June Spent most of the weekend trying to make plans for the future. Every time I come here it seems to us that it could be for the last time.

Monday, 26 June Yesterday at midnight Tatiana, Paul Metternich and I drove over to Marienbad to catch the Vienna train for Berlin. We sat in the carriage in front of the station until five in the morning – no train. Finally we were told that an earlier train had been derailed near Pilsen and that the line was cut. We now gave up as I would never have made it to Berlin in time for the meeting, which had been set for 3 p.m.

This time I am really embarrassed and worried, as this meeting is supposed to be particularly important. Have telegraphed Judgie Richter: 'Zug entgleist' ['train derailed']. It sounds like a bad joke. When Mamma got up she was very surprised to find us all back in our beds.

BERLIN *Tuesday, 27 June* This time our train was on time. But half an hour before reaching Berlin it stopped in the middle of cornfields, as a heavy air-raid had just been announced. Hundreds of planes could soon be seen flying overhead – a most disagreeable sensation, as they could easily have dropped some of their load on us. Everbody became very silent and we all seemed to have lost our colour. Air attacks on trains are among the worst; one feels so totally exposed, trapped and helpless. Paul Metternich alone seemed unconcerned. At first everybody hung out of the windows until an angry old gentleman shouted that 'they' would aim at all those uplifted faces shining in the sun. At which a young girl answered 'Erst recht, wenn sie Ihre Glatze sehen!' ['particularly when they catch sight of your bald pate!']. We were soon ordered to scatter in the fields. Tatiana, Paul and I sat in a ditch in the middle of the corn. From where we were, we could hear the bombs falling on the city and see the smoke and explosions. Six hours later, our train started off again but even then we had to circle Berlin and debarked in Potsdam. *Adieu* once more to my meeting, assuming it was ever held.

We walked over to the Palast Hotel, where Gottfried Bismarck had reserved rooms for us, his house being full. Potsdam itself had not been hit but the whole town was covered with dense yellow smoke from the fires in Berlin.

We washed and changed and then took the S-Bahn into Berlin. I proceeded straight to the office, while the others went over to the Gersdorffs'. As luck would have it, or rather to the contrary, Dr Six was still there and Judgie Richter, who, he says, is getting grey hair because of me, sent me in to him at once.

I assured him that the train really had been derailed but today's holocaust seemed to have softened him, for he was civil. In general, I understand that he rants about me in my absence but to my face he is always polite. Adam Trott hates him with a cold hatred and tells me that however amiable he may try to be, we must never forget what he represents. Six, for his part, seems grudgingly to realise what an extraordinary man Adam is and to be somehow fascinated by him and even to fear him. For Adam is perhaps the only man left in his entourage who is never afraid to speak up. He treats Six with infinite condescension and, curiously, the other one takes it.

At 1 a.m. that night another raid. I hurried Tatiana and Paul a little, as the shooting was already violent. At last they were dressed and we got down to the cellar, a dismal affair, rather like an old dungeon, narrow and high and full of hot-water pipes, which gave one nasty thoughts of being drenched, if hit, in boiling water. I am getting more and more nervous during air-raids. I could not even chat with Tatiana, as *Sprechen verboten* [no talking] was plastered all over the walls, probably so as not to use up oxygen should we be buried alive. Actually, I am even more frightened when Paul and Tatiana are with me than when I am alone and this is strange. Probably one's anxiety is heightened by fear for someone else. But Paul, like me, is anxious to be around just now and is always cooking up pretexts to come up to Berlin. Throughout all the noise, which was loud and frightening, he was plunged in a huge book about his ancestor, the Chancellor. After two hours we emerged.

Thursday, 29 June At eleven this morning there was a big meeting. Dr Six headed the long table; I sat between Adam Trott and Alex Werth at the other end. They are my only support and I would feel desperately lost without them. Adam kept shoving *streng geheim* [top secret] papers to me under the table – mostly news items from abroad. We kept up a whispered conversation *à trois* and smoked while the men were shouted at in turns. This morning Six was in a rotten mood and poor Judgie Richter at his right had a hard time calming the troubled waters. In between outbursts, Adam made sarcastic remarks which were swallowed by all present. I like the way he contradicts

Six. Later, he folded his arms and went to sleep. Meanwhile, I was preparing myself for the onslaught, as soon it would be my turn. Alex Werth whispered encouragement, reminding me of one of my friends, Frau Dr Horn, who, when she was roared at and did not know how to stem the flow, stood up and yelled at the top of her lungs 'Herr Gesandter SIX!' – at which, taken aback, he stopped dead. Sure enough, though I was last on the list, I, too, got a flow of invective. His dream is a German *Reader's Digest*, for which he would like to establish a printing shop in Krummhübel. He accused me of never coming up to scratch under the pretext that all technicians have been mobilised, and yet this is the gospel truth. As usual, nothing tangible emerged from a discussion that had lasted over three hours.

Lunched at the Gersdorffs', after which Tony Saurma drove Tatiana, Loremarie Schönburg and me around town to see the damage caused by yesterday's raid. This time the whole district around the Friedrichstrasse Bahnhof is completely gutted, including the Hotels Central and Continental. I had stayed with Loremarie in the Central for two days the last time I was in Berlin.

I had to leave a message at the Adlon and in the hall ran into Giorgio Cini. He has come all the way to Berlin to try and bribe the S.S. into setting his father, old Count Cini, free. When Italy changed sides last year, the latter (a one-time Minister of Finances of Mussolini) was arrested in Venice and has been in Dachau concentration camp, in an underground cell, for the past eight months. He suffers from angina pectoris and is in very bad shape. The Cinis have millions and Giorgio is willing to pay anything to get him out. He himself has changed a lot since I last saw him just before the war. He evidently is desperately worried. He adores his father and for many months did not know his whereabouts, nor whether he still lived. Now he was waiting for some big Gestapo man. Who knows? With that amount of determination and willpower – and money – he may succeed. He wants them to agree to transfer his father to an S.S. hospital and from there to Italy. His family has stayed on in Rome under the Allies, but he seems to be in touch with them.

In the end Giogio Cini succeeded in buying his father's freedom. He himself was to die in an accident soon after the war. The 'Cini Foundation' in Venice was named by his father after him.

FRIEDRICHSRUH *Saturday, 1 July* As I had to give up my hotel room in

Potsdam, I have moved back into town and am now at the Adlon. Otto Bismarck has asked Paul Metternich, Tatiana and me to Friedrichsruh, the family's famous estate near Hamburg, for the weekend. We have never been there and may never have a chance again, so we have accepted. Spent the morning at the office and then rushed over to the station, where the others were waiting. When we arrived, the Bismarcks were very surprised, as our telegram of acceptance had never reached them. Otto, in pyjamas, was taking an afternoon nap; Ann Mari and Giorgio Cini were in the garden. The latter, looking devastating in a pale blue shirt, reminded me of Venice that last summer of peace five years ago.

Sunday, 2 July Otto Bismarck had arranged a little shooting party – for boar – but nobody hit anything. The only boar we saw, as big as a young calf, stalked straight past Paul Metternich's stand. When Paul, deep in conversation with Ann Mari Bismarck, heard our exclamations, he fired wildly but naturally it got away. Otto was visibly put off, as he had given Paul the best stand.

After dinner we had a long discussion with a famous zoologist about the best way to get rid of Adolf. He said that in India natives use tigers' whiskers chopped very fine and mixed with food. The victim dies a few days later and nobody can detect the cause. But where do we find a tiger's whiskers?

Friedrichsruh is beautfully kept.

BERLIN *Monday, 3 July* Got up at 4 a.m. to get back to Berlin on time. Unfortunately, while leaving off my luggage at the Adlon I bumped into Schleier, our nasty new chief of personnel, who could thus see that I had been out of town (private travel is officially discouraged).

KRUMMHÜBEL *Tuesday, 4 July* Returned to Krummhübel to find that Mamma (whom I had invited to visit me there) had already arrived. F)r the moment she lives with us, but she cannot stay long, as we are not allowed to have guests. Count Schulenburg is still away and Loremarie Schönburg is back in Berlin, this time for good. She has even been allowed to take sick leave there. Everybody is surprised that Schleier has been so decent to her.

Wednesday, 5 July Go for long walks with Mamma, who finds the country beautiful and takes photographs tirelessly. I fear she will not see as much of me as she had hoped, as I spend a lot of time at the office and must be back in Berlin next week.

Madonna Blum gave a little dinner party for her, after which we played duos on our accordions. Count Schulenburg's assistant, Sch., has not returned from a trip to Switzerland. He gave the excuse of a broken leg when skiing, but this does not seem to be the real reason and I fear Schulenburg may have trouble on his account.

BERLIN *Monday, 10 July* I am back in Berlin, staying at the Adlon. Giorgio Cini is still here.

Adam Trott and I dined there together. We spoke English to the head waiter, who was delighted to show how well he still remembers it. Our neighbours began to stare. Adam then took me for a drive, during which, without going into particulars, we discussed the coming events which, he told me, are now imminent. We don't see eye to eye on this because I continue to find that too much time is being lost perfecting the details, whereas to me only one thing is really important now – the physical elimination of the man. What happens to Germany once he is dead can be seen to later. Perhaps because I am not German myself, it may all seem simpler to me, whereas for Adam it is essential that some kind of Germany be given a chance to survive. This evening we had a bitter quarrel about this and both of us got very emotional. So sad, at this, of all moments . . .

By 'imminent events' Adam Trott meant a first attempt to kill Hitler which was planned for the following day and which was postponed at the very last minute because Goering and Himmler (who were to be killed at the same time) were not at Hitler's side.

Tuesday, 11 July Consulted Professor Gehrbrandt, Maria Gersdorff's doctor. Something evidently is wrong with my health, as I am terribly thin. He puts it down to the thyroid and will recommend a long leave of absence.

KRUMMHÜBEL *Wednesday, 12 July* Count Schulenburg is back from Salzburg, where he had been summoned by Ribbentrop. He has been ordered to report to Hitler's H.Q. in East Prussia. At long last they seem to want his expert advice. It seems a little late in the game, but it is rumoured that they are cooking up some separate deal in the East. [*This was the first time Hitler had seen fit to receive Count Schulenburg since his repatriation from Moscow three years earlier.*]

He had lent me the former Rumanian Foreign Minister Gafencu's book

Préliminaires de la Guerre à l'Est. It is very interesting and mentions him often, as both Gafencu and he were ambassadors in Moscow before the war together. Sometimes, apparently, Gafencu is mistaken, but when Schulenburg approached him in Geneva he was decent enough to accept all the latter's corrections. This must wait until after the war, however, for these corrections are so damning to the Führer that they would cause a scandal now.

Here, everything is disintegrating and I will be glad to leave Krummhübel myself, presumably for good, next week.

Thursday, 13 July After lunching with us, Count Schulenburg departed. [*Missie was never to see him again.*]

A letter from Adam Trott, straightening out our last misunderstanding. I answered immediately. He has left for Sweden.

The Russians are suddenly advancing very fast.

In fact, Adam Trott was not allowed to go to Sweden as planned. The last of several trips he made there had been in June 1944 when, despairing of obtaining from the Western Allies the assurances the anti-Nazi plotters had so long sought, he planned to get in touch with the Soviet Ambassador, Mme Alexandra Kollontai, via Professor Gunnar Myrdal. At the last minute, however, he decided against this, essentially because he feared that the Soviet Embassy in Stockholm had been infiltrated by German agents.

Saturday, 15 July It's pouring with rain. Went to the cinema with Mamma and Madonna Blum.

A new decree forbidding the use of trains by civilians. Mamma will have to leave immediately, as this decree comes into force in two days.

Tuesday, 18 July Mamma left this morning. Last night, we dined with Madonna Blum and, on our way home, went over to speak with the Russian Cossacks who are here with their horses and, seeing that there are no more cars, are used for the transportation of senior officials. Mamma gave them cigarettes and they danced and sang and were so happy to speak Russian again. The poor fellows are stranded between two chairs, having opted against Communism and never having been really absorbed into the German army.

At the office, the pre-arranged telegram from Adam: I am expected in Berlin tomorrow.

The traditionally mostly anti-Communist Cossacks were the most ideologically motivated Russian volunteers to fight alongside the German army. They had gone over to the Germans, together with their families, by entire villages. Led by Major General Helmuth von Pannwitz and a mixed contingent of German, ex-Red Army and White émigré officers, they proved themselves particularly effective in anti-partisan warfare in Yugoslavia. In the last weeks of the war, they fought their way through to Austria, where some 60,000 surrendered to the British. As they had done with General Vlassov's earlier-mentioned 'Russian Liberation Army', the latter tricked them into believing that they were being re-settled overseas and then, invoking the Yalta Agreement, forcibly delivered them into Soviet hands. Many (including women and children) committed suicide. The senior officers were hanged; most junior ones shot; the rest vanished into the Gulag, from where few returned.

Missie's note: This entire section was written up in September 1945 from shorthand notes taken at the time.

BERLIN *Wednesday, 19 July* Today I left Krummhübel – I suspect for good. I had packed everything and have taken with me as little as possible. The rest will stay with Madonna Blum until I know what is to happen to me.

We reached Berlin at eleven, but owing to recent air-raids all stations are in a state of chaos. Ran into old Prinz August Wilhelm, the late Kaiser's fourth son, who kindly helped carry my luggage. We finally boarded a bus. The town is enveloped in smoke; there is rubble everywhere. Eventually, I was deposited at the Gersdorffs'.

Now that it is summer, they take their meals in the upstairs sitting-room, although it still has no windows. I found the usual group of people, plus Adam Trott.

Later, I had a long talk with Adam. He looks very pale and strained, but seems glad to see me. He is appalled that Loremarie Schönburg should be back in town and is very unhappy about her unceasing efforts to bring together people whom she suspects of being sympathetic to what I call *die Konspiration* [the plot] and many of whom are already deeply involved and are having a hard enough time as it is staying above suspicion. Somehow she has found out also about Adam's involvement and now keeps pestering him and his entourage, where she has acquired the nickname 'Lottchen' (after Marat's assassin, Charlotte Corday). To many she is a real security risk. He told me that she had even complained about my being unwilling to take an active part in the preparations.

The truth is that there is a fundamental difference in outlook between all of *them* and me: not being German, I am concerned only with the elimination of the Devil. I have never attached much importance to what happens afterwards. Being patriots, *they* want to save their country from complete destruction by setting up some interim government. I have never believed that even such an interim government would be acceptable to the Allies, who refuse to distinguish between 'good' Germans and 'bad'. This, of course, is a fatal mistake on their part and we will probably all pay a heavy price for it.

We agreed not to meet again until Friday. After he had gone, Maria Gersdorff remarked: 'I find he looks so pale and so tired; sometimes I think he is not going to live long.'

As the war dragged on, engulfing more and more countries of Europe, and as casualties, human suffering and material destruction soared and reports of German atrocities multiplied, it became increasingly difficult for the Allies to distinguish between Hitler and his henchmen and the so-called 'good Germans', and to agree on a policy that would enable a Germany purged of Nazism to be reintegrated into the community of civilised nations. All the more so since, apart from the assurances and promises of a few individuals, there had never been any tangible evidence that Hitler did not speak for the whole of Germany. As Anthony Eden had already put it in May 1940: 'Hitler is not a phenomenon but a symptom, the expression of a great part of the German nation.' And on 20 January 1941 Winston Churchill had instructed the Foreign Office to ignore any peace feelers from inside Germany: 'Our attitude towards all such inquiries or suggestions should be absolute silence . . .'

It was this wall of distrust and hostility that Adam Trott and his friends in the anti-Nazi resistance kept trying so desperately to overcome. But the response had been given by President Roosevelt once and for all in January 1943 at Casablanca: 'Unconditional Surrender'. This left even many convinced anti-Nazis with little choice but to carry on to the finish.

Aga Fürstenberg joined us for supper. She has now moved to the actor Willy Fritsch's house in Grunewald, a charming little cottage he left in a hurry after having a nervous breakdown during one of the recent raids. Apparently, he lay sobbing on his bed all day until his wife came back to Berlin and took him out to the country. Aga shares the house with Georgie Pappenheim, a charming fellow who has been a diplomat for years and who has just been called back from Madrid, probably on account of his name (the Pappenheims are among the oldest families in Germany). He plays the piano beautifully.

I have been granted four weeks' sick leave but may only take two at a time and must first train an assistant to take care of things in my absence.

Thursday, 20 July This afternoon Loremarie Schönburg and I sat chatting on the office stairs when Gottfried Bismarck burst in, bright red spots on his cheeks. I had never seen him in such a state of feverish excitement. He first drew Loremarie aside, then asked me what my plans were. I told him they were uncertain but that I would really like to get out of the A.A. as soon as possible. He told me I should not worry, that in a few days everything would be settled and we would all know what was going to happen to us. Then, after asking me to come out to Potsdam with Loremarie as soon as possible, he jumped into his car and was gone.

I went back into my office and dialled Percy Frey at the Swiss Legation to cancel my dinner date with him, as I preferred to go out to Potsdam. While I waited, I turned to Loremarie, who was standing at the window, and asked her why Gottfried was in such a state. Could it be the *Konspiration?* (all that with the receiver in my hand!). She whispered: 'Yes! That's it! It's done. This morning!' Just then Percy replied. Still holding the receiver, I asked: 'Dead?' She answered: 'Yes, dead!' I hung up, seized her by the shoulders and we went waltzing around the room. Then grabbing hold of some papers, I thrust them into the first drawer and shouting to the porter that we were *'dienstlich unterwegs'* ['off on official business'], we tore off to the Zoo station. On the way out to Potsdam she whispered to me the details and though the compartment was full, we did not even try to hide our excitement and joy:

Count Claus Schenck von Stauffenberg, a colonel on the General Staff, had put a bomb at Hitler's feet during a conference at Supreme H.Q. at Rastenburg in East Prussia. It had gone off and Adolf was dead. Stauffenberg had waited outside until the explosion and then, seeing Hitler being carried out on a stretcher covered with blood, he had run to his car, which had stood hidden somewhere, and with his A.D.C., Werner von Haeften, had driven to the local airfield and flown back to Berlin. In the general commotion nobody had noticed his escape.

On reaching Berlin, he had gone straight to the O.K.H. [Army Command H.Q.] in the Bendlerstrasse, which had meanwhile been taken over by the plotters and where Gottfried Bismarck, Helldorf and many others were now gathered. (The O.K.H. lies on the other side of the canal from our Woyrschstrasse.) This evening at six an announcement would be made over the radio that Adolf was dead and that a new government had been formed. The new Reichskanzler [Chancellor of the Reich] would be Gördeler, a former mayor of Leipzig. With a socialist background, he is considered a brilliant economist. Our Count Schulenburg or Ambassador von Hassell is to be Foreign Minister. My immediate feeling was that it was perhaps a mistake to put the best brains at the head of what could only be an interim government.

The thirty-seven year-old Stauffenberg was a relative latecomer to the anti-Nazi resistance, having been recruited only in July 1943. In his youth he, like many patriotic Germans, had believed that Hitler was the man to save Germany from the disastrous consequences and dishonour of the Versailles treaty. While serving with Rommel in Africa, he had been severely wounded, losing an eye, his right arm and two fingers of his left hand – a fateful disability when the hour of reckoning came. In June 1944 he had been appointed Chief-of-Staff of the Replacement Army, the so-called Ersatzheer, whose second-in-command, Colonel-General Friedrich Olbricht, was an old-time anti-Nazi plotter. As such, Stauffenberg had periodically to report personally to Hitler. Since no other resister in Hitler's entourage was able or would agree to assassinate him, Stauffenberg undertook to do so himself on one of these occasions.

Two first attempts – on 11 and 15 July – had been called off at the last minute. By now arrests were multiplying also among the military. Clearly the Gestapo was closing in. When, on 20 July, Stauffenberg was again summoned to Hitler's presence, he decided that come what may, this time he would do it.

By the time we had reached the Regierung in Potsdam, it was past six o'clock. I went to wash up. Loremarie hurried upstairs. Only minutes had passed when I heard dragging footsteps outside and she came in: 'There has just been an announcement on the radio: 'A Count Stauffenberg has attempted to murder the Führer, but Providence saved him . . .'

Actually, the first radio announcement, at 18.25, gave no names. It said merely: 'Today an attempt was made on the Führer's life with explosives . . . The Führer himself suffered no injuries beyond light burns and bruises. He resumed his work immediately and, as programmed, received the Duce for a lengthy talk.' Only in the commentary that followed was there a veiled hint at who the authors were ('enemy work'). But then at first Hitler did not realise that the bomb was part of a much larger plot to overthrow the Nazi regime. Only after he had learnt of the attempted takeovers in Berlin, Paris and Vienna was he to grasp what was happening.

I took her by the arm and we raced back upstairs. We found the Bismarcks in the drawing room, Melanie with a stricken expression, Gottfried pacing up and down, up and down. I was afraid to look at him. He had just got back from the Bendlerstrasse and kept repeating: 'It's just not possible! It's a trick! Stauffenberg *saw* him dead.' 'They' were staging a comedy and getting Hitler's double to go on with it. He went into his study to telephone Helldorf. Loremarie followed him and I was left alone with Melanie.

She started to moan: Loremarie had driven Gottfried to this; she had been working on him for years; if he were to die now, she, Melanie, was the one who would be left with three little children; maybe Loremarie could afford that luxury, but who would be left fatherless? Other children, not hers . . . It was really dreadful, and there was nothing I could say.

Gottfried came back into the room. He had not been able to get through to Helldorf, but he had further news: the main radio station had been lost; the insurgents had seized it but had been unable to make it work, and now it was back in S.S. hands. However, the officers' schools in the suburbs had taken up arms and were now marching on Berlin. And, surely enough, an hour later we heard the panzers of the Krampnitz tank training school rolling through Potsdam on their way to the capital. We hung out of the windows watching them go by and prayed. Nobody in the streets, which were practically empty, seemed to know what was going on. Gottfried kept insisting that he could not believe Hitler was unhurt, that 'they' were hiding something . . .

A little later the radio announced that the Führer would address the German people at midnight. We realised that only then would we know for certain whether all this was a hoax or not. And yet Gottfried refused to give up hope. According to him, even if Hitler *was* alive, his Supreme Headquarters in East Prussia was so far away that if things went well elsewhere, the regime could still be overthrown before he could regain control in Germany itself. But the rest of us were getting very uneasy.

Since 1943 there had existed at Army H.Q. in Berlin's Bendlerstrasse, the so-called O.K.H., a contingency plan code-named 'Valkyrie', which provided for the measures to be taken in the event of internal disorders or large-scale sabotage by the millions of foreigners now working in Germany. A key role, under this plan, devolved upon the Ersatzheer, and the units quartered in or around the capital – the Guard Battalion in Berlin itself and the officers' training schools on the periphery. Ironically, 'Valkyrie' had been approved by Hitler himself! Olbricht, Stauffenberg and their fellow-plotters at O.K.H. had devised a secret addendum by means of which the plan could be used also to topple the Nazi regime, after which a new government would sue for peace. From the outset the plot had fateful flaws. For one thing, of those senior military commanders who, under the 'Valkyrie' plan, would be taking over not only in Germany, but throughout the rest of occupied Europe, only a few knew of the plotters' actual intentions. The others, starting with Colonel-General Friedrich Fromm, G.O.C. Ersatzheer, upon whom so much depended, were expected to 'go along' once their Führer's death had released them from their oath of allegiance to him; in other words, everything hinged on the killing of Hitler. It was also essential that for several hours all communications between Rastenburg and the outside world be cut − to prevent counter-measures being taken. Lastly, the would-be assassin, Stauffenberg, had not only to kill Hitler but to get safely back to Berlin to see 'Valkyrie' successfully on its way, and to compound the problems, the average German soldier was by now so heavily indoctrinated that there was no means of gauging what his reactions would be to an order to seize control of the country's key institutions.

Helldorf rang up several times. Also the Gauleiter of Brandenburg, asking the Potsdam Regierungspräsident Graf Bismarck what the devil he proposed to do, as he, the Gauleiter, understood that disorders and perhaps even a mutiny had broken out in the capital. Gottfried had the impudence to tell him that the orders from Supreme Headquarters were that the Führer wished all higher officials to stay put and await further instructions. In fact, he hoped that the insurgent troops would soon come and arrest the Gauleiter.

As night came, rumours began to circulate that the uprising was not succeeding as well as had been hoped. Somebody rang up from the airfield: 'Die Luftwaffe macht nicht mit' ['the air force isn't going along']; they wanted personal orders from Goering or from the Führer himself. Gottfried now began to sound sceptical − for the first time. He said such a thing had to be done fast; every minute lost was irretrievable. It was now long past midnight and still Hitler had not spoken. It all became so discouraging that I saw no purpose in sitting up any longer and went to bed. Loremarie soon followed.

At two in the morning, Gottfried looked in and in a dead voice said: 'It was him all right!'

Hitler spoke finally at 1 a.m. on 21 July. A very small clique of ambitious, dishonorable and criminally stupid officers, he said, who had nothing in common with the German armed forces and, above all, with the German people, had formed a plot to remove him and at the same time overthrow the High Command of the Armed Forces. A bomb planted by a Colonel Count von Stauffenberg – the only one named – had exploded two meters away from him and seriously wounded several faithful members of his staff, one fatally. He himself was unhurt, except for very minor scratches, bruises and burns, and he regarded this as a confirmation of Providence's decision that he should continue to pursue the goal of his life – the greatness of Germany. This very small gang of criminal elements would now be ruthlessly exterminated. And there followed instructions for the re-establishment of order.

At dawn, we heard the tanks from Krampnitz rolling past again; they were returning to their barracks without having achieved anything.

The cadets of the Krampnitz Cavalry Training School were one of the units the plotters counted on to help take over Berlin. Upon being advised by the Bendlerstrasse that Hitler was dead – assassinated by the S.S. – and that 'Valkyrie' was now operative, they had started out for Berlin and taken up their assigned stations there. But when their C.O. (who was not in the plot) learnt that Hitler was not dead and that some of his fellow-officers were attempting a putsch, *he mustered his tanks and returned them to their barracks.*

Friday, 21 July At breakfast we learnt that Gottfried and Melanie Bismarck had gone to Berlin by car (probably to see Helldorf). Loremarie Schönburg looked like death. I myself returned to Berlin alone, leaving her in bed. We still did not quite realise the scope of the disaster and the dreadful danger they were all in.

On my way into town, I stopped off at Aga Fürstenberg's in Grunewald and left my night things with her. As Potsdam is so far away and the bombs have made life at the Gersdorffs' intolerable, I will try that for a change. Aga was nonplussed by the events but was obviously in the dark as to who was involved. It will be difficult, but from now on one must pretend to know nothing and talk about it all, even to friends, with complete incredulity.

After only a short time at the office, I went to Maria Gersdorff. She was in despair. Count Stauffenberg, she told me, was shot yesterday evening at Army Command H.Q. in the Bendlerstrasse, together with his A.D.C., young Werner von Haeften. General Beck, whom they had planned to make

Chief of State, had committed suicide. General Olbricht, another key conspirator, who had replaced the wavering General Fromm as head of the Ersatzheer, had been shot with the rest.

At Rastenburg, Stauffenberg's plan went immediately awry. Hitler's daily briefings (held normally in an underground bunker) took place now, on account of the heat, in an above-ground wooden hut, the walls of which, when the bomb burst, caved outwards, releasing much of its explosive force. Because with his one hand Stauffenberg could only trigger one bomb (instead of the two originally planned to be placed in his attaché case), the explosion itself was weaker. As Stauffenberg left the room to answer a pre-arranged phone call, a staff officer, finding the case in his way under the map table over which Hitler was bent, shoved it to the other side of a heavy wooden trestle. This, to some extent, screened Hitler from the blast.

At 12.42, with a deafening roar, the hut disintegrated in a cloud of flames and smoke. Stauffenberg and his A.D.C. Haeften, who had been standing some distance away chatting with another plotter – Hitler's Chief of Signals General Erich Fellgiebel – jumped into their car, and bluffing their way through the checkpoints (which had been immediately alerted) made for the airstrip, from where they were soon winging their way back to Berlin.

General Fellgiebel was supposed to telephone the news of Hitler's death to General Olbricht in Berlin and then close down all communications between Rastenburg and the outside world. To his surprise and consternation, he saw Hitler tottering out of the wreckage – bruised, dusty, his trousers in tatters, but clearly alive. He had but the time to signal Berlin in guarded terms that 'a terrible tragedy has occurred . . . the Führer lives . . .' when the S.S. took over his network. Already two key premises for the plot's success – Hitler's death and the plotters' control of Rastenburg's communications – had misfired. Moreover the identity of the would-be assassin was now known and an order was being telexed all over Germany for Stauffenberg's arrest.

The week before, 'Valkyrie' had been set in train, only to be hastily called off again when Stauffenberg postponed his earlier attempts. This time therefore, on receiving Fellgiebel's ambiguous message, General Olbricht delayed giving it the green light until he knew for sure what had happened.

At 15.50 Stauffenberg's plane touched down at an outlying military airport, only to find that his driver had not yet arrived. As Haeften called the Bendlerstrasse to find out what had happened, Olbricht asked him whether Hitler was dead. On being reassured that this was so, he went over to General Fromm to obtain the latter's approval for the launching of 'Valkyrie'. But Fromm was instantly suspicious and, calling Rastenburg, got through to Field Marshal Wilhelm Keitel, who confirmed that there had indeed been an attempt on the Führer's life but that it had failed. Just then Stauffenberg and Haeften burst into the room. Fromm said that 'Valkyrie' was now no longer needed. Whereupon Stauffenberg exploded: Keitel was lying; Hitler was dead; he had seen him dead, in fact he himself had laid the bomb! Besides, it was too late anyway: 'Valkyrie' was already on its way. 'By whose orders?' Fromm asked. 'Ours', replied Olbricht and Stauffenberg. White with rage, but above all fearful for his own future, Fromm ordered Stauffenberg to shoot himself and Olbricht to call 'Valkyrie' off. Instead they disarmed Fromm and confined him to his room.

There was now no turning back and at 5.30 p.m. – five hours later than originally planned – the O.K.H.'s telexes started ticking out the 'Valkyrie' orders to the various military H.Q.s and – yet another aberration – since Rastenburg figured on the original plan's distribution list and no-one had thought of scratching it, it was from the plotters themselves that Hitler now learnt what they were up to. An hour later, Germany's airwaves carried the news of the attempt – and of its failure – together with the first orders of reprisals.

Meanwhile other key figures had begun to converge on the Bendlerstrasse: General Ludwig Beck (whom the plotters planned to make Chief of State), Field Marshal Erwin von Witzleben (who was supposed to take over the army), General Erich Hoepner (who should have succeeded Fromm), Count Helldorf, Gottfried Bismarck and many others. Many of them departed again – some indignant, all alarmed. For they found growing disarray, with nobody clear about what to do next. Beck and Stauffenberg kept urging the various military H.Q.s to follow Berlin's example – with little success. But even in Berlin itself they were losing the initiative: the tanks from Krampnitz had been and gone; the main radio station had been seized and abandoned; the Guard Battalion had started out to take over the government buildings and had then stopped in its tracks.

The only senior Nazi leader in Berlin that day was Goebbels, and he saved the day for Hitler. When Major Otto Remer, the much-decorated C.O. of the Guard Battalion, arrived to arrest him on the city commandant, Lieutenant-General Paul von Hase's orders, Goebbels put him through to Rastenburg, to Hitler himself, who, promoting Remer on the spot to colonel, ordered him to proceed to the Bendlerstrasse and re-establish order there. But by the time he arrived, the putsch *was over.*

For meanwhile, officers loyal to Hitler had taken over the building, released Fromm and arrested the plotters. General Beck was allowed to take his own life and having twice failed to do so, was finished off by an N.C.O. Olbricht, his Chief-of-Staff, Colonel Mertz von Quirnheim, Stauffenberg and Haeften were, after a drumhead court-martial, marched down into the courtyard and shot by the glare of headlights. Stauffenberg (who had been badly wounded in the foray) still found the strength to cry out: 'Long live our sacred Germany!' The bodies were first buried in a churchyard. The following day, however, on Himmler's orders, they were exhumed, stripped of their uniforms and decorations and cremated, their ashes being scattered to the winds.

Months ago, Loremarie had told me that she had once visited General Olbricht on one of her fateful recruitment operations, as she had heard that he was a 'positive element'. He had told her in strictest confidence that he had sacks of over 30,000 letters from German soldiers who had been taken prisoner at Stalingrad in 1943, but that Hitler had ordered them to be burnt. Officially, there were to be *no* survivors of that 'glorious' battle. Although one of her brothers had not been heard of since Stalingrad, Olbricht would not let her see them, however much she begged.

Maria had known Stauffenberg slightly, as some of his cousins are her closest friends. She is terrified for them. I had met young Haeften at Adam Trott's a couple of months ago. One evening, when I was dining with Adam alone, a curly-headed, good-looking young captain had burst in, introduced himself and dragged Adam out of the room. They had stayed away for a long time. Afterwards, Adam was curious to know what impression he had made on me. I answered, 'The typical conspirator, such as one reads about in children's books.' I did not know then what his role was. Now at Maria's I could not take my mind off Gottfried and Adam. Both had been in the Bendlerstrasse at some point yesterday. Would this leak out? And all the time one must look surprised, concerned even, but not terrified . . .

In fact, Adam von Trott, Alex Werth and Hans-Bernd von Haeften had spent the day at the A.A.'s main office in the Wilhelmstrasse, which they were supposed to take over once the putsch *had succeeded.*

Late in the evening Percy Frey dropped by to fetch me. As I did not want any supper, we drove into the Grunewald woods, got out of the car and walked. I tried to make him understand what a terrible, enormous tragedy this is. As it began to dawn on him, he was amazed and sympathetic. Until then he, too, had believed the official version, namely that the whole affair was the work of a couple of adventurers.

I *must* see Adam. But although we had agreed to meet today, I do not dare look him up yet.

Saturday, 22 July This morning all the newspapers came out with an appeal offering one million marks to anyone who would indicate the whereabouts of a man '*namens Goerdeler*' ['by the name of Goerdeler']. What a relief! This means he is still at large.

It is rumoured that Claus Stauffenberg's wife and four children have been murdered. Born a Baroness von Lerchenfeld, she was a godchild of Mamma's, as her parents lived in Russian Lithuania before World War I.

Within days of the aborted coup, *under the recently introduced practice of* Sippenhaft *(kith-and-kin imprisonment), not only Stauffenberg's wife and children, but his mother, mother-in-law, brothers, cousins, uncles, aunts (and all their wives, husbands and children) were arrested (see epilogue for their ultimate fate).*

Addressing the Nazi Gauleiters at Posen on 3 August, Himmler was thus to justify kith-and-kin reprisals: 'Let no one come and tell us that what you are doing is bolshevism. No, that is not bolshevism but a very ancient Germanic custom . . . When a man was outlawed, it was said: this man is a traitor, his blood is bad, it contains treason, it will be exterminated. And . . . the entire family, including its remotest connections, was exterminated. We will do away with the Stauffenbergs including their remotest connections . . .'

On entering Judgie Richter's office this morning, I found the older Haeften, Hans-Bernd (our former chief of personnel), sitting at his desk eating cherries out of a paper bag. And his brother shot the day before yesterday like a dog! He smiled to me and chatted as if nothing had happened. When he had gone out, I asked Judgie whether he knew about his brother. Judgie said yes. Judgie himself looked worried and unhappy, but nothing like how he would look if he knew the truth about Adam Trott.

I went down to Adam's room. I found him with one of his assistants, who soon left. Adam threw himself down on a sofa and, pointing to his neck, said 'I'm in it up to here'. He looked dreadful. We talked in whispers. The sight of him made me unhappier still. I told him so. He said yes, but to me it was merely as if I had lost the favourite tree in my orchard, whereas for him it's everything he had hoped for that was gone. The intercom rang: our boss Dr Six, wanted to see him. We agreed to meet in the evening. I left a note with his secretary, saying I would wait for his phone call.

When I went over to Maria Gersdorff, I told her how anxious I was about Adam. 'But why?' she asked. 'He knew Stauffenberg only slightly, didn't he?

No, I'm certain he is not deeply involved!' – 'No,' I said, 'not really involved at all.'

Adam rang and we agreed to meet at Aga Fürstenberg's after six. I then went over to the Adlon, where I was meeting Loremarie Schönburg and Aga. The latter was furious because, when she met Hasso Etzdorf in the street, he turned his back on her. I assume he, too, is deeply compromised. We assembled at Aga's and had tea on the lawn. Tony Saurma and Georgie Pappenheim were there too. Then Adam joined us. He had been with Dr Six, trying to put him off the scent. He looked like death. I drove back with him to his house and sat on the balcony in the sun while he changed. An air-raid alarm sounded; it had the irritating effect of a swarm of bees, no more. When Adam reappeared, we sat outside and he told me about some of it:

Stauffenberg, he said, was a wonderful man, not only brilliantly intelligent but also with exceptional vitality and drive. He was one of the few plotters frequently admitted to Hitler's presence. He had been to Supreme Head-quarters with his bomb twice before but each time there had been some hitch or else Himmler or Goering or some of the others whom he wanted to kill together with Hitler had stayed away from the meeting at the last moment. The third time he was summoned, he had told his fellow-conspirators that he would go ahead with it, whatever the circumstances. The strain was getting too much for him and no wonder. If only it had been somebody who could fire a gun, the attempt might have succeeded. But Stauffenberg was too badly disabled . . . He has lost in him, Adam said, his closest friend. He seemed completely crushed.

Adam himself had spent the whole day of the 20th at the A.A. in the Wilhelmstrasse, waiting for the military takeover. He said he knew he would be arrested, he was too deeply compromised. I did not ask him to what extent. He was sending away his maid; she had witnessed too many meetings in this house and, if questioned, might talk. He feared that Helldorf, too, might break down under torture (I remember Helldorf telling Loremarie he himself feared this . . .).

Adam wondered aloud whether he should not have a piece published in the London *Times*, explaining what these men represented. I disagreed with this idea, as the immediate reaction in Germany would be that they were in the enemy's pay and now that they had failed, public opinion here would be still less in their favour.

Adam went on to tell me that shortly after France was defeated in 1940, he had received a letter from his old friend Lord Lothian (who was at the time British Ambassador in Washington) in which the latter urged him to work for a reconciliation between Germany and England. Whether Lothian had in mind only a non-Nazi Germany (he knew, of course, Adam's hatred of the regime) was to Adam not quite clear. But to him the thought of any possible 'deal' between the two countries while Hitler was still at the helm was so odious, that he never mentioned the existence of this letter to anyone. Afterwards, he said, he often wondered whether he had not been wrong.

We sat up all night talking and listening to stray sounds outside and every time we heard a car slowing down, I could see on his face what he was thinking . . .

I simply cannot leave him like this. If they come to get him while I am here, I can at least alert his friends. Adam said Alex Werth knows all and that if he is arrested, Alex would know what to do. He thinks that Dr Six suspects something too, as he keeps pressing Adam to go to Switzerland. I, also, insisted that he should go – immediately. But no, he will not, because of his wife and children. He said that if they arrested him, he would deny everything – in order to get out and try again. At 4 a.m. he drove me home and promised to call me later in the morning, so that I would know he was all right.

Lord Lothian belonged to a small but at one point influential group of Conservative politicians, the so-called 'Cliveden set', who, while critical of his methods, viewed with some sympathy Hitler's efforts to wipe out the indignities of the Versailles peace treaty (of which they had always disapproved) and the visible success with which he was tackling his country's economic problems. But above all they were dismayed by the prospect of another European war, which, following so closely the bloodbath of 1914–1918 (of which many of them were veterans), would, they believed, fatally weaken Europe, sound the death-knell of the overseas empires and perhaps even of Western civilisation itself, and open the doors to world Communism. Hitler's increasingly brutal policies at home and his ruthless determination to make Germany the dominant power in Europe at whatever price, had frustrated all their efforts at coming to terms with him and many of them would later be branded as 'appeasers'.

Missie's note (September 1945): Adam had never explained to me the exact nature of his activities. I only knew that his every trip abroad – to Switzerland, to Sweden – though always undertaken under some official pretext, was connected with his untiring efforts to create a platform for peace talks with the Allies, once 'the event' (Hitler's assassination) had taken place.

He sincerely believed that when faced with a 'decent' German government, the Allies would be less uncompromising. I often sought to dispel these illusions and kept insisting that the *one* all-important thing was the physical elimination of Hitler, nothing else. I think that subsequent events proved me right . . .

To the very end of her life Missie was reluctant to admit how much she knew about Count von Stauffenberg's plot prior to 20 July. But the many random hints she keeps inadvertently dropping, starting with that first mention of 'The Conspiracy' on 2 August 1943, through the plotters' persistent urging that she help keep Loremarie Schönburg away from Berlin, and ending with that all-revealing entry of 19 July 1944 with its 'We (i.e. Adam von Trott and she) agreed not to meet again until Friday', show that she was far better informed than she claimed and that she even knew the exact date of the planned coup!

Sunday, 23 July Adam Trott telephoned as he had promised. So far all is well. I told him I was going out to Potsdam and would call him from there.

I found Gottfried Bismarck in a bathing suit splashing around in his fountain. It is very hot. Melanie and Loremarie Schönburg were also there. Melanie seems calmer now; she even intends to return to the country to give their staff the impression that life goes on as usual.

I told them how worried I was about Adam Trott. Gottfried did not think they would arrest him. The man who was most in danger now, he said, was Helldorf. His role in the attempted *coup* had been too conspicuous and he would be unable to produce an alibi.

We discussed Fritzi Schulenburg, the Ambassador's nephew and a former deputy head, under Helldorf, of the Berlin police. It is rumoured that he, too, was shot in the Bendlerstrasse on Thursday. I remember him as a young man in East Prussia before the war; though once a Nazi, he was already violently critical of the regime. Adam told me last night that he had seen Stauffenberg's secretary; she had described how Fritzi ran out of his impromptu office at Army H.Q., was shot in the back in the corridor, wounded, dragged into the courtyard and finished off there.

This turned out to be a false rumour. Arrested at the Bendlerstrasse, Schulenburg was among the first to go on trial before the People's Court. Condemned to death, he was strangulated on 10 August 1944.

In the afternoon we all took a nap, for the tension is exhausting. Later Loremarie told me Gottfried had shown her two large parcels in his office cupboard, wondering aloud what should be done with them. When she asked what they were, he had said 'the left-over explosive from the bomb'. She had begged him to get rid of them, as search parties would certainly arrive soon. He had refused, saying that the explosive had been so difficult to get in the first place, that he intended to keep it for another try. She had at least convinced him to hide it in the cellar.

Telephoned Adam. He was still all right. Dined with Percy Frey.

The explosive – a German compound of Hexogen and T.N.T. used by the Abwehr – had been obtained by the plotters as far back as 1942 at considerable risk, since it was difficult to explain why staff officers (as most of them were) needed explosive. Some of it had been used for various earlier attempts on Hitler's life. The fuses, of British origin, had been captured from the French Resistance.

Monday, 24 July Melanie Bismarck has asked me to hold in the Russian church a memorial service for Thursday's victims, as well as prayers for those who are in danger. There are so many: Adam Trott . . . Gottfried Bismarck . . . Helldorf . . . She does not dare have one in a Catholic or Protestant church, but thinks that the Orthodox one is less conspicuous. I agreed to see Father John Shakhovskoy about this. We also agreed that I alone would attend, in order to attract the least possible attention.

Spent the morning in the office and then, although Adam had already lunched in the canteen, I talked him into accompanying me to Maria Gersdorff's. I gave him an icon of St Serafim of Sarov and told him about Melanie's idea of a Mass. He said we must not worry; Claus Stauffenberg was such a fervent Christian that Masses are surely being said all over Germany. We were joined by some of our friends and we tried to talk of other things. As we parted, Adam told me and Loremarie Schönburg that were none of us to survive, it would be impossible to try again and that from now on, therefore, we must be very, *very* careful, that we must no longer meet, that we were all being watched, etc. This seems to be a theme song with all of them: they *must* try again!

In the evening Gottfried drove us out to Potsdam. We supped with him alone. Helldorf, he told us, was arrested this morning. The Polizeipräsidium provides no information: 'The President went out this morning and has not returned.'

After dinner Hanna Bredow, Gottfried's sister, marched in. She is a character. Clutching her umbrella, she sat down: 'Gottfried, I wish to know how much you are mixed up in this business! You cannot keep me any longer in the dark. I am far too aware of what is going on. I *must* know where we stand!' Gottfried hummed and hawed and told her nothing. Hanna is worried about her daughters; the nineteen-year-old Philippa saw a lot of young Werner von Haeften, Stauffenberg's A.D.C., who was shot with him and who seems to have spoken to her freely, too freely. Later, Hanna read our cards; she is very good at it. None of us three seem doomed just yet. Afterwards, we went over to her house, where Georgie Pappenheim played the piano beautifully. Then he, Aga Fürstenberg and I returned to Grunewald to Aga's for the night.

As early as 16 July there had been rumours in the Bredow household that Hitler's H.Q. would be blown up that week.

An air-raid dragged us out of our beds. This time, the bombs started to fall in our immediate neighbourhood and we took refuge in the shelter – a ridiculous wooden structure under a grass mound. Two mines, chained together, came down quite close to us. They took some time to do so, being suspended to parachutes. We crouched on the floor with helmets crammed down on our heads. Aga looked such a sight with hers all crooked that I could not help giggling at the worst moments. The cook, stone deaf, blessed creature, heard absolutely nothing of the pandemonium and threw herself on the ground only because we did.

This afternoon I saw Father John. He thought it would be too dangerous to have a service in the Russian church but he has a small chapel in his flat and we held it there. I was the only person present and I cried throughout it horribly. When I told Loremarie that I could not remember Helldorf's Christian name at the time, she exclaimed, astonished: 'Aber, Missie! Wölfchen!' ['But, Missie! Wolfikins!']

Tuesday, 25 July Early today I telephoned Adam Trott at home; he was still all right. But later, when I dropped by his office, he was not there, only his secretary – a nice girl and a friend – with a scared expression on her face. Lunched in a hurry at Maria Gersdorff's and then returned to the office. This time Adam's secretary tried to shove me out of his room. I pushed past her and marched in. At his desk a small man in civilian clothes was going through his drawers. Another one lounged in an armchair. The swine! I glanced at them closer to see whether they had anything in their button-holes, but then remembered that they wear their Gestapo badge inside. I asked the secretary ostentatiously: 'Wo ist Herr von Trott? Noch immer nicht da?' ['Where is Herr von Trott? *Still* not there?'] They both looked up. When we had left the room, she looked at me beseechingly and put her finger to her lips.

I took the stairs three at a time and burst into Judgie Richter's office. I said something must be done immediately to prevent Adam from returning to his office, as the Gestapo was searching it. Judgie looked at me in a sickly way and said: 'It's too late. They picked him up at noon. Luckily Alex Werth was with him and drove after them in another car, and hopefully he will soon be back with some indication why Adam has been arrested'. Judgie evidently still suspects nothing. He related that Adam had attended the daily meeting at the main A.A. office in the Wilhelmstrasse. The Gestapo, meanwhile, had walked into his office and demanded to know his whereabouts. The secretary had tried to get away to warn him, but they had seized hold of her and had not let her leave the room. He had walked straight into the trap. State Secretary Keppler (a high Nazi official at the A.A. who used to head the Free India office) was expecting him for lunch in the Adlon at one. For the moment, Dr Six seems interested in his release; he has sent his A.D.C. to find out what the charges were. But I doubt he will maintain this attitude.

I left the office and ran over to Maria Gersdorff. Steenson, the Danish chargé d'affaires, was there and so I could not say much; I merely burst into tears. Maria tried to comfort me: it was clearly a mistake, he could not have had much to do with it, etc. If only she knew! And yet I must not explain anything.

A little later Heinz Gersdorff came home. He, too, is in trouble, as his boss, the Military Commandant of Berlin, General von Hase, whom we knew well, who had organised our visits to Jim Viazemsky in his P.O.W. camp, and who was in the *coup* up to his ears, has also been arrested after a stormy interview with Goebbels. Why didn't Hase shoot the rat then and there?

Several people have committed suicide, among them Count Lehndorff, on whose estate Hitler's Supreme Headquarters at Rastendorf in East Prussia is located. Prince Hardenberg shot himself in the stomach when they came to arrest him and is badly hurt. An early resister, he was under suspicion because Stauffenberg and Werner Haeften had spent their last weekend in his house. The two Gestapo men who had arrested him were killed in a motor accident on their way back to Berlin – at last a welcome piece of news! Our Hans-Bernd Haeften was arrested this morning too. It is rumoured that lists have been found.

Slept on the sofa in the Gersdorffs' living room. It still has no windows, but it is so hot that it makes no difference. At midnight, there was an air-raid and the planes were overhead so soon that we scarcely had time to throw on some clothes and crawl into the cellar of the neighbouring house, which burnt down last November. They dropped mines. For the first time in years I was not afraid.

In fact, Count Lehndorff was first arrested; in Berlin he managed to escape his captors; he was then re-arrested and later hanged.

Some lists were doubtless unavoidable (e.g. that of the plotters' liaison officers with the various military headquarters so as to operate 'Valkyrie'). Others (e.g. the composition of the future government) were more inexcusable, especially since some of those listed, such as Ambassador von der Schulenburg, had not even been consulted.

Wednesday, 26 July This morning Judgie Richter was still comparatively calm. He evidently does not know how compromised Adam Trott and Hans-Bernd Haeften are. He thinks it is all a mistake and that everything will be cleared up soon. But when Alex Werth came in and just looked at me, with an air of despair, I burst into tears. Judgie and Leipoldt were visibly surprised.

I just could not stick it out at the office and went home. Maria Gersdorff is now frantic. Count Peter Yorck von Wartenberg, whose sister is one of her best friends, has also been arrested.

A senior civil servant and a long-time resister, Count Yorck von Wartenberg figured on one of the plotters' cabinet lists.

After lunch Percy Frey dropped in to see me. I led him out to the ruins close by our house and told him that I could not see him anymore; we at Maria's were probably being watched and his brand-new car with foreign plates was too conspicuous. None of us should associate in any way with foreigners just now. We agreed that the best thing to do was for him to telephone me occasionally in the lion's den, i.e. the office.

Shortly before supper I went for a long walk in Grunewald by myself. There I sat on a bench in a puddle of misery for most of the evening, not caring what the passers-by might think.

Tonight Goebbels spoke once more over the radio about the attempted assassination; he threw mud at everybody he could. Public opinion, however, does not seem to be on the government's side. In the streets people appear pale and down-hearted; they seem to scarcely dare look each other in the face. A tram conductor, commenting loudly on Goebbels' speech, said to me 'Alles ist zum Kotzen!' ['It makes one want to throw up!']

In actual fact, S.D. reports on the mood of the population (which came to light after the war and are surprisingly reliable) show that the attempted coup was not well received by either the man in the street at home or the military at the front. Even the churches formally condemned it.

But then, the German resistance was not a mass movement; it consisted of a number of unrelated activities by individuals or groups, only some of which were in contact with one another, these activities ranging from the denunciation of injustices and assistance to threatened or persecuted persons to planned coups d'état and even attempts on Hitler's life. And this last extreme step was ethically unacceptable to many of the most dedicated anti-Nazis.

Thursday, 27 July Today Judgie Richter told me that Adam Trott's case looked worse. The investigator in charge, who is sifting the available evidence, has confirmed to Dr Six's A.D.C. that lists have been found. Adam was to be Under-Secretary of State for Foreign Affairs! Six seems still half-inclined to try and extricate him. Alex Werth is badgering him day and night to do so. At least at the moment he is not making Adam's plight worse. They hope to obtain the intervention of a neutral foreign power, but I think that this would endanger him even more.

Gottfried Bismarck comes to town every day and we meet in the ruins near my house. Today he was still hopeful. He did not think they would kill Adam, but Helldorf, he said, is doomed; Hitler is particularly incensed at him as he was an old party veteran and a top leader of the S.A. It is rumoured that Quartermaster-General Wagner has killed himself.

Gottfried plans to drive tomorrow to Reinfeld, his farm in Pomerania. He thinks that now that a week has passed, during which time he has sat calmly at home to prove he had nothing to fear, it might be healthier to get out of town. He wants me and Loremarie Schönburg to come too, but I cannot. I must keep up the pretence of going to the office, although I do nothing there.

A veteran resister, General Eduard Wagner had fatally incriminated himself by providing Stauffenberg with the aircraft in which he escaped from Rastenburg. He shot himself on 23 July.

Friday, 28 July Went this morning to the hairdresser for a permanent wave.

Goebbels has announced 'Totaler Krieg' (total war), which means the closing-down of all 'superfluous' shops and general mobilisation for all. He evidently hopes that by calling up the entire adult population, any overthrow of the regime in the rear will become well-nigh impossible. The Ersatzheer, which thus far had been staffed by decent officers but was compromised by recent events, is now being put under the command of Himmler. The troops are no longer to give the traditional military salute, but to shoot out their arms and bark 'Heil Hitler'. Everybody is indignant, but these frantic decrees border on the ridiculous.

Nobody has any news of General Fromm, the former Commander of the Ersatzheer. Gottfried Bismarck says that the conspirators did not trust him, as he had not explicitly agreed to participate; they had therefore arrested him at the very beginning of the *coup* and locked him up in his own office at the Bendlerstrasse, General Olbricht taking over.

The Commander of the Grossdeutschland-Wacht-Battalion – the unit that provides the guard for all government offices – a Major Remer, set him free. This man Remer should have been removed before the rising. It appears that Helldorf had suggested this, but the military had ignored his warnings. Actually, Remer had at first seemed willing to go along, but then he had been summoned by Goebbels, who had arranged for him to talk on the telephone with Adolf himself.

After lunch Gottfried and Loremarie Schönburg drove by to say goodbye. They were off to Pomerania and hoped to be back in a week. They tried again to persuade me to accompany them. They are both in great danger, but looked unconcerned. Tony Saurma has gone home to Silesia. All my cronies are now out of town. Only I stay on. But I *must* remain in Berlin.

General Fromm's cravenness on the day of the coup availed him little. Arrested on the following day, he was imprisoned for many months, cruelly tortured and finally executed in March 1945.

Saturday, 29 July Adam Trott's situation is stationary. Much has been attempted; now one must wait. I will try to go to the Pfuels' for the weekend.

In the office this morning the telephone rang. It was Loremarie Schönburg. 'From where?' – 'The Adlon. I am here with Melanie [Bismarck]. Don't tell anybody. It's a surprise. Isn't that nice?' This could only mean that Gottfried Bismarck had finally been arrested. I said I would rush around at lunch time. On arriving at the Adlon, I found them with Otto, Gottfried's eldest brother, who had apparently come down from Friedrichs-ruh in the night. They were going out to Potsdam. Melanie, white but calm, intends to stop at nothing to get Gottfried out. She said she would try everybody. Otto will approach Goering. Loremarie told me what happened. On the way out yesterday Gottfried's car broke down and they continued on by train. At Reinfeld they had just finished supper around three in the morning, when three Gestapo men walked in and arrested Gottfried. They also searched the house. They gave him time to talk to Melanie, then drove him straight back to Berlin. Melanie told me she has been warned that the Gersdorff house is being watched and our telephone tapped. She begged me not to see Percy Frey. I promised at least not to bring him back to the house anymore.

In the afternoon Lore Wolf walked into the office, straight from Lisbon. She is expecting a baby and has returned to Germany for it. She looks as if she were off another planet – new clothes, rested and trim. She is staggered by the changes around here. Before her marriage she used to work for Judgie Richter. Tatiana and Luisa Welczeck were both still unmarried and Josias Rantzau was here. How long ago all that seems!

Met Percy Frey and Tino Soldati at the Zoo station and they drove me out to the Pfuels', an hour away, where we found Aga Fürstenberg and Georgie Pappenheim.

MAHNSFELDE *Sunday, 30 July* When speaking of the 20th July, C. C. Pfuel is pointedly careful. I mention a particular detail, he looks astonished, I change the subject. I wonder whether he knew anything about it in advance. It would surprise me if he did not, as he is with the Abwehr and many there were in the plot; but then everybody is so careful these days . . .

In the afternoon, Percy Frey drove up and took some people over to Buchow, to the Horstmanns', but I stayed at home. I don't wish to see anyone.

BERLIN *Monday, 31 July* Found the office in a state of turmoil. Goebbels' recent declaration of 'total war' has driven panic through all the ranks. Our Information Department must relinquish 60 per cent of its staff, the men going off to the front, the girls into munitions factories. Edith Perfall, Usch von der Groeben and Loremarie Schönburg are all being terminated. I am kept on. One wonders why, seeing that the last technicians, photographers, etc., of my photo-archive are leaving too.

Generally, I have noticed that, ever since Adam Trott's arrest, Dr Six is treating me with unusual consideration, so much so that, at one point, I even wanted to speak to him about Adam, but Judgie Richter begged me not to, as he is, apparently, in fact furious. Adam's arrest he says, has compromised the whole Department. At the same time, he has never uttered Adam's name in public, except during one meeting, where he declared: 'Wir haben zwei Schweinehunde unter uns gehabt' ['We had two dirty dogs in our midst'], meaning Adam and Haeften. Probably, he deemed it necessary to take a public stand at least once. Otherwise he never mentions them. Indeed, Adam's name card is still pinned to his office door, like everybody else's. This comforts me, as if it were the only symbol of his continuing existence. I dread its removal.

Since the spring of 1944, Himmler had been putting out, via Sweden, discreet peace feelers. Some of Dr Six's trips to Sweden had been to further that goal. If even Himmler doubted Germany's victory, the far more pragmatic Six must have sensed what was coming. His attitude towards Trott and even towards Missie herself both before and after the 20th July coup could well have been dictated by a shrewd calculation that when the day of reckoning came, their connections in the Allied camp might come in handy. And true enough, one of Six's confidants, Dr Hans Mohnke, has testified that Six had instructed him and another senior S.S. officer, Dr Schmitz, to draft a letter to Himmler, recommending that even if some of the arrested A.A. officials (meaning Trott and Haeften) were indeed guilty, it would be wiser not to execute them, but to hold them, to be used in potential negotiations with the Allies. Himmler had allegedly endorsed this idea, but when he put it to Hitler, the latter had had a near epileptic fit and had screamed that 'the A.A. were the worst of all and should be hanged to the last man.'

During lunch Paul Metternich telephoned from the Adlon. I am horrified that he should have taken the risk of coming here at such a time. But he is too worried about his friends to stay away. He said he had not told Tatiana where he is, pretending he was making a trip to Prague on account of his other Czech estate. He added that Giorgio Cini is here again. I am happy to have Paul around, but what a moment to come to Berlin!

Later, I joined Paul and Giorgio at the Adlon. Otto Bismarck and Loremarie Schönburg were also there. Aga Fürstenberg's sense of humour is getting the better of her again. On seeing Paul, she called out across the hotel hall: 'Are you too one of the plotters, Paul, that you should look so glum?' She and Tony Saurma are our *enfants terribles* just now. The day after the attempt, Tony met a fellow-officer in the street, clicked his heels and, introducing himself, muttered: 'Stauffenberg!'

Otto soon left with Giorgio for Friedrichsruh and, while Paul was talking to someone else, Loremarie drew me into a corner and told me what she had been doing for the last two days:

Before the Gestapo drove off with him, Gottfried had time to tell her that the explosive left over from Stauffenberg's bomb was hidden in his safe at the Regierung in Potsdam and to slip her the key. Speeding back to Potsdam on the milk-train, she arrived there long before Gottfried and his escort and recovered the two parcels. They were, she said, the size of shoe boxes and wrapped in newspaper. She then took one of our bicycles and, balancing one parcel delicately on the handlebar, rode off into the park of Sans-Souci. On the way she collided with a delivery boy and fell off, parcel and all. Fearing that it might explode – she knows, naturally, nothing about such things – she heroically threw herself on top. Of course nothing happened. She finally dropped it into one of the ponds in the park. It kept bobbing up and she kept pushing it down again with a branch. Finally, despairing, she fished it out again and buried it behind some bushes. She was about to ride off when, looking up, she saw a man standing on the other side of the pond watching her. How much had he seen? Would he denounce her? She sped back to the Regierung, but by now she was too unnerved to repeat the operation with the second parcel and she buried it in one of the flowerbeds of the garden. Anna, the Bismarcks' maid, helped her, not showing the slightest curiosity. Loremarie may literally have saved Gottfried's life, for the house has been searched over and over, the first descent of the police taking place only a few hours after what she had done.

I do admire Loremarie's courage and resourcefulness, even though it sometimes borders on dangerous fanaticism.

After a snack at Maria Gersdorff's, Paul insisted on going out to Potsdam. He wanted Melanie and Gottfried to know that their friends are sticking by them. We arrived quite late. Only Otto and Loremarie were there. We stayed for an hour and caught the last train back. On the way home, I felt so ill that at some station we got down and I was violently sick on the platform, while Paul stood patiently by. It was probably the nervous reaction setting in.

Paul is a great help – quiet and matter-of-fact as usual. He is, of course, right when he says that what is happening now was absolutely inevitable and that we can do nothing about it. Since the *coup* failed, it is natural that all those involved will have to pay for it. Indeed, it provides the Nazis with a long-sought opportunity to get rid of all those they have always hated and feared.

Paul walks around with a cane that once belonged to his ancestor, the Chancellor. He is unaccustomed to using one and often trips over it. It looks deceptively light, being covered with a sort of woven cane-like material. In fact, it's made of solid iron, weighs a ton and, when he drops it, sounds like a pistol shot. The first time I jumped a mile. Paul intends to use it, if necessary.

As another key plotter, Major-General Henning von Tresckow, remarked shortly before committing suicide following the failure of the coup*: 'None of us can complain about his lot. Whoever joined the resistance donned the bloodstained shirt of Nessus. But then the worth of a man can only be gauged by his readiness to sacrifice his life for his convictions'.*

Tuesday, 1 August Paul Metternich left this morning, now that he knows everything. He has been urging me to take advantage of my authorised sick leave to join them all in Königswart. Since the first trial, we are told, cannot be held before another three weeks, I have agreed to do so.

Otto Bismarck came to lunch at Maria Gersdorff's. He is trying hard to help Gottfried, but thus far neither he nor Melanie have been 'received' by any of the potentates. Via the Gestapo they have sent food but do not know whether it reached him. Alex Werth has sent Adam Trott a suitcase but again we do not know whether it reached him.

In the evening I met Percy Frey among the ruins and we discussed various escape possibilities. Loremarie Schönburg has been working on Percy to get those that do succeed in escaping papers for Switzerland. Alice Hoyos (Melanie's sister) has come up from Vienna and is busy trying to find out in which prison they are being held.

Later, Percy drove me out to Wannsee, where Otto and I had been invited for dinner by Anfuso, Mussolini's Ambassador here. The latter is alone with his newly married wife. She is a beautiful Hungarian girl called Nelly Tasnady, a little like Tatiana in fair.

I did not have time to ask Otto whether he intended to mention what has happened to Gottfried, but I soon saw he would not. In a way this surprised me, as he and Anfuso are very great friends; on the other hand, Anfuso is one of the few Italian ambassadors who remained faithful to Mussolini after his downfall and I respect him for it. We had supper and then sat and talked. Anfuso could speak only of 'the bomb'. He was there just after it happened, as he was accompanying Mussolini on an official visit to Supreme Head-quarters. He said that Hitler was the only person, that evening, who seemed outwardly composed; the rest of his entourage were still completely dazed. Anfuso said jokingly that he himself was at first on coals, as he feared that the attempt had been made by a pro-Badoglio Italian; it had been such a relief to be told it was a German. He was full of wisecracks. Otto and I, meanwhile, were trying hard to look unconcerned and even amused.

We left early. Otto drove, his chauffeur sat in the back seat. He asked me in English whether I had seen Loremarie lately, because Melanie had been arrested this evening in Potsdam. Two men and a woman had come to fetch her at the Regierung, where she was still living, as Gottfried continues officially to be Regierungspräsident. They had searched the house, but not the garden. Thank God! Luckily Loremarie has moved to the Adlon. Otto was sure he would be the next member of the family to be arrested and asked me to come with him to the Adlon because, if the police were already waiting there, I could alert his wife Ann Mari in Friedrichsruh. I went along. It was past midnight. Otto carefully examined the hall, the letter-rack, and asked whether anybody had enquired after him; but all seemed quiet. We agreed that I would ring him up next morning at ten. If I was told that he had gone out, I would know something was wrong.

Wednesday, 2 August I myself now live at the Adlon with Loremarie Schönburg. Rang up Otto yesterday at the agreed hour. All seemed well. I also managed to reach Tatiana; Paul Metternich had got back to Königswart safely. I told her I would be arriving shortly.

Tonight there was another raid. We felt too tired to go down, but suddenly we heard two loud crashes, pulled on some trousers and sweaters and scurried down into the bunker. All the hotel guests seemed to have dressed in a hurry; Karajan, usually so spick and span, was barefoot, in a trenchcoat, his hair standing on end.

Thursday, 3 August Loremarie Schönburg spends most of her time now at Gestapo headquarters in the Prinz Albrechtstrasse, where she has made a 'contact'. He is one of Himmler's A.D.C.s whom she knew many years ago. She is trying to squeeze out of him how matters stand with Gottfried Bismarck and Adam Trott. He is totally discouraging, says 'die Schweine-hunde' will pay with their heads. Loremarie, who knows when to turn on the charm, argues with him in seeming innocence. What she is really trying to find out is whether any of the jailers can be bought. She is also trying to get to see Obergruppenführer Wolff, reputedly one of the 'tamer' S.S. generals, who is on one of his rare visits from Italy, where he is second-in-command to Field Marshal Kesselring. Obergruppenführer Lorenz, who is considered, by 'their' standards, a decent man and who has been busy mainly with resettling the Germans repatriated from Eastern Europe, is an uncle of Alex Werth's wife – he has two lovely daughters whom Georgie used to see a lot. He is, apparently, doing all he can for Adam; but he is frowned upon just now, probably *because* he is not as bad as the rest and may therefore not be of much use. On one of her visits to the Gestapo Loremarie ran in a corridor into Adam himself. His hands were manacled, he was evidently being led to interrogation; he recognised her but looked straight through her. The expression on his face, she said, was that of somebody already in another world. They are surely being tortured.

Once on the stairs Loremarie also saw Ambassador von Hassell. He was in a strait-jacket and his arm was in a sling. She had lunched with him a few days before and nothing was wrong with his arm then. At these chance meetings nobody on either side ever shows any sign of recognition.

Many of those arrested were indeed not only savagely beaten but cruelly tortured, the most common practices being finger-screws, spiked leggings and even the mediaeval 'rack'. It is to the lasting credit of the 20th July plotters that only a few were broken. Which explains why, despite the bloodbath that followed, relatively so many survived and why, when the war ended, the Gestapo still did not know all.

Hassell was, together with Count von der Schulenburg, on the plotters' cabinet list as potential Foreign Minister. Once the coup *failed, he wandered about the streets of Berlin for days before returning to his office to calmly await arrest. Most of those on the run refused to imperil their friends by hiding out with them; while others actually went out of their way to be arrested, to save their families from 'kith-and-kin' reprisals.*

This morning I was 'working' in the office, when Peter Bielenberg walked in. He has always been very close to Adam. He had come to see Alex Werth, who was out. We sat on the stairs and I told him all there is to tell. He insisted there *must* be a way of fighting Adam free. He said that he is imprisoned outside Berlin, but every morning he is brought with a one-man escort from the jail to Gestapo H.Q. in the Prinz Albrechtstrasse for interrogation. The way to do it would be to ambush the car, after which Adam would be smuggled over to the Warthegau [German-occupied Poland] and hidden with Polish partisans with whom Peter (who manages a factory there) is in touch. What a relief to hear someone ready to act and willing to take on even the S.S.! Actually, when one considers how many key officers were part of the conspiracy, and not all could have been arrested as yet, this *does* sound feasible.

At first, those implicated in the 20th July coup were held in the cellars of Gestapo headquarters in the Prinz Albrechtstrasse. But as their numbers grew, they were moved to the so-called Zellengefängnis Moabit in the Lehrterstrasse, two-and-a-half kilometres away, from where they would be brought back for interrogation.

It is gradually becoming clear that the *coup* succeeded almost everywhere except in Berlin. In Paris, everything worked out right, all senior S.S. were arrested and the entire Western Front was about to come under the plotters' control. Now General von Stülpnagel, who commanded the troops in France, has shot himself; but he is not dead, only blinded. Marshal von Kluge, G.O.C. Western Front, had had long talks with Gottfried, but does not seem to be implicated as yet. Loremarie tells me that Rommel was part of it too, but he had a terrible accident shortly before the 20th July and is still in hospital.

Many senior officers in the West were in the plot, starting with the G.O.C. Western Front, Field Marshal Hans von Kluge, and the military governor of France, General Heinrich von Stülpnagel. At 6.30 p.m. on 20 July, General Beck had called the latter from the Bendlerstrasse: 'Are you with us?' 'Of course!' was the reply, and within hours, without a single shot being fired, 1,200 key men of the S.S. and Gestapo with S.S.-Gruppenführer Carl-Albrecht Oberg – Himmler's representative in France – at their head had been taken into custody. But when later that night – by then it was known that Hitler was alive and that the putsch in Berlin was aborting – his entourage urged Kluge to go ahead on his own and sign an armistice with the Allies, he backed down and ordered the S.S. to be released. By midnight the putsch in Paris was also over.

As his car passed Verdun (where he had fought in World War I) Stülpnagel ordered the driver to stop so that he could 'stretch his legs'. Presently the driver heard a shot and rushing up found his general, pistol in hand, blinded but still alive. Despite his wound, he was dragged before Freisler's People's Court. On 30 August 1944 he was hanged together with several others of the 'Western Group'. They would be followed by many more.

Though repeatedly approached by the plotters and certainly sympathetic to their cause, Field Marshal Rommel, long one of Hitler's favourite generals, had never committed himself. Following the Normandy landings, however, he had sent Hitler an ultimatum demanding an immediate end to the war in the West. Two days later, while driving back from the Normandy front, his car was strafed by Allied fighter-bombers and he was severely wounded. While recovering at home in Germany, his contacts with the plotters came to light. On 14 October, served in his turn with an ultimatum – to commit suicide or face arrest and trial together with his family – Rommel took poison. For the sake of appearances, Hitler gave him a state funeral.

In Vienna also, everthing went well, but the takeover lasted only forty-eight hours. By that time, all those involved were already so compromised that virtually none have escaped.

In Vienna, as in Paris, the military takeover was completely successful. But when a few hours later the local commanders realised that 'Valkyrie' was a sham to cover up an overthrow of the regime, they backed down, and the S.S. and Gestapo took over.

Contrary to what Missie thought, nowhere else in Germany or German-occupied Europe did the plotters' calls to overthrow the regime meet with any positive response – in itself a telling proof of their lack of support even among the German armed forces.

Tonight Loremarie, Georgie Pappenheim, Tony Saurma and I gathered for supper at Aga Fürstenberg's. Corned beef, even whisky – Georgie's last supplies from Spain. Then Tony drove me and Loremarie back to the Adlon. Thanks to his wounded leg, he is still allowed to use a car. He has become indispensable. He is always fooling, is very helpful, is a pillar of strength and has lots of guts. There are so few like him left . . .

Ever since Adam's arrest I had been trying to reach Hasso Etzdorf, who, I have now learnt, was an early member of the plot. Which is, of course, why he seemed so evasive, even to me. I had heard that he was in town and hoped that he might suggest something. A few days ago he passed me in his car on the Kurfürstendamm, stopped, got out and came back to meet me. Then, taking me by the arm, he steered me through the ruins up the back stairs of the bombed-out house of the fashionable photographer Vog. Only then did we speak. He confirmed the rumour that Fritzi Schulenberg had kept lists of participants and of their future functions. Madness! I told him how desperately I had tried to reach him and how much I was counting on him. He said that the worst of it was that there was nobody left in any influential position to turn to. Nevertheless, he promised to do what he could. I had the feeling that he expected to be arrested any moment himself; he kept looking around and stopped talking whenever he heard a sound. He promised to come and see me in a few days, but I have not heard from him again.

KÖNIGSWART *Saturday, 5 August* This morning I caught an early train for Königswart, where I plan to stay as long as my health certificate permits.

Sunday, 6 August Hansi Welczeck, who is training near Dresden, came over for the weekend. His wife Sigi has been here all summer taking a cure with Tatiana. We spend most of the time lying in the sun on the island and talking about the 20th July. Paul Metternich is trotting out his best wines and Hansi is getting fatter by the hour. Around tea time an immense limousine drove into the courtyard. Thanhofer, Paul's faithful major-domo and secretary, had barricaded all doors. We were convinced that it was the police. Tatiana went down to meet them, trying to look unconcerned. The door swung open and Sigi's sister, Reni Stinnes, alighted. She was driving her boy-friend's car. He is a rather likeable Levantine, who seems to deal in the black market or something. Reni stayed for tea and described Budapest, where she had just been to buy clothes. It sounds like an oasis.

Tuesday, 8 August Front-page news in all today's papers: Field Marshal von Witzleben, Lieutenant-General von Hase, Colonel-General Hoepner, Major-General Stieff, Count Peter Yorck von Wartenburg and several others – eight in all – have been thrown out of the army and put on trial before the dread Volksgericht [People's Court]. This means, evidently, that they will be condemned to death, to be either shot or hanged. The announcement is headed 'High Treason'. None of the others whom we know to be under arrest are mentioned. This gives us a tiny hope that the authorities are trying to play the whole thing down.

As early as 24 July Martin Bormann had warned all Gauleiters that Hitler was anxious that comments about the coup *should not degenerate into an all-out attack on the officers corps. Emphasis should be on the assassination attempt as a lone gesture, not on a wide-ranging conspiracy. For their part, the senior generals promptly did their bit to ward off any possible attack against the armed forces: on 4 August a special Court of Honour, headed by the prestigious Field Marshal Gerd von Rundstedt, stripped of their uniforms all military personnel involved in the plot, thus delivering them into the hands of the hangman.*

The Allied radio makes no sense to us: they keep naming people who, they claim, took part in the plot. And yet some of these have not yet been officially implicated.

I remember warning Adam Trott that this would happen. He kept hoping for Allied support of a 'decent' Germany and I kept saying that at this point they were out to destroy Germany, *any* Germany, and would not stop at eliminating the 'good' Germans with the 'bad'.

It turned out to be singularly difficult to obtain exact information about these Allied broadcasts, which certainly proved fatal to some who might otherwise have survived.

All those responsible for or involved in British wartime broadcasts to Germany whom this editor approached, denied any knowledge of them. And yet their existence is beyond dispute. As Christabel Bielenberg, wife of Peter, put it in The Past Is Myself *(op. cit.): 'There was no comfort anywhere . . . Churchill's ponderous satisfaction at "Germans killing Germans"; or that jaunty crew from* Soldatensender Eins, *usually good for a laugh, but now like macabre boy scouts gleefully hammering nails into coffins by implicating everyone they could think of in what they called "the Peace Plot" . . .' The closest anyone has come to admitting their existence is Michael Balfour in* Propaganda in War: 1939–1945 *(Routledge & Kegan Paul, 1970): 'At the same time,* Soldatensender Calais, *besides nourishing rumours as to the people who had been involved, contributed to the distrust between Party and Army, which was one undoubted result . . .' Both* Soldatensender Eins *and* Soldaten-sender Calais *used formerly German-controlled wavelengths to beam 'black' i.e. demoralising propaganda to Germany. They were run by the Ministry of Information in London.*

Apart from the more sinister motivations that come to mind in the light of the self-confessed role played at the time in British intelligence by Kim Philby in successfully neutralising some of the peace feelers put out by the resisters (see his My Secret War, *Granada Publishing, 1969), the resisters themselves may have been partly respon-sible for these destructive broadcasts by exaggerating the numbers and prominence of their alleged sympathisers in order to impress the Allies.*

The ambiguous attitude of the Allies towards the anti-Nazi German resistance that had so disappointed the plotters prior to 20 July, continued after the failure of the coup. Whereas already on 23 July the Soviet-sponsored 'National Committee for a Free Germany' appealed to the Wehrmacht and civilian population to support the movement even though it had already failed, the British continued to steer clear of any positive stand. In due course the B.B.C. was instructed to interpret the affair not as the beginning of civil war (as it had started by doing), but merely as evidence that the German generals, faced with the inevitability of defeat, considered further fighting senseless. As Winston Churchill put it to Brendan Bracken, when the latter broke the news to him: 'the more Germans kill one another, the better.'

Wednesday, 9 August Paul Metternich has received a postcard from Albert Eltz, who had just spent a few hours in Berlin. 'Dear Paul. Am in Berlin. Am absolutely in despair. What a tragedy! What a mess! All our hopes dashed to the ground! What do you say about the attempt on the Führer's life? Thanks to Providence, our glorious Leader has been saved once more. Your loving Albert!'

Friday, 11 August The papers give details of the first session of the Volksgericht and the cross-examination of the first batch of defendants. Most of their answers, as published, seem to be purest invention – on the pattern of the Stalin show trials. Sometimes they make absolutely no sense and are worded in such a way as to make the plotters seem utterly ridiculous in the eyes of the nation. The presiding judge, a man called Freisler, is quite evidently a cynical swine. Nobody will forget him.

All the defendants have been sentenced to be hanged. General von Hase and his family were good friends of ours; Mamma, particularly, saw them regularly. They had even visited here. Count Yorck was a close friend of Adam Trott. All his brothers and sisters have been arrested too, excepting one, the widow of the late Ambassador von Moltke.

A one-time Communist (he had been converted as a P.O.W. in Siberia in World War I), Dr Roland Freisler (1893–1945) had participated in the fateful Wannsee Conference of 20 January 1942 which mapped the 'Final Solution' of the Jewish problem in German-occupied Europe. In August 1942 he had been appointed President of the Volksgericht, a tribunal established to provide summary justice, in camera *and without right of appeal, to those accused of crimes against the Third Reich.*

Hitler himself had laid down the ground-rules of the trials: 'The important point is that they be allowed no time to make long speeches. But Freisler will see to that. He is our Vyshinsky!' – referring to Stalin's Chief Prosecutor at the Moscow show trials. To ridicule them in the eyes of the handpicked spectators, the accused had their ties, braces and belts removed – thus giving Freisler the occasion to mock the way some of them had to clutch at their trousers.

At a given signal from Freisler, concealed cameras would start to whirr, whereupon he would start screaming invective at the accused to demoralise them and to impress the audience – and especially Hitler himself, to whom the developed films were rushed. The engineers kept complaining that this shouting made the sound track unintelligible, but to no avail. His taunts, sarcasms and vulgar abuse shocked even Justice Minister Dr Thierack (himself responsible for some of the most criminal laws enacted in the Third Reich; he was to commit suicide in Allied captivity): he complained to Martin Bormann that Freisler's behaviour 'is very questionable and impairs the seriousness of this important occasion'. Originally, Goebbels had planned to show the films on the weekly newsreels, but the first one made such a bad impression on the handpicked Nazi audience that the idea was abandoned. Only one copy survived – in East Germany, where it was discovered some thirty years later and screened before a spell-bound audience by the TV stations of West Germany in July 1979.

Saturday, 12 August A letter from Maria Gersdorff. Her style is very hazy. She evidently cannot say very much . . . 'everything so sad and depressing . . .' I cling to the hope that she means this first trial, but am very uneasy nevertheless.

Antoinette Croy and her husband drove over from Karlsbad. She gave us the latest news from Paris. She had seen a lot of Georgie there. Apparently, he had offered to procure from his contacts in the Resistance a false identity card for her, so that she could call off her marriage and stay on in France until the war is over. He had even brought this paper to the station as she was leaving, in the hope that she would change her mind at the last moment!

Friday, 18 August We swam naked in the lake. Our life trickles on in this seemingly leisurely fashion, and all the time one's anguish is like an iron band around one's head that is being squeezed relentlessly tighter. My leave, which, I suppose, has done me some physical good, is over in three days. I feel strangely relieved, as the quiet here is often unbearable. It is sometimes difficult, too, with the parents, who show little understanding, probably because they know nothing but are beginning to suspect something, are worried about me and insist on knowing more. And I don't tell them much, so as not to upset them, and that makes it worse still.

BERLIN *Tuesday, 22 August* Arrived in Berlin early this morning and went straight to Maria Gersdorff. I found her at breakfast. I asked her for the latest news. She looked at me aghast. 'You mean you don't know? Adam, Haeften, Helldorf, Fritzi Schulenburg and many others were condemned to death and hanged last Friday!' I immediately telephoned Loremarie Schönburg, but couldn't get a word out. She said she would be here in a minute. Maria said that Loremarie's efforts were now exclusively devoted to trying to find out where our old Count Schulenburg is. For he disappeared last night.

Loremarie arrived and we sat on the steps, looking blindly into the ruins. She is paralysed by all that has happened. Actually, she is not convinced that Adam *has* been hanged. It is rumoured that he is the only one whose execution was postponed.

On 11 August the A.A. had been informed that Trott would be sentenced to death at

the very next session of the People's Court, on Tuesday 15 or Wednesday 16 August.
But in due course Martin Bormann was informed that 'since Trott has undoubtedly
withheld a great deal, the death sentence handed down by the People's Court has not
been carried out, so that [he] may be available for further clarification.'

Tony Saurma attended the trial, which is in itself astounding, for only a
handpicked audience is allowed in. Loremarie waited outside in his car.
When he reappeared, he broke down and cried. All the accused had admitted
that they wanted to kill Hitler. Haeften said that if he could, he would try to do
so again. He considered Hitler Germany's damnation and a great perpetrator
of evil, who had driven his country to a precipice and was responsible for its
downfall. The Judge, Freisler, asked him whether he realised that what he
was saying was high treason. Haeften answered that he knew he would be
hanged, but this did not alter his views.

Though in fact Hans-Bernd von Haeften had, for ethical reasons, opposed the killing
of Hitler, unlike Trott, he seems never to have doubted what his fate would be once the
coup failed. After driving out to the country to say farewell to his family, he returned
to Berlin, where he was among the first to be arrested.

Adam said that Hitler had come to power by fraud and that many had
sworn allegiance to him against their will. He said that he had wanted to put
an end to the war and admitted having had talks abroad with representatives
of the enemy powers. Helldorf said that he had wanted Hitler's downfall ever
since Stalingrad, that he was a menace to the country. According to Tony,
they all looked pale, but that it was difficult to say whether they had been
tortured. I am sure they were, as Adam's last words to me had been that he
would deny everything in order to get out and try again. Or else the evidence
of their guilt must have been overwhelming, and they themselves were at the
end of their tether.

I dragged myself to the office and up the stairs to Judgie Richter and Alex
Werth, who were alone in their room. We spoke only in whispers. Alex said he
knows that Adam is still alive, for they are in touch with one of the policemen
who is present at the executions. All the others are dead. Helldorf was hanged
last, so that he might watch the others die. It appears that they are not simply
hanged, but are slowly strangulated with piano wire on butchers' hooks and,
to prolong their agony, are given heart booster injections. It is rumoured that

the killings are being filmed and that Hitler regularly gloats over these films at his Headquarters.

The executions took place at Plötzensee prison, a short drive from the Lehrterstrasse prison where most of the condemned were held. As there were no gallows in Germany (the usual way of execution being beheading) ordinary meat-hooks had been fixed to an iron rail set in the ceiling of the execution cell – a separate building within the prison compound. The hangings were filmed, with spot-lights illuminating the scene, and were attended by the Chief Prosecutor of the Reich, a couple of wardens, two cameramen and the executioner with his two assistants. On a table stood a bottle of brandy – for the audience. The condemned were brought in one by one; the executioners fixed the nooses round their necks (Hitler had prescribed piano wire instead of rope so that death would come by slow strangulation rather than from a broken neck); and while they writhed and twisted, sometimes for as long as twenty minutes, and the cameras whirred, the executioner – who was famous for his macabre humour – cracked obscene jokes. The film was then rushed to Hitler's H.Q., where the Führer would gloat over it. The building is today a memorial.

Adam's wife, Clarita, has also been arrested. She was not allowed to see Adam after he was sentenced. I knew her very little, because for the last couple of years she had been staying a lot in the country with her parents-in-law. Their little girls were also picked up by the Gestapo and nobody knows their whereabouts, but Alex is raising hell to get them back.

Upon learning about his arrest, Adam's wife Clarita had rushed to Berlin in the hope of seeing him – without success; while she was away the Gestapo picked up their two little girls, aged two-and-a-half and nine months. On the day of Adam's trial Alexander Werth tried to smuggle her into the courthouse but a charwoman noticed them and denounced her to an S.S. guard. The latter, to her surprise, tried to help her get in too – without success. When she thanked him nevertheless, he muttered: 'We understand everything!' Two days later Clarita herself was arrested.

I now live with Loremarie in Tony's flat off the Kurfürstendamm. It consists of two rooms with hardly any furniture apart from two sofas, a kitchen and a bathroom. Tony commutes back and forth between his unit in the country and town, mainly to keep an eye on Loremarie, who, he is convinced, is next on the list. He does not dare leave us alone at night. There are not enough bedclothes to go around, but it is so hot that it does not matter.

Of course, Loremarie *is* in great danger; she goes to Gestapo headquarters practically every day, trying to get inside information. Otto Bismarck is in touch with the Gestapo inspector who is in charge of Gottfried's dossier; the inspector told him that Gottfried's case was 'very serious'; the Führer, he said, is merciless about the 20th July to the point of obsession; he keeps telephoning Gestapo H.Q. daily to hear how many more people have been hanged. Loremarie's contact there says that when the Gestapo seeks to gain time – and in some cases this seems to be what they are doing, probably so as to discover more about the plot – the Führer flies into a rage and insists that they hurry.

I had thought of moving out to the Bredows in Potsdam, although Hanna, Gottfried's sister, is away, but I have just learnt that three of the Bredow girls have been arrested too. They first fetched Philippa, young Haeften's friend, who is nineteen; then they telephoned twenty-year-old Alexandra, asking her to bring blankets for her sister, and held her; then they rang up the third, Diana, who cheekily asked whether it might not be more practical for her to bring bedclothes for all the family. They answered yes indeed, it might. The only one who has been left alone is Marguerite, who is a doctor in a hospital. They keep summoning her to Gestapo headquarters but when they start putting questions, she acts very indignant and protests that she has an entire ward of wounded to look after. Of the Bredow boys the eldest is at the front – the others are still too young.

Wednesday, 23 August Today, the papers published a long account of Adam Trott's trial, following which all the accused were, they say, executed on the spot. Adam was described as 'foreign affairs advisor of Stauffenberg'. Strangely enough, the dates of these press releases rarely coincide with the actual events – probably to confuse any still existing opposition. After this announcement Adam's name-plate was at last removed from his office door and somebody else's put there instead. It makes me feel faint to look at it. I never do. In fact I avoid his floor as much as possible. His car is still parked in the garden, nobody uses it, it looks already a derelict. Alex Werth, however, tells me that he thinks he is still alive, although Dr Six was informed officially that he had indeed been hanged with the others on the 18th.

Loremarie Schönburg is up to another game. A Luftwaffe colonel who resides at Karinhall, Goering's estate in the country, sat talking with her practically all night. He thinks that he is converting her to National Socialism while she tries to convince him how useful it might be if she met Goering. The latter has withdrawn from the scene for some time now and thus far has refused to see even Otto Bismarck, who was often his host at shoots in Friedrichsruh. He is manifestly terrified of being somehow implicated in the recent events himself.

Melanie Bismarck has had a miscarriage in prison and is now under guard in a Potsdam hospital. Nobody is allowed to see her but one can talk to the nurse.

We have heard nothing of Count Schulenburg since he disappeared last Tuesday. On Monday he had rung up Loremarie from the Adlon, where he had just arrived from Hitler's Headquarters. She had lunched with him and told him about all that had happened. He did not seem to have been *au courant*, was visibly shaken and was particularly upset about Adam. They walked up and down the hotel lobby under the baleful eye of Gesandter Schleier (not very prudent of them) and agreed to lunch together again on the morrow. Next day Loremarie was punctual at the rendezvous, but he never turned up. Whereupon she telephoned the Wilhelmstrasse, but his staff there knew nothing of his whereabouts and were beginning to worry, as they had expected him that morning. We are convinced he has been arrested. But where have they jailed him?

Goerdeler was recognised by a Blitzmädchen [German W.A.C.] five days ago, denounced and arrested. He was hiding out in a village in Pomerania. We suspect that Adam is being kept alive because of him (they had worked closely together) and that they are being cross-interrogated. If only Adam had left the country in time! And how could Goerdeler expect to hide out in Germany, when they had offered a million marks for his capture?

The warrant for Goerdeler's arrest had been issued before the coup, on 17 July. Forewarned, he had gone into hiding, first in Berlin (one of his 'hosts', the former Jewish deputy mayor of Berlin, Dr Fritz Elsas, paid for this with his life) then in the country. Arrested on 12 August, he was sentenced to death on 8 September, but survived for another five months by feeding his 'revelations' in driblets and drafting endless memoranda on the plotters' alleged future plans for Germany. Finally, the Gestapo saw through his game and on 2 February 1945 he, too, was executed.

I will move heaven and earth to get Adam and Gottfried out, and Count

Schulenburg too, if need be. One cannot go on leading an utterly passive existence, just waiting resignedly for the axe to fall. Now that the families of the conspirators are also being arrested and even their friends, many people are so frightened that it is enough to mention a name for them to look away. To achieve this, I have thought of a new approach: I will try and tackle Goebbels. Loremarie also thinks that something could be done through Goebbels, be it only because he is intelligent enough to perhaps realise the folly of all these executions. I don't quite know how to go about this, as the only person I know who knows him well, Frau von Dirksen, would immediately put two and two together. It might be better to pretend that I want a part in a film. I will therefore call Jenny Jugo, who is one of the most popular German stars.

Thursday, 24 August This morning I rang up Jenny Jugo. When I insisted that I had to see her immediately, she sounded alarmed. She said she was filming at the U.F.A. studios in Babelsberg, and that if I took the S-Bahn, she would send a car to fetch me. I arrived in stifling heat and was driven to the studios by a strange-looking youth with long yellow hair and a colourful shirt. I found Jenny in the act of being filmed, with a young man at her feet, clasping her knees. Luckily the shot did not last long and presently she came back into her dressing room to change. She sent away her maid so that we could talk, but even then we only whispered.

I told her I *had* to see Goebbels and that she *must* arrange an interview for me. She said that if it was absolutely necessary, she would of course do so, but that she herself had quarrelled with him and had not seen him in two years: 'Why, are Tatiana or Paul Metternich in trouble?' I said: 'Neither'. She breathed a sigh of relief. I said 'It's my boss', adding that he had been condemned to death but was, we suspected, still alive and that we had to act quickly. After all, Goebbels was the hero of the day – it is he who had crushed the uprising! I would tell him that Germany could not afford to destroy so many exceptionally gifted men who could be of such use to their country, etc. Jenny listened to all this quietly and then took me out into the garden. There she exploded: my idea was total madness. Goebbels is such a swine that he would not dream of helping *anybody*. *Nothing* would induce him to lift a little finger for *any* of them. After Helldorf was hanged, he had refused to see the son who had come to ask for a reprieve – they had been early party friends –

and did not even have the decency to let him know that his father was already dead. She said that he is a cruel, vicious little sadist, that his hatred for all those involved in the attempt on Hitler's life is beyond belief, that he has a visceral loathing for all that they stood for, that he is a real sewer rat, and that if I caught his notice in the slightest way, I would drag the whole family into it, Paul would be arrested, and my own troubles would never end. She beseeched me to drop the whole idea and added that the U.F.A. studios are teeming with Goebbels' spies, who are trying to snoop out potential defectors from among the actors. Two days ago there had been a political meeting and when Goebbels appeared in the hall, there was a huge *'Merde'* written in chalk on the red pulpit at which he was to stand and nobody dared come forward to erase it. Her own telephone is being bugged, she can hear the click whenever she uses it. As she kissed me goodbye, she whispered that if anyone asked about the reason for my visit, she would say that I was trying to get into films.

I returned to town, discouraged and exhausted, to find Loremarie Schönburg and Tony Saurma at the flat, Loremarie completely hysterical. I have never seen her like this before. This afternoon, they said, the police had called; neighbours had complained about our inadequate blackout but, however unimportant the reason, Loremarie is suddenly broken. Tony had more bad news: Marshal von Kluge, the German G.O.C. in the West, had committed suicide, which meant that they are being tortured and that someone gave him away, since practically nobody knew that he was involved.

Kluge's defection on the day of the aborted putsch availed also him little. Though one of Hitler's favourite and most successful commanders, his close contacts with the plotters eventually came to light. Relieved of his command, and summoned back to Germany on 17 August, he suspected that he, too, would be put on trial and committed suicide on the way.

Loremarie got more and more hysterical. None of us, she said, will get away . . . they give you an injection that destroys your willpower and makes you talk. She begged me to marry Percy Frey and leave for Switzerland immediately. Tony chimed in and said that he was willing to take her to Switzerland whenever she liked, as he himself intended to run away at the end of the week; but he must first go down to Silesia to fetch some valuables. For Tony is beginning to worry also about himself as someone has denounced him for shooting in their mess hall in a fit of drunkenness at the

Führer's photograph. Loremarie said that she would not leave with him without marrying him first or her parents would have a fit. For all the horror of the situation, I find this sudden concern for the proprieties rather funny. Tony flatly refused, saying that they could think about that later. Tension mounted and soon everybody around the kitchen table was in tears. Tony jumped up and began to stride up and down, saying that he could not bear the strain and the tears any longer and that he was firmly determined to fly the coop. I said they could do whatever they liked but *I* was staying on and Loremarie should too; in Switzerland she would be without news from her family until the end of the war; she could never take that. In the end we all decided to stay.

Tony then came into my room and told me all about Adam's trial. Adam had caught sight of him, had made no sign of recognition, had looked at him fixedly for a long time and had then started to sway back and forth from the waist in a rocking kind of movement. He wore no tie, was clean-shaven and very pale. Tony had examined the hall where the trial was taking place very carefully and had concluded that there was absolutely no chance of rescuing anybody by force from there. Even the so-called 'public' was made up mostly of thugs and police, all of them armed. He had gone out before the verdict was read out as he knew from the start what it would be.

There are air-raids every night now, but we have a pass from Tony for the Siemens office bunker across the street. They have a wonderful cellar deep underground where one feels really safe. We usually sit it out with the night shift; one of the workmen is a nice Frenchman and we dream together aloud how lovely Paris will be again once the war is over.

Friday, 25 August Loremarie Schönburg has recovered from her brief fit of depression and is again on the war path. We have found out at last that the prison – a military jail – is near the Lehrter station. She has already been there and, with the help of cigarettes provided by Percy Frey, has managed to bribe one of the wardens, who agreed to take Gottfried Bismarck a message scribbled on a tiny piece of paper. He even brought back an answer in which Gottfried complained of the vermin, asked for anti-lice powder and also for a little food, as they only get black bread and he cannot digest it. He has not received any of the packages sent to him, so the only alternative seems to be to bring him sandwiches every day. Loremarie wants to ask the wardens whether Adam Trott is there too, but one must be careful, for officially he is dead and any untoward curiosity might put them on their guard, make an eventual escape still more difficult or even hasten his execution.

Most people, including Loremarie, are shocked because I am so relieved that Adam may perhaps be still alive. Far better to be dead, they say, than to undergo torture daily. But I do not agree and keep hoping for a miracle.

Suddenly I thought of Peter Bielenberg and wondered what happened to his plan of ambushing the car that used to take Adam to Gestapo H.Q. for questioning. He seemed so full of hope and optimism the last time he came to the office. Today I took the bus out to his house in Dahlem. The door was opened by a girl who looked me up and down suspiciously, blocked the entrance and refused to talk; she said only that Peter was not there and would not be returning for some time. I felt that she knew more than she would say but did not trust me, so I told her that I came from the A.A. and that I had been working with Herr von Trott. At that, her face changed, she went back into the house and another girl came out. This one was friendlier; she told me that Peter had vanished, nor had he been seen at the factory outside town where he was working. I asked for his address, as it was urgent for me to reach him. She said she could easily imagine so, but that there was no sense in writing, as letters would not reach him. Which meant that he too has been arrested.

I went away in a daze. Waiting for my bus back to town, I sat on the curb, too tired and discouraged even to stand. Wherever I turn, everybody is disappearing one by one; there is nobody left whom one can ask for help. They are now arresting people who were mere acquaintances or who happened to work in the same office. I do not know whether Peter was himself an active conspirator, but at Göttingen University he and Adam belonged to the same fraternity and were close friends and even that may be enough to compromise him.

At the time of the 20th July coup *Peter Bielenberg was managing a factory in German-occupied Poland. Upon learning, on 25 July, of Trott's arrest, he had taken off for Berlin to organise his rescue, which is when he had discussed his plan with Missie. But hardly had he returned to Poland to put the finishing touches to it when he himself was arrested and imprisoned in the notorious Lehrterstrasse jail.*

And then I remembered Claus B. Though in the past I had always avoided getting too chummy with him because I was never quite sure what his game was, now, I decided, if he was what I suspected, he might be the one person able to help. Back in town I searched around for a still functioning telephone booth and called his office. I told him I had to see him urgently. He told me to wait for him near the Zoo station. We walked past the wrecked Gedächtniskirche along the Budapesterstrasse; I told him everything. When I had finished, he stopped and, looking at me with an amused smile, said: 'So you suspect I am one of *them*?' 'I *hope* you are', I blurted, 'for then perhaps you can do something!' He turned instantly earnest and said that he would try and find out what the situation was and if anything *could* be done, I could of course rely on him. We arranged to meet tomorrow outside the ruined Hotel Eden.

Saturday, 26 August Today I asked Gesandter Schleier whether I could be discharged as I wanted to join the Red Cross and become a nurse. For if anything happens to Judgie Richter and Alex Werth – my last friends here – I will be left alone with this gang. The only problem is that this may be taken as a gesture of solidarity with those who are gone. Schleier was discouraging; Dr Six, he said, will let nobody go of their own free will. The only solution, I conclude, is another illness.

After work this afternoon I hurried over to the Hotel Eden. Claus B. was strolling up and down with a largish newspaper parcel under his arm. Without a word he led me to a bench in what remains of the Zoo. After making sure that there was no one within hearing, he told me that he had enquired into the situation, that there was absolutely nothing anyone – least of all somebody like myself – could do; that Hitler was thirsting for revenge; that none of those implicated would escape; that everyone is so scared that even those who might have a moderating influence would not stir a finger so as not to arouse suspicion. He went on to say that all those who had any contact with any one of the plotters are being watched and that I am now in the greatest danger; that with their methods of interrogation I might be made to talk and implicate others who are still at large, and that at any price I had to avoid arrest. At this point he opened up a corner of the parcel and I saw the barrel of a small submachine pistol. 'If they come for you, don't hesitate, shoot them all and run for it. As they won't be expecting it, you may be able to get away . . .' I couldn't help smiling. 'No, Claus. If I am really in such trouble, then I had better not make things worse by being guilty also of murder . . .' He seemed genuinely disappointed.

After leaving him, I went out to Potsdam to fetch some of my things at the Regierung; I spoke to both servants. They told me that Melanie Bismarck had been denounced by someone on their estate in Pomerania for varnishing her toenails and taking her breakfast in bed and that this had complicated her case as it made her *asozial* as well. She was, they said, very weak and, on getting up in hospital for the first time yesterday, fainted, fell on her face and broke her jaw. It's heart-rending. Her brother Jean-Georges Hoyos had been allowed to see her. She kept asking him: 'Il est mort?' ['Is he dead?'] Later, I bicycled over to the vegetable gardens and exchanged some coffee for two melons which we will try to take to the prison.

On my return to Berlin I found Loremarie at the Gersdorffs'. She related that when the guard brought her Gottfried's dirty laundry today, she asked him in a whisper whether 'Herr von Trott' was still there. He said 'Ja, ja, er ist noch da' ['Yes, yes, he is still here'], and that she could write him a note; he would bring her an answer tomorrow. She wrote: 'Can we bring you anything? Love from Missie and Loremarie'. She asked the man whether Adam was very hungry; he said no, Count Bismarck shared his parcels with him. If only we could be sure that this man is not lying! [*In fact, on this same day Adam von Trott was hanged in Plötzensee prison.*]

We still have no news of Count Schulenburg. We now know that all cells numbered 100 and above are occupied by those who still have a chance of survival; those numbered 99 and below are occupied by those already condemned. Gottfried's cell is number 184; Adam's is 97. It is rumoured that they are in chains.

Alex Werth has been able to rescue Adam's children and they are back in the country, but his wife Clarita is still in prison. The Stauffenberg children are in an orphanage under a different name, but this has leaked out, so it may be possible to find them one day.

The children of the plotters alone numbered about fifty, some of them babies. The Nazis' original plan had been to kill off the parents and the older brothers and sisters and to scatter the others, under new identities, among S.S. schools and families, to be brought up as Nazis. For some reason this plan was abandoned and in October 1944 some of the children were allowed to go home, while the rest were hidden away in ordinary boarding schools. But even after the war was over, some time went by before all the families were re-united.

It is said that Gottfried's niece, Philippa von Bredow, will be tried by the Volksgericht too; they have managed to make her talk and she admitted knowing in advance from young Haeften the date set for the attempt on Hitler's life.

A long talk with Otto and Ann Mari Bismarck, who are both here, trying to get to see someone at the top. Loremarie Schönburg thinks that some of the jailers can be bribed, so long as they themselves can be helped to escape. She hopes that the Bismarck pearls will be sacrificed for the occasion. We ourselves have few valuables to offer. It appears that every prisoner has six jailers. Even if we did succeed in bribing them, this means that we would have to spirit out of the country three prisoners and eighteen jailers. I can just see Percy Frey's face! Whereupon Ann Mari remarks wryly: 'Why not give a cocktail party at Templehof to wave them goodbye?' We discussed all this in the Adlon in one of the upstairs bedrooms.

Gottfried Cramm has come in from the country. I am not happy to see him. Another one to worry about. The last time we met was on 20 July. He too was a friend of Adam Trott's and so at least we can talk openly about him. He now said: 'I don't want to hear what is happening to them. All I want to know is whether any of them will survive and get out, who is still free and when they intend to try again. For if so, they can count on me!' At the same time he is appalled that Stauffenberg's bomb killed one of the plotters' own men, a Colonel Brandt, who before the war had been a famous *concours hippique* champion. He was present at the fateful meeting in Hitler's map room and was killed on the spot. At first, he had been buried with all honours, as one of the victims of the 'cowardly act of treason', but later, when his name was found on some list, his body was dug up again, burnt and the ashes scattered to the winds.

A senior officer with the Operations Section of the O.K.W., Colonel Heinz Brandt, though not an active plotter, was close to many of them and sympathised with their ideas. Once before, in 1943, he had almost perished in an earlier attempt on Hitler's life, when a bottle of brandy – which, unknown to him, contained a bomb – failed to explode in mid-air as the Führer's party was flying back to Rastenburg from the Eastern Front. On 20 July it was he who inadvertently helped to save Hitler's life by pushing Stauffenberg's briefcase out of the way. When the bomb exploded, all those standing to the right of the trestle, including Brandt himself, were either killed or badly injured.

Gottfried wants me to arrange a meeting between him and Alex Werth. The office won't do and I can think of no other place except at Maria Gersdorff's, that is if she does not object. But she is very worried about her husband, who was close to the late General von Hase.

Sunday, 27 August We spent most of the day cleaning the flat. Afterwards Percy Frey drove us over to Aga Fürstenberg's, where we sat sunning ourselves in the garden.

From a letter from Missie in Berlin to her mother in Schloss Königswart, dated 28 August 1944. I enclose several letters from Georgie, which a friend of his who left just before the Allies marched in has brought over from Paris. As you will see, all seems well with him . . . Here in Berlin and the surroundings it has not rained for seven weeks. It is like living in an oven. And to top that, all around so much worry and misery. There are air-raid alerts every night and almost every day, but little happens . . . I myself will probably take some leave in Königswart next week or I will lose it altogether. The day after tomorrow I will be going back to Krummhübel for a couple of days.

KRUMMHÜBEL *Wednesday, 30 August* Early this morning I left for Krumm-hübel. At Hirschberg, I missed the connection and had to wait three hours. As I was getting off the train, I noticed Blankenhorn following me. My first reaction on seeing anybody connected with Adam Trott is to burst into tears. Depositing my suitcase with the left luggage, I wandered out into the street. Blankenhorn still behind me. As he passed, I heard him mutter, 'Go into the park and sit down on a bench. I will join you.' Coming from different directions we reached the bench at the same time. Only then did he dare speak.

He told me that he and Adam had met in the Grunewald woods on the 21st. He had asked Adam whether he had destroyed all his papers. Adam replied that he had. But some papers *had* been found, mainly *aides-mémoires* about his various journeys abroad. What folly! I asked Blankenhorn whether he thought they would kill Adam. He said: 'Without the slightest doubt!' I told him that Count Schulenburg too had disappeared. He did not know this, but said that if he *had* been arrested, they would certainly kill him too. I said: 'Impossible. It would be too much of a scandal abroad!' – 'What do they care about *that*?' He told me that Goerdeler had rented under another name a room at the Hotel Bristol, where he kept a safe with all his secret papers. Last

February, the Bristol was destroyed by an air mine. A fortnight after the attempt on Hitler's life, the safe had been discovered by chance among the rubble and dug out. Not only was it intact, together with all the papers it contained, but some of these were found to be annotated and corrected by Ambassador von Hassell in his own hand. Which explains *his* arrest. Blankenhorn said that more and more people were being arrested daily. We caught the same train to Krummhübel, but agreed not to see anything of each other there. I am so glad that he is still free and pray that they do not also get him.

The day after tomorrow I am going back to Berlin. I am packing my last belongings and sending them to Johannisberg, although only the roof of the castle has as yet been rebuilt. But there will surely be a barn or something where they can be kept. Krummhübel seems utterly remote and to me quite unbearable, and without Count Schulenberg it makes me even more miserable. I dropped by to chat with his staff; they know as yet nothing of his disappearance but his secretary, Fraülein Schilling, and his assistant Sch. (who, thank God, did not stay on in Switzerland as we feared) have been summoned to Berlin. There they will surely find out.

To this day, the exact number of those executed in connection with the 20th July Plot remains a subject of controversy. According to official Nazi sources those arrested after the coup *numbered some 7,000. A total of 5,764 were executed in 1944 and a further 5,684 in the five remaining months of Nazi rule in 1945. Of these, some 160 to 200 were directly implicated in the plot. They included: 21 generals, 33 colonels and lieutenant-colonels, 2 ambassadors, 7 senior diplomats, one minister of state, 3 secretaries of state, the head of the Criminal Police and numbers of high officials, provincial governors and top police chiefs.*

BERLIN *Friday, 1 September* The war began five years ago today.

I arrived in Berlin at lunch time and went straight to Maria Gersdorff's. She looked a little paler than usual and said quite calmly: 'Missie, you will have to stay here for good. Loremarie Schönburg and Percy Frey have brought over all your things' – pointing to a number of sandbags spilling out my belongings – 'Tony Saurma was arrested yesterday morning.' The charge: shooting at a picture of the Führer some time ago and announcing after Stauffenberg's attempt: 'Well, never mind, better luck next time!' Percy had already got hold of a lawyer, a man who works for the Swiss at their Office for the Safeguard of Enemy Interests. He is a well-known anti-Nazi – in itself not so wise a choice! – and a brilliant man; moreover he also lives nearby in the Woyrschstrasse. Loremarie was back at the Adlon and had summoned Tony's mother from Silesia. Tony, too, was being held at the Lehrterstrasse prison but as he is an officer, he will be court-martialled. Which means that if he is condemned, he will be shot, not strangulated. If that is any consolation.

Saturday, 2 September Loremarie Schönburg has now moved to Maria Gersdorff's too; we share Gottfried Cramm's former room. She is too distraught to live alone. Besides we prefer to face the police together if . . .

Papa has been here for two days and returned to Königswart today. He has left me his great-grandfather's Cross which the latter had worn during all Russia's campaigns against Napoleon; he says it saved him then and will save me now.

Meanwhile Loremarie has made friends with a baker near the Lehrterstrasse prison. He is also a part-time jailer there and has already taken letters and cigarettes to Tony Saurma. She now goes there daily, hoping also for an answer to her last note to Adam Trott, but the jailer she had given it to now avoids her, although two days ago he had said 'Somebody ought to do something for Count Schulenburg, he is getting daily weaker'. This is the first confirmation that he is in that prison too. I will be the one to take him some food as we must deal with each case separately as far as possible.

We spent much of the afternoon cutting up bread and roasting a tiny chicken sent by Otto Bismarck. We then divided everything into three parcels, one for the Ambassador, one for Gottfried Bismarck and one for Adam. Loremarie is also taking fruit and vegetables for Tony. The latter is allowed neither bread nor meat, indeed nothing strength-sustaining. They are kept undernourished deliberately – to make them more 'co-operative'!

Percy Frey fetched us in his car and dropped us off at some distance from the prison. Loremarie had told me exactly how to behave but I admit that my knees wobbled. It was the first time I had been there. The building is of red bricks and from the outside looks like any other barracks. We had agreed that I would ask only after the Count, while Loremarie enquired at another entrance about Tony. Only once I was back would she go in again and hand over the parcels for Gottfried and Adam.

At the gates there were two S.S. guards, then came a courtyard and then a large front door flanked by two more S.S. They stopped me. I said that I wanted to speak to the Geheime Staatspolizei [Gestapo]. Whereupon one of them led me along a broad corridor until we came to a huge canary-yellow iron door. On the left of it there was a small window behind which sat a fat man, also in S.S. uniform. He asked me what I wanted. I produced the parcel and said I would like to have it delivered to Ambassador Count von der Schulenburg. He told me to wait and disappeared. Meanwhile the iron door opened several times to let guards out. Each time I took a quick look inside. I could see a large open space with lots of little corrugated iron stairways and platforms at different levels; the cells lined both sides of these platforms; their doors didn't quite reach the top, as in some cheap lavatory. The place was very noisy with guards clanking around in heavy boots, whistling and shouting to each other. It all looked perfectly revolting. Soon the turnkey or jailer or whatever he was returned and asked me what the Count's Christian name was. I hesitated but then I remembered it to be Werner. The man noticed my hesitation and bawled: 'If you are so interested in him you should at least know his name!' This nettled me and I shot back: 'There can hardly be any confusion. There is only one Ambassador Count von der Schulenburg, as everybody knows; and seeing he is past seventy I never called him by his Christian name.' He then made me write it all out on a slip of paper, together with my own name, address, etc. To this I added a few friendly words, asking whether I could bring him anything. My heart sank a bit as I handed the paper over, but by then it did not make much difference, for they can evidently trace me easily anyhow. The man disappeared once more and I saw him conferring with two cronies. Finally he returned, flung the parcel at me but kept my note, and spat out: 'Not here! If you want more information, enquire at Gestapo headquarters, Prinz Albrechtstrasse'. I tottered out feeling completely ill. In a shop window around the corner I caught sight of my face: it was green.

I told Loremarie how things had gone and departed for home while she took a stab at delivering *her* parcels. It seemed a long time before she reappeared at Maria's. She was in tears. She had waited inside the building for the jailer who had earlier taken the notes to Adam. When he had at last appeared, he had again ignored her. Whereupon she had given up and left the building. Another guard had been watching her; he followed her to the Underground and as they walked, whispered to her: 'Why do you go on doing this, day after day? They are making a fool of you! All this time I have been watching you bringing letters, but I tell you: he is dead!' He meant Adam. He probably thought she was in love with him. He went on: 'I can't stand the misery of all these people any longer. I am going mad. I am returning to the front. I never wanted this job anyway. These notes you bring! The others split their sides over them, laughing. *Please*, do what I tell you! Don't come back. Leave Berlin as soon as you can. You are being watched. And the jailer who took your letters has himself been now transferred back to headquarters. They don't trust him anymore either . . .' It was that man who had told her to write to Adam in the first place, 'Er wird sich so freuen . . .' ['He will be so happy']. Loremarie does not know whom to believe.

The Lehrterstrasse prison, a star-shaped building erected in the 1840s after the design of London's Pentonville, consisted of four wings, one of which – a military jail – was administered by the Wehrmacht, while two others were taken over by the Gestapo for political prisoners. Most of the 20th July plotters were held there.

Conditions, as described by surviving inmates, were harsh: four walls; a bed on which it was forbidden to lie down in the daytime; a wooden stool; a small wall-table; in the corner, a w.c.-like contraption for which the guards furnished scraps of weeks-old newspaper; no pencil or paper; no books; no newspapers; no walks in the courtyard; no view of life outside.

The guard consisted of regular prison officers, themselves closely watched by S.S. men who were mostly Volksdeutsche *(ethnic Germans) repatriated from the East and inured to brutality through fighting partisans in Russia. The cells were cleaned, meals distributed and shaving kits passed around by trusties – Jews, other political detainees or Jehovah's Witnesses. With the exception of the latter, who, because of their ethic of non-participation, mostly refused to help their comrades in distress, these trusties were often the sole link between the prisoners and the outside world.*

From dusk to dawn the cells remained lit – unless Allied bombers were overhead. While the guards fled to the cellars, the prisoners remained manacled in their cells, many of them perishing when one of the wings was hit. Curiously, several survivors have testified to the feeling of peace they had among the falling bombs – the only time they were not watched.

Among the inmates (themselves often believing Christians) there were several clergymen. By bribing or otherwise securing the collusion of guards, the Catholic padres were able even to take confession and give absolution: a trusty would bring the former in a closed envelope and take back the latter, together with a consecrated wafer, in another envelope. Thus, despite solitary confinement and the rule of absolute silence, a web of Christian solidarity was spun which even the Gestapo was helpless to break up.

Every day with Percy Frey we visit Tony Saurma's lawyer. He is a young man with prematurely grey hair, an artist in his free time, maybe a bit queer, and certainly intelligent. Today, on hearing Loremarie Schönburg's account of her visits to the prison, he flung up his hands and told her she must leave Berlin immediately: these visits were madness; we will all end up being arrested ourselves; moreover, we were not doing anybody the slightest good. He, too, thinks that Adam Trott is still alive, but he added: 'Better dead than what he must be going through.' I seem to be the only one to hope that the war may end soon enough for him to survive.

We decided that Loremarie must go back to their family home in the country. She can be of no more help to anyone here and if she stays on in Berlin any longer they are sure to arrest her. Aga Fürstenberg will go on bringing things to Tony. At least hers will be a new face. But it is not so easy to get out of Berlin these days unless one has a special pass. True, Loremarie has received a telegram saying that her grandfather is dying; this may enable her to buy a ticket.

Sunday, 3 September Although it is Sunday I had to go to the office – on air-raid duty. I did not do a lick of work but practised the accordion. Late in the afternoon Albert Eltz and Loremarie Schönburg dropped in and we sat around talking. Suddenly Albert whipped out his revolver, yelled: 'Where is Six? Off with his head!' and rushed down the stairs. I hung on to his Luftwaffe uniform, as Dr Six happened to be in his office, working.

Later we dined at Percy Frey's. On the way there Albert kept stopping policemen to ask what they thought of Count Helldorf. He wanted to see how much they knew and would let them go only when they called the whole thing a *Schweinerei* [pigsty]. He is quite mad! One can only explain these hysterical outbursts as a reaction to the constant tension.

There was a heavy raid; we sat it out in the basement facing Percy's house, as we dared not go back to Tony's.

Monday, 4 September Loremarie Schönburg left for home this morning without bothering to obtain an official pass. One of the Gersdorff servants accompanied her to the station and saw her jump on to a train which was already underway; she had got through the wicket with a platform ticket. The last thing the maid saw was that she was being hailed by a conductor. Though I had been urging her to leave, I am very worried as this absurd way of doing so may drag all her past activities into the limelight. But both Tony Saurma's lawyer and Maria Gersdorff are vastly relieved.

I am staying on for a little while longer as Tony goes on trial before a military court for a preliminary hearing tomorrow. The lawyer is pessimistic as regards the second charge, the one about 'Better luck next time'. That alone could cost Tony his head. Luckily his regimental commander has given him a certificate of good conduct. The lawyer finds Tony in good shape and not too depressed. He is coaching him so that he does not act too aggressively. I now regret having talked him out of escaping to Switzerland. He might have succeeded after all.

I remember Tony telling me about the night Gottfried Bismarck was arrested. He himself was driving down to Silesia. The police had laid on road blocks and had stopped him also. They got friendly over cigarettes and he was shown an order to arrest a man driving with a girl in a silver Tatra. He realised immediately that this was Gottfried and Loremarie, as he knew they were on their way to Reinfeld that night. He was convinced they would never make it. In fact they only reached Reinfeld safely because the car broke down, they abandoned it and went on by train.

Tuesday, 5 September Tony Saurma's first day in court. The trial was immediately suspended for a fortnight while they send for further information from Silesia. Any delay these days is a good thing. But the lawyer is worried, as evidence is piling up and none of it is in Tony's favour. All seems to depend now on the decency of the judges. I wrote Tony a letter today, for I myself am leaving for Königswart tomorrow.

At the office Adam Trott's friends now believe that he *is* dead, although Tony's lawyer still thinks otherwise. But none of us can do anything either for him or Gottfried Bismarck or Count Schulenburg. Gottfried's trial too seems to have been postponed thanks to Otto Bismarck's indefatigable efforts to gain time. His name has never yet been mentioned in the press. True, a Bismarck trying to kill Hitler would not sound too good, even *they* realise that. One can only wait and pray that he will survive.

And now the time has come also for me to go. I have still some sick leave due of which I may as well take advantage. I feel relieved at going away but also depressed. We have been under such pressure these last weeks, the mind is so obsessed by all that has happened that nothing else seems to matter anymore. Also, for all the anguish, I am so accustomed now to living among these ruins, with the constant smell of gas in the air, mixed with the odour of rubble and rusty metal and sometimes even the stench of putrefying flesh, that the thought of Königswart's green fields, quiet nights and clean air actually frightens me.

At all events this seems to be the end of my Berlin life. Paul Metternich and Tatiana are meeting me in Vienna in eight days and they will no doubt talk me into staying on in Königswart until I am quite well again. I can resist family pressure from afar, but once we are all reunited I will probably agree with them.

All these weeks I had been fearing that the Allies might broadcast further particulars of the 20th July Plot (as they did in the beginning), revealing the purpose of Adam's trips abroad and thus harming him still more; but in his case they were for long mercifully discreet, starting to write about him only once the German press had announced his execution.

Das Schwarze Korps (the official S.S. paper) has been storming about 'blaublütige Schweinehunde und Verräter' ['blue-blooded swine and traitors'], but a recent anonymous article in *Der Angriff* (the S.A.'s sheet) strikes, surprisingly, a contrary note: no social class in Germany, it said, had made greater sacrifices and had suffered, proportionately, such heavy losses during this war as the German aristocracy. Some of the Nazis seem to be playing it safe.

Since the war much evidence has come to light which shows that as defeat neared, even within the S.S. many began to waver, starting with Himmler himself. As early as 1942 he had asked his Finnish masseur, Felix Kersten: 'What do you think? Is the man mad?' and he had begun building up a medical file on his Führer. Stalingrad shook his faith in Hitler's star further and – as we have seen – by early 1944, Dr Six was seeking on Himmler's behalf to put out feelers to the Allies.

Some of the senior S.S. generals went further. The head of the Criminal Police, S.S.-Obergruppenführer Arthur Nebe – though himself a mass-murderer in the East – was close to the 20th July group and was subsequently hanged. At one point S.S.-Generals Felix Steiner and Sepp Dietrich (the latter commanded for many years Hitler's bodyguard and was his top executioner in the 1934 'Night of the Long

Knives') were planning to attack Hitler's H.Q. Canaris' successor at the head of the joint Abwehr-S.D. intelligence service, S.S.-Colonel Walter Schellenberg, considered kidnapping Hitler and handing him over to the Allies. In Paris at the time of and after 20 July the attitude of S.S.-Obergruppenführer Carl Oberg, Himmler's representative in France, was markedly ambiguous. S.S.-Obergruppenführer Karl Wolff was to play a crucial role in the capitulation of the Axis forces in Italy. And it was again Schellenberg who in the spring of 1945 was to organise the talks between Himmler and the Swedish Count Folke Bernadotte by means of which the Reichsführer-S.S. planned at the last minute to take Germany out of the war.

Pütze Siemens came to lunch yesterday – she is a great friend of Maria Gersdorff's. She was in deep mourning for her brother Peter Yorck, who was hanged at the same time as Field Marshal von Witzleben. This conventional reaction to such an unconventional death seemed somehow pathetically inadequate to express such grief. She questioned me a lot about Adam, who was a friend of theirs, but we did not mention her brother. I could not have found words.

My hands are still covered with cuts from trying to open the oysters that Tony brought us just before his arrest.

VIENNA *Wednesday 6 September* Spent my last evening in Berlin with Aga Fürstenberg and Georgie Pappenheim. Georgie escorted me home in the tram; he played a mouth organ all the way to the enthusiasm of the other passengers. He stayed overnight, as Maria and I were alone and wanted a man about in case of another raid. He slept in the drawing-room on one sofa and I on another. When the old cook, Martha, awoke me this morning, she sniffed: 'In meiner Jugend kam so etwas nicht vor, aber dieser 20. Juli stellt alles aus den Kopf!' ('In my young days, that couldn't have happened, but this 20th July has turned everything topsy-turvy').

Missie's note: Since leaving Berlin on sick leave in September 1944, I had stayed with the family in Königswart and been trying to get back on my feet for what we all knew would be the last round. On my way to Königswart I had spent a few days with Tatiana and Paul Metternich in Vienna, had had a complete medical check-up and had been pronounced by Professor Eppinger 'useless' for a couple of months. He had found an enlarged thyroid, which was the reason for my being so thin – all on a more or less nervous basis. Since then I had been absorbing massive doses of iodine.

KÖNIGSWART *Monday, 1 January* It has snowed heavily and we spend most of the time out of doors, tobogganing clumsily and playing childish snowball games. There is plenty of food but we eat in the kitchen, the servants having gradually dwindled away – the men into the armed forces, the women into the armaments industry. Lisette, the housekeeper, cooks. All our evening clothes have been put away. We play games and enjoy Paul's best wines. For tomorrow we break up again.

Tuesday, 2 January Paul Metternich is about to rejoin his regiment, having been pronounced cured of that dreadful lung abscess he had almost died from last year on the Russian front. I have stayed on one more day to cheer up Tatiana. She is very low.

VIENNA *Wednesday, 3 January* Spent my last day in Königswart having long talks with each member of the family in turn. This time it really looks as if *die grosse Entscheidung* [the great climax] will take place before we meet again. Mamma wants me to stay on, but now that my sick leave is up, I have to go; otherwise I will be in trouble with the Arbeitsamt [manpower board]. Tatiana drove me to Marienbad station in the middle of the night.

Thursday, 4 January In the train the other night the talk was about the air-raids on Vienna which are picking up. Here the Americans do most of the bombing from their bases in Italy, usually in broad daylight. The trams (which are the only public transport inside the town that still functions) run apparently only at midday. I was a bit worried since I had as usual too much luggage, plus a goose (plucked). Luckily, a Russian ex-P.O.W. volunteered to carry my stuff in exchange for a sizeable number of cigarettes. On the long walk home he told me that Stalin is planning an amnesty and that 'we may all go home soon'. He added that he had had hardly anything to eat lately and so when we reached our destination – Antoinette Görne-Croy's two-room flat on Modenaplatz, which I will be sharing with her – I gave him all the food I found there. Antoinette herself is visiting her husband in Yugoslavia.

A summons awaited me – from the local Arbeitsamt. They certainly don't waste any time!

Lunched with Franzl Thurn-und-Taxis at the Hotel Bristol. The Thurn-und-Taxis brothers have been kicked out of the army as 'royals' and are studying at the university here. At the Bristol nothing seems to have changed since I was here with the Metternichs four months ago. Alfred Potocki and his mamma, old Countess 'Betka', who, for all her eighty-three years, is still extraordinarily spry, are in their usual corner. They have had to abandon their world-famous estate, Lancut, as the Russians have entered Poland. It was considered the Versailles of Eastern Europe and had survived until now unscathed because, thanks to Goering, who used to hunt there before the war, it was occupied only by German senior command staff.

Friday, 5 January Dropped in at the Arbeitsamt. They suggested that I go to work as a nurse. That is what Tatiana and I wanted to do when the war started, but we were rejected on account of our Lithuanian passports. They apparently suffer from an acute shortage of nursing personnel and do not seem to care that I have done all in all only twenty hours of basic first-aid training. From friends, I know what a gruelling work this often is now. Which is probably why they were surprised by my happy reaction.

Saturday, 6 January On entering the flat, I stumbled on a pile of luggage – Antoinette and her husband, Jürgen Görne, were back.

She rushed out in curlers to greet me and started to tell me all about her visit to Veldes [Bled], where Jürgen's unit is fighting the Yugoslav partisans. She was very excited, as their car was fired on in the woods – there is a huge hole near the radiator and the ignition was destroyed. Her life down there must have been pretty depressing: she was never allowed out of doors, since the partisans now kidnap people. But the scenery, she says, is magnificent. She is evidently happy to be back.

Ferdl Kyburg dropped in to see me. Since being thrown out of the navy as a 'royal' he, too, has been studying at the university.

Sunday, 7 January This morning, church. Tonight, Görne's orderly roasted the goose I had brought back from Königswart. Never having cooked such an animal before, he sat in front of the oven with a spoon in one hand and a cook book in the other. The result, however, was quite satisfactory and our landlady – the German wife of a colonel presently at the front – was also offered some. Our guests: Franzl Taxis, Ferdl Kyburg and Sita Wrede (who is nursing in a Luftwaffe hospital here).

Thursday, 11 January My birthday.

Sita Wrede has talked the doctors of her Luftwaffe hospital into taking me on to work there. I was interviewed this morning by the *Chefarzt* [head doctor], a swarthy fellow who had lived for eighteen years in India. This is good news, as theirs is considered the best hospital in Vienna. But I may have to take a refresher course, as they want us general nurses to be able in an emergency to replace the male medical orderlies, who are all being sent off to the front. This training includes first-aid under fire (in case we are posted to an airfield), etc. I have been given a Red Cross uniform, a new set of identity papers and a metal tag on which my name is engraved twice and which can be broken in two if I am 'killed in action', one half being then sent back to my 'dear ones' – a rather weird feeling.

In the evening Ferdl Kyburg arrived with a bottle of champagne and we celebrated my twenty-eight years *à trois*.

Saturday, 13 January Had tea with the Trauttmannsdorffs, who live in the Palais Schönburg. It belongs to Loremarie Schönburg's grandfather. Built by one of the most famous architects of his day, Lucas von Hildebrandt, the beautiful small eighteenth-century town mansion stands in the middle of a large garden full of fine trees, but in a relatively inelegant part of the town, and the neighbouring streets are pretty shabby. One of its most attractive features is a smallish, totally round ballroom.

Alfred Potocki had invited me, Gabrielle Kesselstatt and three Liechtenstein brothers to the theatre. Their oldest brother is the reigning prince, Franz-Joseph. They are in their thirties and miserably shy. Afterwards we dined at the Bristol, with poor Alfred making tremendous efforts to draw them into the conversation. Gabrielle lives just across the street in the Hotel Imperial. But Alfred, who is prematurely 'gaga', would not hear of my walking home alone and since none of the Liechtensteins offered to escort me, he produced from nowhere an old lady to whom, he said, he often resorts when his mother wishes to go for a walk.

Tuesday, 16 January The Russians have entered East Prussia.

Thursday, 18 January Together with many other nurses I was summoned to the Luftgaukommando [Air Force Regional H.Q.], where they offered to send me off to Bad Ischl, in the Salzkammergut. This poses a dilemma, for I do not want to leave Vienna just now and yet it is perfectly clear that if I stay on, I may not get out at all, as the Russians are advancing steadily. Finally I made up my mind and told them that I preferred to work on in Vienna. When this evening I told Antoinette Görne and Ferdl Kyburg my decision, they were absolutely horrified.

The Russians have taken Warsaw.

Sunday, 21 January Hungary has signed an Armistice with the Allies.

Despite the presence of a German occupation army, Admiral Horthy had not given up hope of taking his country out of the war. On 15 October 1944 he had denounced Hungary's alliance with Germany and ordered the Hungarian forces fighting the advancing Russians to cease hostilities. Whereupon he and his family were packed off to a German concentration camp and a German puppet, the fascist leader Ferenc Szalasi, was installed in his place. In due course, the Soviets set up a rival Hungarian government, which on 31 December 1944 declared war on Germany. By then Budapest was surrounded. In January 1945 it fell; some 20,000 inhabitants had perished during the seige, which destroyed one-third of the city. The victors indulged in an orgy of plunder and rape, whilst further thousands were deported to the U.S.S.R.

Sunday, 28 January Went to the Russian church and the others – to the Stefansdom [St Stephen's Cathedral]. I had just got back to the flat, when a heavy air-raid started. Ferdl Kyburg has discovered a strong shelter in the cellar of his uncle Hohenlohe's house nearby. I rather dislike going there alone – my perennial fear of being buried alive without anybody knowing where I am – but today it couldn't be helped. When I emerged, I found that our neighbourhood had suffered a lot of damage. Antoinette Görne was nowhere to be seen and I began to worry that something had happened to her.

Sat down to write some letters by the glow of a candle stuck in a bottle, as our district has been for several days without light. Since we have also been without water, I then went over to the Hotel Imperial and had a lovely bath in Gabrielle Kesselstatt's suite. Then Antoinette reappeared and she and I staggered over to the pump down the street and filled two pails each to take home. At first, we had thought that we could fill them with snow and use that, but once it had melted, it turned out to be black, with potato peels floating around.

Monday, 29 January Have started work at the Luftwaffenlazarett. It used to be known as the Kaufmännisches Spital [merchants' hospital] and would be nice, were it not for the fact that it is located on a hill behind the large Türkenschanzpark in the 19th district, which is almost out of town. The tram trip alone takes one hour and since transport, generally, is agonisingly slow these days, the streets being either pitted with bomb craters or covered with snow, I must get up at 6 a.m.

I work as one of two assistants in the internal dispensary, where my boss, Dr Thimm, examines about 150 patients a day. This includes various tests, X-rays, etc. He dictates his conclusions to me. He comes from Königsberg and is quite witty, albeit sardonic. We work until 7 or 8 p.m. with half an hour off for lunch, which consists of a particularly repulsive soup.

Sita Wrede (who got me the job in the first place) works as surgical nurse; she has been doing this almost since the start of the war and is, compared to all of us, a veteran, having before that had a couple of years' nursing during the Spanish Civil War. I am very relieved to know that she is around, but she is upset that I was not assigned to her department and maintains that this was done deliberately, 'because they do not want us aristocrats to work together'! She will come down to visit me, however, every morning and bring me sandwiches, as she has access to special food supplies for the wounded. She will also smuggle in some milk for me, about a baby's bottle a day, so despite the fatigue and although I am run down, I hope to stay fit. It is a bit ironic that I should have left the Foreign Ministry in Berlin, ostensibly for health reasons, and that I should find myself working here infinitely harder than I ever did there. Actually, it is good for me, as this way I do not have time to think . . .

Sita has begun introducing me to the staff and patients. The most serious cases are downstairs in the so-called *Kellerstation* [cellar unit] which is not really completely underground, but where they are relatively better protected during air-raids, for they cannot be moved. Three of our best nurses are attached to this special ward, including one very jolly girl called Agnes, who comes from Westphalia. We have already become quite chummy. Another rather ugly girl called Lutzi is engaged to a young Luftwaffe lieutenant who, poor fellow, was brought here a fortnight ago with both legs torn off during a training flight. Thus far he had been through the war without a scratch. He is called Heini, has a charming face, is about thirty, but his hair is already grey. Although he and Lutzi are in love, they must not show it, as personal relations between nurses and patients are forbidden.

Tuesday, 30 January As I do not yet nurse, the *Oberschwester* [matron], who is a pet, allows me to go about without the traditional uniform cap. But there have already been protests, with some of the other nurses complaining about my *Hollywood Allüren* [Hollywood airs]. In Germany, nowadays, to pass muster one must look like a mud patty! But as long as the doctors and the matron do not object, I refuse to put that cap on. I am already having to get accustomed to going without lipstick, but even that I do gradually. This puts Sita Wrede into fits; she keeps begging me to wipe it off.

Today the matron ordered me to be examined by our *Truppenarzt* [staff medical officer], Dr Tillich. This, Sita assured me, is no laughing matter, as he is, reputedly, the Gary Cooper of the establishment. She maintains that when she had tonsillitis she would not let him touch her. She even went in a flap to the matron about it and when I went to be X-rayed, there she stood, arms akimbo, prepared to face the Devil himself. But she had to leave me alone with him eventually, which she did with visible reluctance. We had a long chat – with me in abbreviated attire – about my fall off the horse in Berlin a couple of years ago and my subsequent injury to the spine. It was all very professional. But he is certainly attractive. He is, I gather, the star pupil of Professor Eppinger, thanks to whom I got out of Berlin in the first place.

Tuesday, 6 February Jürgen Görne had been insisting that Antoinette leave

Vienna now, before it is too late. Her family in Westphalia, too, were getting very nervous. Yesterday, therefore, she left to go and stay with a school chum near Tutzing, in Bavaria. I am going to miss her terribly. Görne had sent his orderly over to help and yesterday we packed also my things, as I don't want to stay on alone with the *Frau Oberst*. I will try to move back into the Hotel Bristol (where I have stayed on earlier trips to Vienna) and make some permanent arrangement with them for the tiniest room I can get (I still have very little money). This may be feasible, as I am working in a *kriegswichtiger Betrieb* [war-essential enterprise].

I am also running out of ration cards and had to borrow some from Christian of Hannover. He is living at the Imperial and studying at the university, after being kicked out of the army because he, too, is a royal prince; moreover, he is related to the British royal family.

Since I had the morning off, I discussed my housing problems with Herr Fischer, the manager of the Bristol, who sounded hopeful.

Wednesday, 7 February This morning there was again a heavy raid. I sat it out in the cellar ward where the badly wounded lie. This is not much help, as one hears every bomb whistling down and feels every explosion. On such occasions I make a point of sitting with the worst cases, as when one sees how helpless *they* are, one feels stronger oneself. I am glad Antoinette Görne got off, as this time the main railway station was hit.

Thursday, 8 February Another heavy raid.

Tatiana telephoned from Prague, where she is once more undergoing medical treatment. It was good to hear her voice.

Herr Fischer has told me I can move into the Bristol at the end of the week.

Saturday, 10 February The raids are getting worse. This is the third one in as many days. Our head doctor has issued orders that those patients who are able to walk, as well as the younger nurses, may no longer stay on at the hospital during these raids but must take shelter in the long railway tunnel that runs through the Türkenschanzpark, about five minutes' walk away. As the whole neighbourhood seems to think this is the safest place, over eighty thousand persons crowd into it daily. They start queuing up at 9 a.m. and by the time the sirens sound, there is a seething mass milling around the entrance, trying to force their way in. Since one cannot possibly face this sort of situation daily, which is made worse by the fact that we have to stay on at the

hospital until the very last minute and so are invariably the last to arrive, we
have only been there a couple of times. I must admit, however, that my nerves
(which are bad enough as it is as a result of all those raids I lived through in
Berlin) are not improving and when the bombs start crashing here in Vienna
as well, I am pretty shaken each time.

Sunday, 11 February Have the day off and can therefore move into the
Bristol, where they have given me a tiny, but spotless room. However the
manager, Herr Fischer, is doubtful that I can stay there very long, as the hotel
is chock-full of S.S. But I don't see why, since I am such a hard-working
member of the community, I cannot also have a decent roof over my head.

Lunched with Franzl Taxis and Heinz Tinti. As the former's flat has been
badly damaged, he has stowed away the remains of his belongings in the
Grand Hotel next door. There we found two bicycles and rode them along
the hotel corridors before proceeding to my flat. We loaded them with my
belongings and then pushed them back to the Bristol. There the manager told
us that the last time he was here, Paul Metternich had left behind two bottles
of Napoleon brandy. Since they are unlikely to survive the raids, we wheedled
them out of his reluctant hands and uncorked one.

Monday, 12 February Air-raid.

Tuesday, 13 February Air-raid.

Wednesday, 14 February Air-raid.

The only thing that still functions in Vienna is the Philharmonic Orchestra.
After the hospital, I go to their concerts nearly every day.

The Allied conference in Yalta is over. My little wireless set gets only
German stations and they say naturally very little about it.

It is rumoured that Dresden has been razed to the ground by two
successive Allied air raids.

The Russians have entered Budapest.

*At this last Allied summit of the war, which had met on 4–11 February, Churchill,
Roosevelt and Stalin had agreed on the strategy to wind up the conflict and in effect
had settled the boundaries of post-war Europe as they exist to this day.*

*On the eve of the conference the Allies had decided to resume massive air strikes
against civilian population centres to impress Stalin with their war effort, crack
German morale and create new hordes of refugees who would disrupt the movement*

of troops and supplies. At the time, Dresden was virtually undefended by fighters or flak, the few military targets were outside the bombing zone, as were the main communications objectives. On the other hand, the city was a treasure house of baroque architecture. In a series of massive raids that started on 13 February and went on until April, the R.A.F. and U.S. Eighth Air Force virtually wiped out this ancient historical city. Some 90,000 to 150,000 townspeople and refugees (some estimates go as far as 200,000) perished in the resulting fire storms. The deliberate destruction of Dresden ranks now among the more unjustifiable atrocities committed by the Western Allies during the last war. Even Churchill – himself one of the authors of the policy of indiscriminate 'area bombing' – was stirred to belated pangs of conscience and when the bells of victory sounded, there was not a word of recognition for Air-Marshal Harris and his Bomber Command.

Thursday, 15 February Am beginning to feel ill. Yesterday because of the air-raid I had to interrupt work for three hours and make up for it afterwards. Towards 9 p.m. I felt so terrible that while the doctor was examining a patient, I took my temperature; it showed 39.4° C. Rubbing his hands with glee, Dr Thimm said that this was simply because I was tired; by today it would have dropped and I could come back to work.

Just as we were finishing, two American pilots, who had been shot down yesterday morning, were brought in. They arrived supported on either side by a German soldier. They seemed badly injured and could barely drag their feet. One had a burnt face that was quite black, with yellow hair standing up stiffly. By now we have about thirty American pilots in our hospital. They are treated well, but are taken down into our basement shelter only during exceptionally heavy raids. I would have liked to speak to them, but this is strictly forbidden. One nurse, who had been a governess in England before the war, brought one of them some flowers; she was fired on the spot. However, once during a raid Sita Wrede took me to the special ward where they lie. Some of them look very nice, but most are so badly injured that they are almost totally bandaged up. Nearly always they suffer from severe burns.

The patients in my department are all in more or less bad shape. Most are over fifty or under twenty years of age. Usually they have just been called up and it's up to our Dr Thimm to figure out whether they are truly sick or just malingering. Because of his rather perverse sense of humour, this leads to sometimes pathetic, sometimes hilarious dialogues.

The trip home was again endless.

Saturday, 17 February Today, for the first time in ten days, there was no raid. My fever has dropped and in the afternoon I got up, took a lot of aspirin and tottered over to the hairdresser, praying that I would not find myself face-to-face with one of our doctors. Friends dropped in to see me. Luckily, the hotel sends up my meals.

Sunday, 18 February Air-raid.

Spent the morning in the hospital basement; then I saw our Gary Cooper, Dr Tillich. He diagnosed acute tonsillitis and told me to go home again and stay away until Wednesday. I have no voice at all.

Sita is annoyed at me for falling ill so soon after joining the hospital: 'What will they think of us aristos if you collapse so easily?' Somehow *that* consideration had not entered my mind!

Tuesday, 20 February Air-raid.

Wednesday, 21 February Today's raid was particularly bad. I was still at the hotel when it started. We all assembled in the basement as far down as we could go: Vinzi Windisch-Graetz, Martha Pronai, the Potockis, the Sapiehas, Etti Berchtold and her mother, etc. The noise was deafening – the crashes and tinkling of splintering glass never seemed to end.

After the all-clear I walked down the Ring with Veichtel Starhemberg. We had heard that the Liechtenstein Palace had been hit. On reaching it, we saw that the roof was gone but otherwise the building did not seem badly damaged. The debris of a shot-down American plane was scattered all over the pavement in front of it; it was still burning merrily and now and then there were little explosions – the ammunition going off. Nearly all the crew had perished. Only one of them bailed out but got stuck on a roof gable, which tore off both his legs. All through the raid, some bystanders told us, one could hear his screams, but no one dared leave the shelters and by the time they finally got to him, he was dead.

We strolled on. Near the Burgtheater there was an unexploded time bomb. The whole area had been cordoned off, but we wandered past it without giving it a thought. The town was still full of smoke and on the Karlsplatz, just across the Ring from our hotel, there was a huge bomb crater.

Thursday, 22 February Am totally hoarse. As public transport has broken down completely since the last raid, I had to go to work on foot. This took me two hours.

Friday, 23 February Spent the night at the hospital. Sita Wrede was on duty, so I could use her camp bed, which is in her boss's study.

Saturday, 24 February Spent another night on Sita Wrede's camp bed. It's so much more convenient to sleep on the premises than to walk back and forth for miles every day.

Dr Tillich has suggested that I become his assistant, as the nurse I was replacing in the Internal Dispensary is about to resume her duties. I am not too happy about this. He is very pleasant and attractive but he is also our Politischer Leiter [political officer] and, as such, is responsible for staff morale. Every Monday in the chapel there are lectures on political subjects which we are all supposed to attend, however busy we may be elsewhere. The day I arrived, he gave us a brief lecture about 'the duties of a nurse in this fifth year of the war'. The gist: not too much compassion since many of the patients are malingerers; doctors had to be stricter, as the front needed every able-bodied man; on the other hand, if we ever observed unduly harsh treatment, we were to intervene. By way of a deterrent, 'in strictest confidence', he also mentioned the case of one nurse who had given a young wounded soldier – a friend of her son, who had been killed – an injection that had temporarily disabled him, thus saving him from being sent back to the front. 'She was given ten years!' We were standing with our backs to the wall, he added. There was no alternative but to fight to the last man! Etc., etc. All this sounded so grim that I have not been back, making my excuse the never-ending flow of fresh patients. I have been expecting trouble for some time but Dr Tillich has never once said a word.

The matron, on the other hand, says that I may be appointed to work with Prince Auersperg, our leading neurologist, a slightly batty but fascinating man who is one of our local celebrities. So it looks as if nothing has been decided about me yet.

I was just about to go home when the sirens started to wail. Dined with friends, after which Meli Khevenhüller took me to a party where there was a very good jazz pianist in the style of Charlie Kunz. We sat up very late chewing bacon and listening to him.

Sunday, 25 February Mass at the Stefansdom. The streets are filled with people. Nowadays thousands of Viennese from the suburbs crowd into the centre of the town because the ancient catacombs are, reputedly, the safest shelters of all; nobody trusts the ordinary cellars, which collapse too easily and in which already hundreds of victims lie buried. Most of these people come from the working districts, having walked for hours to get here.

Lunched with the Potockis, who had made an exceptional effort, as they are entertaining a Frau Heryz, who is married to a German millionaire from Lodz, in German-occupied Poland, and from whom they hope to hear from her about their home. The food was delicious; there was even *foie gras*!

My diet seems to fluctuate between watery soups at the hospital and occasional feasts at the hotel. If only my ration cards would last a little longer! As it is, after the first ten days of the month I have none left. *Schwester* Agnes feeds me occasional egg-nogs that are especially concocted for the badly wounded; fortunately they don't seem to like them as much as I do, so there is always something left.

Sisi Wilczek, who has worked for the past four years as a surgical nurse at the hospital in the Hofburg, dropped in to see me. We visited friends for coffee and then went for a long walk. In front of the Palais Liechtenstein the debris of the American plane that had been shot down on Wednesday was still lying around, though souvenir hunters have carried off most of them. 'Be' Liechtenstein appeared in the doorway with a large mauve-coloured accordion which he is leaving with me, as he, too, he told us, is leaving Vienna 'for good'.

For some reason I am becoming the custodian of all the gear people leave behind in Vienna when they take off to escape the Russians. The ironical thing is that, if *anyone* should get out ahead of the Russians, it is *I*; and when I myself *do* get out – *if* I ever manage to do so (which is by no means certain) – all this will have to be abandoned anyway.

We ran into Geza Andrassy, another refugee from Hungary. He said his sister Ilona had refused to leave Budapest, where she, too, is a Red Cross nurse. We all ended up at the Wilczek Palace in the Herrengasse. I then went home to bed. I am so tired that in the evenings I hardly go out anymore.

Monday, 26 February The Taxis boys had received a goose from their family estate in Bohemia. We cooked it today at Meli Khevenhüller's. Though we were five, it made for quite a feast, for we are all most of the time undernourished.

'Puka' Fürstenberg's father has died. He was a charming Austrian diplomat of the old school. There is an enormous difference, I find, between that generation of Austrian aristocrats, who still ran their Empire, and the present generation, who grew up in an amputated, stinted little country with no future. The latter are, nearly all of them, basically provincial and even when there is still plenty of money around, they can barely speak a foreign language and few of them have been outside Austria for any length of time. Moreover, though full of charm and delightful company, they are, by and large, lightweights, with few of the fundamentally solid qualities that still characterise good Germans of the same generation, of whom I have known so many in Berlin. This, of course, may be partly due to the 1938 *Anschluss*, with its various subsequent constraints (military service, labour service, etc.), which was followed almost immediately by this war.

Tuesday, 27 February Finished work a little earlier today and so had time to see the hospital dentist.

In the evening, Sisi Wilczek brought Geza Andrassy around and we cooked supper in my room on my little electric heater; we even made some delicious coffee, thanks to a machine that Christian of Hannover has given me.

Wednesday, 28 February Tatiana telephoned. She is still in Prague but is about to join the Otto Bismarcks in Friedrichsruh, near Hamburg, as Paul Metternich has been transferred to neighbouring Lüneburg. Gottfried Bismarck, who has at last been released from the concentration camp where he had been interned since his acquittal last autumn, is said to be on his way there too, but somehow I can't believe he has really been let out; he was far too compromised in the 20th July Plot. This coming trip of Tatiana's worries me, as nowadays passenger trains are constantly bombed too.

Friday, 2 March Two days ago, during a raid, we had to change the dressing of Heini (the airman with the two amputated legs). *Schwester* Lutzi, his fiancée, was away; the lights had again gone out and I had to hold two oil lamps over the doctor and nurses as they worked. What poor Heini goes through each time is unbelievable, for both stumps are completely mangled, with the bones shattered into many little pieces; they keep popping up and have to be fished out with tweezers. Sita says that if I can look at that without feeling queasy, I can face anything. At first I did not think I could. But, strangely enough, it *is* bearable, especially when one is oneself helping. There is such a total concentration on one's job and also such a curious kind of detachment from the patient, that one is hardly aware of anything else. Thank God!

Saturday, 3 March No raid today, so for once we could go home on time.

At the hospital it has become very cold, as we have run out of coal and even hospitals, nowadays, no longer get priority supplies.

Sunday, 4 March I was just leaving for the Stefansdom with Hansi Oppersdorff when the sirens started. He usually accompanies me these days, as he is undergoing treatment after being shot in the vocal cords; he can speak only in a whisper.

Later I dropped by to see Meli Khevenhüller. Working in a munitions factory, she will not be allowed to leave when the Russians arrive. However, she is having a cart and two horses smuggled in from the family estate in the country in case we have to flee at the last moment.

Today I received a parcel sent by Mamma from Königswart on . . . 2nd January. It had been in the mail for two months – thus far, a record.

Tuesday, 6 March The Fugger grandmamma has died. Her son, 'Poldi', who is a general in the Luftwaffe, has been here these past few days. Sisi Wilczek urged me to ask him to have me transferred to some other air force hospital further west. He wields some influence as he was an air ace in World War I and wears the famous *Pour le Mérite* – the highest award for valour in Imperial Germany. Sisi herself is being transferred with all her staff to Gmunden, near Salzburg. But she, too, does not want to leave Vienna just now and is procrastinating. The Hannovers own a castle in Gmunden, which is now a hospital, and Christian has suggested that both Sisi and I live in his parents' house (a transformed mews) if and when we get there; he promises to make all the necessary arrangements. This is very reassuring, for, assuming we escape at all, ours will no doubt be a last-minute headlong flight.

Wednesday, 7 March Sisi Wilczek took me to meet Poldi Fugger. He has white hair but his face looks still quite young. He is extremely good-looking and full of charm. He promised to put my case to the Luftgauarzt [the regional air chief M.O.], who, to us, is God Almighty but who happens to be a friend of his. Actually, I am doing all this mainly to reassure my friends, who do not think that Vienna can hold out for more than another ten days and who are horrified that I am still here. Indeed, the Russians are advancing steadily and if they do not arrive sooner, this will certainly not be due to German resistance, which, we hear, is slackening visibly.

This evening Vladshi Mittrowsky invited me, Gabrielle Kesselstatt and Franzl Taxis to dinner at the Hotel Sacher in a private dining-room. The atmosphere was still utterly antediluvian – waiters in white gloves, pheasants shot personally by our host, champagne in a bucket, etc. He continues to live the life of a wealthy landowner, although the front is now only a few kilometres from his doorstep!

Thursday, 8 March Air-raid. We had therefore again to work late to catch up.

The Allies have crossed the Rhine and according to the radio, they are now fighting around Cologne and Bonn. But though they are advancing everywhere, German resistance in the West seems still very stiff. This I do not understand. One would think that, as between the two, they would wish above all to hold off the Russians.

Saturday, 10 March A Herr Mühlbacher (whom I have never met) brought me a letter from Antoinette Görne and Ferdl Kyburg (he too left Vienna last month). They are both in Munich and beg me to leave Vienna immediately. I met him in the hall of the hotel, as he is supposed to help organise my departure. This will not be easy, as, one week ago, all private travel was banned. He handed me a blank travel permit made up by the Rüstungskommando [armaments unit] in Munich. I need only fill in my name and address, he said. But even such a permit is no good, for I cannot leave the hospital until conditions become totally chaotic: and by that time there will be no more trains running and, generally, it may be too late. Nevertheless I am touched by Antoinette's efforts.

In the middle of the night Marianne Thun called from Karlsbad over a Wehrmachtsleitung [armed forces telephone line] on behalf of Mamma, who, she says, worries madly. I gave her my latest news.

Back at the hotel I found a telegram from Mamma. Good news from both Irena in Rome and Georgie in Paris. Extraordinarily, even these days personal messages still seem to get across all front lines, probably via Switzerland. She asked me to ring her up, but although I have had a call running to Königswart every night, it is impossible to get through.

Monday, 12 March A dark day for Vienna.

Sita Wrede burst into my office at the hospital with the news that large enemy air formations were on their way. I had so much to do that I could not rush off with her to the tunnel. She likes getting there early, when it is less packed. By the time I was ready, she had lost patience and said we might as well stay where we were. I felt a bit guilty, as I was to blame. But many others seemed to have stayed on too – the basement shelter was full of wounded and nurses. I joined the former. One of them, a Captain Bauer, is a famous air ace with Oak Leaves to his Knight's Cross. He has a bad shoulder wound, but is up and walking. We talked a bit, but then the lights went out and soon the noise outside deafened all conversation. I looked in at the *Kellerstation* and found *Schwester* Agnes perched on a table, sobbing; a young surgeon was patting her back. Though such a good and happy person otherwise, she always goes to pieces during raids. I sat with her on the table and we clung to one another. There was such a whistling and roaring as I had never heard in Vienna before. We have an observer on the roof, who is not supposed to leave it whatever happens. He now sent down a message that the tunnel had had a direct hit. We immediately thought of our many patients and nurses who had sought cover there. And, sure enough, about ten minutes later, when the noise had lessened a bit, people came running in with stretchers loaded with the men and girls who had walked there happily less than an hour earlier. It broke one's heart! Some were screaming. One, who had been hit in the stomach, caught my foot and begged: 'Narkose, Schwester, Narkose! . . .' ['anaesthetic, Nurse, anaesthetic! . . .']. He went on whimpering without end. Several were operated on right there in the cellar, where there is neither light nor water, but that poor boy soon died. The head doctor kept shouting at those who had stayed on in the hospital against his express orders. He was furious to find virtually the whole staff assembled here: 'Wenn wir einen Volltreffer bekommen hätten, so wäre ich meine ganzen Leute auf einmal los!' ['Had we received a direct hit, I would have lost my entire staff at one blow!']. It appears that the bomb fell in front of the entrance to the tunnel just as some of the inmates had come out for a breath of fresh air. Some say there was a false rumour that the raid was over. Anyway fourteen persons were killed on the spot and the scene in our cellar when the survivors were brought in is something I will never forget.

Later, we climbed on to the roof and looked out towards the town.

Professor Auersperg said he could see the Opera House burning, but there was so much smoke that one couldn't really tell what had happened.

In the evening, Willy Taxis appeared. He had heard about the tunnel and was worried about me. He waited until I had finished and we then walked all the way back to town together. There was wreckage everywhere. He said that the centre had been badly hit – the Opera, the Jockey Club, even our Hotel Bristol. I asked him whether my room still existed. He didn't know. By the time we reached the centre, it was night and yet in many places one could read a paper by the light of the flames shooting out of the buildings. There was also a very strong smell of gas. Like Berlin in the worst days.

We first went around to the Wilczeks, in the Herrengasse to reassure them. Sisi was in bed with tonsillitis and a high fever. Everybody was a bit hysterical and acting sort of half-drunk. The most ghastly disaster, we heard, was that of the Jockey Club, where 270 people perished in the cellar. The building is still on fire and nobody can get near. Josy Rosenfeld told me that during the worst moments she had clung to Poldi Fugger, feeling that a bemedalled air force general was the safest person to be with in an air-raid!

For Poldi is still here to bury his mother. So far he has been unable to do so because of the shortage of coffins. It appears that at first people made them out of the cardboard panels that in many buildings have replaced smashed window panes, but now there is a shortage even of that. A few days ago Meli Khevenhüller told me that she forbade me to die just now: 'Das kannst Du uns nicht antun!' ['You can't do that sort of thing to us!'], implying that my funeral would pose too many problems! Not only is there a shortage of coffins, but friends and relatives must dig the graves themselves, as all the gravediggers have been called up. As it is, in many places there are piles of improvised coffins awaiting burial. As long as the winter lasts, this is merely weird, but God knows what it will be like when spring comes and the snow melts. The other day a solemn funeral of a defunct colonel took place. There was even a military band. Just as the coffin was being lowered into the grave, the lid slipped and the face of a grey-haired old woman appeared. The ceremony continued!

From the Wilczeks' we continued on our round. The Opera House was still burning. The Bristol had not a single window pane left and from the street one could walk straight into the dining-room. People were scurrying around, dishevelled and smelling of smoke.

I dined with Poldi Fugger, his daughter Nora and his sister Sylvia Münster. Poldi's ex-wife married Kurt Schuschnigg, the former Austrian Chancellor, just before the war and they are both now in a concentration camp.

In July 1934 Dr Kurt von Schuschnigg (1897–1977) had succeeded the assassinated Dolfuss as Chancellor of Austria. Having to the end resisted Hitler's Anschluss *in March 1938, he had been arrested and, with his wife, had spent the war years in concentration camps. Released by the Americans in 1945, he was to spend his last years teaching in the U.S.A.*

The management of the Bristol is amazing: there are no lights, just a candle on each table, but otherwise the restaurant is functioning as usual. Afterwards we walked over to Peter Habig's shop next door and watched the Opera House still burning. Peter had tears in his eyes. For the Viennese, the destruction of their beloved Opera is a personal tragedy.

The Opera had been inaugurated in 1869 in the presence of Emperor Franz-Josef with Mozart's Don Giovanni. *By a curious coincidence, the last opera to be staged there before its destruction was Wagner's* Götterdämmerung. *With it perished the sets for some 120 productions and about 160,000 costumes. For all the hardships of post-war life, the Opera House's reconstruction was given top priority and its re-opening in November 1955 symbolised better than anything else the rebirth of a 'civilised' Austria.*

Wednesday, 14 March Again I had to walk to the hospital. It now takes me four hours to get there and back. I will soon start hitch-hiking, but for the moment the streets are so blocked by rubble that no vehicles can get through and everybody walks.

Thursday, 15 March I have been given a couple of days off. I am to take over another job: Wehrbetreuung und Fürsorge [troop advisory services and welfare]. It is not quite clear to me what this involves, but I gather that it includes correspondence with the Luftgau concerning the granting of promotions and awards to the wounded in our hospital, as well as advising them about their personal problems. One has to deal with a vast variety of people and the head doctor seems to think that I am good at just that.

Unfortunately I also have to handle anything to do with deaths and since our tragedy in the tunnel shelter, there are many sad interviews with next-of-kin. Today the fiancée of one of the boys who was killed came to see me; she wanted to know all the grisly details.

Friday, 16 March This morning, another raid. I crossed the Opera square to the Hotel Sacher, as their cellar is supposed to be safer than that of the Bristol. The Taxis boys and Heinz Tinti joined me. We were stuck there for four hours and though this time all ended well, everybody seemed more nervous than they had been thus far. After the all-clear, Josy Rosenfeld (whose family has an estate near Linz) headed straight for the station, although we are told that there are no more trains. She has become frantic and does not want to stay another night in Vienna. She left me some eggs.

Saturday, 17 March Sita Wrede and I spent several hours in the Sacher cellar again. It does indeed seem rather solid, but then one never knows at what angle the bombs will fall.

Ever since these heavy raids began, the family keeps sending frantic letters, which I cannot answer, as no mail leaves Vienna anymore.

Sunday, 18 March Church with Hansi Oppersdorff. Then visited Sisi Wilczek, who is still in bed. The day the Opera was destroyed her uncle Cary wrote me a letter dated 'der schlimmste Tag, den Wien je erlebt hat' ['the worst day Vienna has ever experienced']. Poor man; he is completely broken; so is Sisi's father. Franzl Taxis tells me that to their generation Vienna was like our bedrooms are to us: every corner 'belonged' to them; they were familiar with every stone . . .

Lunched at the Bristol with Gabrielle Kesselstatt and a Prince Sebastian Lubomirski, yet another refugee from Poland. The Potockis left three days ago. They kept postponing their departure. It seems so strange without them. We had become a sort of family. Each departure leaves a void. We then had coffee at Gabrielle's hotel across the street. She has just bought herself some new hats – the one article of clothing one can still get without coupons. She is leaving by car any moment now thanks to her Liechtenstein passport (she is a cousin of the reigning Prince).

Monday, 19 March Another nightmarish day.

This time a so-called *Bombenteppich* dropped onto the hospital compound.

We were inside the tunnel where that last tragedy had occurred. Since then, we have a direct line between the hospital and the tunnel, so that we can pass on the reports of the look-out on the roof. Today three bombs hit the tunnel itself. Sita Wrede shouted: 'Kneel down!' – for I am taller than most of the people here and she feared the effects of the blasts. The inmates behaved first like a herd of cattle, shouting and stampeding, but after a while they calmed down. Though the pressure from each blast kept toppling people over, no one was hurt and the tunnel itself held out. Seven other bombs landed in the hospital grounds. One hit the surgery and went through three floors before coming to rest, unexploded, just on top of the basement shelter. But all the windows are shattered.

One American plane crashed in the Türkenschanzpark nearby and some of our staff were sent out to bring in the crew. They found four of them, but the fifth had vanished.

We went to work cleaning up the debris, staggering around among piles of glass and rubble. The girl I am about to replace had hysterics: she had been caught by the raid as she was on her way to work and had to sit it out in a shed. I sent her home and went on to pile up bits of wrecked furniture, blown-in window frames, etc.

Towards 6 p.m. I myself started out for home. On the way someone threw a broken window pane from an upper floor into the street; it cut my hand badly. An army car stopped to pick me up and drove me to the Wilczeks', where I had hoped to find Sisi. She was out, but her father wrapped my hand up in a towel, which lasted until I got back to the Bristol, where the Sapiehas took over. I was, they say, quite a sight.

Things have become particularly uncomfortable because the town has been virtually without water for several weeks now. How they can still cook our meals I do not understand. None of us trust ourselves to drink tea or coffee anymore. There is still no light and I am rapidly using up the Xmas candles Sisi gave me. In the evenings I sit in my room in the dark and practise the accordion.

Tuesday, 20 March Carpets of glass litter the streets. I now hitch-hike to the hospital. This is not easy, but twice running I have been picked up by the same army car and the driver promises to look out for me, as he drives my way daily. Peter Habig has promised to lend me his newly-acquired bicycle,

which he does not need in the daytime. This will make me a little more
independent.

Another air-raid. No damage.

Wednesday, 21 March An air-raid lasting five hours, but again without
damage. They flew in from Italy and continued on to Berlin – quite an
achievement!

One of Georgie's letters has just reached me somehow. He is still in Paris,
working in some news agency and at the same time continuing his Sciences
Po studies. He advises us 'to stay together' – as the Russians say, 'swim to the
shore' advice. For, meanwhile, Tatiana and Paul Metternich are up north;
the parents are in Königswart; and I am stuck here in Vienna! But Georgie
means well.

Saturday, 24 March Every evening Sebastian Lubomirski and I go down to
the basement and fetch water in large jam pots, as, although the hotel puts a
tooth-glassful in every wash basin daily, one gets very dirty because of the all-
pervading smoke. Lately I have been taking baths at the hospital – during the
air-raids – but these have become so dangerous now that I no longer dare do
so; besides, even there water is very scarce. The P.O.W.s, including those
shot-down American airmen who are fit enough, are sent to fetch water from
a neighbouring reservoir; this water, which is admittedly highly polluted, is
used even for cooking. Hygiene is deteriorating rapidly and we nurses are
now being vaccinated against cholera, as an epidemic has broken out in
Budapest. But we are kept so busy that we do not really have much time to
think or worry.

I am about to move to the Wilczeks'. Sisi leaves with her hospital next week,
but her brother Hansi, though badly wounded, is a reserve officer and must
stay on until the Russians arrive. At least he will keep me informed about their
progress. I have already started taking my belongings over to the
Herrengasse.

They have at last managed to burrow their way through the rubble to the
collapsed cellar of the Jockey Club and are beginning to dig out the bodies.
The smell is nauseating and clings to one's nostrils for days. I usually bicycle
around the Stefansdom to avoid that particular street.

Monday, 26 March The first day on my new job. Was kept very busy.

Yesterday I and Uncle Cary Wilczek were heading for Mass at the

Stefansdom (it is the first day of Western Passion Week) when the sirens started. There was much dust around, but the sun was out. We sat on the steps of the church in the Michaelerplatz, where Franzl Taxis would join us occasionally and report where the planes were.

Uncle Cary told me that on Saturday, when the Sapiehas were finally allowed to leave Vienna with their possessions (which they had brought out from Poland in a lorry), they had rung him up in the middle of the night to say that as they had some extra space, they could take along some of the packing cases which the Potockis had to leave behind and which are now stored in the Palais Liechtenstein. Uncle Cary had immediately gone there and loaded those that were within immediate reach. Now, after they had left, he had checked the inventory. The Potockis' celebrated estate Lancut contained a world-famous collection of porcelain, furniture, pictures by Watteau and Fragonard, etc., which an ancestor, who was in Paris at the time of the Revolution, had picked up for a song when the Palace of Versailles was being looted. All this, thanks to the intervention of Goering, had landed safely in Vienna. But what, Uncle Cary said with an embarrassed grin, went off with the Sapieha truck were the liveries of the Potockis' private orchestra! True, they, too, dated back to the eighteenth century; but one can just imagine poor Alfred's face when he opens those cases . . .

Tuesday, 27 March At the hospital there has been a slight misunderstanding: I have decorated several soldiers for bravery, not realising that this is the sole prerogative of the head doctor. The orders had landed on my table with a note that they should be carried out at once. He is furious, as he takes these solemn occasions very seriously.

On getting home I saw Geza Pejacsevich's car parked in the Michaeler-platz. He is Sisi Wilczek's brother-in-law. At the sight a load fell off my chest, for nobody here has more guts and initiative or is more of a daredevil. Though by birth a Hungarian, he carries a Croatian passport, as their family estate is in what used to be Yugoslavia. He has just been fired from the Croatian diplomatic service because his brother, who was Croatian Ambassador in Madrid, has gone over to the Allies. Geza had come to fetch Sisi and is now stuck in Vienna until he can find enough petrol to move on.

Later I rode over on my bicycle to the Bristol to pick up my accordion. I was trying a short-cut back to the Herrengasse when the blasted accordion fell off

– just as I was passing that tragic Jockey Club. As I bent down to pick it up, I bumped against a lorry parked before the ruins. There was still that ghastly smell and, as I looked up, I saw that the lorry was loaded with loosely tied sacks. From the one nearest to me a woman's legs protruded. They still had their shoes on but, I noticed, one heel was missing.

Geza drove me back to the hospital, where I found Sita Wrede in the strangest mood. She slipped into my office and whispered that she must get something off her chest: since the destruction of our surgical ward, our wounded are terribly crowded. In the cellar we used to have a so-called *Wasserbad-Station*. This is a special Austrian invention that works wonders. It consists of bath tubs in which those suffering from spinal injuries lie day and night in tepid water; they are never lifted out and even sleep that way. This prevents the marrow from running out of their bones and also relieves the pain. I used to visit a Soviet P.o.W. there; he was very young, had terrible injuries and cried all the time. I hoped that by just speaking to him in his own language I would cheer him up. And true enough, very soon he was playing the mouth organ and feeling fine. But after the water supply ran out, we had to put these wounded back on dry beds. One of them, a Serb, was suffering from some sort of internal gangrene and smelled so badly that it was impossible to keep him in the same ward with other patients. Finally he was left alone in one ward with eight other empty beds. The doctors had given him up some time ago but he lingered on, and in order to fill the vacant beds, they had now, in a top-secret session, decided to 'put him out of his misery'. Sita had just found out about this and was terribly upset. She took me to see him, to show me how hopeless his condition is. We went up to his bed, she lifted the sheet and touched his arm. It was coal-black and her finger went straight through it. He kept looking at us with searching eyes. It was terrible!

Geza fetched me after work and we drove up to the Kahlenberg and sat there for a while, sorting out our thoughts. Then we returned to town. I said goodbye to Gabrielle Kesselstatt, who is finally off tonight. Dined with Vladshi Mittrowsky at the Bristol. On the way there I saw an old man pushing a small wheelbarrow with a coffin on it. It was inscribed 'Herr von Larisch' – probably the one who perished in the Jockey Club. I wheeled my bicycle around and only realised when I was about to touch his sleeve that I intended to ask him . . . where he had got the coffin!

The Palais Wilczek is slowly emptying too: Sisi's parents and Renée,

Hansi's wife, left ten days ago. There now remain Uncle Cary, Hansi, Sisi herself, Geza, the Taxis boys (their palace was also destroyed two weeks ago) and myself.

The Russians have crossed the Austrian frontier and are approaching fast. German resistance, we hear, is minimal.

What was left of the Phillipshof, the building in which the Jockey Club was located around the corner from the famous Hotel Sacher, was blown up in 1947 and a public garden laid out on its site. Most of the bodies were never dug out and lie still underfoot.

Wednesday, 28 March Sita Wrede had been insisting that I have a talk with Dr Thimm, the head doctor, and explain to him that as a White Russian, it would be 'unhealthy' were the Red Army to find me here. Today I did so. He replied that he is an amateur astrologer and that by his latest calculations the Führer will live another ten years. Ergo – the war is not yet lost! Then, working himself up into a passion, he screamed that I had better not spread panicky rumours, that he could have me arrested for defeatism, etc.

I walked out, firmly decided never to raise the issue again, but to simply take off any way I can when the time comes. But quite aside from my personal case, it is incredible that no arrangements have been made to evacuate the wounded and staff. And yet the Russians have reached Wiener Neustadt, which is virtually a suburb.

Geza Pejacsevich again drove me home.

Thursday, 29 March Sita Wrede is now on the war path. Today she had a thundering interview with the head doctor and demanded to be transferred to Bayreuth. Whereupon he threatened, 'if there is any more defeatism in the ranks', to have us all sent off to the front.

This evening I was working peacefully in my office, when Sita burst in with the news: orders had just come through from the Luftgau that the entire hospital – wounded, staff and equipment – was to be evacuated to the Tyrol at once.

Geza Pejacsevich drove me home and I tried to send off telegrams to the family to reassure them at long last; but no telegrams are accepted. No trains are running. The whole town is in a state of panic.

Friday, 30 March Spent all morning at the office, packing what I consider important and finishing the more urgent business. We are to burn all that is not indispensable. This I rather enjoy, as much of it is just red tape anyway. But there are also many wounded who need help and advice and I am kept busy all day.

At 4 p.m. the matron told me we must be back this evening at nine, when the first batch of wounded and staff would be leaving. Sita Wrede and I are in this first batch. Geza Pejacsevich and I raced back to the Sacher to warn Sita, who has the day off, but we did not find her. We left her a note and I rushed home to pack.

Actually, Geza does not believe that the hospital will, in fact, get off and keeps urging me to escape on my own with him, Sisi Wilczek and Sita. But first he has to obtain permission to take his car out; and we have to get the hospital's permission to leave or else we might be considered deserters.

Baldur von Schirach, the local Gauleiter, who used to head the Hitler-Jugend, has plastered the walls of the town with posters which proclaim that Vienna will be turned into a fortress and will stand to the last man.

An early Nazi enthusiast (despite his mother's American background), Baldur von Shirach (1907–1974) had headed the Hitler-Jugend from 1931 to 1940, when he had been posted to Vienna as Gauleiter *(i.e. Governor). Though in time even his faith in Hitler waned, he had lent his hand to the persecution of the Jews and, in the aftermath of the 20 July fiasco, to the hounding of the anti-Nazi resisters.*

In front of the Sacher I came upon Nora Fugger, Poldi's daughter. She was in tears, as the lorry in which she was to leave had not turned up.

Sita and I then took off for the hospital with whatever we could carry. There we found total confusion. Nobody had left yet; indeed nobody knew whether we *would* be leaving after all. Sita had a talk with the matron and finally we were given our *Marschbefehle* [travel orders]. We may leave Vienna by whatever means we choose, but must report to the Luftwaffe base hospital at Schwarzach-St Veit in the Tyrol by 10th April. This gives us exactly ten days to get there. It is now a general *sauve-qui-peut*. Ran into Professor Högler, who said he was staying on, as he had many patients too ill to be moved. Many doctors feel likewise. They are now in conference and, it is whispered, are even considering giving injections to the hopeless cases, so that they do not fall into Russian hands.

Loremarie Schönburg's eldest brother, a wounded officer lying in a hospital in Prague, was to be dragged out of his bed there and murdered in cold blood just a few days later. Loremarie was to lose altogether five brothers in the war.

Saturday, 31 March Sita Wrede returned to the hospital to see how they were doing. Some of the wounded and the youngest nurses had already left. The others were surprised that we are still here.

At midday, a *coup de théâtre*: no Hungarian car may leave Vienna and those that attempt to do so will be confiscated by the authorities. And Geza Pejacsevich has a Budapest number plate! Despite this blow, he is still foraging around for petrol. Meanwhile I make the rounds to say goodbye. Peter Habig sounded surprised that everybody should be so eager to get out; he is staying; but then he is an elderly man and does not risk much; besides he thinks that it will all drag on as Berlin is doing. I do not agree. Berliner sind Berliner und Wiener sind Wiener! – a different kettle of fish altogether. Near the gutted shell of the Opera House I bumped into Wolly Seybel. He was wearing a bowler hat and swinging an umbrella – a plucky but most incongruous sight. But then he is a well-known Vienna Beau Brummell. 'C'est épouvantable, mais que faire? Je reste!' ['It's ghastly, but what can one do? I'm staying!']

We put the finishing touches to our luggage. Sisi Wilczek kept packing and unpacking her one rucksack over and over again. Laszlo Szapary and Erwein Schönborn came over to help us squeeze in last-minute items. Both had just dug themselves out of the Palais Schönborn, where a bomb had crashed into the courtyard before they could reach the cellar. The building is pretty battered and they are now fishing among the wreckage for Erwein's shooting trophies; he had many ivory tusks mounted in silver, as well as two stuffed orangoutans; all these are now probably lost. Laszlo intends to try and get back to his estate, but in that direction one can already hear gunfire. The Russians are now near Baden-bei-Wien.

Geza is in his element: he has three different appointments at different places set for the same time and in between, he keeps meeting shady characters in bombed-out cellars who promise him petrol in exchange for U.S. dollars at exorbitant prices – in short, he is exasperatingly enjoying himself while we three women sit disconsolately on our bundles and wait for the miracle to happen.

I took him over to the Hotel Imperial, where Sandro Solms (an official of the A.A.) presides over the fate of the puppet governments of Rumania, Bulgaria, etc., whom he is evacuating to the outskirts of Salzburg. We dared not confess to Sandro that Geza has been kicked out of his own Foreign Service and produced his Croatian diplomatic passport to justify his being in possession of a Hungarian registration plate. Poor Sandro complained that since Baldur von Schirach assumed full powers, he himself had no more say: he advised us to go over to the Ballhausplatz – the famous palace of the former Austrian Imperial Chancellors, which is now Schirach's office.

I sat in the car while Geza bearded Schirach's underlings there. He stayed away a long time. I was tempted to go in after him but dared not leave the car for fear that it would be impounded. At last he reappeared. He had not achieved anything and now blamed himself for our being still in Vienna. The underlings, he said, were friendly but firm: the Herr Gauleiter signs everything himself and he is out of town. Come back tomorrow!

At the Wilczek house everybody is in a dither. Hansi's barracks are on standby alert and a most colourful crowd keeps trooping past the porter's lodge – Anni Thun with pails of water; Erwein Schönborn with a ladder (he is still digging hopefully for his orangoutans!); Fritzi Hohenlohe with a black, hirsute beard, his chest covered with medals – he has just escaped from Silesia and is full of hair-raising stories about how the Soviets are treating the women there (mass rape, quite a lot of random killing, etc.). This makes our men, starting with Uncle Cary Wilczek, frantic. Sisi and I have decided that if Geza does not work anything out by tomorrow, we will leave on foot, for otherwise Uncle Cary might do something rash and get into trouble.

At the end of the war, some 10 million Germans fled or were hounded from their homes in Eastern and Central Europe. Of these, more than half a million perished; many of the women were raped.

Lunched with Franzl Taxis; we ate huge schnitzels bought with the last meat ration cards Tatiana had sent me, cooked on a spirit lamp – very greasy but delicious – and washed down with some of the Taxis' far too good wines, which Franzl has rescued from the cellar of the bombed-out Thurn-und-Taxis palace; but it seems a pity to leave them to the invaders. Franzl's brother Willy seems to have joined some Austrian underground resistance movement and rushes around looking mysterious.

This was the so-called '05', a military organisation which co-ordinated the activities of the various underground anti-Nazi groups. Once the war was over, its members were to play a key role in re-establishing a democratic Austrian state.

This evening Franzl organised a real farewell dinner. We have now been joined by Geza's brother-in-law, Capestan – what a name! – Adamovich, who has just escaped from Croatia with his wife and many children and who sits around expecting Geza to get him further westwards. Sisi Wilczek's cousin Gina Liechtenstein (who is married to the reigning Prince) had sent her a special nerve tonic; we took gulps from the bottle in turns and it was soon empty. I cooked coffee ceaselessly on my spirit lamp and Paul Metternich's last Napoleon brandy was now sacrificed.

Katalin Kinsky with her two daughters and Freddy Pallavicini are in the same position as Geza on account of their Hungarian licence plates. Gigha Berchtold had arrived with a car packed with victuals; he was stopped by the Gestapo, who took away everything, confiscated the car and told him that he could proceed on foot. He was one of the great beaux of his day. As was Pali Pálffy, who is also stuck here.

Until now most of these people had spent the war years as in 'the good old days': living on their huge estates; free from hardship or privation, let alone danger; in a country where the shops were until lately still bursting with goods (Budapest was a real mecca for the rest of German-occupied Europe); often not knowing – or even caring – what the war was about. And now, virtually overnight, their whole world has collapsed and the Russians have overrun their homes, sweeping everything before them. As their armies advance, the nationality of the refugees changes apace – the latest wave is from the Bratislava area in Slovakia, just across the Danube.

The Russians have marched into Danzig, which is where it all started.

Sunday, 1 April Easter Day. Attended High Mass at the Stefansdom, wondering whether I would ever see it again, especially that Virgin in the right-hand chapel which Tatiana likes so much. Later I dropped in to say a prayer in the little church of St Anthony of Padua in the Kärntnerstrasse.

Meanwhile, Geza Pejacsevich had gone back to the Ballhausplatz, where he was told that Baldur von Schirach was still out of town. At this Sita Wrede took things in hand – as usual. Saying that she knew exactly where he was –

sitting things out in the special shelter that has been built for him on the Kahlenberg – she added that she knew Wieshofer, his personal A.D.C., and would tackle *him*. Whereupon she and Geza drove off while Sisi Wilczek, Meli Khevenhüller and I lunched, in a state of acute suspense, off horrible sandwiches in a nearby tea room.

Meli is still calmly planning to slip out of Vienna at the last minute with her horse-driven cart. We discussed the young men we knew here, most of whom seem to have evaporated without so much as saying goodbye, let alone helping us. Perhaps one cannot really blame them, since they are probably in even greater danger than we girls are. Nevertheless we cannot help feeling that the so-called 'weaker sex' is not being offered the protection it was entitled to expect. Here again the difference between older and younger generations is striking! Were it not for Geza, who is wonderful to us all, we would be left entirely to our own devices.

Baldur von Schirach's hysterical proclamations are appearing like mushrooms overnight. He keeps harping on the need to defend the 'land of our ancestors' against this 'latest horde of barbarians'; Jan Sobieski and his victory over the Turks in the seventeenth century crop up frequently.

Sita and Geza returned. This time it was Geza who had stayed in the car, while Sita charged into the holy-of-holies. Waving all minor minions aside, she pounced on Wieshofer, Baldur's A.D.C. – the sometimes peculiar friendships of the Wrede twins *do* prove useful once in a while! – and presently she was ushered into Baldur's presence. Invoking her acquaintanceship with Heinrich Hoffman (Hitler's court photographer, who happens to be Baldur's father-in-law), she asked him to issue a special permit that would allow Geza to leave Vienna. At first Baldur seemed prepared to do so, but after he had made a phone call, his whole tone changed: 'I have just been informed that Count Pejacsevich is no longer a Croatian diplomat!' Sita said she knew nothing about that and explained that he was driving three nurses to rejoin their units. Whereupon Baldur replied that he could do nothing, that at a pinch Geza could join a diplomatic column which included the other members of his embassy; or else he could simply stay on in Vienna. And that was that! Back with us, Sita shed a tear about Wieshofer (the A.D.C.), who had said, apparently, as they parted: 'We shall never meet again. Here we stand and here we will fall!' I doubt this very much; they will probably bolt at the last minute.

As Vienna fell to the Russians, Baldur von Shirach did indeed escape to the West, where he easily found work with the Americans. In due course, however, he gave himself up. Brought to trial in Nuremberg, he was condemned to twenty years' imprisonment for crimes against humanity. He had been among the few to plead guilty, blaming himself for having brought up a generation of young Germans to believe in one who turned out to be a mass-murderer.

Of course Geza cannot rejoin his ex-colleagues, as they detest each other cordially. Finally, we girls decided to take off on our own in order to give Geza a freer hand. He will surely manage better without three women to worry about. Franzl Taxis (one of the few remaining 'loyals') was now dispatched to the station to enquire about trains. He came back with the news that most lines were cut, but that we could still try the Donau-Ufer Bahn – the local line that skirts the river Danube, linking up all the little wine-growing villages between Vienna and Linz. A train was due to leave at 4 a.m.

Sita was sent home to the Sacher to take a nap; Sisi vanished into Hansi's room, where they spent most of the time chatting; while Geza and I cooked coffee. None of us undressed. Geza told me that he was now in touch with three shady S.S. of minor rank who were prepared to issue him fake car papers and registration plates if he agreed to drive them out of Vienna. So the rats are beginning to flee the sinking ship! He was sorely tempted to do so, as he saw no other alternative. Actually, in the present state of chaos, this may even make sense.

We said our goodbyes at the Herrengasse. Poor Uncle Cary Wilczek looked very unhappy; who knows when or whether we shall ever see him again. Then Geza drove Sisi and me to the Franz-Josef station, picking up Sita on the way. We have left all our heavy luggage behind, including our fur coats; Geza has promised to bring all he can out with him. If he can't, *tant pis!*

DORF-AN-DER-ENNS *Tuesday, 3 April* At the station controls were rigid, nobody being allowed to board the train otherwise. Fortunately, we are travelling legally – something we had no longer hoped to do – with officially stamped travel orders. Mine read: 'DRK Schwester Maria Wassiltchikoff kommandiert nach Schwarzach-St Veit zum Vorkommando des Luftwaffen-lazaretts 4/XVII' ['German Red Cross nurse M.W. is being posted to . . . the Advanced Unit of Air Force Hospital 4/XVII']; they specify further that any trip that is not on the direct line to the above-mentioned destination may be construed as an act of desertion.

The train, naturally, was packed, so Sisi Wilczek and I squeezed into one carriage, Sita Wrede into another. We departed punctually, plagued by worry about Geza Pejacsevich. The train crawled. We had had hardly anything to eat and were soon hungry. About noon, shortly after Krems, the first enemy fighters appeared. They showed some interest in us. We crept into a tunnel and remained there for six hours while enemy bombers battered Krems to pieces.

Theirs was the last train to leave Vienna, for this raid severed all remaining rail communications.

In addition to her rucksack and other odd bags, Sisi hugs to her bosom a parcel the size of a shoe box. It contains several million marks and as many Czech kronen – in fact, the entire cash fortune of the Wilczek family. It is supposed to be handed over to her parents in Carinthia. It is bound to be a headache all the way.

As we were beginning to suffocate in the tunnel, we got out and walked around outside the entrance. We could see many bombers overhead, flying towards Vienna. By the time we moved on again, it was dark. The train kept stopping and each time Sisi would get down and stretch out alongside the tracks. We were cramped and felt already exhausted. By now, Sita had joined us, lying full length on the floor under one of the benches. At the Herrengasse, just before we left, she had picked up everything Sisi had discarded as useless – old cork-soled pumps, topless thermos flasks, fake jewellery – and all this is now travelling with us, for, as she says: 'One never knows . . .'

At 2 a.m. a freight train pulled up alongside of us. Sisi went to investigate. She learnt that it would be leaving ahead of us, so we decided to switch. We scrambled down, forgot the money-parcel, returned for it and boarded the freight train, which consisted of open cars packed with people wrapped in blankets; they turned out to be refugees from Hungary. Sita sat down on one of them by mistake and somebody shouted: 'Vorsicht! Frisch operiert!' ['Watch out! He's just been operated on!']. We were now moving again. It was a beautiful moonlit night, but cruelly cold. And then the sun rose beyond the Danube. We stopped for quite some time at Schwertberg, the family seat of the Hoyos – Melanie Bismarck's family. We now heard that the train we had left was rapidly catching up with us and that it would overtake us and proceed ahead. Sita, speechless with indignation, buttonholed the stationmaster, showed him our travel orders and insisted that we were entitled to top priority. He merely stared at her dully. She then tackled the engine driver and offered him cigarettes – with no more success. Our former train puffed into the station and groaned to a halt. In a jiffy we were back in it again and presently we were on our way to St Valentin, on the river Enns, which is the terminal station of this line.

In St Valentin we staggered across torn-up tracks to another train, which took us to Dorf-an-der-Enns (where Josy Rosenfeld's estate is located), where we arrived at 9 a.m. It is here that we had arranged to wait for Geza Pejacsevich. By now we had been travelling for more than twenty-four hours and had not eaten a thing. Josy's house is a half hour's walk from the station. We trudged along, sick with hunger, and collapsed at her feet, rucksacks, bags, money-parcel and all. We must have been quite a sight!

Josy took us in hand. First we had breakfast. Then we had a bath. Two hours later we began to look civilised again. The house – like many country manors of these parts – is built around an open, arcaded courtyard and the atmosphere is very *fin de siècle* and picturesque. Josy lives here with her mother and her two maiden aunts – good-natured but fussy old ladies who gaze at us somewhat horror-stricken. But she has no intention of staying here under the Russians and is already packing feverishly. The aunts refuse to move and the situation is made even more complicated by the presence of two Hohenberg children, aged eight and one, with their nurse. Their father, Prince Ernst, the second son of Archduke Franz-Ferdinand of Austria (whose assassination at Sarajevo sparked the 1914 war), was one of the first Austrians to be interned in Dachau at the time of the *Anschluss*. Their mother is English. The parents have stayed on in Vienna, where the Prince hopes to be of some use to Austria later on.

We are glued to the wireless, but about Vienna there is nothing new. We are also helping Josy pack vast quantities of rather hideous silver into laundry baskets. With the assistance of a handful of friendly French P.O.W.s (who work as farmhands on the estate) these are then sealed in cement drainpipes and buried in the garden. The Frenchmen – all of them jolly *méridionaux* – then join us at the house for a glass of wine. All this is done by the light of candles, so as not to arouse the suspicions of the surrounding population.

There is naturally much whispering and laughter, but it is strenuous work.

These French P.O.W.s were employed in agriculture all over Germany and Austria and they proved almost invariably remarkably nice, helpful and resourceful. Once the war ended and they were free, they would offer protection to whoever needed it, often providing a bodyguard to their former employers during their flight westwards. They were to do so also in the case of Paul and Tatiana Metternich. Whatever their political opinions (and quite a few were leftists), most of them chose to walk all the way back to France rather than await the arrival of their Eastern European 'liberators'.

Wednesday, 4 April Still no sign of Geza Pejacsevich. We have decided to wait for him for another twenty-four hours, after which we will go on to Gmunden without him.

GMUNDEN *Thursday, 5 April* We got up at 4 a.m. and left while it was still dark. Josy Rosenfeld accompanied us part of the way; she was hoping to find a hairdresser in nearby Steyr. We ran into two drunken soldiers; they had walked all the way from the Hungarian border and thus far had not been stopped once. Which shows in what state the German army as a whole must be.

By 10 a.m. we were in Linz. The station area was one mass of ruins with crowds of people milling about. The whole scene was totally depressing. Hitler had dreamt of turning Linz into a major art centre. From what we could see, not much was left of it.

As the train to Attnang-Puchheim (our next destination) was leaving only at 2 p.m., and there was nowhere to deposit it, we wandered off, Indian file, into town, dragging our gear with us. It was very hot. Sita Wrede trailed behind, hung with little baskets crammed with the old shoes, the topless thermos bottles and the rest of Sisi Wilczek's junk. We beseeched her to throw all this away, but she was adamant.

At last we found a small undamaged hotel, where they allowed us to wash and rest. We then looked for a post office from where we could send off telegrams to our families. In vain, I went in search of a butcher and returned, quite proud, with half a pound of sausage. But both Sisi and Sita were convinced that it was made of horse or, worse, dog meat and refused to touch it. We gave it to the waitress, who was delighted. After gulping down some thin soup, Sisi and I went and sat in the sun on a bench in the park. We were surrounded by bomb craters. The sirens started to wail. We collected Sita and our luggage at the hotel and hurried back to the station. For whatever happened, we did not want to get stuck in Linz and to avoid this, we had also to avoid the shelters.

The station was in an uproar. Nobody seemed to know where to go or what to do. Sisi spotted a train on another track; it had its steam up and seemed to point our way. We climbed aboard and awaited events. We were very lucky, for instead of leaving on schedule, it took off at once to avoid getting caught by the coming raid.

Attnang-Puchheim is an important railway junction for trains to Gmunden and Salzburg. We alighted and went into the village. It consisted of one street. We were given soup at a Red Cross distribution centre which had taken over all the inns here. Streams of wounded, we were told, keep coming this way. We were pleasantly surprised at the sight of the pretty sunburnt nurses, all looking crisp and friendly. Here the war seemed much further away. At the post office even my telegram to Mamma was accepted; I wonder whether it will ever reach her. Tatiana is in Hamburg, too far away to even try to contact.

At 5 p.m. we boarded a train for Gmunden, where Sisi and I got off, while Sita continued on to Altmünster further down the line. Next week we will join up again and proceed on to Schwarzach-St Veit.

Our first impression of Gmunden was not too favourable. We had to wait a long time for a tram, but then we have become accustomed to these interminable delays. It took us to the market square in front of the principal hotel, the Schwan, near the lake. Here too there is much confusion, as lorries keep arriving, loaded with fugitives from Vienna. Having nowhere to go, they are simply dumped and sit around on their bundles. Among them I recognised a Spanish diplomat.

We walked up a steep hill to the Königinvilla. Built originally by a Duke of Cumberland, it now belongs to Christian of Hannover's unmarried aunt, Princess Olga. It looked deserted. I wandered over to the stables to see if I could find anyone, while Sisi was kept at bay by a large wolfhound, who circled around her, barking furiously. There were several signs with 'Böser Hund' [fierce dog] and we were rather worried. We were finally admitted by the refugee wife of a German colonel, who is here with two little daughters. Fräulein Schneider, a typical old-fashioned lady's maid, with pince-nez and a highly perched *chignon*, was alerted and she took us upstairs and installed us in the master bedroom. It is small, with a narrow bed and a *chaise-longue*. We drew lots. Fräulein Schneider was upset, as, although Christian had told her to expect us, she did not know the exact day of our arrival and could not make better arrangements. But we are so grateful to Christian for making even this possible that we don't dream of complaining. The colonel's wife invited us to supper. She is very kind. Afterwards we revelled in the supreme luxury of a bath in a room plastered from floor to ceiling with family photographs of European royalty of the Victorian period.

Suddenly we heard the hooting of a horn. It was Geza Pejacsevich! He was with his brother-in-law, Capestan Adamovich. They were safe and sound and had even brought along all our luggage, coats, etc. But that's not all. Somewhere Geza had discovered a trailer, which he had hitched to the back of his car and into which he had piled the abandoned belongings of many other friends. It is amazing how much one determined and gutsy man can achieve even in times such as these! Only my mauve accordion and one of Sisi's suitcases had to be left behind.

We insisted that they stay overnight, but where? The house is quite large, but every room is stacked with furniture from the neighbouring castle, which is now a hospital. In the end we girls both slept in the tiny bed, Geza got the *chaise-longue* and Capestan was installed on an improvised sofa in the bathroom. But first we had them tell us about what happened in Vienna after we had left.

Events there evolved so rapidly that Hansi, Sisi's brother, marched out with his regiment to Amstetten the very afternoon we left. Geza and Capestan left the following morning, together with the three S.S. deserters who had provided the petrol, the papers and the registration plates. In exchange, Geza had to bring out also all their luggage. To our amazement, one of these S.S. turned out to be a friend, the deputy-manager of the Hotel Bristol, Herr Rusch. As he was far too nice a fellow to be an S.S., I suspect that he, too, was travelling with false papers – in order to get out. Geza's specify that he is on a secret mission for the Gestapo! They are valid for one month. They allow him to circulate freely about the entire Salzburg area. He is supposed to surrender his car to the three S.S. at St Gilgen, but this he is not prepared to do, as he feels he has done enough for them. Meanwhile, he has dropped them off in Linz.

BAD AUSSEE *Friday, 6 April* We unloaded the car and the men drove on to join Geza Pejacsevich's wife Ali (who is Sisi Wilczek's sister), their two children and Capestan Adamovich's wife Steff and *their* four children, who have been staying at the Eltzes' in Bad Aussee. We plan to join them there for the weekend.

But first we had to obtain official permission to stay in the Königinvilla. The Nazi Kreisleiter of Gmunden was very unfriendly, but the Bürgermeister turned out to be a decent fellow and upon hearing our names (which Christian of Hannover had mentioned to him), he immediately allowed us to stay where we were. Christian had also spoken to the gardener, who has allowed us to help ourselves to any fruit and vegetables available, so it looks as if we shall survive. Sisi is lying low, as the hospital here in Gmunden, to which she is assigned, knows as yet nothing of her arrival. We lunched at the Hotel Schwan, where a recent arrival from Vienna told us that already yesterday the Russians were hanging Nazi party members from trees in Floridsdorf, a suburb of Vienna.

In the afternoon we took a train to Bad Ischl and visited the Starhembergs. Geza fetched us there and we drove on to Bad Aussee. Mamma Eltz has no news from any of the boys, but rumour has it that Albert is hiding out in the woods nearby.

Saturday, 7 April Breakfast *en famille*, followed by a walk with the children to look for dandelions. They make very good salad. Then the hairdresser's. Steff Adamovich cooks for us all, which is difficult, since none of us have any ration cards.

GMUNDEN *Sunday, 8 April* In church this morning there were many refugees from Vienna – Hohenlohes, Pálffys, etc. After lunch the Pejacseviches drove Sisi Wilczek and me back to Bad Ischl. On the road we were stopped by an S.S. patrol. Dreadful moment! Geza produced his faked papers. They asked for ours. Mine say I should be on my way to Schwarzach-St Veit, which is not at all where we were heading, and this immediately made them suspicious. They argued about the dates, wondering why I am still so far from my destination. I explained that I had left Vienna much later than the date of my travel orders. The sergeant in charge ended by saying that if he were not so good-natured, he would haul me out of the car and set me to dig trenches. I answered that I thought that 'in this sixth year of the war' nurses could be more usefully employed. The exchange was not a pleasant one and we proceeded on our way rather shaken. At Bad Ischl Sisi and I caught a train back to Gmunden. We now plan to rest for a couple of days.

Monday, 9 April The weather is beautiful. We sun ourselves on the terrace of the Königinvilla, which has a lovely view over the lake and mountains behind. Sisi Wilczek must report in at her hospital down in Gmunden pretty soon now.

At the Hotel Schwan today we ran into the Erbachs. He was the last German Minister in Athens and his wife Erzebeth is the sister of Katalin Kinsky. They have just fled Hungary. They told us that the S.S. had stopped Katalin in Linz and had confiscated everything she was carrying – mainly bacon, flour and sausages – which she had brought all the way from Hungary and on which she hoped to keep her children going until the end of the war. The Erbachs may stay at the hotel only one night and seem completely at a loss. We feel very guilty living so comfortably; and yet without the Hannovers' permission (and they are all in Germany) we dare not take anybody in.

Tuesday, 10 April Sisi Wilczek had a talk with the head doctor of the so-called Cumberland Hospital up at the former family castle nearby; he suggested that she work there. This would be most convenient, as all she would have to do is walk through the park; but she hesitates, for it has no operating facilities and she has worked all through the war in surgery.

Wednesday, 11 April The colonel, whose family lives above the stables here, drove down from Lambach to visit them. He does not think that the war can last more than another fortnight and advises me against trying to reach Schwarzach-St Veit. He heads a Sprengkommando [demolition team] and sees often Gauleiter Eigruber in Linz, who is virtual king of this part of Austria. The latter is a particularly obnoxious individual, who continues to make fiery speeches about 'resistance', 'honour', etc.

By now we have learnt that none of our wounded reached Schwarzach-St Veit; only the younger nurses and some of the doctors got through. But I have my marching orders and much as I would prefer to stay and face the *Zusammenbruch* here among friends, it seems wiser for the moment to obey. Geza Pejacsevich will drive me part of the way.

Thursday, 12 April The colonel drove Sisi Wilczek and me down to

Gmunden station, for, though some of my things have gone on ahead, my bags are still quite heavy. The little local train to St Gilgen was so crammed that we stuffed our luggage in through the windows and stood on the lowest step of the carriage, clinging to whatever we could hang on to. The guard came by and made us get off; we ran round and, just as the train started moving, climbed on to a step on the other side. Sisi stood with each foot on a different carriage. We went hurtling along and did not feel safe at all. We were saved by an army doctor, who jumped on behind us and prevented us being brushed off our precarious perch by odd branches and the walls of narrow tunnels. In St Gilgen Geza and Ali were at the station to meet us.

That day President Roosevelt died in Warm Springs (Georgia)

Friday, 13 April The drive to Radstadt turned out to be a nerve-racking experience. Road blocks have sprung up everywhere and when it is not the army's Feldgendarmerie, it's the S.S. In the latter case Geza would produce his false Gestapo papers; in the former, his Croatian diplomatic passport. As army and S.S. hate one another more than ever, he had to keep his eyes open so as not to confuse the two. This was not easy, as, seen from afar, their uniforms are practically identical. We were told that beyond Fuschl (Ribbentrop's late hideout) the road block was particularly strict; several cars had been confiscated and their occupants evicted. At one of the S.S. road blocks these gathered around us ominously, but then, seeing Geza's papers, they waved us on muttering 'Kolonne der Geheimen Staatspolizei' ['Gestapo column'] and even proffered warnings to be careful: one of their group had just been shot dead by a driver disguised as a Feldgendarm, who they were now looking for.

We reached Radstadt just in time for me to hop on to a departing train. It was already moving when Geza threw me a bunch of ration cards. An hour later I was in Schwarzach-St Veit. On the way we passed through a place called Bischofshofen and I was shocked to see barbed wire strung along both sides of the track. This, I was told, was a camp for Russians or Poles; they gathered at the fence to watch us go by and stared at us dully.

Schwarzach-St Veit itself is a tiny village hemmed in by glowering unattractive mountains. When I alighted it was six o'clock. I was told that the head doctor, Dr Thimm, was having supper in some inn and that I should report there. In the market-place I ran into the arms of *Schwester* Agnes with two other nurses, all of them in attractive dirndls. She greeted me with a screech of joy and gave me all the local gossip: everything is at a standstill; there will be no work for another fortnight; the hospital here is apparently split into two rival clans, one of which has moved on to Bad Gastein . . .

Finally I found Dr Thimm, who was dining with six or seven other officers. His first question was: 'Where is Carmen?' – by whom he meant Sita Wrede. Then he asked whether I had found a place to live, for he had absolutely no room for me; everything was full up; he could only offer me his own bed! I suggested timidly that I should perhaps leave and join another hospital. He said that he had thought Sita and I had deserted and had reported us as such to the Regional Air H.Q. in Bad Ischl – this with a broad wink; then he added: 'No, no, I absolutely insist that you work in the surgery here. We are opening it in ten days' time.' Meanwhile I could go back to Gmunden, but then I was to return with Sita without fail. He also suggested that a colonel who was dining with him give me a lift. I hastily gathered together all my luggage – that which I had sent on ahead here and the bundles I was carrying now – and at 8 p.m. we departed. The colonel, who sat with his driver up front, seemed nervous. In the mountains, he said, there were now partisans everywhere. After a big detour via Salzburg, we finally got to Gmunden only at one in the morning.

Saturday, 14 April Although I am exhausted from so much travelling, I walked to Altmünster – about two hours there and back – to tell Sita Wrede the good news.

Yesterday, the Russians occupied Vienna. There was, we hear, hardly any resistance.

In fact, the battle for Vienna, which had started with the city's encirclement on 6 April and lasted barely a week, saw some of the bloodiest and most destructive street fighting of the whole war.

Gauleiter Eigruber has been thundering over the radio that Oberdonau – the Nazi name for the province of Upper Austria – must stand to the last man; there is no escape now; women and children will not be evacuated, however tough things get, for there is nowhere for them to go. In his rhetoric he copies Adolf, but at least he is frank and does not try to hide the gravity of the situation. By way of compensation, he has promised the population a special distribution of rice and sugar.

Sunday, 15 April Spent the day resting and re-arranging my room. I have at last unpacked.

Monday, 16 April As there are no more trains (for lack of coal), I bicycled over to Bad Ischl, forty kilometres away, to fetch a fur coat and a rucksack which I had left at the Starhembergs'. The expedition took five hours! The country around here is beautiful. But at one point alongside the road there was another concentration camp. One could see the barracks in the distance. It was entirely enclosed with barbed wire. It is called Ebensee. Nobody seems to know who exactly is locked up there, nor how many they are, but it is supposed to be one of the worst camps in Austria and just passing close by is in itself a sickening experience.

Ebensee concentration camp (a subsidiary of Mauthausen) was renowned for its harsh conditions and high death-toll. As General Patton's Third Army approached, the S.S. Commandant prepared to blow up the 30,000 remaining inmates in a tunnel filled with explosives, but the camp guards (most of them Volksdeutsche repatriated from the East) refused to obey his orders and the inmates survived. The site is now a memorial cemetery.

Wednesday, 18 April Geza Pejacsevich rang up from St Gilgen to say that he had seen someone who had run into Paul Metternich in Berlin. Having at last been kicked out of the army, he was on his way home to Königswart. We expected this to happen much sooner, firstly because he is a prince (albeit not royal), and secondly because he has a foreign mother and a foreign wife. But all this seems to have dawned on the authorities only recently. Tatiana was with him. Now we must pray that they get out before the ring around Berlin closes. The fighting there is already in the outskirts of the city.

Thursday, 19 April Sisi Wilczek and I are having a hard time getting enough food. The shops have nothing more to sell, the inns are crowded and what you do get there is terrible. As neither of us is working – at least the hospitals have canteens – we are on the verge of starvation. Even so, Sisi keeps on postponing her return to her hospital. She is in a state of complete exhaustion, sleeps for hours on end and looks very unwell; five years of surgery are beginning to tell. She is so pretty that to see her in such a piteous condition is sadder still.

Friday, 20 April Adolf's birthday. A ridiculous speech by Goebbels: 'Der Führer ist in uns und wir in ihm!' ['The Führer is within each of us and each of us is within him!']. How far can one go? He added that to re-build all that had been destroyed would be no problem. Meanwhile, the Allies are advancing on all sides and the air-raid warnings last all day. The colonel's wife, for one, seems to believe these announcements. She is convinced that Germany has a secret weapon that will be used at the last minute; she cannot conceive how they could make such pronouncements otherwise. She insists that we breakfast with her. This is very kind of her, for it is our only daily meal.

Saturday, 21 April At 11 a.m. Sisi Wilczek called me up to the roof. The sky was filled with planes. They were flying in from all directions and shone silver in the sun. It was a beautiful day, but proved to be a tragic one for Attnang-Puchheim down in the valley below. We could see the bombs raining down. The planes were never out of sight and after they had finished their job, they flew once more over our heads. The raid lasted three hours. I had never observed one at such close quarters, as usually when they came, we were crouching in cellars. This time I could see it all. The earth literally rocked with the explosions. It was horrible and beautiful at the same time.

Sunday, 22 April It is pouring with rain. We went to church. On the way back a lorry full of soldiers passed us. We hitched a ride but to our dismay it suddenly veered off and headed for Linz. We had great difficulty catching the attention of the driver and making him stop. Some of the soldiers were wearing the Ritterkreuz. They were being sent back to the front. They offered us bacon.

Apparently, yesterday's raid on Attnang-Puchheim caused huge casualties, as several Red Cross trains were on sidings at the station. I thought of all those pretty sunburnt young nurses who had been so kind to us when we stopped off there on our way from Vienna a fortnight ago! The stocks of rice and sugar promised by Gauleiter Eigruber to the starving population have also gone up in smoke.

Eger was taken by the Russians today. This means that Königswart is also in their hands. Did the family get away?

Monday, 23 April Sisi Wilczek has at last reported back to her hospital down in Gmunden. I bicycled again over to Bad Ischl. At lunch in an inn there I talked with someone who had got out of Vienna on the 11th. He told some gruesome tales about last-minute fighting between Volkssturm [territorial militia] and S.S.

Tuesday, 24 April Sisi Wilczek spent the day at her hospital washing dirty bandages. There seem to be still no operating facilities there. She now has a fever. I keep searching for food for her. It is again pouring with rain.

Wednesday, 25 April At last a sunny day. We tried to get a little brown on the terrace. In the afternoon we went for a long bicycle ride around the lake. As we sat at the edge of the water, the mountains around us grumbled and seemed to shake. There must have been a raid on somewhere, but we could not figure out where. It seemed so near and yet we could see no planes. On getting home we heard that this time it was Berchtesgaden, some fifty kilometres away, and it only sounded close because the mountains produce an echo. Sita Wrede gave us later the details on the telephone. She referred to Berchtesgaden as *der Fels* [the Rock].

That day the U.S. and Soviet armies met on the banks of the river Elbe, near Torgau. The Nazi Reich was now cut in two.

Thursday, 26 April This morning Sita Wrede drove up to see us. There was another raid in the vicinity. We lay *en deshabillé* on the terrace watching the planes. A little later one of them returned and began circling the lake. As they seldom fly alone, Sita thought it was an American bomber that had been hit. Our eyes followed it lazily as it banked and all of a sudden it swept down towards us. We scrambled to our feet and rushed back into the sitting-room, convinced that it was about to ram the house. We had not yet recovered our senses when it crashed into our park. We raced over but by the time we got to it, it was burning so fiercely that nobody could approach it. We were told that the crew had bailed out, but this seemed hardly possible in so short a time. Perhaps the pilot tried to crash-land on the lawn and just missed. We were very shaken.

The colonel has sent over some men, who are planting a vegetable garden in the park. The worst one must now begin to fear is widespread hunger.

On that day Mussolini, his mistress Clara Petacci and a number of Fascist leaders were shot by Italian partisans and their bodies strung up by the heels in the main square of Milan.

Friday, 27 April Coming home this evening, I found a huge grey car parked before the door. I recognised the driver of Antoinette Croy's husband, Jürgen Görne (the one who had roasted our goose in Vienna four months ago!). Jürgen said he had just spent a few days with Antoinette in Bavaria. He had been ordered to proceed to Czechoslovakia to join Field Marshal Schörner's army, which is about to be surrounded there; but his men are stuck in Klagenfurt. He is clearly playing for time. We told him how rough the food situation was and he promised to help.

We have heard over the radio that the Bismarcks' house in Friedrichsruh was bombed and destroyed and that there are several dead. What a relief to know that Tatiana and Paul Metternich are no longer there, but where can they be? Eger and Marienbad seem to be in the hands not of the Russians but of the Americans. And what about all the Bismarcks?

Although the Allies are closing in on all sides and to continue the war seems utterly senseless, the German troops in our part of the country remain by and large disciplined and obedient.

Sunday, 29 April We have put Jürgen Görne and his A.D.C., Auer, up in our house, as they have nowhere to go. The manager of the Hannover estate, Herr Stracke, is getting nervous because of all these constant comings and goings, but in times such as these he can hardly object; besides, thus far everybody who has stopped off at the house knows the Hannover boys personally and *they* would certainly not mind. Jürgen does not think that I should return to Schwarzach-St Veit. The war will be over in a week, he thinks.

The weather has changed, it rains again heavily and has even snowed. We bicycled down to church but otherwise stayed indoors. Then Geza Pejac-sevich drove up to see Sisi Wilczek and discuss future plans. He has obtained passports for his family and is taking them all to Switzerland. He wants Sisi to join them, but she bursts into tears and refuses to go.

I have talked with the head doctor at the Cumberland Hospital up at the castle. But he can only take me on if I am discharged from the Luftwaffe by the Regional Air Chief M.O. in Bad Ischl, as all the hospitals here are army. The three of us have decided to go there. If I can swing this, I will accompany

Geza and Sisi for a few days to Moosham, where the Wilczeks have a castle, in which they intend to sit out the end of the war. After which I will return to work here. Though Sisi will not hear of going to Switzerland, she has agreed to visit her parents. There may not be another chance to drive there and at Moosham she will at least have something to eat. For her part, Sita Wrede has decided to ignore all orders and to volunteer for work in a local hospital.

In Caserta that day, following secret negotiations that had gone on for months, SS-Obergruppenführer Karl Wolff surrendered all German forces in Italy to the Allies.

MOOSHAM *Monday, 30 April* We took off under showers of rain. I was again dragging along a lot of unnecessary luggage in case my interview in Bad Ischl failed and I had to continue on to Schwarzach-St Veit after all.

In Bad Ischl I had some difficulty finding the Regional Air Chief M.O., who was already at supper with a group of fellow-officers. Luckily I was in uniform and he took me into his office. I described the conditions at Schwarzach-St Veit, whereupon he gave me a certificate releasing me from my obligations to the Luftwaffe, which meant that I may now work for any hospital I choose. I was immediately under his charm.

We could now all leave for Moosham. Geza Pejacsevich headed the column with Ali, Sisi Wilczek and myself. Steff Adamovich followed with all the children. The third car, belonging to Jakob Eltz, was driven by Capestan. Each car was loaded with all sorts of nondescript luggage, including some sacks of flour and rice and tinned food collected at various points during the Pejacsevich/Adamovich clan's exodus from Hungary – and miraculously preserved.

As we drove through Bad Aussee, we caught sight of Dicky Eltz. This was a lovely surprise, but he looked miserable and lost; his only wish, he said, was to return to their home in the Balkans!

We were moving along quite nicely when Capestan suddenly vanished. We waited and waited and finally got out to stretch our legs a bit. He re-appeared and we drove on. Six kilometres later Sisi uttered a piercing shriek: she had left her handbag with all her personal papers and the parcel box with the Wilczek family fortune on the side of the road where we had stopped. Steff turned around and drove her back. On arriving at the spot where we had rested, they spotted the parcel but not the handbag. Driving a little further, they caught up with two women on bicycles. Sisi's bag was dangling off one of the handlebars. A nasty confrontation followed with the woman insisting on taking the bag to the police. But in the end she relented and presently we were again headed in the right direction.

After Radstadt comes the Tauernpass. Here it was snowing heavily and our car got stuck. Sisi and I pushed and shoved, all very uncomfortable in uniform at four o'clock in the morning. Suddenly around the bend two horses appeared pulling a cart on which Meli Khevenhüller sat perched, surrounded with bundles – the caricature of a refugee. True to her word, she had driven in this manner all the way from Vienna and was now heading for Schloss Hoch-Osterwitz, the family castle in Carinthia. We finally all got across the pass and down the mountainside, reaching our destination at 5 a.m.

Schloss Moosham turned out to be an ancient mediaeval battlemented fortress containing an entire village. It gave the impression of being the end of the world. We awakened Renée Wilczek, Hansi's wife, who hastily set about organising things. Sisi and I share a large four-poster bed. Tomorrow we will look around and plan our next moves . . .

That same day, 30 April, Adolf Hitler committed suicide in his Berlin bunker.

Missie's note (September 1945): A few days later Sisi Wilczek and I returned to Gmunden, where both of us were taken on by the Cumberland Hospital in the castle just across our park. But conditions there were so atrocious that almost immediately we came down with a very serious case of scarlet fever, brought on probably by delousing the innumerable soldiers coming through from the East; and aggravated, of course, by our state of under-nourishment and exhaustion generally.

As we lay ill, the American Third Army reached Gmunden. For us the war was over.

During all the subsequent period, needless to say, I kept no diary notes. The struggle for sheer physical survival amidst the chaos and total disintegration throughout Germany and Austria during the first post-war months absorbed all one's remaining reserves of energy and nerves – to the exclusion of virtually everything else. The only other thing that kept me, personally, going was my need, at all cost, to re-establish contact with the scattered members of the family, about whose fate I knew absolutely nothing and who, I realised, must be worrying just as desperately about me as I worried about them.

General Patton's U.S. Third Army reached Gmunden on 4 May and the following day saw the surrender of all German forces in Bavaria. Four days later, on 8 May, the war in Europe came formally to an end.

Sisi Wilczek (now Countess Geza Andrassy) has described this missing period in Missie's diary: One day an American jeep with two officers drove up to the Königinvilla. Since neither the estate manager, Herr Stracke, nor Fräulein Schneider spoke any English, Missie, who was working in the Cumberland Hospital across the park, was summoned to interpret. The two American officers visibly took an instant interest in Missie and, allegedly because the Russians were advancing and they wished to protect her from them, tried to persuade her to drive away with them. She refused, saying that she wouldn't leave me in the lurch; it was agreed that they would return in a couple of days. Meanwhile they forbade us to leave the house. Two days later they re-appeared and again urged this time both of us to go away with them. We refused. Whereupon they again forbade us to leave the house, saying that otherwise we would be shot. We now realised that the story about the allegedly approaching Russians was a sham and that they had something quite different in mind. Luckily we never saw them again.

Shortly thereafter we both came down with scarlet fever and, loaded onto a horse-drawn uncovered ambulance, were driven down to Gmunden, where we were installed, the two of us in one bed, in the isolation ward of the hospital in which I had until then been working, almost completely oblivious of what was going on around us. At some point there was the noise of many vehicles grinding to a stop outside, of shouting, of orders being barked – in American. Then some soldiers in unfamiliar khaki-coloured uniforms and helmets and bristling with weapons burst into our room; and were pushed out again by some of our doctors and nurses. A few days later we were told that the war was over.

I remember very little of the time we spent there. I recall dimly, for instance, that one day we found a cookery book with reproductions of bread, milk, meat, etc., and tried to picture ourselves partaking of all that. Another time I crept down into the hospital garden and stole a glassful of red currants. One of the nuns caught me red-handed and scolded me, calling me a thief, while I, still clutching my precious glass, scurried back to our room, where we hastily gobbled down the berries before anybody could retrieve them. After about six weeks we were released – in a state of total starvation.

When we got back to the Königinvilla, we found that the main house had been requisitioned by the American C.I.C. [counter-intelligence corps], headed by a Major Christel. Of the period that followed, what I remember most vividly is, again, the constant sensation of acute hunger. From the Cumberland Hospital (to which, though on convalescent leave, Missie was formally still attached), we would get our rations of horse meat and the like, which we were allowed to heat up in the Americans' kitchen. I still recall how our mouths would water at the sight of all the delicacies being consumed by our 'house-guests'. Finally, out of sheer desperation, Missie and I resorted to a trick. Just about the time when the Americans sat down to eat, we would creep up to the windows of the dining-room and start fussing around with the flowerpots, pruning the roses, etc. And, sure enough, we would almost invariably be invited to share their meal (for in those early post-war days any form of 'fraternisation' with Germans was still officially banned!). And after downing mouthfuls of peanut butter and bowls of real coffee, we would stay bolt upright all night, quite unable to sleep!

Major Christel turned out to be a very nice, courteous and considerate man. He went out of his way to see to it that the constantly changing personnel under his command behaved towards us correctly. This was all the more necessary – and appreciated by us – inasmuch as the house was soon turned into a weekend 'recreation centre', with all that this implies. We only realised what was going on at night in the ground-floor apartments as we were about to leave – to be demobilised.

In this latter connection Major Christel worried especially about Missie. She had told him about her Berlin experiences, particularly the 20th July period, and he feared that this might cause her to be detained for further interrogation. Fortunately, his fears turned out to be unfounded.

One day we were loaded on to a convoy of open trucks and horse-drawn carts and, together with a group of quite young boys in S.S. uniform, taken under heavy guard to Mauerkirchen, where the screening took place. The S.S. kids were released almost immediately – it was clear that they had been called up in the very last weeks of the war and stuck into S.S. uniform without even a by-your-leave. The rest of us had to pass through the hands of a veritable chain of interrogators installed in three railroad cars, who asked us hundreds of questions and kept comparing our names with voluminous lists to make sure that we had not been prominent Nazis. Missie, needless to say, was a mystery to them, starting with her flawless English and the fact that she claimed to be Russian. If so, they kept asking, why wasn't she in Russia? They had, apparently, never heard of a White Russian refugee! Finally we were allowed out of the last railway car, given a daub of white paint on each leg – to show that we had been 'whitewashed' – and, after a further long wait, told that we were free to go where we wished. For us both, at long last, the war was truly over.

That same evening, after another long journey, partly on foot, partly hitch-hiking, we were back at the Königinvilla in Gmunden, where Major Christel had prepared a delicious welcome-home feast.

We remained in Gmunden a few weeks longer, visiting various relatives and friends who had found refuge in the neighbourhood – my parents at Schloss Moosham, the Eltzes in Aussee . . .

Missie resumed her diary only four months later:

BAD AUSSEE *Thursday, 23 August* Sisi Wilczek and I have left Gmunden for good.

I now want to try and rejoin the family in Germany by any means I can, that is assuming they managed to escape in time from Königswart (which is now in Czech hands).

I left most of my luggage with the Starhembergs at Bad Ischl and accompanied Sisi to Bad Aussee for the day. At the station we ran into Wilhelm Liechtenstein, who was on his way from Switzerland to Styria and fed us bacon, cheese and crackers out of his suitcase. This was very welcome, as we are faint for lack of food. He also had seven little bottles of schnapps concealed about his person which he intends to offer to those drivers who agree to give him a lift. He told me *en passant* that Paul and Tatiana Metternich are in Johannisberg, Paul's bombed-out wine estate on the Rhine, which is now in the U.S. occupation zone of Germany. This was the first news I had had of them since April! He accompanied us to Aussee, helping us with our luggage.

STROBL *Friday, 24 August* Spent the morning in Bad Aussee chatting with Albert Eltz's mother. She has had no news from her daughter Stephanie

Harrach, who has stayed on under the Russians in Czechoslovakia. Dicky Eltz was captured in the very last days of the war and is still in an Allied P.O.W. camp on the Bavarian frontier; apparently they are very badly treated; and yet Dicky was such an anglophile! I will try and help him through Jim Viazemsky, who was himself freed from his P.O.W. camp near Dresden by the advancing Russians.

Late at night two Americans from the Königinvilla – they are both called Jim – drove up to ask us over to Gmunden for a party tomorrow. One of them is engaged to a French girl.

Saturday, 25 August Ali Pejacsevich and I tried to hitch-hike to St Gilgen to look at some rooms that may be available. But no vehicles drove by and we ended up in a cart driven by two German ex-soldiers who stopped at every house they saw in a vain search for hay for their horses. We soon parted company with them. While I stretched out in the sun on the edge of the road, Ali sat down in the middle, the better to intercept passing traffic. We finally walked to St Wolfgang and hitched a ride on a jeep from there. It had taken us three hours to travel the twelve kilometres!

The rooms proved a dismal disappointment and we were just wondering how to get back when we ran into our two Jims on their way to pick us up for their party. When we arrived, we found many of the girls fairly dressed up. We felt very D.P.-like in our plain dirndls. Spent most of the evening chatting with Jim No. 1, who is about to rejoin General Mark Clark's staff in Vienna. I myself am planning to leave for Johannisberg on Tuesday.

Sunday, 26 August In the afternoon Geza Pejacsevich, Sisi Wilczek, Alfred Apponyi and I walked several kilometres to visit Karl Schönburg, a cousin of Loremarie's, who lives in a farmhouse several villages away. It belongs to his brother, who has disappeared in Czechoslovakia. Karl himself had also stayed on under the Russians at first, but the Czech administrator of the estate, a decent fellow, persuaded him to leave, as things were getting dangerous. Now his castle there has become a Russian hospital. He offered us delicious fresh milk and schnaps. We accepted both gratefully. He also filled two rucksacks with potatoes for us to take home to the Apponyis. All the way Geza kept complaining that his feet hurt; he has never walked as much before. Finally an American jeep gave us a lift. To the drivers' glee Sisi and Alfred yodelled all the way.

Monday, 27 August Sisi Wilczek and I share the same bed, face to feet; sometimes our toes tickle each other's noses. But since they dumped us into the same bed in hospital when we had scarlet fever, we are getting used to this 'U-boat crew' position.

Went to Salzburg to see a Herr von Lehn. With the help of the Austrian authorities he is trying to repatriate several hundred German refugee children who had been evacuated to Austria from the bombed-out cities of northern Germany during the war. He suggested that I join the escorting Red Cross personnel. But the organisational side takes ages. In the afternoon I had tea wth Puka Fürstenberg's mother, a charming old Hungarian lady, in her very pretty house. She gave me some English books to read, as well as some macaroni and sardines to take back with me. This was terribly welcome, as, not being registered with the authorities here, none of us have food cards and we are again beginning to starve. Every day we go to the woods and look for mushrooms, which make up our main diet. The other day I was barefoot and sliced my toe open. It bled profusely and Geza Pejacsevich insisted on sucking it out to avoid blood poisoning. We take our meals with the Apponyi family, who are ever so sweet and hospitable, but who have very little themselves.

Tuesday, 28 August Today Ali Pejacsevich and I went to St Wolfgang in the Apponyi carriage in the hope of getting some food on my Gmunden cards. Strobl being in Land-Salzburg and Gmunden in Upper Austria, they are not valid here. We were successful and brought back my one week's ration of food – one loaf of black bread, a quarter of a pound of butter and half a sausage. So far, so good.

We then visited the Thuns, who are living with their three children and his mother in four rooms. They gave us tea and told us more hair-raising tales of adventurous escapes from the East. On our way home, we stopped in front of every plum tree we could see and, with the help of the coachman, gave it a good shake.

Vladshi Mittrowsky (another last-minute escapee from Vienna) has given me a tin of sardines. This is a very valuable gift, as I have made no preparations for the journey and may be travelling for days.

Wednesday, 29 August After lunch, Gina Liechtenstein (wife of the reigning Prince), her father Ferdinand Wilczek and Geza Andrassy, Sisi Wilczek's future husband – they have just become engaged – appeared in a car flying the Liechtenstein flag. They have had news of the Metternichs via Gabrielle Kesselstatt, who stopped off in Johannisberg to see them on her way down from Trier to visit her family in Vaduz.

After supper Gina departed, leaving several bottles of gin, and we and the Apponyis got pretty tiddly. It was really a goodbye party, as Geza and Ali Pejacsevich leave for Altmünster and then for Switzerland tomorrow, and my own departure is also at last in sight.

Thursday, 30 August Ali and Geza Pejacsevich have gone. The room looks very empty without their belongings. I too have started to pack. Herr von Lehn gave me my last instructions. The children's transport with which I am going back to Germany leaves tomorrow at 5 p.m.

Herr von Lehn accompanied us to the Mittrowskys', where we had some wine. As my train is going through all of Germany to Bremen non-stop, Christl Mittrowsky gave me the address of someone there, in case I do not manage to hop off on the way. We walked home rather late and got stopped by a patrol of M.P.s. We had forgotten our papers and got scolded.

As my departure looms, I feel more and more nervous. It is the first time I will be returning to Germany since I escaped from Berlin almost exactly one year ago.

Excerpt from a letter from Sisi Andrassy-Wilczek dated 1979: The last time I saw Missie was on the station platform at Strobl, where she was joining a transport of refugee children returning to Germany. As we hugged each other farewell, we made one another a solemn promise: not to marry for a long time, but to 'stay free' . . . Within less than a year Missie had broken that promise!

Friday, 31 August [Written up in Johannisberg-am-Rhein in September 1945] Wrote a letter to Irena in Rome. Then, donning my newly-washed Red Cross uniform for the last time (for I am travelling as a nurse), I took a last walk around Strobl, lunched, and escorted by Sisi Wilczek, Albert Eltz and Vladshi Mittrowsky, headed for the station.

Herr von Lehn was meeting us in Salzburg. We took six hours to get there, for two American lorries had collided across the track and much time was needed to pull them apart.

At Salzburg I was told to join the Führungsstab [H.Q. staff] in another train. There a charming nurse helped me settle down. Only two benches were free, as the rest of the car was packed with loaves of white bread and quantities of butter, sausage and cheese – all courtesy of the U.S. army. This is the food ration of eight hundred children and forty grown-ups for two days. We waited a long time, as we were expecting several hundred more children from Berchtesgaden. Finally everybody was aboard and we started off.

There are forty-five carriages in all. Each one contains children from a different refugee camp, as well as their teachers. Most of the kids look clean and well-fed. They are visibly thrilled to be going home. They have been without news of their families for the past year, having been evacuated to Austria after Bremen was destroyed.

Our H.Q. staff consists of Herr von Lehn, a doctor, a secretary, we two nurses and a lady with a four-year-old girl who lived in the Lehns' house in Strobl. We also have an American escort made up of an officer and four men.

After being held up for a long time at the Bavarian frontier, we arrived in Munich at 2 a.m. All that remains of the station is a huge iron skeleton. The local Red Cross had arranged for coffee and sandwiches to be distributed to the children, who took turns being served, carriage after carriage load. We sleep badly – there is too little space and the benches are hard.

Saturday, 1 September Six years ago the war started. It seems a lifetime.

Early this morning we passed through Augsburg, where some of my companions tried to wash under a pump on the platform. I slumbered on. We continued through Nuremberg, Bamberg and Würzburg. Seen from the train, all these towns look alike – the same ruins, the same desolation. In Würzburg we stopped for quite some time. I alighted and had a thorough wash. We then started work on our stock of provisions, cutting the loaves (more than eight hundred of them), buttering the bread, slicing the sausage, etc. We were busy until dark.

Whenever we stop, people try to board the train. They are mostly soldiers who have just been discharged. Theoretically, nobody is allowed on, but our American officer is good-natured and lets them into the luggage van. We are privileged insofar as, being a special convoy, we have priority. I have not yet seen a single other passenger train since we started out. All civilians seem to be travelling nowadays in freight trains. Moreover there are no travel schedules. Generally, Germany is a sorry sight.

We pored over a map, trying to figure out the best place for me to get off. Some of my companions advise me to continue on to Bremen and then try to reach Johannisberg from there. I would like to see that part of Germany (which is controlled by the British) for curiosity's sake, but it seems a preposterous detour and does not really make sense.

Tonight we stopped somewhere and began distributing the food. I stood outside, the children filed by, camp after camp, and the provisions were handed down from the train. They looked sweet, seemed very grateful, especially for the white bread, and there were lots of *danke schöns*. When we were through, many of the civilians who have been allowed on to the train came up asking for food for their own children and, as we have more than enough, we fed them too. We have stuck candles in mugs and everybody is getting more cheerful, particularly the nurse and the secretary, who are both from Salzburg and are returning there in two days. They sing Viennese songs, in which the rest of us join. We again discussed what I should do. One of the conductors said he was getting off one station before Fulda, where the train would stop for two minutes. He suggested I get off there too; he could fix me up in the station for the night and next day I could take a train to Frankfurt. Fulda itself, he said, should be avoided – the town is blasted to bits and almost deserted and there is no more station.

As we neared the town in question, we gathered at the door of the car. The conductor had a lantern. Herr von Lehn and the girls held my luggage in readiness. We passed slowly through the station but the train did not stop. The conductor jumped out nevertheless and waved his lantern frantically to signal the driver to stop and let me off too. Instead, we picked up speed. So it was to be Fulda for me after all.

Herr von Lehn was very upset and tried to dissuade me, but I refused to go on to Bremen. Meanwhile the others had gone back to sleep. We kept watching for Fulda and when we saw what appeared to be like it looming up in the distance, I prepared to jump, for I no longer believed the train would ever stop. And indeed it did not, but at least it slowed down sufficiently for me to slither off on to the tracks. Herr von Lehn hurled my luggage after me and called out that he would be passing through Johannisberg in a fortnight to see whether I had arrived safely.

Luckily, I had fallen into the arms of a railway worker with a large lantern who had jumped off the train too and was likewise heading for Fulda. He helped me with my luggage and we stumbled in pitch darkness towards what is left of the station, along torn-up, mangled tracks, across gaping holes and loose wiring that got entangled in our feet. I felt totally miserable and the prospect of staying up all night on a platform once we had reached Fulda chilled me even more. My guardian angel had disappeared ahead in order to reconnoitre. Suddenly, I saw the headlights of an engine steaming slowly towards me. I waved frantically and just as it loomed above me, it stopped. I asked where the driver was going. He answered: 'To Hanau!' (Hanau is near Frankfurt) but that he must first shunt a freight train elsewhere; I could hop on if I liked.

The idea of driving around on an engine all night seemed a bit less dreary than that of hanging around a bombed-out station. With his help, therefore, I clambered up. There were two men on board and they hung my bags on hooks around the engine driver's cabin. Then my first companion, the railway worker, came running up through the dark and we hoisted him aboard too. Though sparks kept showering down on me, I felt grateful to be there, as the furnace kept me warm; but I hated to think what my spotless uniform would look like the next day. The three men were good-natured but at first monosyllabic. The railway worker was getting off soon, as he was nearing his home. He suggested that I come along too and wait for the Frankfurt train at his house, where he could offer me coffee and cakes, 'alles von den Amis' ['all from the Yanks']. I was touched but refused, hoping to get to Frankfurt sooner by staying aboard the engine.

We hurtled off into the darkness at what seemed to me breakneck speed. The countryside around us is so scarred that time and again the rails seem about to end in nothingness. We reached a place called Elm, where they stopped and uncoupled the freight cars. Both drivers then disappeared while I dozed on a stool in front of the furnace. Presently they re-appeared, very angry. Though they had been working for twenty hours non-stop, the *Direktion* wanted them, before returning to Hanau, to take another freight train from here to Würzburg, which we had passed ten hours earlier. I was ready to cry! The chief driver, a tall burly fellow, then said that having promised to take me to Hanau nothing would induce him to go anywhere else. First, they tried to ease out of the station on the sly, but the points had been cleverly switched. Then they decided to stall all night. If anybody came around, I must not show myself, as that might cause trouble. I tried to find out on the map where we were but could not see anything. My idea of no-man's-land! I got down and trudged to the station, pretending I had come from nowhere, and was told that the next train to Frankfurt was the day after tomorrow.

The engine driver had followed me. He now told me he had driven Goering and Hitler in their day and now he had driven Eisenhower twice; that he had been offered a job in the United States for two thousand dollars a month (here he only earns 400 marks) and that in Germany one was treated like a dog. He had had enough of it! Would I like to come to America with him? 'Ich bin schon halb verliebt in Sie! Das wäre doch eine Sache!' ['I am already half in love with you. *That* would be something!']. I trudged back to the engine, hoping for protection by the other chap, and found him fast asleep. It was getting very cold; I tried to stoke the fire – unsuccessfully. I woke the man up and urged him to add more coal. But now my admirer had re-joined us. They told me not to worry – Germany, they said, had practically no engine drivers left; the *Direktion* would have to give in or they would simply refuse to work. I remarked that it was a good thing the war was over or they would both have been hanged for sabotage. They agreed.

Sunday, 2 September An hour later it started to get light. The engine drivers grabbed their bags and took off, assuring me they would soon be back. At 7 a.m., at last, the stationmaster, having telephoned all and sundry, gave in and signalled us to be off. He needed the track for other convoys. They started up the engine and presently we were off to Hanau at an exhilarating pace, my bags swinging wildly, through beautiful country – or so it seemed to me in my relief.

We arrived in Hanau at 9 a.m. and one of the men carried my luggage into a room at the station marked in English 'Off Limits'. Friendly goodbyes; grateful handshakes; and the last of my cigarettes!

The American sergeant in charge looked up at me surprised, said: 'Do you want to wash?' and handed me a mirror. My face was streaked with black and my uniform with the white apron and cap were a sight. He brought me some water in his helmet and after much exertion, I managed to look a little better. A girl was sitting on another soldier's knee on a camp bed in a corner. She told me she had been waiting for a train to Cologne for the last two days but now seemed reconciled to a different fate.

After some enquiries, I found another engine driver, who was leaving for Frankfurt in ten minutes. He agreed to take me with him. This time several other people clambered aboard too. Two American soldiers helped me with my luggage and we were soon off again. We steamed slowly through Frankfurt – yet another desolate mass of ruins. I counted six bridges over the Main, all wrecked. Two pontoon bridges replace them. At Höchst I waited three hours and a half. Then an hour's train ride to Wiesbaden; then two more hours waiting there; and lastly another train to Geisenheim, the little village at the foot of the hill on which stands Johannisberg. A girl who had got off there with me offered to help carry my luggage up to the Ursulines' cloister nearby. We set out up the hill through Paul Metternich's famous vineyards, me hoping that he and Tatiana had not gone away for the weekend.

It took me quite some time to reach the ruined castle. It, too, is a sorry sight. Only one of the gatehouses still stands. The first person I saw was Kurt, the butler from Königswart. He told me Tatiana and Paul had left ten days ago by car for Salzburg – to look for me!

By then, I was too exhausted even to cry and simply collapsed in what I assumed was the housekeeper's sitting-room. Soon Lisette, Kurt's wife, appeared and suddenly it felt like old times. Under their kind ministrations, I crept into the only bed of a very polished-looking new bedroom suite. Tomorrow we will see. For now, I want only to sleep. And forget.

Monday, 3 September Today I started looking around a bit. This gatehouse is the only building left more or less intact in the 1943 Allied bombing of Johannisberg. The little flat I am in used to be the housekeeper's but is now where Tatiana and Paul Metternich live, the housekeeper having moved upstairs. It consists of a sitting-room, a bedroom and a bathroom. The windows look across a round flowerbed – now a spinach patch – and a wide square entrance yard on to the ruins of the castle. Through the latter's gaping window frames one can see the Rhine valley below. The place is teeming with Metternich retainers from their various estates in what is now again Czechoslovakia, who have converged here in the hope of finding some sort of employment and who have literally nothing to do all day. It is all very depressing . . .

I have now learnt that two days after the Americans arrived at Königswart, Tatiana, Paul, Mamma and Papa left with a cart drawn by two horses and escorted by seven French ex-P.O.W.s, who had been working on Paul's estate. The local American Commandant, who happened to be a friend of cousins of ours in the U.S.A., had warned them that the Americans would be relinquishing that part of Czechoslovakia to the Soviets shortly, and had advised them to leave instantly. They had taken twenty-eight days to cross Germany, spending the nights in farmhouses or barns or, occasionally, at friends'. Kurt and Lisette (who are looking after me now), together with their daughter and son-in-law and Thanhofer, Paul's secretary, had followed in another horse-drawn cart a few hours later. They had left most of their possessions behind and are very unhappy. Tatiana and Paul, too, seem to have taken very little with them; when they arrived they didn't even have blankets for their beds, everything here having perished in the 1943 bombing. Mamma and Papa are now in Baden-Baden, in the French zone (where we lived for many years as children).

I am told that two of our relatives, who are serving with the Allied forces, have already come by to find out where we are and whether they can help us: Jim Viazemsky, who is now a liaison officer between the Soviet and French high commands, and Uncle Gherghi Shcherbatov, who is a Lieutenant-Commander in the U.S. navy and who was an interpreter at the Yalta Conference.

Spent most of the morning trying to get myself a permit to visit the parents in the French zone. Thanhofer does not leave my side; he even accompanies me to look for mushrooms. He does not trust the Americans, some of whom have taken over the Mumms' house next door. They have apparently been behaving very badly, throwing the furniture and china out of the windows, distributing Olili and Madeleine Mumm's clothes to the village girls, etc.

Then Brat Mumm appeared, just released from an Allied P.O.W. camp near Rheims. During the German occupation he had gone back to Paris to take care of the family champagne business there (which had been returned to the Mumms after being confiscated following the 1914–1918 war) and the French have not been forgiving. He looks well, though he was a prisoner for four months and they had hardly anything to eat. He is now staying with his family at the Ysenburgs', north of Frankfurt, his own house here having been declared off-limits to him. He took some of the letters I had brought from Austria back with him to Frankfurt and promised to send them on from there – a weight off my mind. He told me Freddie Horstmann was apparently alive and well, having survived the Russian capture of Berlin by living in a tent in the woods.

This evening Thanhofer took me down to Geisenheim to see a Countess Lucie Ingelheim, who works for Major Gavin, the U.S. Commandant of Rüdesheim. She is a cousin of Claus Stauffenberg, who tried to kill Hitler last July. She promised to help me get a permit for Baden-Baden.

Tuesday, 4 September Olili Mumm came by with a Lobkowitz, who has just arrived from the British zone. He said the British are correct but most unfriendly and inclined to plunder. For one thing, they had 'requisitioned' the horses he had evacuated from his estate in the East.

The food here is very uneven. We have lovely wine; there is plenty of milk; we grow our own fruit and vegetables; but there is absolutely no meat. Nevertheless, Kurt insists on serving our frugal repasts in white gloves, whispering the vintage year into my ear. All the servants are falling over each other, so eager are they to be of some use on this devastated estate.

Wednesday, 5 September Brat Mumm re-appeared with the news that Alfy Clary had escaped with Lidi from Czechoslovakia and is rumoured to be in the neighbourhood. I will look for them at once.

On my way back from the local cobbler's, where I left all the shoes I own, I bumped into Joe Hamlin, one of the Americans I had met in Gmunden. He is now a major. He told me that in Hanau he had met an American W.A.C. to whom he spoke about me and about what I had told him about wartime Berlin and how little he had believed me until he got to Berlin himself. Whereupon she had told him that she knew Tatiana and had given him their address here. He had now driven over to Johannisberg to meet them and tell them all about me, only to find not them, but me! He is driving straight back to Austria. I begged him to take me along but he is afraid to do so, as in Germany there is still a ban on so-called 'fraternisation' and I, to all intents and purposes, am regarded as a German. He has agreed, however, to take some letters. We emptied a bottle of Paul's wine together and then he was off.

In the afternoon I walk over to our neighbours, the Matuschkas, to borrow some English books. They have been very lucky. Their beautiful castle is still intact; they do not even have anyone billetted there. But then he was in the anti-Nazi resistance.

Friday, 7 September I have resumed work on my diary. After the 20th July I only wrote in shorthand, and a personal one at that. I fear that if I put things off any longer, I may forget all that has happened or be unable to re-read my jottings.

Saturday, 8 September Went mushroom-hunting with Kurt. We did not find many, as the season is practically over. This is disastrous, for they replace the absent meat.

Joe Hamlin is back. He has seen Tatiana and Paul Metternich, who are at the Fürstenbergs' in Strobl. He has brought letters. They ask for 300 bottles of wine, probably as exchange currency. Joe now regrets that he did not take me along. He is off to Berlin, but will try to find some job for me that can justify my accompanying him back to Austria to rejoin the Metternichs. If this cannot be arranged, I will go down to Baden-Baden to visit the parents.

Hans Flotow appeared today with two friends from Heidelberg. He is already back at work and seems well. We hadn't seen each other since Berlin. He told me that Loremarie Schönburg is working with the American C.I.C. in a village close to the place where I spent the whole night on that engine.

This evening an ex-officer arrived from Königswart with letters for Paul. He had gone back there with a friend six weeks ago, caught diphtheria, been imprisoned by the Czechs and got out again. What he relates is very discouraging. The Americans, who are still installed in the house, throw parties to which they invite the local village girls. These appear with empty suitcases and leave with them filled. They now go around in our clothes. The Königswart gardener writes: 'Es war ein Jammer zuzusehen, wie an dem schönem Schloss gesündigt wurde' ['It was tragic to watch the beautiful castle being so sullied']. The officer also brought a letter from Marguerite Rohan, Loremarie's cousin; it had reached Königswart by ordinary post from the Russian-occupied zone of Czechoslovakia. She and her five sisters, aged fifteen to twenty-two, have been made to work as servants in a hotel in Turnau. The Czechs have plundered their Schloss Sichrow (where I had stayed in 1944), and removed all the furniture to Prague. I wonder what has happened to the beautiful family portraits by Mignard, Nattier and Rigaud which the Rohans had brought over to Bohemia with them from France during the Revolution. Marguerite is trying desperately to get back to Austria to join her fiancé. They are being helped by one of Prince Franz Joseph Liechtenstein's brothers who is able to travel back and forth.

The Sudeten Germans are certainly paying a heavy price for having voted in 1938 to be re-absorbed by Germany. The Czechs are now evicting them mercilessly and settling their own people into their homes. Paul's estate agent has been arrested and his wife and children thrown out of the country without being allowed to take anything with them. The head forester at Plass, another Metternich estate in Czechoslovakia, was murdered together with his sister, the housekeeper. Meanwhile, the Americans look on.

Sunday, 9 September My tiny wireless did not survive the strains of the trip. I have given it to be repaired, but meanwhile I am totally without news of what is happening in the world. All I can do is read. And work on my diary.

Monday, 10 September Spend the days reading, writing, sleeping and walking in the beautiful woods. It's a little eerie, for I never meet anybody.

Thursday, 13 September Supper at the Ingelheims'. A young Stauffenberg was also there. He was interned in Dachau for many months and says that one of the 20th July conspirators, a Herr von Schlabrendorff, has survived and has much documentation about the anti-Nazi resistance which he intends to publish. It is indeed high time that the true story came out, as, so far, very little is known about it all by the general public. The truth about Rommel's alleged 'suicide', for example, has only just now come to light. I remember Adam Trott, just before his arrest, wondering whether the London *Times* should not be given the true story now that they had failed, and how violently opposed I was to this, fearing that it would merely endanger them even more. Now, however, it is different. If only as a tribute to their sacrifice.

Dr Fabian von Schlabrendorff's book, Officers Against Hitler, *which came out in 1946, was the first eye-witness account of the German resistance to be published. It is still one of the most reliable.*

Friday, 14 September More news from Königswart. The Alberts are under arrest, accused by the Czechs of espionage. Why on earth did they stay on?

Saturday, 15 September This morning I borrowed Lucie Ingelheim's bicycle and rode over to Wiesbaden to fetch my wireless. It was a long ride and a fruitless one. The Phillips lamp that was broken cannot be replaced. I had taken a bottle of Paul Metternich's wine to pay for it and had to lug it back. It's sad not to have any music.

Wiesbaden is teeming with American soldiers careening around in jeeps and with Allied military uniforms generally, but, contrary to Salzburg, no Russians are to be seen anywhere. The town is a wreck.

On the way home, I stopped off at Eltville and visited the Eltzes. Jakob's mother looks young and is still beautiful. Her mother, old Princess Löwenstein, is also there, together with several other refugee ladies. I can remember Sargent's portrait of her and her beautiful sister Thérèse Clary, Alfy's mother, at Teplitz. What a contrast with their present plight – the Edwardian Golden Age and now this! Alfy and Lidi are, I'm told, at the Löwensteins' in Bronnbach. They got out of Teplitz safely, after having been made to dig in the fields for potatoes. Marcus, their only surviving son, is a prisoner-of-war in Russia.

Sunday, 16 September The clock has been turned back an hour, which gives me fourteen hours' sleep. I am catching up on the many short nights of the past months. In church today, the local priest – a pocket Savonarola – uttered a fiery sermon with much ranting against the Nazis. Now! . . .

Bicycled over to the Matuschkas' for lunch. We were interrupted by one of the Johannisberg maids who had bicycled over to say that an American general had just driven up and was asking to see me.

He turned out to be a Brigadier-General Pierce, who had until recently commanded the U.S. forces in the Königswart area. He had driven up especially to give the Metternichs the latest news about their home before going back to the States. It appears that the Czech authorities have agreed to let U.S. Ambassador Laurence Steinhardt take it over as a summer residence; this may guarantee its future survival, or at least of what remains of it. General Pierce had also brought a letter from the Alberts, who are still under arrest.

Monday, 17 September Joined the Matuschkas, who drive around all day doing political work. A new Christian Democratic party is being formed.

This was to become the Christian Democratic Union (or C.D.U.), which with its Bavarian counterpart, the C.S.U., has been in and out of power in the Federal Republic since the end of the war.

Drove back to Johannisberg via Bad Schwalbach through the beautiful forests of the Taunus. The silence there is total, the sense of quiet and peace pervasive . . .

Here my diary ends.
(About this time, I met my future husband, Peter Harnden.)

FINIS

Marie Vassiltchikov-Harnden
Berlin 1940 – London 1978

EPILOGUE

Missie married *Peter G. Harnden* in Kitzbühel (Austria) on 28 January 1946. After wartime service with U.S. Army Intelligence, Peter was at the time a captain on the staff of the U.S. Military Government in Bavaria. An eye-witness, *Hans von Herwarth* (himself an early anti-Nazi resister, who was to become one of West Germany's most distinguished post-war diplomats) has described the scene: 'As Missie was Orthodox, the wedding was celebrated in a Catholic Gothic chapel by a Russian priest who had fled from the Soviet Union. One sunny day we walked in procession to the chapel. Following the Russian tradition, my child walked in front carrying an icon. Next came Missie and Peter in American uniform, followed by the three best men, Captain Count de la Brosse in French uniform, and Paul Metternich and myself who had both served as German officers. The three of us had alternately to hold a heavy crown over the heads of the young couple. We were aware of the significance of this ceremony, which united people from four nations that, a short time before, had fought a grim war against one another'. ('*Against Two Evils*', Collins, London, 1981).

Following Peter's demobilisation, he and Missie settled in Paris where, after a brief spell with the Marshall Plan, Peter set up his own architectural business which was to gain wide international recognition. He died in Barcelona in 1971, when Missie moved to London, where she was to live her last years. They had four children, two of whom now have families of their own.

Many months were to pass before the scattered members of the Vassiltchikov family were able to visit one another again.

Missie's mother died in Paris, run over by a car, in November 1948; her father died in Baden-Baden in June 1969.

Her sister *Irena* spent the post-war years in Italy. Since 1980 she has lived in Germany.

Once the greater part of Schloss Johannisberg had been rebuilt, *Tatiana* and *Paul Metternich* made it their permanent home. Until recently Paul was prominent in international motor sports. Tatiana is active in Red Cross work.

After the war, Missie's brother *Georgie* became an international conference interpreter, first at the Nuremberg war trials and later with the United Nations. He was married and has two children. At present, he is in business.

Like all other German 'royals', *Konstantin of Bavaria* had been cashiered from the army early in the war. Thanks to this, he not only survived but, like most of them, was able to complete his higher education. When war ended, he was among the first to achieve prominence – as a journalist with the newly-created free German press, and as a lecturer in the U.S.A. He then went into politics, being elected a deputy to the Bonn parliament. He died in an air crash in 1969.

Following his arrest, *Peter Bielenberg* was questioned for months by the infamous Gestapo inspector Lange; he never disclosed a thing. He was then long held in solitary confinement at the concentration camp of Ravensbrück. He and his family now live in Ireland.

Though *Gottfried Bismarck* was repeatedly beaten and tortured, his lawyers had succeeded in postponing his trial for many months. Finally, on 4 October 1944, he appeared before Judge Freisler's People's Court, where, to everyone's astonishment, he was acquitted – as it later transpired, on Hitler's orders. Re-arrested by the Gestapo, he was imprisoned in a concentration camp, from which, in the spring of 1945, he was released. Himmler, at the time, was putting out discreet feelers to the Allies via Sweden, where Gottfried's sister-in-law, the Swedish-born Ann Mari, had influential connections. In the early post-war years he and his wife Melanie lived on a family estate near Hamburg. They were killed in a road accident in 1947 on their way to Johannisberg to visit the Metternichs.

Once the war was over, *Herbert Blankenhorn* became one of the founders and later General Secretary of the Christian Democratic Union (C.D.U.). A close associate of Chancellor Konrad Adenauer, he played a key role in establishing the West German state, as well as in setting up the European Coal and Steel Community. He then rejoined the Foreign Service and was successively Bonn's Ambassador to N.A.T.O (1955), France (1958) and Great Britain (1965). He now lives in retirement.

After the war, *Gottfried von Cramm* was for a while back in the forefront of international tennis. He was briefly married to Barbara Hutton. For many years he was President of the West German International Lawn Tennis Club. He died in 1976 in a car crash in Egypt.

Both *Albert* and *Dicky Eltz* survived the war unscathed. They now live in Austria.

Hasso von Etzdorf probably owed his survival to the fact that, in the closing months of the war, he was posted as Consul-General to Genoa. With the establishment of the German Federal Republic, he rejoined the Foreign Service, where he held a number of prominent posts, including those of Ambassador to Canada (1956), Deputy Under-Secretary for Foreign Affairs (1958) and Ambassador to Great Britain (1961–1965). He now lives in retirement near Munich.

On 3 February 1945, with the advancing Soviet armies only a hundred kilometres away, Berlin was hit in broad daylight by the heaviest U.S. air-raid ever. Coming after two months of respite – owing to winter weather – it took the city by surprise. Some 2,000 persons perished (roughly one for each ton of bombs dropped), 120,000 others were made homeless. One bomb set ablaze the Gestapo's H.Q. in the Prinz Albrechtstrasse. Another hit the People's Court in which Hitler's 'hanging judge', *Roland Freisler*, was interrogating a prominent resister, Dr Fabian von Schlabrendorff. Judges, guards, prisoners and spectators were hurried down into the building's shelters and there, after the all-clear, Freisler was found, crushed to death by a falling beam, still clutching Schlabrendorff's file. Though he was to spend the rest of the war in concentration camps, this raid saved Schlabrendorff's life.

After the execution of the Berlin Commandant, General von Hase (on whose staff he had long served), *Heinz von Gersdorff* was drafted into the Volkssturm. For many months after the war, his wife *Maria*, who had stayed on in Berlin, had no news of him. In the winter of 1945 she was told that he had been killed in the final battle for the capital, whereupon her nerves broke and she committed suicide. *Heinz* himself lived on until 1955.

Despite the destruction by Allied bombs of the *Horstmanns'* country home at Kerzendorff, *Freddie* had refused to abandon what remained of his collections, and the arrival of the Soviet army found him and *Lally* hiding out in the woods nearby. Even then he would not flee and eventually he was arrested. He died of hunger in an East German concentration camp in 1947. Lally's reminiscences, *Nothing for Tears* (London, Weidenfeld and Nicolson,

1953) was a best-seller. She was to die some time thereafter in Brazil.

After parting from Missie in August 1945, the *Pejacseviches* made their way, via Switzerland, to South America, where *Geza* still lives.

After a spell in U.S. captivity and a few years in German local government service, *'C.C.' von Pfuel* was, for almost three decades, representative in Bonn of the European Parliament in Strasburg. He now lives in semi-retirement in Bonn.

Carl-Friedrich von Pückler-Burghaus – who had, in 1941, denounced Missie's mother to the Gestapo – had himself transferred from the army to the S.S., in which he rose to the rank of Brigadeführer and Himmler's police chief in Prague. As Prague was being liberated in the first days of May 1945, he committed suicide.

When Bucharest fell to the Russians on 31 August 1944, German diplomats and their families were immediately interned. The women and children were eventually able to make their way home, but the men were all deported to the U.S.S.R., where *Josias von Rantzau* is said to have died in Moscow's Lubyanka prison.

At the end of the war *Judgie Richter* and his family found themselves in Westphalia. There he and his wife opened an interpreting-translation bureau which prospered. In 1949 he joined Lieutenant-General Gehlen's office, which was later to become the Bundesnachrichten Dienst (better-known as the B.N.D.), the newly-constituted intelligence service of the German Federal Republic. He died in 1972.

Tony Saurma survived the post-20 July terror thanks to the decency of his commanding officer, who succeeded in having his court-martial adjourned, 'pending additional evidence'. When the court finally reconvened, much of this evidence had become too circumstantial to justify conviction and in consideration of his war wounds, he was merely cashiered. In the closing days of the war he managed to make his way from his family estate in Silesia to the West, where he eventually found employment with the U.S. occupation authorities as a lorry driver. In due course he was able to acquire a vehicle of his own, then several, until he had a whole trucking business. He now lives with his family on a farm in Bavaria.

Ambassador *von der Schulenburg* had never been an active resister. But as the war with Russia sucked Germany ever closer to disaster, he offered his services as a possible intermediary with Stalin. This seems to have been the purpose of his summons, early in July 1944, to Hitler's H.Q. (which Missie records). But he had also been in touch, via Ambassador von Hassell, with some of the plotters, who, without his knowledge, had listed him, alongside Hassell, as a future Foreign Minister. When these lists were discovered, he was arrested, held for several months in the Lehrterstrasse prison and finally, on 4 October 1944, brought to trial before Judge Freisler's People's Court – together with Gottfried Bismarck. Less lucky than the latter, he was sentenced to death and hanged on 10 November.

Loremarie Schönburg was yet another miraculous survivor of the 20 July Plot. After her precipitate departure from Berlin in August 1944, she lay low at her family's estate in Saxony until the advancing Soviet armies forced them to escape to the West. There, once the war was over, she soon found work with the U.S. Army's C.I.C. In due course, she married an American officer and lived for a while in the U.S.A. In her later years she became obsessed with environment problems, to which she dedicated herself with the same single-mindedness she had shown in her fight against Nazism. She was to die in Vienna in July 1986.

For all his damning record, S.S. Brigadeführer *Six* turned out to be, if for different reasons, a survivor too. The war was barely over when he was 'recuperated', together with the notorious Klaus Barbie and many other former S.S., by the U.S. army's C.I.C. But soon his past caught up with him. Arrested in the spring of 1946, he was brought to trial in the case against the former mass-murdering Einsatzkommandos and, for all his assurances that he had been 'but a scientist, never a policeman', he was sentenced in 1948 to twenty years' imprisonment. He evidently had some powerful protection, for in 1951 his sentence was cut to ten years and in 1952 he was amnestied altogether. Soon after, he was again 'recuperated', this time by General Gehlen's new West German intelligence service, where he found many former S.S. and Gestapo colleagues whom Gehlen had chosen to shelter as 'experts' of some sort or another. Six's particular 'expertise' involved setting up groups of agents recruited from among former Soviet P.O.W.s or D.P.s for infiltration into the U.S.S.R. – a function he combined with that of publicity manager for Porsche-Diesel, a subsidiary of the powerful Mannesmann group. At his trial in Jerusalem in 1962, Adolf Eichmann described Six as the man who had descended lowest from the pedestal of a self-professed 'intellectual' to the depravity of mass murder, only to bounce back after the war as the confidant and advisor of both the American and German governments.

Tino Soldati was to make a brilliant career, which culminated as Swiss Observer to the United Nations and Ambassador to France.

Despite Himmler's ominous threats after the 20 July Plot, only two *Stauffenbergs* perished: *Claus* and his brother *Berchtold*, a naval jurist, both of them active plotters. The rest of the family were first sent to Dachau, the children being separated from their parents and hidden away in a different camp under the name of 'Meister'. As the Allied armies advanced into Germany, they were moved from camp to camp; more than once they were close to summary execution, before being finally freed by U.S. troops just four days before the war ended, on 4 May 1945.

Together with several other Germans who perished in the last war, *Adam von Trott zu Solz's* name is honoured on the memorial tablet of Balliol College, Oxford. His widow *Clarita* was released already in September 1944 and reunited with her children shortly thereafter. She has become a distinguished psychiatrist and lives now, as do her two daughters, in West Germany.

When France was liberated, *Henri de Vendeuvre* joined the French army advancing towards Germany; he was killed in Alsace, aged twenty-three, in January 1945. His brother *Philippe* became one of General de Gaulle's A.D.C.s.

The end of the war found *Alex Werth* in the Soviet occupation zone, where in due course he was arrested, spending many years in East German prisons. Though he was eventually released, escaped to West Germany and became a successful businessman there, his ordeals had shattered his health. He died in the mid-1970s.

Sisi Wilczek also soon broke the promise she and Missie had made to one another when they parted in Austria in August 1945. She married Geza Andrassy and now lives in Vaduz (Liechtenstein).

Sita Wrede and her twin sister *Dickie* spent the early post-war years with their mother's family in Argentina. Eventually, Sita married a West German diplomat, *Prince Alexander zu Solms-Braunfels*, whom Missie mentions briefly in her 1945 Vienna reminiscences. He held for many years ambassadorial posts in Latin America. They now live in Monte-Carlo and Munich.

GLOSSARY

A.A.–abbr. for Auswärtiges Amt. German Foreign Office.

Abwehr Germany's military counter-intelligence, foreign intelligence and sabotage service. Long headed by Admiral Wilhelm Canaris and a safe-house for many anti-Nazi resisters, it was, starting in 1943, gradually absorbed by and finally amalgamated with the S.D.

Afrika Korps Special German unit formed to aid the Italians in North Africa. Became in January 1942 part of the German panzer army under Rommel.

Der Angriff lit. 'The Assault'. The organ of the S.A.

Arbeitsamt Manpower Board.

Arbeitsdienst Obligatory labour service for all able-bodied citizens of the Third Reich.

Atlantikwall German fortified system which extended from the North Cape in Norway to the Pyrenees.

Ausweichquartier Emergency quarters for an evacuated German service.

Blitzmädchen Women auxiliaries.

S.S. Brigadeführer S.S. Brigadier.

D.D. Abbr. for Drahtloser Dienst – the News Service of the German Broadcasting Corporation.

Das Reich Weekly publication, of which Dr Joseph Goebbels was editor-in-chief.

Drahtfunk lit. 'cable radio'. German wartime device linking telephones to news broadcasts.

Ersatzheer Reserve army.

Feldgendarmerie Military police.

Flak abbr. for Fliegerabwehrkanone. Anti-aircraft gun.

Fristlos entlassen Cashiered.

Führerhauptquartier Hitler's Supreme Headquarters.

Führungsstab Headquarters staff.

Gauleiter Nazi provincial party leader; in fact, provincial governor.

Generaloberst Colonel-general.

Gesandter Minister Plenipotentiary.

Gestapo abbr. for Geheime Staatspolizei i.e. 'Secret State Police'. Created in 1933, the Gestapo became the executive arm of the S.D., the S.S. security service, with branches all over Germany and occupied Europe. Its longtime chief, an efficient and ruthless police officer by the name of Heinrich Müller, vanished without trace in the last days of the war, possibly 'recuperated' by the Soviets, of whom he may have long been a secret agent.

Kreisleiter Nazi district party leader; in fact, local administrator.

Landjahr-Mädchen Young women's compulsory rural labour service in Nazi Germany.

Luftgau Provincial air command.

Luftgaukommando Provincial air H.Q.

Marschbefehl Military travel orders.

N.S. or Nazi abbr. for N.S.D.A.P., i.e. 'National Socialist German Labour Party'.

N.S.V. abbr. for Nationalsozialistische Volkswohlfahrt. Nazi 'People's Welfare' organisation.

S.S.-Obergruppenführer S.S. lieutenant-general.

O.K.H. abbr. for Oberkommando des Heeres. Supreme Command of the German Land Forces.

O.K.W. abbr. for Oberkommando der Wehrmacht. Supreme Command of the German Armed Forces.

Ostarbeiter abbr. for persons of Eastern European origin who volunteered or were indentured for work in wartime Germany.

Panzer Armoured vehicle or formation in German army.

Politischer Leiter Nazi political officer; equivalent of Soviet Communist commissar.

Polizeipräsident German police chief in a major city.

Polizeipräsidium Police H.Q. in a major German city.

Pressechef Head of the Press Office.

Protektorat Nazi name for the provinces of Bohemia and Moravia (formerly, with Slovakia, part of Czechoslovakia) annexed by Germany in March 1939.

Regierung lit. 'government'; in this case residence and office of the local civil governor.

Regierungspräsident Local civil governor.

Ritterkreuz lit. Knight's Cross of the Iron Cross. Until superseded by additional ornaments to it, wartime Germany's top award for valour.

S.A. abbr. for Sturm Abteilung, lit. 'storm detachment'. Private army of the N.S.D.A.P.; designed originally to protect Nazi meetings and fight political rivals. Was modelled after the German army and was at first led mostly by ex-officers. After the 'Night of the Long Knives' of June 1934, its place was taken more and more by the S.S.

S-Bahn abbr. for Stadt-Bahn, Berlin's elevated municipal trainline.

Schwester Hospital nurse.

S.D. abbr. for Sicherheitsdienst, i.e. 'Security Service'. Created originally as the S.S.'s internal intelligence arm, it gradually infiltrated its agents everywhere, becoming, together with the Gestapo, an all-powerful instrument of information and terror that kept watch over all aspects of German life. With its absorption in 1943 of the Wehrmacht's Abwehr, it also took over foreign intelligence and sabotage.

Das Schwarze Korps Official weekly newspaper of the S.S.; mouthpiece of Heinrich Himmler.

Sippenhaft lit. 'kith-and-kin detention'. Retaliatory measure against the families of opponents of the Nazi regime.

Sprengkommando Pioneer unit entrusted with demolition.

S.S. abbr. for Schutz Staffel, lit. 'Protection Squads'. Originally Hitler's personal bodyguard. Later transformed by its leader, Heinrich Himmler, into a mass army and all-pervasive administration upon which was ultimately to rest all Nazi power.

Störflug Nuisance raid.

Streife Patrol or road block.

Streng geheim Top secret.

U.F.A. abbr. for Universum Film A.G. Largest pre-1945 German film production company.

Volksdeutsche lit. 'ethnic Germans' living in countries other than Germany.

Volksgericht lit. 'People's Court'.

Volkssturm Home Guard type of militia created towards the end of the war.

Wachtmeister Staff sergeant in the German armed forces.

Wehrmachtleitung Armed forces telephone line.

Wehrmacht Armed forces.

INDEX

A NOTE ON THE TYPE

The text of this book was set in a digitized version of Ehrhardt, a type
face first released by The Monotype Corporation of London in 1937.
The design of the face was based on a seventeenth-century type, probably cut by Nicholas Kis, used at the Ehrhardt foundry in Frankfort.
The original cutting was one of the first type faces bearing the charac-
teristics now referred to as "modern."

Printed and bound by Maple-Vail Book
Group, Inc., York, Pennsylvania.